'A salivating reminder on why, what ███████ food culture that nourishes us and the earth.'
HANNAH MALONEY, AUTHOR, PERMACULTURE DESIGNER AND TEACHER

'The quintessential guidebook for anyone who cares about what they eat. A pillar of the Australian food literature canon.'
LAURA DALRYMPLE, FEATHER & BONE FOUNDER AND AUTHOR

'Matthew Evans teaches without preaching. He writes without dithering. And he knows what great food is. You'll read this from cover to cover!'
NAGI MAEHASHI, RECIPE TIN EATS FOUNDER, COOK AND AUTHOR

'This book is for the chef as much as the home cook. Matthew's talent for making the raw produce accessible to the reader is second to none.'
ROSS O'MEARA, CHEF, GAME HUNTER AND AUTHOR

'Country folk often gauge each other's kitchen skills over their batch of scones or seasoning of a humble roast chook, which are the first recipes I'm drawn to in these seductive pages. This book is packed with wise-old-bugger tips that all underpin Matthew's true commitment to agrarian living and cooking from the land.'
SEAN MORAN, SEAN'S PANORAMA, CHEF AND AUTHOR

'*The Real Food Companion* is a must read for anyone interested in how to ethically source, prepare, and eat real produce. A great resource that I always recommend to my team.'
PETER GILMORE, QUAY, CHEF AND AUTHOR

'A rallying cry to eat like it matters, in a world out of balance. The glorious fundamentals of real food, coupled with the why and the how of cooking it with love.'
KIRSTEN BRADLEY, MILKWOOD FOUNDER AND AUTHOR

'A wonderful, gritty, generous gift to the world (and Hedley!). If we consider our role as current-day decision makers but ancestral thinkers, a book like this is just the tome to kick us into action.'
JADE MILES, FARMER, AUTHOR AND PODCASTER

The Real Food Companion

The Real Food Companion

MATTHEW EVANS

Photography by Alan Benson

murdoch books

Sydney | London

CONTENTS

PROLOGUE

When I first sat down to write Real Food, *it was a love letter to my unborn child. At that time I was also single, and our son wasn't even a twinkle in anyone's eye. Despite that, I wanted to distil some of what I'd learned — all of what I'd learned — about how to choose and cook food, for the generation to come. I wanted to bring all the pleasures I'd found in and around the dining table to one place, to help those I love learn how best to eat.*

The book took a long time to write. By the time that first edition was finished, our son Hedley was thrust, screaming, into a wintry Tasmanian night, all wrinkled and purple and looking for all the world like a skun rabbit. I fell immediately, and irretrievably, in love. By that time, I'd also considered how the simple act of growing, shopping and cooking can embellish anyone's life. The frivolous became vital. The thwack of the cleaver, the gentle stirring of the pan, the licking of the spatula — they mean more than words. More than just fuel. What I write is not just for my son, it's also for all those babies already born and yet to come.

Hedley is now old enough to read this book and many things have changed, not all of them in a good way. In that time, the last great kelp forest off Tasmania's coast — one I was lucky enough to swim in — has vanished. Fires, floods, pandemics and pestilence (in the form of rodents) have ravaged the country I love. As I type, the Arctic is 30°C (85°F) warmer than it should be for the time of year. The Antarctic is 40°C (105°F) hotter than previously recorded. Globally, insect numbers have plummeted, soil has been lost at astonishing rates, and the world population has kept climbing, mirrored by atmospheric carbon dioxide. What that means, in terms of what my son and his generation will experience, both at the table, and more generally in life, is unclear.

Knowing something of the changes that will be encountered in any human life, The most important thing I could want for anyone is a good sense of humour, a good heart and a good knowledge of food. The how, the why, the where. That's because in challenging times food is comforting. In happy times it uplifts and sustains. If we show respect for ourselves and what we put into our bodies we will find strength and happiness. Dine in front of the television at your own peril. Keep your self-esteem intact and your front door open to visitors. Keep the pantry full and the larder enriched. Keep the invitations going to those who seek refuge, as well as those who come to bring joy. Be generous with the ladle and cavalier with the wine. What I want for my son is not a degree, or boundless riches, it's an appreciation of the simple pleasures that matter. I want him to cook, because hospitality is the glue that binds humanity together.

As Covid finishes its apocalyptic ride across the sky, it's good to remember a lot of things. We need to recognise that our collective good is in our collective humanity. We don't thrive in a vacuum, we thrive when we work in concert.

It's worth remembering, for a moment, all those multinationals who encourage us to buy online instead of at our local shops. If every dollar that used to be spent locally has gone offshore, never to be seen again, there's less of a pie to share. And I quite like pie.

Now is the time to look at our systems and fix them. We all know people who think it's quaint, a bit yokelly, and not sustainable to support local farmers. That economies of scale and agribusiness and Amazon are the only way forward. That it is just fine to send money overseas every time you buy a book, a pair of shoes, a glass of cider made from concentrate. A kettle. Every time you have home delivery or catch a ride. It might take something like a pandemic to realise that spending money close to home recycles that money close to home. Buying locally gives our neighbours, our town, our community, purpose. When we give ourselves purpose, we give our kids, our elderly and others hope.

What life has taught me is that every soul in our circle is vital to our wellbeing. What can we do to strengthen those ties? Know this: over 70 per cent of the world's food is grown by small farms, and consumed locally, despite what farming may look like near you or in your imagination. How you spend really does matter.

So do other things. I want people to cook for each other. Care for each other. Read books. Write books. Write a love letter. Bake a cake. Tell jokes.

Cooking allows us time to pause. Time to think of those who are less firm. Less able, emotionally as well as physically. It's never a bad time to offer soup. To invite someone over who lives alone. To quote poetry. Cooking and sharing mealtimes are beautiful things, so store them away in your hearts and minds for when we may not have beautiful things in front of us.

The art of the table, the choosing, preparing and serving of food, gives us pause to reassess what is important. Who is important. How community is built by us, not foisted upon us, or something that only exists on shows like *SeaChange*. It allows us to witness the incredible goodness in each other. To be honest about our failings, our vulnerabilities, our strengths and our hopes.

Knowing and caring about what you eat isn't the preserve of any particular colour, religion, class or race of people. It's what connects all of us. Yes, the world is changing in ways that are hard to predict. What we do know is that what happens at the table can contain all the laughter, tears, pain, courage, joy and pleasure that humanity is capable of. That's the brilliance of a life well lived.

Why write about food, when other challenges confront humanity? It's a good question. By 2050, one-third of Australia's cropland may be blighted by salt or desertification. About 80 per cent of the globe's crop biodiversity has already been lost, and natural ecosystems are under great threat.

I write about food because that's what I know and how I find joy. But also, because while agriculture may have harmed Earth at times, it is also our great hope.

Regenerative agriculture, ecological farming, it doesn't matter how you frame it: growing food in a way that replenishes soil and ecosystems is not only possible, it is practical and sustainable. It's happening right now, all over the globe. How you shop, what you buy, has impacts way beyond your front door. It affects the very health of the land that gifts us life. The good news is that better farms usually produce better-tasting food. It's a win for the environment, a win for the globe, a win for you.

I also write about food because there's great potential in what individuals are doing to preserve old ways, old varieties. There are producers, provedores, cooks and fishers out there who bring great pleasure to dining tables, giving us all an excuse to come together, break bread, and build culture as we eat.

And for this reason, to celebrate those people, and those at home who can benefit from that care, I've condensed everything I've found out about food in one place, this book.

A CAMPAIGN FOR REAL FOOD

It started with milk. For a while I was the best-fed person in the country, dining at the finest restaurants for my work as the chief restaurant critic for The Sydney Morning Herald, *and what amazed me most was milk. Good, simple whole milk. Milk with the cream on the top, milk that had been caressed into being, from lush grass that the cows fed on, to the gentle pasteurisation that preserved its flavour. Forget your fine dining restaurants, your million dollar fit-outs — it was old-fashioned unhomogenised, full-cream milk that blew my mind.*

Good milk set me on a course to find the best produce, and to find out what made it the best. It even got me to grow my own vegetables and milk my own cow. What I learned about milk I related to every ingredient I could get my hands on, from beef to kale, from carrots to figs. Just what is it that makes some foods better than others? Is there a way to tell what is likely to taste better out there, before you buy? How do we get the proverbial cream from the top of life?

Often the great joys I discovered turned out to come from farmhouse producers. Often they were overlooked ingredients, or just plain old-fashioned fresh flavours that can be found across the nation at farmers' markets; simple food, truly seasonal food that real people can find and eat. Food that makes good cooking easy.

What I have discovered is a country on the ascendancy. Unlike France and Italy, countries that I once visited regularly and which are striving to preserve their gastronomic integrity, in Australia we are now more aware of what we have, what we can do, and are starting to question just how sustainable it is. While older nations are scrambling to maintain the quality of their markets, their traditional recipes and ingredients, we are building a repertoire of ever greater produce.

This book encapsulates a 'whole food' philosophy. Mediocrity is not something to aspire to. If large corporate food manufacturers say something is great, that probably means it's not. This is an anti-marketing book, celebrating resolute flavours, integrity and the joy of good home cooking. It's not going to tell you to buy a packet of my own brand sauce. It won't point you to one supermarket or another; in fact, I hope it helps alleviate the need for supermarkets in your food shopping life.

My biggest concern with mass-marketed food is that it promotes mediocrity. It has to. Price points, the weekly and seasonal variations in everything from coffee to pork to seafood, means you can't brand things (or sell them widely) if they're fabulous. Fabulous, fresh, unbelievably good food is — virtually without exception — too rare, too fleeting, to be given a brand and sold nationally. Nature, by very definition, creates diversity — the enemy of consistency. So consistency promotes mediocrity. If a big brand gets its hands on something marvellous, they have to bring it into line and make it 'consistent'. They have to dumb it down because if they sell you something marvellous one day, you may expect it all the time.

When I worked for various food magazines I too faced this dilemma. Here we were, trying to promote the unique, the brave and the most downright amazing food producers in the land. But the advertising dollar came from elsewhere. Only big companies, only those organised into conglomerates, the antithesis of most good food, had the money to buy a page of advertising. Each issue, as with just about every magazine, was a compromise between what the advertisers wanted, and what the punters should hear about. It was a constant tug-of-war between commercial and artisan, between corporate and seasonal, between mission statements and regional variation. The truth is, the small guys are at risk of being shunted out of the market, but more importantly, they aren't lauded enough for their wisdom, ingenuity or moral stance, because they're not big or fancy and they don't have deep enough pockets to get into our collective psyche.

Know this truth: the best food is being grown and cooked by people you've never heard of.

This book isn't meant to be just some glossy tome giving faint praise to producers and avoiding the hard topics. Part of me is ashamed to live in a nation where our national dish, the meat pie — a meal at once both as humble as a shoe and as majestic as a star — is by law allowed to contain as little as 25 per cent meat. And 'meat' can include everything on the beast, from eyebrows to bum holes to blood vessels and cartilage. The only thing that 25 per cent can't include is pure fat and solid bone. Or a foetus.

And that's why this book talks about producers. It offers an easily digestible but detailed insight into the way food is made, handled, sold and cooked. It's a cookbook with a focus. It will empower you when you visit a farmers' market, butcher and baker. It debunks myths, gives honest information on what is happening to our food, and looks internationally to show where we succeed, and where we fail. It has an organic emphasis, but remains sceptical of the hype. It is earthy like the real food within its pages — like the growers, producers, fishers and farmers who provide such bounty for our tables.

It's all I know about food, in one volume.

A NEW FOOD PHILOSOPHY: ONE DEGREE OF SEPARATION

Call it slow food, call it ethical eating, call it organic, sometimes, or biodynamic if you please. But the modern cook needs a new philosophy. It's not enough to support inhumane treatment of animals by omission or naivety. It's not enough that a simple pasta sauce from a supermarket can contain twenty ingredients and take just as long to cook as a homemade sauce.

Our kids are overweight, our lives too full, our food too fatty, sweet and packed with natural or added MSG. How does intensive pig farming — where the sow may never in her adult life be able to turn around — make us a better place or make better food?

Does what we're eating, and how we eat it, give us a true sense of place? And if it doesn't, and that matters, what should we do about it?

The whole genesis of this book is to help you know how your food is made and grown. The ideal is to be one step away from the source of your produce: if you can't make it yourself, hopefully someone you've met or someone you know has made or grown it for you. I know what you're thinking: it's easy for me, because I own a farm, and can produce just about everything I eat within my fence line. Yes, we do produce our own meat, our own dairy, our own fruit and vegetables.

But this isn't some ode to an unachievable foodie nirvana that never existed except for the privileged few. It's a concept I have worked on since I lived in Sydney and Melbourne, our biggest cities, and had a tight food budget, just like everybody else. It's possible to achieve the One Degree of Separation on some levels for most of us — and it's important, too. Every step of separation means you can have less faith in the freshness and production of your food. For many of us, the closest we'll get to achieving the One Degree is to shop at local farmers' markets. The second degree of separation means the shopkeeper or stallholder knows the grower, even if you don't. After that, it's all just stuff for sale in a shop, and any personal assurances count for nothing.

I'm just one voice in a greater chorus arguing for wiser food decisions when you have the choice. I want you to feel that every time you buy something, you hold in your hands the power to make a good, bad or hurried choice, and that the more good decisions we make, as a society, the better we'll eat, and the better the world will be when we leave it.

All we have to do is make the right choices when we shop. Sounds easy, but it isn't.

Yes, as individuals we will fail. There are times when you will have no choice but to buy the kind of factory, fast-fattened chicken you suspect was plucked while still alive. There could well be times when you won't have the money, or the option, or the energy to care. But if we do the right thing most of the time, then good operators — those who produce food with real flavour, with arguably better nutrient value, whose philosophies are kind to the Earth — well, maybe they will survive and thrive, too.

I don't expect it to be easy or quick. While Australia continues to be seduced by sugar and Uber Eats and takeaway coffee, it shows our collective heart is yet to be won by the simple pleasures of real food, real company, and the flavours of simply great produce, handled with care and cooked with passion.

But change is coming, and good produce is thriving already. So too food cooked from the heart and brought steaming to the table. The recipes I've shared with you in this book are based on my upbringing, and Aussie culture. I live surrounded by a mix of nationalities, but my cooking is grounded in my Anglo history, laced with Italian sensibilities and the occasional Asian flourish. It's my food. Food that you and I could cook together at home without having to spend a month shopping (with the good base ingredient hopefully procured direct from a farmer), and without having to become a scholar of another cuisine.

In this book I have tried to ask some of the big questions surrounding the ethics of the food we eat — such as, should such a dry nation as ours really be growing rice? And if we do, shouldn't this at least be done in the tropics, where there's the certainty of at least one wet season a year? Should the dry heart of the nation be populated by cattle beyond the point of sustainable capacity, who are then put on feedlots for the last days of their lives?

But I appreciate that it is still the small questions that are most important.

Like, what are we having for dinner? And how can I make it taste good?

THE ETHICAL ISSUES: AN OVERVIEW

We used to see food as our friend. But thanks to the relentless marketing of those who would sell us 'healthy' food, the media's love affair with any new nutritional study that comes to light, and the often draconian health regulations that mean processed food is considered safer than fresh food, we're no longer sure. Thanks to unsavoury farming techniques, such as those surrounding mad cow disease or swine flu, our concept of food security has been compromised.

The fact is, food is still our friend. Sure, being dense with nutrients means other bugs may find it attractive, but that's the whole point. Food is full of what most life — including us — uses to survive. Raw milk from a healthy cow, by definition, is safe to drink because it's the food intended for young calves. It's usually only what we do to it afterwards that can make it risky.

If you know the origins of your food, if you can trust your food, and if you look at every meal as an expression of those who cooked it, then food really is on your side. Having said that, it is important to know and understand some of the ethical issues surrounding food in modern society so you can make the best decisions before you buy.

THE ETHICS OF EATING ANIMALS

There are reports that it takes 16,000 litres (28,155 pints) of water to create 1 kilogram (2 lb 4 oz) of beef. Scary, really, except the figures are fudged (they allow for grain feeding and and irrigation of hay paddocks), and most of that falls as rain on pasture — grass that you and I can't digest anyway. That said, it's obvious that too much meat eating, and dairy eating, may not be good for the environment. I've written extensively about the ethics of eating meat, particularly in my book *On Eating Meat*, so I won't go into detail here. We're all grown-ups and can make informed choices, and for some that might include eating meat. The fact is many of us in wealthy nations do eat too much meat — particularly too much poor-quality and badly produced meat — for both the environment and our health. But not all production systems are bad, and many are restorative and sustainable. As is often said, it's the how, not the cow.

GENE POOLS

We've passed the peak. About 80 per cent of the genetic variation in the world's agricultural crops has been irretrievably lost. What we've squandered in the last century is greater than what all the labs in the world set up for genetic modification could produce in the next century. All this in the name of progress.

Humans have always modified the genetics of their crops, through natural pollination of crops and cross-breeding of animals. We've favoured certain characteristics over others. The original corn was probably a dry, shrivelled thing smaller than your little finger, the original tomato a mean-looking tiny, sour fruit. There were many originals, and we've selected constantly over generations to create the fruit, vegetables and domestic livestock we know today.

The problem comes not with this selection, but rather with where that selection has been leading us. We used to breed for flavour, or for food to be cooked in a certain way. Now, however, crops and animals are being bred to cope with petrochemical sprays, easy transport and intensive farming. Much of the good work we've done in breeding has been destroyed over the last one hundred years. We now breed to make life better for the grower, without giving much thought to the consumer who will eat it.

WHAT ABOUT FLAVOUR?

If you spend much time researching breeds of apples, cherries, nectarines, sheep or cows, you'll come across the same thing, time and time again. What matters to those who write complicated papers on the topics, or those who run industry lobby groups, is efficiency, profitability and transportability. What they don't talk about is taste. They're the robbers of our palate — those who would have us eat green tomatoes, gassed to make them blush, because it suits the retailer and the grower, even if it doesn't suit us.

I have a theory about flavour. The more I see, the more I'm convinced that our food lacks the flavour that it used to, and it's changing the way we cook. In the old days, Anglicised nations spiced their food. Recipes from the 1600s in the UK talk about using lots of cinnamon, cloves, ginger and nutmeg. But, over time, as we got better at breeding animals and plants for their inherent flavour (about the end of the 1700s), heavily spiced food started to fall out of favour. After all, if a carrot tastes sweet and juicy and ultimately of carrot, that's a good thing. No need to scent it with lots of nutmeg or mace. If meat isn't on the turn, if a simple piece of juicy, marbled, slow-grown pork is as good as it can be, there's no need to drown it in an anchovy and clove sauce. A little, maybe, but not too much. If there's no boar taint or funky smell to hide, if the breed is good enough to eat unadorned, then we let the ingredients speak. For a few centuries good breeding helped us rediscover the pure, true flavour of things.

Turn the clock forward and you can't fail to see that these days most people like to flavour chicken breasts. They think these should be marinated, or put into red curry sauce or cooked with apricots and a packet of chicken noodle soup to give them flavour. And they're right. The flavour has been bred, or force-fed, out of them. Cattle are fattened quickly, and sold before they reach full maturity and flavour. In an attempt to make pork lean and cheap, we've lost the flavour of the breeds, and so pork is considered a dry, boring, flavourless meat — because it usually is.

The good news is that properly reared, grown, harvested and marketed food is on the rise. The upsurge in farmers' markets in Australia, in the UK and across the New World has not only given the ordinary punter access to the great produce usually reserved for those who live in the countryside, but, even more importantly, it's given feedback and impetus to those who do the right thing by what we eat. It's meant that farmers have been able to hear just how good (or not) their produce is, when there are no intermediaries.

ORGANICS

If there's a growth industry in agriculture it's probably organics. In a time of 'biosecurity' fears, you could be forgiven for thinking that organics is just an excuse to charge double the amount for food that often looks a bit flyblown. I do, however, like the idea of organics. Certified organic farmers can generally say they're doing the right thing by the animals and land that they tend. The increased price, many would say, is the true cost of sustainable agriculture.

There's some contention about the nutritional benefit of some organic foods, but the thing to remember is it's unlikely that organic produce will ever be worse than conventional food. And into the bargain you'll be ingesting less pesticide residue, promoting less crop spraying, and arguably restoring some of the land to a better standard than when the farmer arrived.

Uncertified organic farmers abound. We tend to use organic techniques at home, as do many small market gardeners. It's about logistics as much as anything else. Small-scale operators have the time, the space, and the nous to be able to do things naturally. But certification is complex and expensive, and probably won't increase their bottom line.

SUSTAINABILITY

The issues surrounding sustainable agriculture are many, and I strongly suspect the topic will become increasingly important in the next fifty years. Hopefully, we can learn from past mistakes.

Look at the one-time food bowl of the Middle East — the Fertile Crescent, the birthplace of agriculture as we now know it. It's fertile no longer. Desertification is a growing problem across the globe. Salinity is striking at the heart of agriculture in Australia. Add to this a reliance on petrochemical-based fertilisers, the wholesale rise of industrial farming, and a lack of government will to regulate the industry, and you'll see we're addicted to unsustainable agriculture. It's estimated that, globally, we've abandoned 40 per cent of our agricultural land because the soil is no longer fertile.

But as with all things, the pendulum is swinging back. There's a lot of talk about food miles — the distance each ingredient has travelled to your plate. This has bred a tiny but well-publicised 'locavore' movement, where people try to eat food harvested within 100 miles (160 kilometres) of where they live. Small farmholding is no longer a fringe activity even in our expansive nation. Where I live, rare-breed chooks have tripled in price. Homesteaders are trying to rear old, slow-growing house pigs in free-range settings because they've heard about the horrors of factory farming, and have been disappointed at the taste of factory-farmed meat. People who milk their own house cow are swamped with requests for real, raw milk. So much so that raw milk is the new moonshine.

While most people, most of the time, are driven by price, convenience and consistency, there is a much smaller, dedicated band of people who want the chance of magic. Consumers who want their chickens to have seen the sun, their pigs to have tasted grass, their vegetables to be grown using age-old techniques and not plumped with fertilisers and sprayed with toxins. How sustainable is conventional and factory farming? Only time will tell.

WHAT ABOUT GENETIC MODIFICATION?

Genetically modified (GM) food isn't created through selective breeding, the method we've used to improve breeds for thousands of years. It's a much more brutal process where a gene from a completely different species (which means it can't be transferred by selective breeding) is inserted into a crop or animal. You can put a firefly gene in corn to make it glow in the dark (apparently it's been done, just to prove a point), or alter a microbe that lives on strawberries so it produces an equivalent of antifreeze to help prevent frost attack. There's even a variety of sweetcorn that has a gene inserted into it to make it produce its own insecticide.

I'm sceptical about GM foods. Proponents say they offer a quick fix to environmental problems and world hunger, because crops can be bred to resist disease or produce a better yield. I worry about unintended long-term consequences. It's only since the 1990s that GM crops have been in the public domain, but we're yet to see them alleviate world hunger or improve farming practices.

From a world hunger point of view, GM is a furphy. We have enough food to feed the world already. Have done, probably since time began. There's enough food in the world for about 2–3 kg (4 lb 8 oz–6 lb 12 oz) of food per person, per day; a 2002 report from the Food and Agriculture Organization estimates there's enough food for 2720 kilocalories per person per day — that's about 15 per cent more than we could possibly need. The problem isn't food production, or genetics. It's political. We lack the political will to end world hunger. Don't blame lack of genetic variation. Most of the problems they're trying to correct come about because of farming practices.

Instead of looking at what's wrong with modern farming, we're looking to science to help us continue doing it. It could be that it's intensive farming that's broken. Massive monoculture farms fight nature.

So what does GM food promise or currently do? There's some promise of higher yields, though much of this isn't borne out by the studies. There's the promise of more food for the Third World, where poverty is the main cause of malnutrition, so I can't see how having to constantly buy hybrid seeds — when in the past people would have collected seeds year on year — will help. There are crops bred so you can spray them indiscriminately with pesticides or herbicides — the sprays, curiously enough, sold by the same companies that patent the genetic code for the GM crop and sell the seed. To my mind, patent rights are a big part of the rub. A company can own the rights to a gene that exists in nature because it has the technology to isolate it and insert it into other crops.

While the debate about GM crops can be divisive and emotive, and there's some evidence that on average they have helped some local economies, they do tie the farmer to the multinationals that own the rights to those crops. In growers' terms, that's always a risky strategy. And from what I can see, little research looks at how those crops affect soil health. So what do we know?

We know that transgenic material has passed from GM corn into native corn in Mexico. We know that the transplanted genetic material can be passed from canola into charlock, a native weed. We've seen conventional canola contaminated with the altered genes of GM crops because of open pollination. We know that most users of GM crops use more herbicides and pesticides, and that an area of the US way bigger than my home state of Tasmania has rampant super-weeds because of unfettered herbicide use. There's also concern that the crops inserted with a gene to produce *Bt* (*Bacillus thuringiensis*), a toxin used in organic farming, will lead to *Bt*-resistant pests, as always tends to happen in nature. *Bt* kills nematodes, the most abundant multicellular life on Earth, of which 90 per cent live in soil. We probably kill them at our own peril. And at least 185 million hectares of soil has crops that have *Bt* in them thanks to GM.

Is it too late? Probably. If you eat any corn or soy-based products, you're probably eating GM food. By some estimates, 75 per cent of all processed products in the US now contain

an ingredient using GM technology. Thankfully, there's very little evidence that GM foods have any impact on human health, and let's hope there isn't more evidence to find.

There is work being done on trying to grow meat in a lab, from stem cells, so no animal will die in the process. It sounds far-fetched, but they can already create the fibre of meat on a petri dish, so in theory it's not a large jump from a few cells to a sirloin steak. Or is it? Having seen first-hand the effect of years of breeding, of exercise and diet on the taste and texture of meat, fake meat is unlikely to have any that complexity. There's also GM used to make fake meats out of pea protein and potato starch and the like, which will find a place in the market with all the world's other processed foods.

You may ask: isn't GM food tested as safe? The answer is yes and no. To be approved for sale, a GM crop only has to show that it isn't 'substantially different' from a conventional crop. There is no way to know if GM foods have an impact on our collective health until a lot of people have consumed them for a long time, research is carried out and the results analysed.

FUNCTIONAL FOODS AND NOOTROPICS

You've got to hand it to the marketing boffins. This sounds great, doesn't it: food with added nutrients, antioxidants or cholesterol-reducing properties — so-called superfoods. And nootropics — drugs that help with brain function and health ('smart drugs' or 'cognitive enhancers'). As if food isn't functional when it has been grown well, sold fresh and cooked properly.

Functional food is the marketing spin for food with extra bits added. Perhaps you want milk with fish oil in it? (Because, well, you don't want to eat fish or eat properly.) Or orange juice with calcium (don't ask me why)?

Nootropics is the fast-growing field of finding micronutrients and either refining or boosting them in supplements, so you can supposedly get your brain food in pill form.

Functional foods and nootropics rely on the fact that people have forgotten what real food is, what it tastes like and how to cook it. They rely on the laziness of communities as a whole, and promise a magic bullet. By exclusion they imply that real, wholesome, naturally grown and reared food is dysfunctional.

But the truth is these are frankenfoods — strange concoctions invented in a lab not because they taste good, but because somebody wants to make money out of them. They're not needed, so much as being foisted upon us. Look at the rise in obesity following the introduction of low-sugar and low-fat products in much of the Western world. Once we've forgotten how to balance our diets, how real food should look, feel and taste, then the companies who sell these foods will have enslaved us forever.

SOIL TO STOMACH

While the idea of 'paddock to plate', or 'farm to fork' has taken hold, the truth about what you eat is even more base than that. Really, we should be talking 'soil to stomach'. What exists in food is the result of countless interactions between the living things in soil, living plants and animals. The origin of much of what we think of as flavour is in the ground beneath our feet. Soil not only inoculates our immune system (literally fortifying our own microbiome), it can imbue the food we eat with a myriad of biological chemicals that nourish our gut, bolster mental health and fortify our health, at the same time as they make it taste better — more complex, more nuanced, more ... flavoursome.

Any home gardener knows this, that food grown in healthy soil, eaten in season, not long after harvest, is simply yummier. How that translates into the modern day, when we buy rather than grow most of our food, is what matters. (For those who want to delve more into the fantastic world of soil and all its wonders, I wrote a book called, enigmatically, *Soil* a few years back.)

If I had to paraphrase this entire tome, it's this: the flavour of food represents the soul of the grower, and the soul of the grower is expressed in their treatment of soil.

Chapter 1

DAIRY

DAIRY

*If there's one place where quality counts, where the flavour of the
raw product is affected by everything from the animal and its pasture
to the way the ingredient is pumped and treated, it's milk. That's right,
that fresh, seemingly mundane product which gives us all those miracle
foods — yoghurt, cream, butter and cheese — is easily transformed,
and harmed, by the way it is handled. Good butter can lift sourdough
bread from ordinary to extraordinary. Good cream can transform the
most humble porridge. Yoghurt, when made with milk from a single
herd and gently set, can be a revelatory experience. And cheese, well,
cheese can scale the greatest heights of any food that humans produce.*

At their best, dairy products are an expression of place, of the artisan or the maker,
and the care of the primary producer. At their worst, they're processed and standardised
to become bland, boring and disappointing.

The good news is that there's been a surge in artisan producers, including a
rediscovery of farmhouse cheese, in the past several decades. What was once an
experience only for those willing to travel to continental Europe has now started to
blossom at home. Cottage-made butter, smelly cheese, great-tasting milk that hasn't
been fiddled with and still has the cream on top — these are the kinds of products
that appear in great foodstores and farmers' markets thanks to a small but dedicated
band of producers.

MILK & YOGHURT

On top is a millimetre or so of cream, set seductively firm by being left a couple of hours in the refrigerator. Underneath this gentle, forgiving crust lies the yoghurt itself, a spongy, virginal white mass, the texture of marshmallow meringue. There's the nuances of fresh pasture and a hint of cashew, or is it hazelnut? Underlying it all is the hint of sweetness, a mellow, trance-inducing flavour of unbelievably fresh milk. It's defined — like fresh fish — as much by what you don't taste as what you do. Welcome to the yoghurt of Billawarra dairy, which was made with one of the finest milks in the land.

To make a living as a dairy farmer in Australia, you need to have 300 cows. That's modern thinking, anyway. But Billawarra had only two or three cows in milk at any one time. Go in February or August, and you'd find none. And there was never any milk to sell, either. I managed to try their milk as a guest at their house in the early 2000s, but they weren't licensed to sell it. They could only sell cheese and that unbelievably good yoghurt.

Maureen Dowd and Annie Nutter were the dairy delights of Western Australia. When I visited their modest dairy just outside Denmark in the south of the state, their cows were being hand milked, a daily production of a mere 22 litres (39 pints) each — whereas dairy cows in the rest of the country average 28 litres (59 pints) each; the Australian record for one cow is 110 litres (232 pints) a day. This milk was being made into relatively simple fresh cheeses and yoghurt.

Billawarra was the benchmark Australian dairy. Forget throughput, output and cost-benefit analysis, this was milk like it's supposed to taste. And even though they never had a licence to sell the milk, it was a lesson in how important the flavour of the milk is to the end product, and a lesson in just how good milk can taste. Exactly how the milk got its flavour is not certain, because every step of the way the cow and their feed were nurtured by the people who hand milked the cows in a way that was in stark contrast to mass-produced dairy products.

Each morning 'the girls' lined up to be milked. On my visit, Tulip, a jersey, joined the queue, even though she was supposed to be dried out. She kept producing a couple of litres a day, just enough for Maureen and Annie's coffee, and a couple of tubs of thick cream-topped yoghurt ready for the weekend market. Libby, another larger jersey, was the real worker, producing most of the herd's production. If you can call three a herd. Daisy was a short-legged dexter, an Irish breed, and her milk was naturally lower in fat. In the pan (she's too short for a full-sized bucket, dear thing) it looked a slightly greener hue than her paddock mates'.

You can be sure the best milk is always being drunk by a dairy farmer, but some great milk is available commercially. Joe and Antonia Gretschmann are at the pointy end of milk production. Their soft-eyed herd of cows are all named, and live a very cosseted life chomping the lush green grass of Elgaar Farm. The Gretschmanns run Elgaar on organic principles, from the growing of their own feed to the steam, rather than chemical, sterilising of equipment. They use glass bottles to hold the unhomogenised milk and offer you a refund on the bottles' return so they can be re-used. Situated under the shadow of the Great Western Tiers in a fertile valley in northern Tasmania, this is real milk, with real flavour.

What makes it good? It's hard to say. If you buy from one herd, you'll notice how the milk isn't one consistency or one flavour all year. Milk changes not only with the season, but with the breed of cow and how far into her lactation she is. The milk also changes as she gets older, and most dairy cows are only used for a half dozen or less years.

For 13 years I've milked my own house cows, and can attest that every cow, every season, every day is different, an expression of time, place, breed and the individual cow. Milking cows and drinking their milk is the ultimate way to taste and know a place.

WHAT'S THAT, YOU DON'T LIKE MILK?

I blame the former Australian government. When I was growing up in the seventies, the government stipulated that all school children be given milk to drink each day. The result of this is that an entire generation of Australians grew up with free milk that had been sitting in the sun outside the school canteen. Many of us were less than impressed with the stuff and might be afraid to drink a glass of milk these days. Particularly one with a layer of cream on the top, the marvellous, least adulterated milk, the unhomogenised version — the type you used to get delivered in a glass bottle at the front door.

Just about all milk (and I know, because it was my first job to deliver milk, door to door) was unhomogenised. All that ended in the 1980s, however, when cartons took over from bottles and cream on top of the milk became too scary to contemplate.

I was that boy in short pants put off by being forced to drink milk. I can still taste the lightly turning contents of those sun-ripened little bottles we were made to drink at school, now, several decades after the event. But if you want to know more about pure food, if you want to get back to basics, to find the true flavour of things, milk is the perfect place to start.

WHAT IS HOMOGENISED MILK?

Homogenised milk is by far the largest selling milk in most Western nations these days. It's milk that is forced through fine tubes or plates, where the resultant turbulence emulsifies the cream by splitting the butterfat globules into smaller parts. This means, simply, that the cream won't rise to the top. For some reason it is whiter in colour and has a thinner mouthfeel than unhomogenised milk (the sadly now rare stuff where the cream still rises to the top).

Unhomogenised milk is widely regarded as more flavoursome. This is probably because homogenisation causes virtually flavourless proteins to surround the aromatic fatty molecules of milk. It masks flavour. Unhomogenised milk does, however, tend to sour more rapidly than homogenised milk. The rich cream seems to be a fine place for bacteria to flourish, though it still keeps well for more than a week. Even though a generation of people raised on the homogenised version are unaccustomed to so much flavour in their milk, purists will love unhomogenised milk for its richer, fuller flavour.

Homogenisation is done for aesthetic reasons only. Many customers these days find the occasional clot of cream, or the look of a film of cream on the top of milk, disconcerting. They think it's off, when it's actually the way milk should look. As we've lost contact with our food, and the confidence to know when milk is off or not, we've favoured milk that doesn't get a layer of cream on top. For those who like their food to look and taste real, however, this lack of homogeneity is actually a selling point. And if you get to the bottle first, it's a simple joy to spoon off the cream to use on porridge, in coffee, or on a bowl of summer strawberries. Or, as I am wont to do, simply enjoy it off the spoon.

WHY DO I GET BUTTER FAT DROPLETS ON MY TEA WHEN I USE UNHOMOGENISED MILK?

Not having the cream homogenised into the milk can go awry in the processing stage. If milk is overheated during pasteurisation, the cream clots into thicker than desirable lumps, the butterfat sticking fast together. In this case, it's hard to shake the cream back into the milk, and it will split into butter and milk when you put it in or on anything hot — such as your tea or coffee, or hot porridge. It's a fault in the pasteurisation, and the only thing you can do about it is complain to the company that produces the milk.

WHAT IS PASTEURISED MILK — AND WHAT EXACTLY IS 'RAW' MILK?

While homogenisation is done for aesthetics, pasteurisation of milk is done for safety reasons. Discovered by Louis Pasteur, the ability of heat to kill pathogens has led to the pasteurisation of most milk in Western countries. Milk is heated to kill some pathogens, and to reduce the likelihood of dangerous microbes breeding and causing health concerns (some say to kill 99.999 per cent of viable micro-organisms). The heating process — typically of milk to 72°C (162°F) for 15 seconds as the milk passes between hot plates — alters the flavour of milk, and some choose to try to find and drink so-called 'raw' milk, which is another name for milk that comes straight from the cow (okay, so it is filtered and chilled).

Some producers favour a lower temperature pasteurisation that renders the milk just as safe, but takes a longer time. Called 'batch pasteurisation', it differs in that milk is heated for longer — for 30 minutes at 63°C (145°F) — in individual vats, not as it passes through heated pipes. While it has its own risks (because it needs to be done in large vats, which are more difficult to sterilise than a flushable, one-way pipe), it does leave more of the true flavour in the milk, and less of the caramel, off-almond eggy flavours that occur in normally pasteurised milk.

Ultra-pasteurised milk is a marketing moniker for UHT (ultra-high temperature) milk. It has been super heated under pressure to 138°C (280°F), altering the flavour of the milk substantially. The upside is that unopened UHT milk keeps for months out of the refrigerator.

Cold-pasteurised milk is a new, expensive variation, where bacteria are killed by putting the milk under intense pressure. This industrial process, however, does destroy much of the milk's character and natural flavour.

WHAT ON EARTH IS PERMEATE?

Technological advances have allowed milk to be pulled into some constituent parts. Even fresh milk usually goes through this process, using ultrafiltration. Milk permeate is the term given to a runny liquid retained after the milk solids (mostly fat and protein) are removed. The fat and protein are called the retentate.

Ultrafiltration is an increasingly common process of pulling apart milk into some of its constituents so it can then be reassembled and various components used in different applications. Sometimes milk is pulled apart just to be put back together again. Industry proponents like to think of this as standardisation; which means milk can meet the minimum fat and protein contents required by law. It's a modern means of making milk consistent, because, as mentioned, milk composition alters by the month and also by cow age and breed, in terms of fat, protein, lactose, vitamin and mineral content.

As a process, it undoubtedly alters the end flavour. It has also been suggested that dairy conglomerates use milk permeate to 'water down' milk, attempting to meet the low-cost contracts offered by supermarkets for their home-brand milks. The dairy industry says consumers deserve confidence in the consistency of milk, and using permeate to achieve this result is in consumers' interests.

WHY SOME VEGETARIANS DON'T DRINK MILK

Commercial dairy herds are, by their very nature, focused on producing milk, not rearing baby cattle. And to get a cow to produce milk, first the mother must give birth. (In this respect, cows are just like all mammals, humans included.) Some small dairies and farms rear the boys to adulthood and sell the meat, but many take the young males from their mother on the first day and shoot them. A few live on to become veal. In a move to use the calves of dairy cattle, and make a marbled beef sought after in much of the world, wagyu–friesian cross cattle are being fattened in feedlots for the beef market. Full-bred young friesian or jersey girls, typically, are reared to be the next generation of milkers. For a full discussion of veal, see pages 213–14 in the meat chapter.

I'VE HEARD ABOUT HORMONES IN MILK?

All milk does contain some hormones that are natural in mammalian milk, but of more interest are hormone supplements. In some countries, dairy farmers use a genetically modified bovine growth hormone to stimulate milk production. Because this causes an increased incidence of disease in cows (the inflammatory udder condition, mastitis, mostly), it's outlawed in many countries, including Australia. Moves are afoot, however, to promote its use more generally because it is believed it can cut the greenhouse emissions of cows (burps and farts, mostly of methane).

IS JERSEY MILK OR CREAM ANY DIFFERENT?

The two main milking breeds of cow used in commercial milk are the friesian (holstein), with its archetypal black and white markings, and the soft-brown coloured jersey. Less common are tiny little dexters for small farmholders, guernseys and brown Swiss among others. In the past, the jersey was the milker of choice for its wonderful cream content. But as tastes have changed, and friesians have been bred to produce more than 40 litres (70 pints) a day, the lower producing jersey has fallen out of favour. Some herds have a smattering of jersey cows to boost the fat content of the milk (which can make it worth more). Jersey milk contains, on average, about 5 per cent fat, compared to about 3 per cent for milk from friesians (though this varies with the cow, their age, how many calves they've had, the feed and the season). Many people, myself included, prefer the flavour of the milk from a jersey, and particularly the sweet, silky cream from a grass-fed jersey cow. If you get the chance to buy jersey cream from a single herd, try it and make up your own mind.

SOUR MILK

Mass-produced milk doesn't sour quite like milk from smaller herds, for reasons that aren't well explained. But even big brands of milk can sour and still be used for cooking. Soured milk has better baking properties and can be used in place of buttermilk, or instead of adding lemon juice to recipes, as some people do. Sour milk is milk that has just turned — use it on the first day you notice that it has a slightly sour smell. If it has changed colour at all, or smells off rather than just sour, don't use it.

WHAT IS YOGHURT?

Yoghurt is a great method of preserving milk, although unlike butter, which uses cream, or cheese where the whey is drained off (see pages 72–73), it uses whole milk.

To make yoghurt, milk is warmed and cultured with live, lactose (milk sugar)-eating bacterial cultures. As they consume the lactose they produce acids, making the yoghurt taste sour, and form bonds that thicken the yoghurt into a gentle mass. If you cut into a naturally set yoghurt, you can see a line where the curds are set. There are several bacteria used in making yoghurt, with more expensive yoghurts usually using a mixture to get a more complex flavour, and cheaper yoghurts favouring just one or two.

Because yoghurt is simply set milk, which means it lingers on the palate longer than milk, the better the flavour in the milk, the truer the flavour in the yoghurt.

WHY DOESN'T MOST YOGHURT RESEMBLE REAL YOGHURT ANYMORE?

Just check the ingredient list. Yoghurt, which was once a light, sprightly acidic way of preserving milk, has been debased by the addition of milk powder, emulsifying gums and sugars of various sorts. The reason? It's pretty similar to the reason milk is homogenised — aesthetic factors. Yoghurt that is set in a tub will leach out a watery whey when you cut into it. One way to help avoid this is to stir the yoghurt well, but that actually loses the light, gently melting structure of tub-set (or pot-set as it's sometimes known) yoghurt — and texture is as important as flavour in good yoghurt. This whey is flavoursome, but can make the yoghurt look curdled (though I like to use it on my muesli or on fruit and bugger the way it looks). You can buy tub- or pot-set yoghurt in most decent supermarkets these days, often under organic brands. Big manufacturers have discovered that you can avoid any weeping or splitting by adding vegetable gums or gelatine. They've also found that you can intensify the flavour using milk powder, but if you've ever drunk milk made from powder, you'll know this is not the most desirable flavour to use. It adds a caramel sweetness, but is nothing like the pure flavour of real, fresh milk. From tastings I've done, the closest thing you can get to real milk is to buy organic yoghurt.

Some brands now drain the yoghurt for you, leaving a richer, creamier-textured yoghurt. Beware the added gums and sugars, though, which are also often added to stop yoghurt separating and increase its immediate sweetness and smooth mouthfeel.

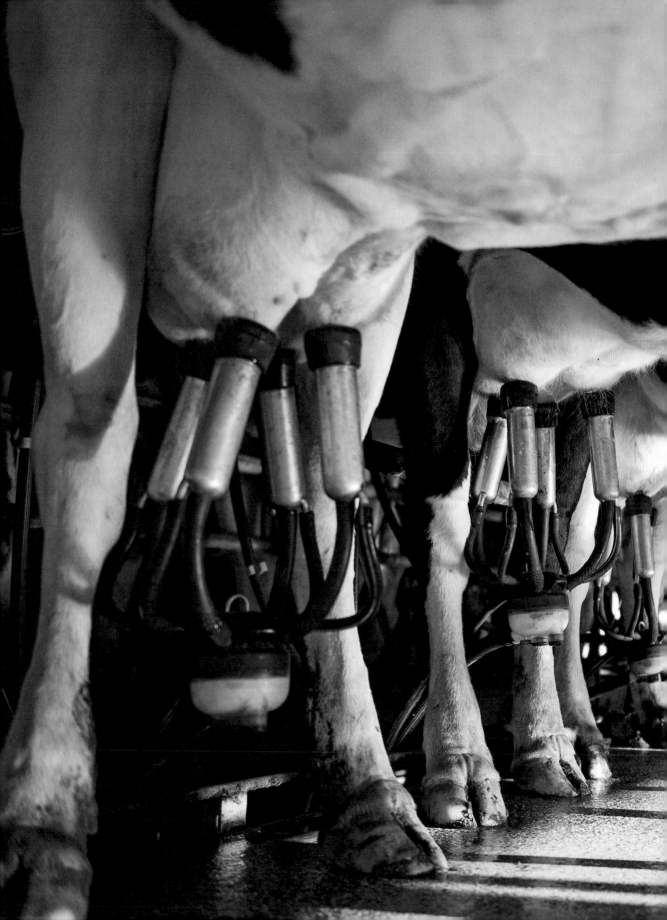

USE-BY DATES

Milk lasts longer today than it did thirty years ago (often up to twice as long, according to best-before dates). That's because every farm's microbial counts are far stricter, hygiene is better, and the milk is chilled at every stage of handling and processing these days, ensuring better shelf life. It may also have something to do with the way milk is treated through ultrafiltration, as the milk I buy, with cream on the top and from a single herd, goes off within three days of opening, regardless of the use-by date.

500 ml (17 fl oz/2 cups) full-cream
   (whole) milk
100 g (3½ oz) caster (superfine) sugar
4 eggs, beaten
½ whole nutmeg, freshly grated
   (about ½–1 teaspoon)

Baked nutmeg custard

This baked custard is a flourless, just-set milky pudding, heady with the fragrance of fresh nutmeg. For a more indulgent custard, use a mixture of half cream to milk, and replace the eggs with 4 egg yolks.

SERVES 4

Preheat the oven to 150°C (300°F/Gas 2).

Heat the milk in a saucepan over medium heat until hot but not boiling. Beat the milk, sugar and eggs together in a bowl until well combined. Strain into a 1 litre (35 fl oz/ 4 cup) ovenproof dish and sprinkle half the nutmeg over the top, stirring to combine.

Place the dish into a deep baking tray and pour in enough boiling water to come one-third of the way up the side of the dish. Bake in the oven for 30–40 minutes, or until the custard has set.

To check, bump the edge of the tray gently to see if the middle wobbles in the same way as the edges. Cooking times can vary because of the heat of the milk, water and the oven, so you want to get it out of the oven just as it sets. Once set, the custard can start to bubble and overcook, which alters the texture; if it curdles it is not quite as good to eat (and a bit ugly to look at), but it's still quite edible.

Sprinkle with the remaining nutmeg and serve warm.

1 litre (35 fl oz/4 cups) goat's or
    sheep's milk
1 vanilla bean, split lengthways
180 g (6¼ oz) caster (superfine) sugar
3 teaspoons powdered gelatine

Balsamic strawberries
500 g (1 lb 2 oz) strawberries,
    hulled and halved
icing (confectioners') sugar, to taste
2 tablespoons good-quality
    balsamic vinegar

Goat's milk latte cotto

In Italian, panna cotta literally means 'cooked cream', and latte cotto is a lighter version meaning 'cooked milk'. You need to use super fresh, sweet-tasting milk if it's from your own herd. Sheep's milk works just as well.

SERVES 8

Put the milk and vanilla bean in a saucepan over high heat. When the milk is hot, and nearly boiling, remove from the heat and set aside for 15 minutes to allow the flavours to infuse.

Return the milk to high heat and add the sugar. Bring to the boil, stirring to dissolve the sugar. Remove the vanilla bean and discard, then remove the pan from the heat and whisk in the gelatine until completely dissolved.

Remove from the heat, pour into a bowl and allow to cool to room temperature. Whisk again and pour the mixture into eight 150 ml (5 fl oz) dariole moulds or small plastic cups and refrigerate for a few hours, or preferably overnight, to set.

To make the balsamic strawberries, put the strawberries in a bowl and toss with the icing sugar and balsamic vinegar. Set aside for 10 minutes.

To serve, turn the latte cotto out of their moulds by dipping the base of each mould into hot water, then inverting over a plate — run a knife down the side of the latte cotto to break the vacuum if necessary. If you're making them in plastic cups, you can also make a little hole in the bottom of each cup to help it slide out easily.

Serve the latte cotto with the balsamic strawberries on the side.

1 litre (35 fl oz/4 cups) full-cream
  (whole) milk, preferably organic
  and unhomogenised
2 tablespoons natural yoghurt,
  whisked lightly

Homemade yoghurt

*Homemade yoghurt is nothing like most commercial varieties
(see pages 36–7). Those who make it every week tend to find their
own way to get it to set perfectly — it's not hard to do and worth giving
a go. It should go without saying, but the better the milk, the better the
yoghurt will taste. Choose a natural plain yoghurt to put in it that has
a flavour you enjoy (different cultures have different flavour profiles).
Low-fat milks make a thinner, more sour yoghurt, so use full-cream
(whole) milk for the best effect. Replacing 100 ml (3½ fl oz) of the milk
with cream makes a more Greek-style yoghurt.*

MAKES 1 LITRE (35 FL OZ/4 CUPS)

Heat the milk in a saucepan over high heat
until it just starts to froth at the edges,
but hasn't quite boiled. If you have a
thermometer, aim for 92°C (198°F).
Turn the heat right down and stir often,
keeping the milk hot for 10–15 minutes;
this ensures a better set.

Turn off the heat and let the milk cool
until you can leave your hand comfortably
on the outside of the pan — it should still be
warm, but not scorching. I cover the pan with
a lid to stop a skin forming.

Pour the milk into a gently warmed dish
that you can store it in — a ceramic bowl is
a nice idea.

Stir in the yoghurt, cover the dish well
with plastic wrap and then wrap the entire
dish in several layers of cloth to insulate it.
Leave it to sit overnight on the bench —
this allows the yoghurt cultures to breed.
The ideal temperature is about 20°C (68°F)
— depending on the time of year it could be
better to make it in the daytime. After about
8 hours the yoghurt should be set. Transfer
to the refrigerator and eat within 1–2 weeks.

You can use this yoghurt to start your next
batch, but sometimes the cultures may need
refreshing with another bought yoghurt.

2 litres (70 fl oz/8 cups)
    full-cream (whole) milk
2 tablespoons white vinegar

Ricotta

Homemade ricotta isn't the same as real ricotta (see explanation on pages 79–80), but it is far superior to the long-life product they sell as ricotta in supermarkets. For subtlety and texture, this ricotta recipe is hard to beat.

MAKES 440 G (15½ OZ/1¾ CUPS)

Put the milk in a saucepan over high heat. Cook until the milk reaches 93°C (200°F) — the best way to check this without a kitchen thermometer is to heat the milk to the point where it has foam on top, but isn't boiling. Turn off the heat. Stir the milk and when it's moving rapidly, toss in the vinegar and stir just until evenly spread. The milk should curdle immediately and form a raft of clotted curds on top — this will become your ricotta. Let the curd clump up (this makes it much easier to remove), then lift it off gently with a slotted spoon.

Put the curds into a fine sieve, seasoning with a little salt, to taste. Gently pour the liquid (whey) from the saucepan over to catch the last few curds in the sieve.

Turn the ricotta out onto a plate and serve hot with just a drizzle of olive oil for a sensory thrill, or chill it down and store, well covered in the refrigerator, for use in other dishes.

It keeps well for about 4 days, and after that you may want to use it cooked. Let your taste buds be your guide.

500 ml (17 fl oz/2 cups) full-cream
    (whole) milk, plus 2 tablespoons extra
2 strips lemon peel
2 tablespoons wheaten cornflour
    or 3 tablespoons pure cornflour
    (cornstarch) (see page 126)

2 eggs
100 g (3½ oz) sugar

Good old-fashioned cornflour custard

*Real, old-fashioned English custard has a soft, cushiony mouthfeel that
you just don't get with the French anglaise (which has no flour in it).
To me this cornflour custard is more comforting, homely and satisfying,
just like slipping on a well-worn woollen jumper instead of a polar
fleece. This recipe makes enough custard for four people to eat with
pudding and can be flavoured with either vanilla or lemon. If you
wanted to, you could use an extra 100 ml (3 ½ fl oz) warmed milk
to adjust the consistency.*

MAKES 500 ML (17 FL OZ/2 CUPS)

Put the milk and lemon peel in a saucepan over high heat. Remove from the heat just before it starts to boil. Set aside for about 10–15 minutes to allow the flavours to infuse. Remove the lemon peel.

Put the extra milk and cornflour in a bowl and whisk to dissolve the cornflour. Whisk in the eggs and half of the sugar, combining well.

Add the remaining sugar to the milk and reheat over high heat. Whisk the hot milk into the cornflour mixture. Return to the heat in a clean saucepan and whisk until it comes to the boil. (The clean pan isn't essential, but it helps to prevent the custard from catching and burning.) Remove the custard from the heat and place a sheet of plastic wrap onto the surface of the custard while still warm if not serving straight away.

Variations: To make a bay leaf custard, add 1 fresh bay leaf when you add the lemon peel and be sure to remove it once the flavours have infused. Continue with the method above.

To make a vanilla custard, omit the lemon peel, only heat the milk once, and add 1 teaspoon natural vanilla extract after the custard has thickened and been taken from the heat.

250 g (9 oz) butter, cubed and softened
300 g (10½ oz/1⅓ cups) caster
  (superfine) sugar
3 eggs
1 teaspoon natural vanilla extract

250 ml (9 fl oz/1 cup) sour milk
  (see page 36)
400 g (14 oz) self-raising flour, sifted
100 g (3½ oz) frozen raspberries

Raspberry sour milk cake

Soured milk (see page 36) makes this cake so much better than using regular milk. If you don't have milk that has only just turned, add a bit of buttermilk, yoghurt or a good tablespoon of lemon juice to the milk to help sour it. You can also substitute chunks of baked quince (see page 425) or poached pears (see page 555) for the raspberries if you like.

SERVES 12

Preheat the oven to 180°C (350°F/Gas 4). Grease a 26 cm (10½ inch) round spring-form cake tin and line the base and sides with baking paper.

Beat the butter and sugar together in a bowl until light and pale. Beat in the eggs, one at a time, making sure each is well incorporated before adding the next one. Add the vanilla extract and stir to combine.

Add half of the milk and half of the flour, in two batches, stirring until the batter is just combined. I like to add 1 or 2 extra tablespoons of milk if it seems too thick. Stir in the raspberries (they should still be frozen) until combined, then pour the mixture into the prepared tin.

Bake in the oven for 35–45 minutes, or until a skewer inserted into the centre of the cake comes out clean. Cool in the tin for 10 minutes, then turn out onto a wire rack to cool completely.

This cake can be stored in an airtight container for up to 5 days.

1 kg (2 lb 4 oz) Greek-style yoghurt
a pinch of salt
500 ml (17 fl oz/2 cups) extra virgin
    olive oil
fresh or dried herbs, such as thyme, bay
    leaf, oregano, peppercorns or chilli

Labna

Labna (or labne) are tangy balls of drained yoghurt that resemble a soft, curd-style cheese. They're terrific for spreading on bread or eating as part of an antipasti platter. This recipe uses Greek-style yoghurt, which is creamier than natural yoghurt, so in its absence, add a little pouring (whipping) cream (35% fat) to natural yoghurt for a richer effect. The labna can be eaten straight away, or stored in oil in the refrigerator and used for up to 1 month.

MAKES ABOUT 50 SMALL BALLS

Put the yoghurt and salt in a bowl and whisk well to combine. Line a sieve with a piece of muslin (cheesecloth) and sit the sieve over a large bowl. Pour the yoghurt into the sieve, cover with plastic wrap and refrigerate for 1 day to allow the whey to come out. Take care that the muslin isn't sitting in liquid.

After the first day, turn the yoghurt out onto a fresh piece of muslin, discard the used muslin and any whey from the bowl and return the muslin-wrapped yoghurt to the sieve. Cover with plastic wrap and refrigerate for another 1–2 days. When ready, the yoghurt should be just firm enough to roll into balls. I like to drain it even more using paper towel if it's a bit thin.

Take 1–2 teaspoons of the drained yoghurt at a time and roll into balls. Place the balls into a sterilised airtight jar and fill with the extra virgin olive oil and your preferred mix of herbs.

Raita

Raita is a very simple side dish that's great to serve with curries. Black salt is a wonderful, complex, sulphurous salt from India, available at Indian food stores. If you can't find any black salt, use table salt instead.

100 g (3½ oz) natural yoghurt
a pinch of black salt
a good pinch of freshly ground black pepper
2 Lebanese (short) cucumbers, finely diced
1 tablespoon chopped coriander (cilantro) leaves

MAKES 375 G (13 OZ/1½ CUPS)

Whisk together the yoghurt, salt and pepper until well combined. Stir through the cucumber and coriander and serve with the Taxi Driver's Lamb Curry (page 254), Stir-fried Chicken Thigh with Black Pepper and Curry Leaf (page 171), the Beef, Coconut and Lime Leaf Curry (page 229), the Dark Curry of Venison with Cardamom (page 295) or the Goat Shin Curry (page 294). Raita is best used straight away, but can be stored, covered in the refrigerator, for up to 1 day.

CREAM & BUTTER

Cream is simply the rich, fattier portion of unhomogenised milk that rises to the surface and is skimmed or spun off. It has a higher proportion of butterfat than milk, and has long been considered a very good reason to keep a cow. Traditionally, before the advent of refrigeration, cream was often soured and preserved in some way. The ready availability of fresh cream is a very recent phenomenon.

Butter, that glorious emulsion of butterfat with a little water and milk solids, is made by the simple action of churning cream. The cream will go thick like whipped cream, then split into butter and buttermilk (the runny bit). It is then washed to rinse out extra buttermilk, before being patted or massaged into blocks. At its most pure, butter is simply made from cream, though sometimes it has a culture added, and salt is often used, particularly in Britain and areas influenced by the UK, including the US, New Zealand and Australia.

A FEW CREAM DEFINITIONS

SCALDED CREAM This is cream that has been simmered, which alters the flavour and texture, adding more caramel hints; it thickens up after cooking and cooling (see page 59).

CLOTTED CREAM Traditionally an English soured cream, which is heated very slowly (and to a lower temperature than scalded cream) until it reduces in volume and gets a brown crust on top. Clotted cream thickens as it cools, and is usually about 55 per cent butterfat when set. It is often called scalded cream in and around Cornwall, where it originates and reaches perfection (see page 61).

SINGLE CREAM Not used as a term where I live, but a lovely light cream of about 16–18 per cent butterfat. It won't whip, but is delicious poured on strawberries and the like. In some places they have 'half cream' that is 12 per cent fat and good in coffee.

POURING (WHIPPING) CREAM This cream has about 35 per cent butterfat and is suitable for whipping. In Australia this is just normal pouring cream, while in the UK it is known as whipping cream.

THICK (DOUBLE/HEAVY) CREAM This cream has about 45–55 per cent butterfat. It is a naturally thick cream and will usually separate into butter if lightly whipped or even stirred too much. Sadly, much of the 'thick' cream sold in supermarkets is thickened using gum or gelatine rather than being naturally thick.

WHAT IS CRÈME FRAÎCHE?

To most English-speaking nations, crème fraîche means sour cream, but the origins of the expression are French, and to them the term simply means, literally, fresh cream. Traditionally, fresh cream in France was cultured, which soured it lightly, and allowed the French to keep their cream a little longer. Most crème fraîche in France is lower in fat and acidity than the more acidic sour cream we are familiar with in Australia, the Americas and the UK. It has a subtler, often more complex flavour. So while the literal translation of crème fraîche is 'fresh cream', a lightly soured cream is the actual result.

To make crème fraîche at home, simply add about 2 tablespoons of live yoghurt to 300 ml (10½ fl oz) warmed cream (just a little warmer than your hand when you touch the dish). Cover lightly with plastic wrap and let it stand at 15°C (59°F) for about 12 hours before transferring to the refrigerator (a cellar would be good, or something similar). If you live in a hotter climate, cut the time shorter. Ideally, you should leave the cream for 2–3 days before using it. In the absence of a live culture, you can create crème fraîche by adding about 2 teaspoons of freshly squeezed lemon juice to 300 ml (10½ fl oz) cream and refrigerating overnight before using.

WHAT IS MASCARPONE — AND WHY ISN'T IT CHEESE?

Mascarpone isn't a cheese, because it isn't made using rennet, or a live culture. Instead it's scalded (boiled) cream that is soured using an acid such as vinegar, lemon juice or tartaric acid, and is then drained of whey. Traditionally in the north of Italy, where mascarpone originates, it may also be cultured, in the same way as buttermilk, by using live bacteria, but most of the time it is simply soured. It can be used in the place of thick (double/heavy) cream in many instances, and is typically quite high in butterfat.

Homemade mascarpone (see page 62) is better than most commercial brands.

BUYING BUTTER

A lot of butter you buy in a supermarket has been frozen in large blocks to preserve it, because the spring flush of milk means more butter can be made in the warmer months, and much less over winter. Butter can be yellow or pale, mostly depending on the feed of the cow, though in some places it's artificially coloured, either through the feed of the cow or when made. The butter where I live is a bright golden hue, because the cows are virtually always feeding on fresh grass and the beta-carotene in the grass lends the butter a yellow glow. Cows fed on dry feed, like those who must live indoors over winter in really cold climates, tend to produce a very pale butter by comparison.

Some butter is made from the whey left over after cheesemaking. If you put the whey through a centrifuge, the small amount of fat that is left in it can be salvaged and makes an interesting butter, lightly acidic from the cultures used in the cheese, and often very pale. Some butters, such as those made from Italian Grana cheeses (Parmigiano and Padano) use the cheese as a marketing tool for the quality of the butter. Butter can also be made by centrifuging milk.

Butter can also be made from other milks, including buffalo and yak.

WHAT IS CULTURED BUTTER?

In some places, Europe in particular, the cream that butter is churned from is cultured to help preserve it. This lightly acidic cream produces a butter that is fuller in flavour, and less likely to leave a waxy feel in the mouth. English butter is more likely to be salted, but it too may also be cultured. This culture in salted butter is usually used to allow the maker to redeem more butter from the cream, rather than for any culinary advantage. Some modern 'cultured' butter is the result of very quick processing, and has no discernable higher quality, merely a slightly sour profile. Typically in Australia only artisan cultured butter is fermented the old-fashioned, flavoursome way.

Good-quality cultured butter has a lower water content, and this, combined with its clean mouthfeel, makes it ideal for pastry, despite a sometimes prohibitive price.

WHAT IS GHEE?

Ghee is a heated, clarified butter. Butter, being about 80–85 per cent fat, has some water and some milk solids in it. Heating it causes the liquid to drop below the butterfat, and some solids to rise. If you skim the solids and drain off the liquid butterfat, the remaining clear yellow liquid is called clarified butter. If you heat the butter even longer until the liquid underneath evaporates and turns a nut brown colour, then siphon off the clear liquid, this is called ghee, much used in Indian cookery (the milk solids and browned base are discarded, usually).

Because ghee has no water or milk solids in it, it can be heated to higher temperatures than butter before it burns. The scorching of the fat when it is made also creates antioxidants, which means, along with its lack of water, that ghee stays fresher for longer than pure butter or clarified butter, before turning rancid.

WHY DO SOME PASTRIES LEAVE A WAXY FEEL IN THE MOUTH?

Most commercial pastry doesn't use butter. Sadly. That's because butter, with its low melting point, can be difficult to work, and it's more expensive than margarine.

So the miracle that is butter is often replaced, at least in part, with very strange-textured margarines, some very specific products that allow the most amazing layers to be worked up in puff pastry, even by a complete novice or a computerised machine. These artificially solidified fats create pastries that suit the unskilled or the processing industry. The downside is the flavour, texture and after effects of this margarine. Pastries made with these margarines don't boast a lot of flavour (hence you can eat more pastry than is good for you), they don't melt in the mouth, and they leave an awful waxy texture on your tongue and the roof of your mouth. In other words, they're margarines designed so that the rolling and baking of pastry is easier, and they store better, but they're not designed with the actual eating in mind.

WHAT IS REAL BUTTERMILK?

Buttermilk, as its name suggests, is the runny liquid that separates out during the process of making butter. Whipping, churning or centrifuging cream clumps fat globules together, leaving buttermilk as a byproduct. This is usually cultured, so it's a lightly sour, whey-like liquid, with the occasional blob of butterfat that will rise to the top if left to stand. It's a most refreshing drink and remarkably full of flavour.

These days, however, buttermilk isn't actually buttermilk. It's fresh milk cultured much as you would yoghurt, usually given extra body by the addition of skim milk powder or other milk solids. It's not a bad product, but it's not real buttermilk, despite being labelled as such. In cooking, often the substitution of full-cream (whole) milk with some yoghurt is as good as using factory-made buttermilk. So fundamental has been the change, that virtually no modern recipes use the old-fashioned, real version of buttermilk.

DID YOU KNOW?

The quantity of milk fat in butter has changed in the past few decades — down from 84 to 80 per cent, which means manufacturers are leaving more buttermilk or water in the butter, which helps their bottom line, but makes the butter a much lesser product to use. Good local and French butters have a higher fat content (hence less water) and are far better for all cooking, particularly for making pastries and frying.

Scalded cream

Scalded cream is just that: cream that has been heated; in fact, it is best barely simmered. It is a cross between a panna cotta (which is set with gelatine) and clotted cream (which is cooked over a lower heat). Sometimes clotted cream (see page 61) is called scalded cream. All you do for my scalded cream is boil up cream and pop it in the refrigerator. It's much faster to make than clotted cream and seriously yummy, because it has caramel flavours and a richer texture than if it hadn't been heated. Use it as you would any rich cream.

---

300 ml (10½ fl oz) pouring (whipping) cream (35% fat)
100 g (3½ oz) thick (double/heavy) cream (over 45% fat)

MAKES 400 ML (14 FL OZ)

Put both creams in a large saucepan over medium heat and bring to just simmering — the cream will bubble at the sides and a skin will form on top. Keep the cream at this temperature for about 5 minutes, adjusting the heat to keep it gently simmering and being careful that it doesn't boil over. Remove from the heat and transfer the cream to a shallow serving dish, scraping in all the skin from the edge of the pan as well. Allow to cool, cover with plastic wrap and refrigerate to set until needed. It will keep for up to 10 days if stored correctly.

600 ml (21 fl oz) pouring (whipping)
cream (35% fat)

600 g (1 lb 5 oz) thick (double/heavy)
cream (over 45% fat)
2 tablespoons natural yoghurt

Clotted cream

Clotted cream (see page 54 for a definition) is an incredible cream that tastes of so much more than plain old whipped or thick (double/heavy) cream. The sign of true clotted cream is the crust that appears on the top from long, slow cooking. You can make it in a double-boiler, but cooking it in a low oven (in an ideal world, a cooling woodfired oven) works best, and is how the cream was traditionally cooked in England, where this recipe originated. Just be sure your oven actually works at such a low temperature, as many older ovens don't. Lightly souring the cream by leaving it at room temperature for a few hours without the addition of yoghurt is an inexact process, but you may want to try it as it does make the cream taste better. Whatever you do, make sure the creams are pure — no gums or thickeners added. Use it on any pudding or cake that you'd use a rich cream on. I've actually dipped fresh dates into clotted cream and pretended it was dessert. Start 2 days in advance for best results.

MAKES 750 ML (26 FL OZ/3 CUPS)

Place both creams and yoghurt in a bowl and whisk until just combined. Pour into a 30 x 20 x 6 cm (12 x 8 x 2¹/₂ inch) baking dish, so the cream is about 2 cm (³/₄ inch) deep all over. Set aside at warm room temperature (about 20°C/68°F) for 6 hours to lightly sour the cream. This step isn't essential, but will improve the taste. Dip your finger in and see if it has soured slightly. If it tastes awful, it's too sour so don't go any further.

Preheat the oven to 100°C (200°F/ Gas ¹/₂). Put the dish of cream in a deep baking tray and pour in enough water to come one-third of the way up the sides of the dish. Bake for several hours (more than 12 hours is usual) until a crust forms on top and the cream has thickened and set — the cream should have reduced by about one-third, though this may not be apparent.

Allow to cool, cover with a lid or plastic wrap, then refrigerate for at least 1 day, preferably 2 days, to let it set completely (there may be some whey-like bits at the bottom — these are perfectly edible, but not so nice as the clotted cream on top). Make sure you scoop out a good layer of cream and crust when you serve it. The clotted cream will keep for up to 1 week in the refrigerator.

Variation: To make using the stovetop, pour the cream into a stainless steel bowl and place over a saucepan of hot water (it should not be boiling or even simmering) — they say 82°C (180°F) is best, but this is hard to measure without a thermometer. Keep over the water on low heat for about 2–3 hours, or until the cream has the requisite crust — it won't reduce much in volume. Allow to cool, then cover and refrigerate for 2 days before using.

600 ml (21 fl oz) pouring (whipping)
    cream (35% fat)
1 tablespoon freshly squeezed lemon
    juice, strained

Homemade mascarpone

*Mascarpone is one of the world's most exciting creams. But often the
stuff you buy isn't as good as it could be. By making it yourself, you
won't have to pay exorbitant prices and will also get a better result than
if you were to buy a commercial variety. This recipe is also handy for
people who live in country towns and may not have mascarpone available
on supermarket shelves. You can replace the lemon juice with lime juice
in this recipe, or add 1 teaspoon citric acid and a vanilla bean to the
simmered cream and let it infuse for 15 minutes.*

MAKES 350 G (12 OZ)

Put the cream in a saucepan over high heat.
Bring to a simmer, add the lemon juice and
cook for 1 minute. Remove from the heat
and allow to cool completely.

Line a sieve with a double layer of muslin
(cheesecloth), and drain the cream into this
muslin over a clean bowl.

Refrigerate in the sieve for 1–2 days until
firm. Discard the liquid. The solids are your
mascarpone, ready to flavour and sweeten
if you desire, or just serve it as you would
a rich cream.

Store the mascarpone covered with plastic
wrap in the refrigerator for up to 1 week.

3 teaspoons powdered gelatine
1.25 kg (2 lb 12 oz/5 cups) sour cream
180 g (6¼ oz) caster (superfine) sugar
balsamic strawberries (see page 43),
   to serve (optional)

Sour cream panna cotta

Panna cotta should be gently wobbly and very light on the lips — a barely set jelly that lingers like butterfly kisses. I prefer it served in individual cups rather than made rubbery and tipped out of moulds, but these amounts should give you the chance to get them out of the mould and still keep that sexy texture. It can be served on its own, with a sauce of some kind, or with balsamic strawberries like the latte cotto on page 43 — although panna cotta is richer in flavour and more filling.

SERVES 10-12

Put the gelatine in a large bowl with 4 tablespoons cold water and stir to dissolve the gelatine.

Put the sour cream and sugar in a saucepan and bring to the boil over high heat, stirring to help dissolve the sugar into the melting sour cream. Remove from the heat and gradually whisk into the bowl with the gelatine. Stir well to completely dissolve the gelatine. When it has cooled to room temperature whisk well and pour the cream mixture into ten or twelve 150 ml (5 fl oz) dariole moulds or plastic cups. Refrigerate for at least 4 hours to set, or overnight.

Turn the panna cotta out of their moulds by dipping the base of each mould into hot water, then inverting over a plate — run a knife down the side of the panna cotta to break the vacuum if necessary. (If you're making them in plastic cups, you can make a little hole in the bottom of each cup to help it slide out easily.)

Serve the panna cotta on its own or with balsamic strawberries if you like.

Variations: You can use pouring (whipping) cream instead of the sour cream in this recipe if you prefer. Add a little buttermilk to the cream if you want a sour flavour. For a coconut version, you can use coconut cream, or half coconut cream and half cream, with a little pandan leaf (a South-East Asian substitute for vanilla that is used for flavouring sweets) thrown in while the cream heats, for excitement. Make sure you discard the leaf before pouring the mixture into moulds.

Treacle ice cream without a machine

600 ml (21 fl oz) pouring (whipping) cream (35% fat)
6 eggs, separated
125 g (4½ oz) treacle
100 g (3½ oz) glucose syrup (corn syrup)

SERVES 8–10

Whisk the cream to soft peaks. Whisk the egg yolks and treacle in a bowl until well combined. Stir into the cream, then mix until evenly textured.

In a separate bowl, whisk the egg whites with the glucose syrup and a pinch of salt until soft peaks form. Gently fold one-quarter of the egg white mixture into the treacle mixture until nearly combined, then fold this into the remaining egg white mixture until combined.

Spoon into an ice-cream container and freeze for at least 3–4 hours before serving. Store ice cream in an airtight container in the freezer for up to 2 weeks.

270 g (9½ oz) self-raising flour, plus extra, for sprinkling
2 tablespoons full-cream (whole) milk powder (optional)
2 teaspoons baking powder
1 tablespoon sugar
a pinch of salt
40 g (1½ oz) butter, chilled and cubed
185 ml (6 fl oz/¾ cup) buttermilk, chilled

Buttermilk scones

Scones benefit from minimal handling (preferably with cold hands). They say your scones should be ready in the time it takes from the unexpected squeaking of the front gate to the knock on the front door — that's minimal handling!

Curiously, these scones taste much better using milk powder rather than normal milk. I rescued them from a recipe book brought back from Norfolk Island. They differ from a regular scone recipe in that they include buttermilk (and even provide a measurement for it!) and a hint of sugar. They're light and delightfully textured, although you have to smother them with red berry jam and lightly whipped cream to enjoy the full effect.

MAKES 12

Preheat the oven to 220°C (425°F/Gas 7). Line a baking tray with baking paper.

Mix the flour, milk powder, baking powder, sugar and salt in a large bowl. Using your fingertips, rub in the butter until no large bits remain. It doesn't have to be perfect. You can use a food processor if you prefer, but it is preferable to chill the bowl first so the butter stays quite firm and doesn't melt into the flour.

Make a well in the centre and add the buttermilk. Mix together with a spoon until the mixture starts to stiffen, then continue mixing with your fingers, kneading until the mixture just comes together — be careful not to overmix or the scones will be chewy.

Dust the bench with flour and sprinkle a little over your fingers, then press the dough out to about 1 cm (½ inch) thickness all over. Use a sharp 4–5 cm (1½–2 inch) round pastry cutter to make rounds. Place the rounds close together on the prepared tray. Press out any left-over dough and continue cutting out circles to make 12 rounds in total. These final few scones will be a little tougher in texture, but it's better than letting the dough go to waste.

Bake the scones in the oven for about 10–15 minutes, or until lightly coloured on the top and bottom.

600 g (1 lb 5 oz/2⅔ cups) thick
(double/heavy) cream (45% fat)
3 cm (1¼ inch) strip citrus peel (lemon,
lime or tangelo)

1 vanilla bean, split lengthways
6 egg yolks
2 tablespoons caster (superfine) sugar,
plus extra for burning

Crème brûlée

The name crème brûlée literally translates to 'burnt cream', and is the dessert restaurants love to serve, because it costs virtually nothing to make and they can charge like a hog on heat for it. Crème brûlée should be very dark on top. It is very rich, so is best served in small quantities.

SERVES 8

Put the cream and citrus peel in a saucepan over high heat. Scrape the vanilla seeds into the pan and add the bean. Bring to a simmer. Remove from the heat, whisk and set aside for 15 minutes to allow the flavours to infuse. Strain the cream through a fine sieve, discarding the peel and bean.

Beat the egg yolks and sugar together in a bowl until pale. Whisk in the cream, then pour into a clean saucepan over low heat, stirring constantly, until the cream thickens — the mixture should coat the back of a spoon. Don't overcook the custard or it will scramble. Pour into eight 100 ml (3½ fl oz) heatproof dishes, such as ramekins, cover with plastic wrap and refrigerate overnight.

Just before serving, sprinkle an even layer of caster sugar over the top of each custard. Caramelise the top using a blowtorch, or cook under a preheated grill (broiler) — the top of each brûlée should be dark, but not black; the time will vary depending on how well your grill heats up. Allow to cool slightly before serving (otherwise your guests may lose a few of their taste buds).

3 eggs, separated

2 tablespoons icing (confectioners')
    sugar, sifted

½ teaspoon natural vanilla extract

250 g (9 oz) homemade mascarpone
    (see page 62)

2 teaspoons caster (superfine) sugar

200 ml (7 fl oz) hot espresso coffee

160 ml (5¼ fl oz) Tia Maria or similar
    liqueur, such as Kahlua

250 g (9 oz/about 12) savoiardi
    (lady finger) biscuits

unsweetened cocoa powder,
    for dusting

Tiramisù

Try to find a good soft mascarpone, for this recipe, rather than a coarse, thick one — or better still, make your own (see page 62). The important thing is to make sure the biscuits are wet and soft right through, so if you run out of the coffee mixture, make more. I also like to use a little bit of Strega in the mascarpone, an Italian liqueur that adds extra flavour, but isn't that easy to find in bottle shops. In its place, Frangelico is a lovely substitute.

SERVES 4

Beat the egg yolks, icing sugar and vanilla together in a bowl until pale and light. Fold in the mascarpone until just combined — take care; some mascarpone will split if over-handled.

Whisk the egg whites until soft peaks form, then fold into the mascarpone mixture.

Dissolve the caster sugar in the hot coffee and stir in the Tia Maria. Dip half of the biscuits, one at a time, into the coffee mixture until softened all over and place in an even layer in the bottom of a 2 litre (70 fl oz/8 cup) round serving dish with a 20 cm (8 inch) diameter. Top with half of the mascarpone mixture.

Repeat this step to create another layer of coffee-soaked biscuits and mascarpone. Dust the top with cocoa and (if you're strong-willed) refrigerate for a few hours before eating so the biscuits and mascarpone have a chance to mingle flavours and the mascarpone can set a little.

Remove the tiramisù from the refrigerator about 30 minutes before serving.

CHEESE

It's 2015. Hans and Esther no longer hand milk, unless the goat is old or unwell. Their twenty-six toggenburg goats are milked in a portable milking shed, perched high on a hill near Cygnet in southern Tasmania. Esther misses the interaction she had with each girl when she did it by hand. It's a long way from the alps of Switzerland, where Hans and Esther learnt their craft, to Tongola dairy, though the softly tinkling bells around the goats' necks make the hills resound like those of the Matterhorn.

This is true, handcrafted, artisan farmhouse cheese. The goats are a single herd. They're milked twice a day, every day, during the warmer months, and the cheese is made by the people who milk the goats. Between them, Hans and Esther are the living face of an ancient craft — cheesemaking at its most pure, where animals are milked on the same farm where the cheese is made. A visit to Tongola revealed how little has improved in the art of cheesemaking in the past few centuries. Despite Tongola moving to Leap Farm further north at Marion Bay, traditional cheesemaking is still at its heart thanks to dedicated owners Iain and Kate Field.

Nick Haddow, from Bruny Island Cheese, is another, perhaps more modern, face of the cheesemaking fraternity. Nick has started his own dairy 25 minutes from our farm, and his cheeses are variants on themes. About fifteen types appear in a twelve-month cycle, while Tongola specialise in just four.

The cheeses from both properties are nothing like mass-produced cheese. They both source milk from single herds. Both mature their cheeses using natural rinds and ancient techniques, and the end result is cheese that speaks not only of the milk, but also of the skill and care of the cheesemakers themselves.

Cheese is preserved milk. That's it. Despite the hundreds of varieties, the European system of preserving names and traditions, and the myriad styles, flavours, textures and maturing techniques, cheese is really just an old-fashioned way of storing an excess of milk for another day. Thankfully, it's also an incredible thing to eat.

Cheese is just the more solid part of the process left when curds and whey are separated out after acidifying and culturing milk. Whey is the watery bit; curds the slippery, wobbly, sweet/sour bit that's left.

Making cheese involves a series of steps. First the milk is cultured using bacteria, as you might yoghurt, but using a much lighter culture than yoghurt. It's then set using rennet, the enzyme used to make junket. This mixture is then known as curd, but every time you cut, stir or move the curd, it will drain out the more watery whey.

How you cut, stir, salt, heat, massage or press the curd has an impact on the texture of the final cheese.

If you cut curds, wash them in warm water or heat them, or all three, they drain out more whey and dry differently. Cheeses are also ripened using moulds, blue and white, both usually added early in the cheesemaking process. Then the final stage in making cheese lies in ripening and ageing to produce different results. At its heart it's a beautifully simple technique, an age-old method of keeping the goodness of milk for times when you're not near the cow, or she's no longer milking.

But cheesemaking has changed. No longer is most cheddar aged in cloth, the outside releasing moisture, the inside a living mass that becomes more complex; now it's aged by being vacuum-packed in big plastic bags. No longer are most white mould cheeses best eaten on a certain day of a certain week; they're now stabilised to stop them over-ripening (which means that they never actually ripen). Artisans are under pressure from rigid health regulations and a system that favours the large, industrial cheesemakers over those who concentrate on interesting, complex, endlessly variable flavours.

This isn't just a New World problem. An article in the *Wall Street Journal* from 2000 quotes the director-general of a large French cheese company, Celia, as saying, 'No matter what people say, what they want to eat is cheese that is creamy, tender and bland.' Celia aims to sell to the entire French market, and you never go broke catering to the lowest common denominator. In the same article it was claimed that French dairies focusing on the mass market strive to produce a cheese that is unctuous and bland. Worse still, it should be 'without typicity' so it is generic. (Typicity is a word usually reserved for wine; how the wine is an expression not only of the type of grape, but also of the place where it was made; each region produces a wine with unique typical characteristics.)

Mass-produced cheese is insipid by comparison with true farmhouse or artisan cheese. The good news is that for those obsessed by flavour, those who want their cheeses to taste of mushrooms or earth, who like a bit of bracing acidity, a whiff of something forbidden, a little bit of sex in their fromage, great artisan cheese is still being made.

WHAT MAKES GOOD CHEESE?

To make good cheese you need a few things. It helps if you start with good milk. Add good, sound, proven techniques to ferment and culture it, then mature it well, using moulds and bacteria to the best advantage. Simple really. But of all these, the ingredient most important for good cheese is the technique of the craftspeople who make it.

Cheese can be made from almost any milk, but the four main commercial milks used for cheese are cow, goat, sheep and buffalo. Each has its own distinct flavour, each can be made into hard or soft cheeses, and each milk is very much at the whim of the cheesemaker, whose art is in the transformation of liquid to culinary gold.

A real cheese is handled. If a firm cheese has a natural rind and is going to be aged, it needs to be turned and rubbed to reduce the moulds on the outside. As each cheese is lifted from the maturing board, the wooden shelf is rubbed, too. A white mould cheese is also turned, but gently, ensuring an even blanket of mould flourishes on the outside. An artisan washed rind cheese is physically washed with brine.

Most cheese, if it is matured at all, is matured in plastic bags. This allows the flavours to change (some say not for the better) without managing to create the same flavours that you'll get in naturally rinded cheese. Some say that bagged cheeses get a bag taint; a formaldehyde hint, or other off aromas. Why do manufacturers do it? Well, it's far cheaper to put a cheese in a vacuum-sealed bag than to have to rub it to reduce moulds, worry about the humidity in the cheese room and turn the cheeses regularly, which is the artisanal way of doing it. Sadly, many so-called 'farmhouse' cheeseries have fallen for the easy way out, using plastic bags (at least one calls them 'maturation bags'), and their cheese suffers by comparison.

CURD

The first stage of cheesemaking, curd is a very soft, subtle cheese that is spoonable because it still contains lots of the watery whey that is drained out when making more mature cheeses. Best eaten within a couple of days of making, it's a very good expression of the flavour of fresh milk. Cottage cheese is an example of a very fresh curd, with the whey washed out of it. Real, fresh cottage cheese is sublime. The stuff you buy in a supermarket, with its very long shelf life, is just texture, really. In France, a good country to compare ourselves with because they know and love cheese probably better than any nation, they eat over 7 kg (15 lb 12 oz) of fresh (under a week old) cheese each a year, from over 20 kg (45 lb) cheese in total. It could be curd, or fromage frais, or cottage-style cheese. In Australia we eat closer to 800 g (1 lb 12 oz) of fresh cheese a year, out of a total of 9 kg (20 lb 4 oz) of cheese.

SOFT CHEESE

Soft cheeses can be broken up into a few categories, but the main thing is that they are soft (oh, derr). This means they're usually young, relatively simple cheeses, such as a one-week-old salted curd, or perhaps a six-week-old white mould cow's milk cheese, or a washed rind cheese (although washed rind cheeses can also be firm cheeses).

An interesting variant on the soft cheese is mozzarella, which is made by heating and stretching the curds to form balls of layered curd that trap some of the milky whey inside. The best mozzarella is made from buffalo milk and is an art perfected in Battipaglia and Caserta near Naples in southern Italy. It's at its best eaten immediately after making, and loses quality by the day.

HARD CHEESE

As the curds drain, the cheese dries and you end up with a firmer end result. These cheeses can be aged for many months, and the insides form glutamates, which have a very, very satisfying effect (umami) on the palate. Think of the flavour of aged cheddar or Parmigiano Reggiano and you'll get the picture.

Even ricotta can be pressed and dried to produce a hard cheese, as can other soft cheeses, including cantal from France. Gouda is an example of a washed curd cheese that is rather sweet, mild and semi-hard when young. It becomes a hard cheese, as do so many cheeses, when aged for long enough — and some are aged for years. It's been said that you can buy a wheel of gouda to celebrate a child's birth and cut it on their twenty-first birthday. Three-year-old gouda is hard enough to cut; I can't imagine one twenty-one years old.

Parmigiano Reggiano and Grana Padano are the two most famed Italian parmesan-style hard cheeses. Reggiano is older, made with better milk, using more artisan techniques. Grana is younger, more commercial. But both, interestingly, have a natural rind. They're no longer rubbed by hand in most maturing rooms (the size of aircraft hangars, by the way), but the exact same motion is done by machine. Pretenders to the crown of either of these cheeses are usually sour. Australian parmesan tastes like heartburn.

CHEDDAR CHEESE This classic, hard English-style cheese takes its name from the gorge in Somerset, England, where it was originally made. It is 'cheddared' — a process where the curds are massaged with salt after being cut, which gives its characteristic dry texture and tang.

Real cheddar still comes from in and around Somerset in the UK, is matured in cloth, and has a natural rind because of it. Sadly, they don't own the rights to the name, so cheddar made in industrial quantities that's matured in plastic bags is also called cheddar. (The EU does, however, protect the name West Country Farmhouse Cheddar.) The non-traditional 'cheddar' has a few different names, at least in Australia, to define how much flavour it has. Below is a guide, though you can pretty much guarantee the cheese will be at the lower end of each age scale.

- Mild — 'matured' for up to three months.
- Semi-matured — matured for three to six months.
- Matured or tasty — matured for six to twelve months.
- Vintage — matured for twelve to twenty-four months.
- Colby — takes its name from a place in the US; it's a rubbery, fresher style cheese. The stuff I can buy (which isn't the American version) is a poor excuse for a cheese.
- Club cheese — Industrially produced cheddar is often sold on to other cheese companies that make 'club' style cheddar. This is a cheese that's been shredded or milled and packed back together, which makes it quite crumbly, and possibly more interesting than the cheese from which it came. It's not a bad technique in some ways, but doesn't make up for dodgy cheesemaking skills in the first place.

COOKED CURD CHEESE

These semi-firm to hard cheeses are most famous in their home around northern Italy, into Switzerland and Austria, and over to the French Alps. Think gruyère, emmental, comté, fontina and piave. They're nutty, melting-textured cheeses made by gently heating the curds to exclude more whey when first made. Typically cow's milk, they can also be made from sheep and goat's milk, too.

Parmigiano Reggiano and Grana Padano, two of Italy's famed grating parmesan cheeses, are both hard cheeses, which are made with a cooked curd (see page 75).

BLUE MOULD CHEESE

This category includes cheese that has introduced blue-green (*Penicillium roqueforti*) moulds throughout. The curd is usually inoculated with the mould when made. After it is drained and formed, then matured for either a long or short period, the cheese is spiked with metal rods that encourage the mould to form inside the cheese. Contrary to the myth that the mould follows the lines of copper wires, it is simply an aerobic mould that needs air to grow, so it breeds up in the cheese along the holes left after it is spiked. Blue cheese can be sweet and mild, or strong and acidic, and made from any milk you can make cheese with. It can also be used in conjunction with other cheesemaking techniques, such as white mould, or brevi, the bacteria used to flavour washed rind cheeses.

WHITE MOULD CHEESE

While brie and camembert are the most famous, there are plenty of other white mould cheeses in France, including many goat's milk cheeses that use the *Penicillium candidum* (or *P. camemberti*) mould on the outside to ripen. The cheese ripens from the outside in, breaking down just under the rind and going from a firm, almost chalky interior, to a liquid-centred cheese when fully ripe.

As the mould breaks down the protein structure of the cheese, the flavour becomes more complex, lightly acidic and cleansing, but with a real buttery richness. It is, in fact, sublime. A good white mould cheese, ripened well and served at room temperature, isa thing of rare and utter beauty.

Much of the so-called brie and camembert that is made outside (and increasingly inside) France is stabilised so it stops ripening, meaning you usually end up with a rubbery, relatively flavourless cheese. This works well for cheesemakers and fromagers (cheese merchants), because it means they can sell the same cheese for a month, not just for the week it is at its peak. Cheesemakers often overcome the cheese's lack of full, ripened flavour with the use of extra fat — hence the rise of so-called double cream and triple cream brie. Unlike traditional white mould cheeses, which have spores of the mould stirred into the curds, some white mould cheese is now sprayed with the mould so it develops a nice bloom on the outside, but doesn't invade the cheese much.

A good white mould cheese, of the style they make in small farmhouse cheeseries in France, may have some grey or orange mould/bacteria on the outside. If a white mould cheese has a perfect rug of white mould on the outside, it may not be as good as one that has a more mottled, rustic appearance. In fact, it's usually quite dull by comparison, and in France it's not considered ripe.

WASHED RIND CHEESE

Some cheeses are washed in a light brine solution to encourage the formation of a flavourful bacteria, *Brevibacterium linens*, which has a pungent smell not dissimilar to that of the socks of a fourteen-year-old boy. No wonder, because it's the same bacteria. Typically these cheeses get a sticky orange rind, which harbours most of the smell, but the interior (in soft cheeses) breaks down to soft, fudgy consistency and is more delicate and sweet. For this reason, many people discard the rind of washed rind cheeses.

Most types of cheese can have their rinds washed, though the most common are soft cow's milk cheeses. Apart from brine, cheese can also be washed in wine or strong alcohol such as grappa. Washed rind cheeses include taleggio, münster and Pont l'Evêque.

SMOKED CHEESE

Guess what? Most smoked cheese, like so many hams, bacons and smoked oysters these days, has never been 'smoked' in the sense that it's been put in a smokehouse. It's usually substandard, young, often processed cheese that has simply been flavoured with a smoky-tasting syrup. That said, there are some smoked cheeses (Pugliese smoked scamorza from southern Italy comes to mind) that are naturally smoked and taste incredible.

FLAVOURED CHEESE

If a cheese needs a flavour added, such as pepper, dried herbs, sweet chilli, or anything, really, it's usually a substandard cheese that is so awful to eat on its own that it has been flavoured to make it palatable. It's cheesemaking for dummies. I know, I know, it's sad. I used to love it too.

VEGETARIAN CHEESE

Traditionally cheese is made with animal rennet (apart from a small number, made with a rennet from thistles or artichokes), which is a coagulant enzyme found in the stomachs of young animals. To get it, the animal was killed, hence the problem vegetarians have with eating cheese made with calf rennet or similar.

These days some very good non-animal rennets are used in cheese, but many traditional cheeses from Europe still use animal rennet. If you're concerned, check the ingredients on the packet —though if you're really concerned about the unnecessary death of calves, you won't be eating any dairy (see page 214).

WHY IS SOME AMERICAN CHEESE BRIGHT ORANGE?

Food colouring. Simple as that. They use annatto, a colouring agent from the achiote tree, beta-carotene (the stuff that makes carrots orange), paprika and other food dyes to make it orange. I have no idea why.

WHAT IS PROCESSED CHEESE?

Look at the label. Why on earth the simple name 'processed' doesn't turn people off, I don't know. It's not like the stuff is called 'real farmhouse cheddar'. What's more, the ingredient list looks like a range of lab chemicals, not the sort of things that go into cheese. Good cheese should list milk, rennet, cultures and salt as the only ingredients.

Processed cheese has some cheese in it (more than half in most countries), is heated with emulsifiers, has preservatives added, and perhaps some colour, and is often watered down with water and other milk byproducts, such as whey powder and the like. It doesn't taste like cheese, has the texture of plastic, and is beloved in the manufacturing industry because it doesn't split like real cheese does when heated for any length of time. It's a way for the industry to use off-cuts, cheese with some errant mould, or misshapen cheeses.

Cheese spreads or other 'cheese food' products not called processed cheese may have as little as 15 per cent real cheese in them, plus a cocktail of additives to try and make them runny/yellow/taste good. There are also cheese analogues — scary substitutes used on top of manufactured pizza that actually contain no cheese, but rather a substance developed to behave like cheese.

WHAT IS REAL RICOTTA — AND WHY CAN'T YOU BUY IT AT A SUPERMARKET?

Real ricotta, the Italian stuff from whence it takes its name (meaning literally re-cooked), is made by adding an acid to the whey that is left after cheesemaking. (Lemon juice is good, vinegar is more consistent.) The whey is heated and then, when the acid is poured in, miraculous clouds of sweet, milky white ricotta appear and float to the top. These puffs of ricotta are drained and sold the same day or the next. It's not really a cheese, but rather a byproduct of the cheesemaking process — and a very good one at that.

Ricotta you buy anywhere other than Italy is usually made of full-cream (whole) milk, so it's heavier in texture, fattier in substance and is treated to allow it to last a long time. This mass-produced product is pretty boring by comparison. For a taste of real ricotta, head to an Italian delicatessen and buy it straight from the basket. A very good substitute (that uses a lot of milk) is the homemade version of a milk ricotta on page 45.

Paneer, the Indian cheese, is actually made in a virtually identical way to my full-cream (whole) milk ricotta. There's no rennet or culture added. Paneer comes from the solids that float from acidified milk, which are pressed as they are scooped from the pot.

IS WAX ON MY CHEESE A GOOD THING?

Wax is a good thing in some ways. It protects the cheese when it is bumped. It stops it going mouldy, or drying out. And it's a great way to market an average cheese that could just as easily have been matured in plastic.

HOW TO STORE CHEESE

The best advice is, don't. Good cheese, that is sold ripe, should be eaten while it's at its peak. If you are lucky enough to buy an unstabilised white mould cheese that is runny in the middle, eat it straight away and give thanks. Any soft or fresh cheese should be eaten almost immediately.

If you do need to store a hard cheese, it's a balancing act trying to keep enough moisture around it, and not too much. Just like in the maturing room, where it's, say, 12°C (54°F) and 70 per cent humidity, that's the environment you're trying to recreate. Wrapping a hard cheese tightly in plastic will probably cause it to sweat and get mould on it. Leaving it unwrapped will probably dry it out, especially in most refrigerators, which are very dry environments. I opt for one of two methods. First I use zip-lock bags, which create a micro-environment for the cheese to sit in. It's best to open it every few days so it doesn't sweat. If you're eating it often, this will just be part of the eating routine. The other option, for bigger pieces, is to use a well-sealed, re-usable airtight plastic container. Big enough so there's some air around the cheese, but not so big that it can dry out. And again, open it on occasion. If you can't open it for a while (say if you're going away for a week), a piece of paper towel around the cheese can help slow the growth of mould, which will eventually take hold on the cheese anyway, as it does in cheese maturing rooms. Feta can be stored in the brine it comes in, as can any cheese sold in brine (such as mozzarella) or oil (marinated cheeses).

DID YOU KNOW?

The older a cheese, if it is naturally rinded, the more it has dried out. This means it's more intense in flavour. So a fresh curd has more water than an aged Parmigiano Reggiano. A lot more. And the price you pay will often reflect that.

WHAT ABOUT RAW MILK CHEESE?

The use of raw, unpasteurised milk to make cheese is contentious. Those who make cheese, or many of them, say you can't make great cheese, as good as artisans do in Europe, without raw milk. And then there are those who say it's too risky, that pasteurisation (see page 34) reduces the risk to consumers.

It's illegal, at the time of writing, to make and sell raw milk cheese in Australia, New Zealand and some parts of the US without following some quite serious regulations, resulting in harder-style cheeses that meet a so-called pasteurisation equivalence. (These regulations cover elements such as moisture content, pH, and age at sale, and are quite complex.) To muddy the waters, however, some of the greatest cheeses in the world, which are imported into these countries and sold legally, are made from raw milk — including Roquefort, comté, gruyère, Parmigiano Reggiano and Grana Padano, among others. What's amazing is that a lot of cheese we used to eat, at least in Australia, was made from raw milk up until just a few decades ago. As the science of food-borne illness flourished, the death knell came for raw milk cheese (as it did for sawdust on the floor of butchers' shops). Paradoxically, even as milk quality has improved, and bacterial counts, refrigeration and other methods of ensuring milk safety have proliferated, raw milk cheese has slipped somewhat further out of reach for many producers and consumers.

Interestingly, those most frightened of raw milk cheese these days seem to be the big manufacturers. Despite strong consumer demand for raw milk cheese at the pointy end of the market, it is unlikely to ever threaten the viability of large manufacturers who make a profit from pasteurised cheese. The absence of a plethora of safe, delicious raw milk cheeses, however, means the full variety of cheese flavours, textures and regional variation may never be known.

4 thick slices rustic white
  sourdough bread
2 teaspoons dijon mustard
2 tablespoons sour cream
a pinch of hot paprika

lemon juice (optional)
2 slices gruyère cheese
6–8 rocket (arugula) leaves, rinsed
2 thin slices leg ham
lashings of butter, for spreading

My croque monsieur

This is my version of the classic Parisian toasted cheese sandwich. It can be made with brioche or ordinary sliced bread, but I prefer a decent sourdough. Most are made using a white sauce scented with mustard, but I find the whole process of making white sauce just for this a drag, and I also prefer the lightly acidic flavour of sour cream. In fact, a couple of drops of lemon juice make it even livelier.

SERVES 2

Place the bread slices on a clean work surface. Mix the mustard, sour cream and paprika together in a bowl and season with freshly milled black pepper, to taste. Now's the time to add a few drops of fresh lemon juice, if you have it.

Top two slices of bread with the cheese, then spread with the sour cream mixture. Lay half of the rocket leaves over each, and cover with a slice of ham. Place the remaining bread slices on top to create two sandwiches.

Butter the tops and bottoms of each sandwich and slide them into a cool frying pan. Place over medium heat and gently fry until brown on the bottom. Turn over to brown the other side. With any luck the cheese should've melted as it cooks. Serve warm and often.

Variations: You can create your own version of the croque monsieur and make up your own unique name to fit. Croque madam is the same as the monsieur with the addition of a fried or poached egg on top. While travelling through Paris I've also seen a croque provençal, using olives and tomato in the sandwich; a croque marsellaise, using a few good-quality anchovies either draped over the top or in the middle; a croque normande, using famous Normandy camembert; and a croque mademoiselle, which may refer to a number of variations, including the addition of tomato or champignons, a smaller version of the monsieur and even an open-faced monsieur.

84

12 plump figs, cut in half through
  the stem
2 tablespoons good-quality balsamic
  vinegar
1 small head radicchio, leaves torn,
  washed and dried

1 tablespoon walnut oil
200 g (7 oz) goat's cheese, chopped
  or crumbled

Balsamic fig & goat's cheese salad

Really good balsamic vinegar brings out the best flavour of fresh figs by matching their sweetness with gentle, vague acidity. Have this dish for lunch or as an entrée when you have someone over who you want to impress. Like family.

SERVES 4

Toss the figs in a bowl with the balsamic vinegar and let stand for a good 30 minutes or so. Toss the radicchio in a separate bowl with the walnut oil to coat. Add the figs and goat's cheese, plus any left-over balsamic from the bowl.

Use your fingertips to combine, and season with salt and freshly milled black pepper to taste. You may like to add a touch more walnut oil or balsamic vinegar.

250 g (9 oz) good-quality naturally
  matured cheddar cheese

Cheddar crisps

These luscious crisps are pure cheese — like the best bits that dribble out of a toasted cheese sandwich and into the pan.

SERVES 6 WITH DRINKS

Preheat the oven to 140°C (275°F/Gas 1). Line a baking tray with baking paper.

Simply grate the cheddar and arrange the cheese in small circles on the tray as you would biscuits. Beware; the cheese will spread. Bake for about 8–12 minutes, or until the cheese bubbles and starts to colour. When cool, they will crisp up. Serve with drinks. Cheddar crisps can be stored in an airtight container for up to 2 weeks.

- 250 g (9 oz) plain sweet oatmeal biscuits (cookies)
- 100 g (3½ oz) butter, melted
- 1 generous pinch of ground ginger or cinnamon (optional)
- 330 g (11¾ oz) cream cheese, at room temperature
- 330 g (11¾ oz) ricotta cheese or cream cheese, at room temperature
- 200 g (7 oz) caster (superfine) sugar
- 120 g (4¼ oz) sour cream
- 4 eggs
- 1¼ teaspoons natural vanilla extract
- finely grated zest of 1 large lemon
- 100 ml (3½ fl oz) lemon juice

Baked New York-style cheesecake

Back in the 19th century, British cheesecakes, such as the Yorkshire curd cheesecake, were made using a mixture of almonds, egg and lemon, and contained no cheese at all. While these are good, they are not as yummy as the baked cheesecakes that were popularised by the Americans and use cream cheese. I don't like eating cheesecake hot, so plan on making this cake early in the day, or the day before you want to eat it. It should keep for a few days.

SERVES 8–10

Preheat the oven to 230°C (450°F/Gas 8). Grease a 20 cm (8 inch) round spring-form cake tin and line the base with baking paper.

Place the biscuits in a food processor and blitz until they resemble very fine crumbs. Pour the crumbs into a bowl over the melted butter, add the ginger, if using, and stir to combine. Press this mixture into the tin to create an even layer in the base and all the way up the sides. I use a straight-sided glass or cup to do this, starting with the sides and finishing with the base. Place the tin in the refrigerator while you get the filling ready.

In a big bowl or even better, an electric mixer, mash the cream cheese until soft and smooth, adding the ricotta, sugar and sour cream as you go, beating until smooth. Beat in the eggs one at a time, then add the vanilla, lemon zest and lemon juice and combine until smooth.

Pour the cheese mixture over the biscuit base, place on a baking tray and place in the oven, towards the bottom and preferably not on fan-forced, but don't worry if it is. It will take on a bit of colour with this cooking method.

Bake for 10 minutes, then reduce the oven temperature to 130°C (250°F/Gas 1) for 70 minutes, or until it is set when you wobble it gently. Turn off the oven and allow the cake to cool in the oven for 30 minutes. Remove from the oven and cool completely before removing from the tin and serving.

Store the cheesecake in the refrigerator, covered with plastic wrap. It is best eaten within 2 days and served at room temperature.

4 tablespoons extra virgin olive oil

5 garlic cloves, crushed

2 kg (4 lb 8 oz) broad (fava) beans,
    double peeled (see page 391)

½ teaspoon salt

500 g (1 lb 2 oz) short pasta,
    such as penne

100 g (3½ oz) grated pecorino cheese,
    to serve

lemon wedges, to serve (optional)

Pasta with broad beans & pecorino

*Frank Spagnolo, a greengrocer in Canberra, gave me the inspiration
for this pasta recipe when he told me stories about his mother's cooking.
It has broad beans in it, and glorious as they are, it's actually the cheese
that makes the dish stand out. A good-quality pecorino cheese that isn't
as sharp as a mother-in-law's tongue is the only cheese to use in this
recipe. In its absence, use Italian parmesan or another firm cheese,
such as a manchego or a similar style firm goat's cheese.*

SERVES 4

Heat half of the oil in a frying pan over medium heat. Add the garlic and cook for 30 seconds, then stir in the broad beans. Add 125 ml (4 fl oz/½ cup) water and add the salt; cook for about 5 minutes, stirring regularly, until the beans have softened. Mash the beans with a fork until they have broken up but are still a bit chunky.

Meanwhile, cook the pasta in a saucepan of salted boiling water for 8–10 minutes, or until *al dente*. Lightly drain and return to the warm pan, reserving a little of the cooking water just in case you need it.

Add the bean mixture to the pasta, add the remaining oil and toss through with half the cheese — the sauce should be a little brothy; add a little of the cooking water if necessary. Season with freshly milled black pepper and serve with the remaining pecorino and perhaps with some lemon wedges on the side for squeezing over.

The world's best cheese biscuits

My mum's cheese biscuits are simply the best cheese biscuits in the world.

170 g (6 oz) cultured unsalted butter, chilled and cubed
250 g (9 oz) plain (all-purpose) flour
a pinch of salt
a good pinch of cayenne pepper
150 g (5½ oz) good-quality naturally matured cheddar cheese,
    finely grated

SERVES 10 WITH DRINKS

Preheat the oven to 200°C (400°F/Gas 6). Line two baking trays
with baking paper.

    Put the butter and flour in a bowl and use your fingertips to rub
the butter in until the mixture resembles breadcrumbs. You can use
a food processor if you like. Add the salt and cayenne pepper, then
knead in the cheese until just combined. Press the mixture out as you
would shortbread into a rectangle about 5 mm (¼ inch) thick all over.
Cut into 2 cm (¾ inch) squares or diamonds and place on the trays.
Bake for about 15 minutes, or until the biscuits are golden. Allow to
cool, then try and eat just one! Store in an airtight container for up
to 2 weeks (if you're strong-willed).

92

Chapter 2

GRAINS, PULSES & FLOURS

GRAINS, PULSES & FLOURS

At the heart of most great cuisines is a great grain. And while wheat has conquered much of the world, with its magical properties that allow it to make bread, cakes and pastry, other pretenders to the throne abound. Just look at rice, and how it's part of the cuisine of much of Europe (paella, risotto), as well as throughout the East. Soya beans dominate much of Asia, corn is the pre-eminent grain in the Americas, and increasingly in the foodbowl of China (though much is grown there for stock feed or alcohol) — and where would the cuisine of the subcontinent be without pulses such as chickpeas and lentils?

A good grain has flavour. It has texture and starch that can be used in various ways. Used well, a good grain is what makes the meal, be it properly twice-steamed couscous, bread in a sandwich, burghul (bulgur) or rice. The Chinese way of asking how you are is a simple, but telling: 'Have you eaten rice today?' Imagine Mexican food without the corn, Italian food without the flour to make pasta or pizza, Paris without pastries. Life is much better with the right, and right variety of, grains.

GRAINS

*John Bignell leaps around the old mill like a man possessed.
A sixth-generation farmer, he knows a thing or two about mills,
and this beautiful specimen has all the levers, flywheels and cogs that
you'd expect of something built in 1872. Bignell is no stranger to mills.
On his property in the Tasmanian Highlands, Thorpe Farm, there's
also an even older mill — a water mill dating from 1823 that he and his
brother restored in the 1970s. It sits idle now, while the granite stones
of this slightly more modern cast-iron mill are used to do the artisan
grinding of the wheat and rye they grow on the property.*

Grains don't have the same need for quality assessment as some things. It's not as
important that they're fresh, like leafy greens, or free-range, like pork, or ripened
slowly, like bananas. They just need to be grown well, stored well and treated with
respect to keep off things like rust or mildew. And yet, the farmer's treatment of the
soil in which they're grown can be tasted in grains, particularly whole grains.

The flour from John Bignell's wheat, which he grows and grinds with his son
Will, comes from the whole grain, and the granite stones that tear the wheat leave
it slightly coarser than modern roller mills. It's also a fresh, unbleached flour that
flows from between the grindstones, which makes it tacky when formed into dough.
If they're grinding low-gluten wheat, you'll find Bignell's flour fairly useless for
making a light, airy bread. But it's brilliant for cakes, for use as a thickener or as a base
for biscuits. Put your head in a bag of the flour and it's like inhaling the scent of a
granary, it's so fresh.

Bignell also grinds rye flour. This highly flavoured, slightly grey-coloured flour is
always low in gluten, so it's suited to European-style dark, heavy breads.

WHEAT

This miracle seed from a grass plant has been known in most of Europe for 5000 years,
and in China for 4000 years. It was the grain of choice during Roman times, but fell
out of favour somewhat in the Dark Ages in Europe because it requires a certain
amount of infrastructure and cooperation. Wheat's great beauty, however, when you
do get organised, is in the flour that it produces, and in its ability to hold up bread,
stretch into pasta and thicken stews. The main reason we love it, apart from that
glorious flavour, is that it contains gluten, a protein that allows it to hold up a raised
batter or dough, and to hold together when rolled.

The wheat grain, like most grains, can be divided into three parts. The bran, which is the very outer part, is tan in colour and full of minerals and roughage. Then there's the germ, the high-fat part, which is the fertile portion of the wheat. And then there's the endosperm, the nutrient-dense part of the seed that the young plant would use as its first food.

Wheat can be sold whole, ground as various flours (see pages 126–29), rolled or turned into semolina. Durum wheat is famed for being very high in gluten, and so producing an excellent hard flour and high-gluten semolina, both of which are prized in bread baking and dried pasta. Freekah is the name of wheat picked green, then roasted.

SEMOLINA

When the endosperm (the middle bit lacking the bran and germ) of wheat is cracked during the first milling process, it's called semolina. This semolina can then be ground into flour. Hard, durum wheat semolina is a yellowy colour and is used to make semolina gnocchi, couscous, and Middle Eastern sweets such as halva. Soft wheat semolina is usually a little finer, a much whiter colour, and is used as a breakfast dish much like porridge. In some places it's called by a brand name, Cream of Wheat. Confusingly, as well as the difference in the grain they come from, there are different grades of fineness, and they're all just called semolina. Let the colour and the coarseness be your guide.

CRACKED WHEAT & BURGHUL (BULGUR)

Cracked wheat is just as it sounds, while burghul is cooked (usually steamed) before being broken into bits. Cracked wheat takes quite a while to cook; burghul just 10–15 minutes. They can be used in tabouleh, wholegrain breads, and couscous-like dishes.

CORN

Corn, or maize as it probably should be known, originated in the Americas and is the largest grain crop in the world. While one version (sometimes called sweetcorn) is sold fresh for use as a vegetable, the varieties used for flour are starchier and less sweet. Corn is ground into cornmeal (for polenta, corn bread and the like); the centre of the grain is used for cornflour (cornstarch), a noted thickener, and masa, a lime-treated product used in Central American cooking. Corn is also used in just about every processed food product in the Americas — often as high-fructose syrup, or in its simplest form, glucose.

SPELT

An old relation of wheat, with a very hard grain and moderate gluten. It has a very attractive aroma and nutty flavour in breads, and some use the whole grains to make a risotto-style dish. The grain is encased in a very spiky, hard to remove husk, which can add substantially to its already high cost.

RYE
Another close relative of wheat, but with a low gluten content. This makes rye suitable for dense breads, or mixing with normal flour for a light rye bread, which has a gloriously sweet nutty aroma. It's little used in sweet cookery, but used extensively in the brewing industry. Rolled rye can also be used in place of oats.

KAMUT
A brand name for khorosan wheat. This is a hardy grain with a high protein content, and is used in the baking industry.

FARRO
Also known as emmer, another ancient wheat variety, farro is finding new popularity in modern Italy. It is used as a grain to replace rice in risotto, as a texture in soup (not dissimilar to barley), and ground into flour to make wholegrain pasta and bread.

BARLEY
A firm grain often sold 'pearled', meaning it is hulled (the hull is super coarse), then polished to remove the outer bran. Before pearling, the whole grain is called scotch barley. Pearl barley is also sometimes sold rolled, and can be used as a substitute for oats.

OATS
Most oats are steamed to deactivate enzymes that will cause the germ to go rancid. They are then usually rolled. Smaller-cut oats are rolled for fast cooking, while instant oats are precooked. Steel-cut oats aren't rolled, but cut into slivers. Oatmeal is the term for ground oats that probably haven't been rolled (although it can refer to cooked porridge made from oats, too). In some countries, Scotland in particular, oatmeal can be bought coarsely or finely ground, depending on the intended use.

BUCKWHEAT
Not a true grain, buckwheat is grown in cooler climates. The ground seeds are used in pasta in northern Italy, blinis (little pancakes) in Russia and in breads throughout eastern Europe.

TRITICALE

A hybrid of wheat and rye, first developed in the late 1800s, triticale has a more nutty, complex flavour than wheat, is higher in protein, and can be better for soil health. Despite its suitability for humans, it requires different milling to wheat, and is therefore often used only as animal fodder.

QUINOA

This gluten-free South American grain has grown enormously in popularity due to its complete protein profile and relatively high micronutrient content. The UN even declared an official Year of Quinoa in 2013, which took it out of reach of the very peasants who've been eating it for centuries. It is naturally coated in very bitter saponins, and needs multiple washings to cleanse it of these. Most quinoa is sold pre-washed.

AMARANTH

Domesticated some 8000 years ago and used by the Mayans, Incas and Aztecs, amaranth is enjoying new-found popularity further afield than the Americas. It's a tiny seed, about the size of a sesame seed, with a sweet, malty, nutty flavour, and is gluten free. Cooked alone, the flour can go gluey, so it's usually mixed with other flours.

MILLET

Millet is a catch-all name for a multiplicity of ancient tiny grains (some domesticated 7000 years ago), but usually refers to pearl millet, popular in Indian and some African cuisines. It has more natural sweetness than most grains, but a milder overall flavour that some say is earthy. It's often toasted to bring out more flavour. It's also gluten free.

SORGHUM

Sorghum is the name of an ancient grain from several species of grasses, including some from Africa. Like triticale, it is more tolerant of varied soil conditions and drought than wheat, and is useful to help keep soil healthy in crop rotations, but is usually relegated to stock feed simply because of wheat's dominance. The flavour is earthy, sometimes nutty or musky, and it is gluten free, so suitable for coeliacs. In parts of Africa, many people often eat a porridge of sorghum.

RICE

The second most cultivated grain in the world after corn, rice tends to be long or short grain, and white or brown (or black or red), with different varieties bred for different culinary uses, based on their individual starch content. Rice grains rich in amylose stay firmer when cooked, whereas those with amylopectin become softer and stickier.

BASMATI This famed fragrant long-grain rice of the Indian subcontinent is reputed to get better with age, with the Pakistani version being the most prized. Almost always eaten as white rice, it tends to stay loose when cooked.

CALASPARRA A rice grown in the Murcia province of Spain, calasparra (and another rice called bomba) is a very dry rice ideal for paella. It is reputed to expand in width, not length. You can substitute risotto rice as the next best thing.

JASMINE This long-grain white fragrant rice of South-East Asia gets its name from the hints of jasmine in the fragrance, and is a particular specialty of Thai cuisine. It needs slightly more water to cook than basmati rice, and the grains aren't quite as long and stick together just a bit more.

RED RICE Several countries have a red rice, including France, Spain and Bhutan. The red colour is from the outer husk. These rices are unpolished, and hence require more cooking.

RISOTTO RICE The medium to short-grained white rice (arborio, carnaroli, vialone nano) used by Italians to make risotto. because the rice releases the starch amylopectin from the outside of the grain when stirred during cooking. Arborio is usually the cheapest, but I prefer carnaroli and vialone nano because they tend to stay firmer in the centre, so you can be a bit more relaxed with cooking times. Their centre is mostly amylose, so you get a creamy sauce, but still have rice with bite.

STICKY RICE Otherwise known as glutinous rice, sticky rice is popular in South-East Asian countries and comes in two varieties, white and black. Black sticky rice is an unpolished rice that takes about 25 minutes to cook. White sticky rice can be soaked and steamed, and is nearly entirely made up of amylopectin, hence its sticky nature. Both rices may be used for sweet and savoury purposes.

SUSHI RICE A short-grain rice that tends to stick together when cooked, thanks to a high proportion (80 per cent) of amylopectin. It isn't, however, sticky rice. Koshikari is the most common variety from Japan. In Australia, Calrose rice is an okay substitute.

WILD RICE Not a true rice, but a very long, rice-like grain gathered from swamp plants of North America. Despite its moniker, 'wild' rice is mostly now cultivated. It is very flavoursome, but usually used in small amounts with other things, or to flavour white rice.

HOW TO WASH RICE

Some rice needs washing before being used, such as those for pilaf and sushi, or if you want a good steamed rice. However, whether to wash it, and how much to wash it, depends not only on the rice and on the end product, but also on your energy levels.

Put the rice in a bowl or the pot it will be cooked in. Add just enough vaguely tepid water to wet the rice, so it sloshes, but isn't soupy. Gently use your hand, mostly the heel of your hand, to rub the rice grains together. This friction helps to free some of the loose starch, although you'll get less friction if there's too much water. The starch dissolves in the water, creating a white, milky-coloured liquid. Drain the rice well and repeat until the water runs fairly clear.

The Japanese repeat the rinsing up to ten times, but I find two or three washes (maybe because I live off rainwater tanks) is usually enough.

If you don't wash your rice, then cook it by the absorption method — although the result can be stickier or slightly gluggier than if you were to wash it.

185 g (6½ oz) coarse semolina or
   use packet couscous
1½ tablespoons extra virgin olive oil
1 tablespoon unsalted butter
2 tablespoons caster (superfine) sugar
½ teaspoon rosewater or orange
   blossom water (see page 504)
80 g (2¾ oz/½ cup) blanched almonds,
   roasted and roughly crushed

50 g (1¾ oz) walnuts, roughly crushed
30 g (1 oz/¼ cup) raisins
6 fresh dates, pitted and chopped
2 tablespoons pistachios, cut into slivers

Sweet couscous

This sweet couscous is perfect for breakfast. You don't need to use the classic hand-beaten, copper couscousièr to cook this dish, although it does look pretty cute on the stove. Instead, you can cook the couscous in a colander, sieve or steamer over a saucepan of rapidly boiling water. The steaming of the couscous can be done ahead, and the cooked couscous kept in the refrigerator for 3–4 days before using.

SERVES 4–6

Bring a large saucepan of water to the boil over high heat. Put the semolina and olive oil in a large stainless steel bowl and mix well. Place a colander or sieve over the saucepan and sprinkle in the semolina (the steam helps keep it there). Cover with a tight-fitting lid and steam for 30 minutes. (If your colander or sieve has a gap where it sits on top of the saucepan you can use scrunched-up foil to fill the gap.)

Remove the colander from the heat, place over the sink and pour a cup of boiling water through the grains. Cover, return to the heat and steam for another 10 minutes. Empty the couscous grains into a large bowl. Add 185 ml (6 fl oz/³/₄ cup) of the cooking water with the butter and mix well.

Spread the steamed couscous out in a large flat dish or tray and allow to cool, then use your fingers to break up any small lumps. Sprinkle over the sugar and toss to mix through.

To serve, add the rosewater and spoon into serving bowls or plates. Sprinkle over the almonds, walnuts, raisins and dates, and garnish with pistachios. Serve alone, with petal-scented custard (see the variation to Lady Grey Custard on page 422) or even with milk as you would a cereal.

2 teaspoons salt
350 g (12 oz/2⅓ cups) polenta
100 g (3½ oz) butter

100 g (3½ oz/1 cup) grated Italian
 parmesan cheese (Parmigiano
 Reggiano or Grana Padano)

Soft polenta

You can use white polenta made from white corn, if you can find it, for a more subtle and arguably better result. Use the polenta as an accompaniment to a ragu of some kind, or the osso buco on page 236. Alternatively, you can add about 100 g (3½ oz) extra cheese (fontina or a good sheep's milk cheese will work well) to make a richer, more lip-smacking dish —although you may need to reduce the salt at the start.

SERVES 6–8

Put 2 litres (70 fl oz/8 cups) water in a saucepan over high heat and bring to almost boiling. Add the salt and sprinkle in the polenta, stirring constantly. Bring to the boil, then reduce the heat and simmer gently for at least 40 minutes — continue stirring in the same direction, using a flat-bottomed spatula to stop the polenta sticking to the pan (you can pause at times, I've done it, and the polenta still ends up delicious).

As the polenta thickens it may become hard to stir — add a little more water, though this should only happen in the last 10 minutes (don't add too much or the flavour will end up watery too). Some say it's important that the polenta burns your stirring arm when it spits as you cook it because that's the right, thick consistency.

Stir the butter and cheese through the polenta until both have melted and the mixture is smooth. Season with salt and freshly milled black pepper, to taste. Serve immediately — this polenta also goes well with Simple Tomato Ragu (see page 386).

- 2 tablespoons butter
- 1 onion, finely chopped
- 2 tablespoons chopped flat-leaf (Italian) parsley
- 4 thin slices prosciutto, chopped
- 200 g (7 oz) risotto rice
- 1.5 litres (52 fl oz/6 cups) homemade chicken stock (see page 163) or water
- 250 g (9 oz/1⅔ cups) fresh or frozen peas
- 50 g (1¾ oz/½ cup) grated Italian parmesan cheese (Parmigiano Reggiano or Grana Padano)

Risi e bisi

While those in Venice love their risotto all'onda (meaning wavy, because it's quite wet compared to the risotto of Milan), their famed dish risi e bisi isn't actually risotto. It translates from the Venetian for 'rice and peas', and is a cross between a runny risotto and a soup. The good thing for those with ankle biters or other pressing matters is that, unlike risotto, risi e bisi doesn't need constant stirring.

SERVES 4 AS AN ENTRÉE

Heat the butter in a large saucepan over low heat and fry the onion for 5 minutes, or until soft. Stir in the parsley and prosciutto and continue frying for about 5 minutes, without colouring the onion. Add the rice to the pan and cook for 2 minutes, then stir in the stock and season with freshly milled black pepper. Bring to a boil, then reduce the heat and simmer, stirring occasionally, for 10 minutes.

Stir through the peas and continue cooking for a further 10 minutes, or until the rice is cooked through. If you need more liquid, because the rice has become thick or is catching on the bottom of the pan, add some extra chicken stock or water.

Just before serving, stir in the cheese.

1 tablespoon vegetable or olive oil
2 bay leaves
2 large onions, chopped
2 large carrots, chopped
4 celery sticks, chopped

4 lamb shanks
3–4 thyme sprigs
150 g (5½ oz) pearl barley

Lamb shank & pearl barley soup

The flavour of good lamb and the nuttiness of barley tastes wonderful in this soup that can warm even the coldest of hearts. Make a big pan, because this slow-cooked soup is brilliant to pull from the freezer on days when you simply don't have the time to cook it from scratch.

SERVES 6–8

Heat the oil in a large heavy-based (preferably cast-iron) saucepan over medium–low heat. Add the bay leaves, onion, carrot and celery and cook for 10 minutes, or until tender, but not brown. Add the lamb shanks to the pan and just enough water to cover. Bring to the boil and skim off any scum that comes to the surface.

Add the thyme and barley, cover with a tight-fitting lid, and reduce the heat to low, or transfer to a 150°C (300°F/Gas 2) oven, for about 2 hours, or until the meat falls easily from the bone.

Skim the top of the soup again to remove any excess fat. Remove the lamb shanks carefully with tongs, and set aside until cool enough to handle.

Remove the meat from the bones, discarding the bones, and cut the meat into bite-sized pieces. Return the meat to the soup and season with salt and freshly milled black pepper, to taste. Bring the soup back to the boil, then reduce the heat to low and simmer for another 20 minutes to meld the flavours even more.

Serve the soup in the biggest bowls you have, with slices of buttered bread, on days when you want to feel loved.

2 tablespoons ghee or butter
1 large onion, finely chopped
1 garlic clove, crushed
1 bay leaf
2 thyme sprigs
10 peppercorns

300 g (10½ oz/1½ cups) basmati rice,
    washed and drained (see page 101)
500 ml (17 fl oz/2 cups) homemade
    chicken stock (see page 163) or water
a large pinch of saffron threads

The perfect pilaff

Pilaff is a flavoured rice that cooks like steamed plain rice, rather than being stirred like a risotto. It could, at a pinch, be served as a meal on its own with a little fried egg on the side or some left-over meat, but it's also great as part of a larger meal. This recipe is perfectly simple and delicious – though the cooking temperature and timing can always take more perfecting, depending on your stove. You can put it in a moderately low oven for 30 minutes instead.

SERVES 4

Heat the ghee in a heavy-based saucepan over medium heat and fry the onion, stirring often, for 10 minutes, or until golden. Add the garlic, bay leaf, thyme and peppercorns and continue to fry for 2 minutes.

Add the rice to the pan, stirring constantly, until the rice starts to catch slightly on the base of the pan (this adds a certain nuttiness to the dish). Add the stock, saffron and a pinch of salt and bring to the boil, stirring to combine. Reduce the heat to low, cover with a tight-fitting lid, and simmer for 12 minutes. You shouldn't look in the pan because the water level will drop, and lifting the lid will alter the steaming of the top level of the rice. Turn off the heat and allow to rest for at least 5–10 minutes; do not lift the lid

during this time because the remaining heat and steam will redistribute the moisture in the pan. Lifting the lid makes it less likely to cook evenly.

Remove the bay leaf and peppercorns and fluff up the rice grains with a fork before serving.

Variation: You can also cook the pilaff in the oven. Preheat the oven to 180°C (350°F/ Gas 4). Prepare the pilaff as per the method above in an ovenproof dish on the stovetop until after you have covered it with the tight-fitting lid. Cook it in the oven for about 30 minutes, then remove from the oven. Remove the bay leaf and peppercorns, fluff up with a fork and serve.

625 ml (21½ fl oz/2½ cups) full-cream (whole) milk

125 ml (4 fl oz/½ cup) pouring (whipping) cream (35%)

90 g (3¼ oz) raw (demerara) sugar

1 vanilla bean, split lengthways

80 g (2¾ oz) short-grain rice

1 whole nutmeg, grated

Granny Fletcher's rice pudding

There's something fabulous about pudding that isn't trying too hard to be fashionable. I didn't go to boarding school, so although the skin on a rice pudding may be known by some as the fly's walk, I still adore it. My dad always had the right to scrape the rice pudding dish, eagerly lapping up the remnants of the skin stuck to the sides. Now I'm all grown up, I can make rice pudding for myself and just eat the skin without having to compete. Sorry Mum, this isn't your recipe, it's better.

SERVES 4–6

Preheat the oven to 140°C (275°F/Gas 1).

Put the milk, cream and sugar in a casserole dish and scrape in the vanilla seeds, adding the bean. Stir to dissolve the sugar. Stir the rice into the milk mixture to combine.

Sprinkle the nutmeg on top and cook in the oven, stirring occasionally for 90 minutes, or until the rice is tender. The pudding may be a little runny, with the rice grains plump yet still retaining their integrity, but it will thicken up more as it cools.

Remove the vanilla bean and serve the pudding warm. Remember that the cook gets to keep the serving dish to scrape!

50 g (1¾ oz) butter
2 leeks, white part only, rinsed and diced
2 carrots, diced
2 celery sticks, diced
2 litres (70 fl oz/8 cups) homemade
    chicken stock (see page 163) or water

100 g (3½ oz/1 cup) rolled (porridge) oats
¼ poached or roasted chicken, meat
    shredded (optional if you want a
    lighter soup)
1 handful parsley, chopped

Chicken, leek & oat soup

Sometimes we want a granny to spoil us. Sometimes we need a hug and a reassuring word. Sometimes we need the silliness of a child and the gentle feel of a warm hand on the neck. But always we need a soothing chicken soup. This is a gorgeously therapeutic soup that uses oats, which are much faster cooking than barley. For a creamier consistency, you can substitute milk for some of the stock.

SERVES 4

Heat the butter in a large saucepan over low heat and gently fry the leek, carrot and celery for 5–10 minutes, or until very soft but not brown. The longer and slower you do this, the better your soup will be. Rush it and it will still be good, but not great.

Add the stock and oats to the pan and cook for about 10–20 minutes, or until the oats have softened — the cooking time for oats can vary greatly, although you can speed it up by using instant oats if you wish. Bring to the boil for a few minutes — this will help the butter emulsify into the soup.

Reduce the heat, season with salt and freshly milled black pepper, to taste. Add the chicken and parsley, and simmer for about 2–3 minutes, just to heat through. Serve hot, with well-buttered bread on the side.

PULSES

Many legumes can be eaten immature and fresh, but most are matured and dried for later use; these are known as pulses. Almost all dried legumes benefit from soaking in cold water overnight. They can still be cooked without soaking, though the cooking time can increase considerably. The general consensus is to cook them without salt, as it can toughen the skin and make the centre mealy, though in some long, slow dishes, such as cassoulet, adding salt helps prevent the beans from overcooking. A little bicarbonate of soda (baking soda) in the soaking water can greatly speed up cooking times, particularly for chickpeas, but you should really only consider it if you want a purée or very soft bean at the end.

DRIED BEANS

There are many varieties of dried beans, from haricots and lingots to pinto beans, black beans and cannellini beans. Most are best soaked before cooking, and to some extent they're interchangeable. Black-eyed beans (sometimes called black-eyed peas) cook more quickly than many beans. When cooked, they are starchy and have an attractive texture, earthier than most other dried beans.

CHICKPEAS

The dried chickpea is a thing of wonder and is used throughout the world — whether whole; or cooked and ground; or ground into flour. Think of the chana dhal of India, the hummus dip of the Middle East, or of farinata, a kind of flat bread popular in northern Italy. The immature green peas can be eaten, though they do inhibit some nutrient uptake, so it's best not to do it all the time.

SOYA BEANS

A miracle bean, the products made from soya beans are as varied as those from milk. Ground, the resultant 'soy milk' can be turned into tofu, which can be dried, fermented, and more. Soya beans are made into flour and pastes, which can also be fermented (think soy sauce or miso paste). Fresh soya beans, known by their Japanese name edamame, are delicious steamed in the pod. Like corn, soya beans are beloved by the food-processing industry thanks to the many uses their components can be put to, including starch, protein and emulsifiers.

SPLIT PEAS

Just as the name suggests, these are the result of splitting dried peas. Great for soups, they can also be used in Indian-style dhal, as can dried mung beans.

BROAD (FAVA) BEANS

In their dried form, these coarse-textured beans can be quite hard work. Some soak them, remove the skin, and boil the insides. They take anywhere up to six hours to cook properly, but can make excellent dips and dishes.

LENTILS

There are a whole range of lentils out there, most notably the green (brown) lentil, the red lentil, and a smaller green lentil made famous by Puy in France and Castellucio in Italy. Lentils tend to cook much faster than other pulses and don't really need soaking, particularly smaller ones, which should cook in half an hour or so. The fastest-cooking are red lentils.

PREPARING PULSES Most dried pulses are best washed before using; I like to give mine a quick rinse before soaking. They also benefit from being cooked in a different water than the one they are soaked in. If you're in a modest hurry, try soaking them in warm or hot (not boiling) water to speed the process, or use a pressure cooker to get them going (but don't overfill it, because the starch released during cooking can clog the valve).

Many pulses are blamed for causing a bit of gas in those who eat them. A good way to reduce this effect is to cook them for half of their time in one lot of water, which you discard, and cook them in fresh water for the remaining time. You usually can't do this with lentils, however, as their cooking time is too short.

1 tablespoon olive oil
2 onions, diced
1 garlic clove, crushed
400 g (14 oz) potatoes, peeled and diced
375 g (13 oz/2 cups) small green lentils,
    rinsed and drained

1.25 litres (44 fl oz/5 cups) homemade
    chicken stock (see page 163) or water
1 teaspoon lemon juice, strained
extra virgin olive oil, to serve

Green lentil, potato & lemon soup

*This recipe makes a very satisfying, simple lentil soup thanks to
the gorgeous, calm, nurturing taste of the pulse. You can replace
the small green lentils with other types, such as larger green (brown)
lentils, but the basic premise is of an earthy-flavoured soup, chunky
with potato and sprightly from the addition of lemon.*

SERVES 4

Heat the olive oil in a large saucepan over
low heat and gently fry the onion for
5–10 minutes, until just starting to colour.
Add the garlic and cook for 1–2 minutes,
but don't let it colour.

Toss the potatoes into the pan with
the lentils and stock and bring to the boil.
Reduce the heat and simmer for about
1 hour, or until the lentils are very soft. If the
soup is becoming too thick, more like a stew
or porridge than a soup, you may need to add
extra water.

Add the lemon juice and season with
salt and freshly milled black pepper, to taste.
To serve, ladle into bowls and drizzle a thin
swirl of extra virgin olive oil on top.

150 g (5½ oz/¾ cup) dried cannellini or
    white/northern beans
250 g (9 oz/about ⅓ loaf) stale, crusty
    bread, cut roughly
125 ml (4 fl oz/½ cup) extra virgin olive oil
1 large onion, diced
6-8 garlic cloves, crushed
2 carrots, diced
3 celery sticks, diced
2 tomatoes, diced, or use 400 g (14 oz/
    1⅔ cups) tinned chopped tomatoes

100 g (3½ oz) cabbage, shredded
100 g (3½ oz) pancetta, rind removed
    and cut into bite-sized strips
3-4 thyme sprigs
2-3 litres (70-105 fl oz/8-12 cups)
    homemade chicken stock (see page
    163) or water
100 g (3½ oz) cavolo nero or 250 g (9 oz)
    English spinach, stems removed

Ribollita

*A few beans, some decent vegetables, a little cabbage and olive
oil are all good additions to a soup. For best results, use the best-quality
olive oil, preferably one that is peppery and green-tasting. Add enough
stale bread to make it thick and satisfying and you've got one of the most
warming meals on the planet.*

SERVES 6-8

Put the cannellini beans in a bowl and cover
with cold water. Set aside to soak for at least
5 hours or overnight. Don't worry if you
haven't soaked them, they'll just take longer
to cook. Either way, rinse and drain well.

Soak the bread in water until well
softened, then squeeze to remove the excess
moisture and mash a bit between your fingers
to break it up — the water softens the crust
and crumb, turning the bread into a
wonderful thickener for the soup.

Heat 1–2 tablespoons of the olive oil in
a large saucepan over low heat and fry the
onion and garlic until the onion is softened.
Add the beans, carrot, celery, tomato,
cabbage, pancetta, thyme and 2 litres
(70 fl oz/8 cups) of the stock.

Bring to the boil, then reduce the heat
to low and simmer gently for 1 hour — the
beans should be very tender, but not soggy.

It could take 90 minutes or longer, especially
if the beans haven't been soaked. Season with
salt and freshly milled black pepper, to taste.

Add the bread and cavolo nero to the
soup and simmer for about 15 minutes,
stirring occasionally to avoid it sticking to the
bottom of the pan. The bread should break
up a bit and thicken the soup. Add more
stock as needed — the consistency should be
more like runny porridge than soup.

Remove from the heat and stir in the
remaining olive oil. Allow to cool — the
ribollita should be refrigerated overnight to
allow the flavours to meld. Reheat the next
day, or 3 to 4 days later, adding water if
needed to make sure the soup is still sloppy
rather than stodgy.

Variation: You can use bacon, ham or speck
instead of the pancetta if you like.

250 g (9 oz) dried chickpeas
1 tablespoon olive oil
1 large red onion, diced
1 garlic clove, crushed
1 red capsicum (pepper), seeded,
    membrane removed and chopped
1 green capsicum (pepper), seeded,
    membrane removed and chopped

400 g (14 oz/1⅔ cups) tinned chopped
    tomatoes
200 g (7 oz) semi-dry chorizo or
    Portuguese chourico, peeled and
    sliced on an angle
4 eggs

Chickpeas stewed with chorizo

This delightful stew is honest fare that comes from the heart, and ends up with you smacking your lips with satisfaction.

SERVES 4

Put the chickpeas in a bowl and cover with water. Set aside to soak for at least 5 hours or overnight. Don't panic if you haven't soaked them, they'll just take longer to cook. Either way, rinse the chickpeas and drain well.

Place the chickpeas in a large saucepan. Add enough water to cover them by at least 2 cm (³/4 inch) and place the pan over high heat. Bring to the boil, then reduce the heat and simmer for 30–40 minutes, or until half cooked. You're looking for something that you can chew through, but it should still be a bit starchy in the middle. Drain the cooked chickpeas, reserving the cooking liquid.

Meanwhile, heat the oil in a large saucepan over a medium heat and fry the onion for 8–10 minutes, or until golden. Add the garlic and sauté a little longer, to take away its raw smell. Toss in the capsicum and fry for about 10 minutes, or until soft, then stir in the tomatoes.

Add the chickpeas to the capsicum mixture, stirring well. Add the chorizo and 1 litre (35 fl oz/4 cups) of the reserved cooking liquid. Season with salt and freshly milled black pepper and simmer until the chickpeas are cooked through and the sauce has thickened.

Preheat the oven to 220°C (425°F/Gas 7). Divide the chickpea stew between four 300 ml (10 ½ fl oz) individual serving dishes — earthenware would be nice. Crack an egg on top of each and bake for about 10 minutes, or until the egg has set. Serve hot.

Variation: You could actually poach the eggs in the sauce if you put it in a large frying pan. Crack the eggs into the simmering sauce and put a lid on to let them cook through, allow about 5 minutes.

200 g (7 oz/1 cup) dried cannellini or
    white/northern beans
2 brown onions
2 garlic cloves
1 sage sprig
2 teaspoons salt

400 g (14 oz) slab bacon or speck,
    cut into 2–3 cm (¾–1¼ inch) chunks
400 g (14 oz/1⅔ cups) tinned chopped
    tomatoes
1–2 tablespoons treacle

Homemade bacon baked beans

Pulled from the freezer or fridge, these beans, topped with an egg and served with fresh bread, make a good meal in minutes. They do, however, take hours to cook from scratch. It'll take you about 4 hours, but you can be asleep for most of this.

SERVES 4–6

Put the beans in a bowl and cover with cold water. Set aside to soak for at least 5 hours or preferably overnight. If you haven't soaked the beans you can still make this recipe, the beans will just take longer to cook. Either way, rinse the beans and drain well.

Peel both onions and cut one of them into dice and set aside. Place the beans, the whole onion, garlic, sage and salt in a large saucepan and pour in enough water to cover by at least 2 cm (³/4 inch). Bring to the boil, reduce the heat and simmer for about 1 hour, or until the beans are nearly but not quite cooked. Test after 30 minutes and every 10 minutes after that.

Preheat the oven to 150°C (300°F/ Gas 2). Drain the beans, discarding the onion, garlic and sage. Place the beans in an ovenproof dish such as a cast-iron pot or casserole dish, with the bacon, diced onion, tomatoes and treacle. Pour in just enough water so the beans are wet but not swimming.

Add more salt if it needs it and a bit of freshly milled black pepper.

Cover with a lid and bake slowly for 3 hours (check and reduce the oven temperature if it is boiling rapidly). I tend to turn the oven right down to 120°C (235°F/ Gas ¹/2), but some ovens can be less accurate that low. Check occasionally for moisture and top up with water to just below the level of the top beans if needed. The beans will be buttery soft but not broken if you get the temperature and water right. When the beans are done, take the lid off and taste the beans, seasoning as needed.

Increase the oven temperature up to 180°C (350°F/Gas 4), pull whatever meat you can find to the top of the dish, and continue baking for a further 30 minutes to darken the bacon and caramelise the sugars.

Serve the beans hot, with some bread and perhaps a salad to break up the richness.

200 g (7 oz) dried chickpeas

1 onion, halved

2 bay leaves

4–5 garlic cloves

1 tablespoon tahini (sesame seed paste)

2–3 tablespoons extra virgin olive oil,
  plus extra for drizzling

2–3 tablespoons lemon juice, to taste

1 teaspoon salt

¼ teaspoon ground cumin

paprika, to serve

Hummus

This homemade chickpea dip is one of life's great pleasures. Perfect for smearing on sandwiches with left-over warmed roast lamb, excellent on hamburgers, great for crudities (as we like to call batons of carrot and celery), and just heaven smeared on bread at a picnic or barbecue. The secret to making excellent hummus is to add just enough water to give it a smooth, moist texture, and to purée the chickpeas while they're still hot. If you're really keen, the finest hummus is made with chickpeas that are skinned after boiling, by being gently rubbed between your fingers.

This recipe makes a generous amount, which is perfectly fine because some think hummus tastes better if left to sit, refrigerated, for a day or two before eating. A good trick is to use 1 teaspoon of bicarbonate of soda (baking soda) in the cooking water to make the chickpeas soften faster.

MAKES 770 G (1 LB 11 OZ/ 3½ CUPS)

Put the chickpeas in a bowl and cover with water. Set aside to soak overnight. If you haven't soaked the chickpeas you can still make this recipe, the chickpeas will just take longer to cook. Either way, rinse the chickpeas and drain well.

Place the chickpeas in a large saucepan over high heat. Pour in 1 litre (35 fl oz/ 4 cups) water and add the onion and bay leaves. Bring to the boil, then reduce the heat and simmer, covered, for 1–2 hours, or until the chickpeas are very soft. You may need to add more water during cooking to keep the chickpeas covered. Drain the chickpeas and reserve the cooking liquid, discarding the bay leaves and onion.

Put the garlic in a food processor with some of the still-hot chickpeas and process until smooth. Add the remaining ingredients and chickpeas, taking care not to overload the machine, and process to combine. Add a little of the reserved cooking liquid to produce a smooth, but not runny, paste. You may have to do this in batches to suit your machine. If so, mix all the batches together in a big bowl, seasoning with freshly milled black pepper to taste. Allow to cool.

Check the consistency of the hummus as it will thicken slightly as it cools. Adjust the seasoning (cold food needs more salt than hot food to taste as lively). Serve with a sprinkling of paprika and a drizzle of extra virgin olive oil.

Hummus keeps well stored in an airtight container in the refrigerator for up to 1 week.

FLOURS

Since shortly after humans discovered seeds, we've been trying to make things with them. One of the finest things we've discovered, in my view, is flour — in particular wheat flour, with its all-important gluten, a protein that allows it to be stretched and hold its shape.

Flour can be made of other things, such as corn, or rice, or potato, not to mention chickpeas, mung beans and chestnuts. Even wheat flour can be made differently, lending it a variety of characteristics. Each flour has a purpose, be it for making bread, pastry or pasta, thickening sauces, or bringing crispness to batters.

PLAIN (ALL-PURPOSE) FLOUR A wheat flour of moderate protein content (9–11 per cent gluten) that is ground from the endosperm of the wheat. It is stripped of bran (the coarse outer covering of the wheat), and the germ, which can go rancid, being high in oil. Plain flour can be bleached or unbleached and is good for just about all uses, though it's better for pastries than for cakes or bread. Because it lacks the germ and bran, it keeps for years, rather than weeks or months.

SELF-RAISING FLOUR Plain (all-purpose) flour with a raising agent added. The raising agents used are equivalent in content and action to baking powder (a soda and an acid), which — when wetted — react to create bubbles of carbon dioxide. To make self-raising flour from plain flour, add 7 g (¼ oz) baking powder to each 200 g (7 oz/1⅓ cups) plain flour (some say 1 teaspoon per cup).

CORNFLOUR AND REAL CORNFLOUR (CORNSTARCH) Cornflour, as its name suggests, should come from corn. However, in Australia the main cornflour available for most of my lifetime has been 'wheaten' cornflour — in other words, a fine flour made from wheat rather than corn. Confused? You're not the only one.

What we in Australia call cornflour is often known as wheat starch in the rest of the world. It's the starch that's left after most of the gluten (a protein) is removed from wheat flour. It's very fine, brilliant at dissolving, and used to thicken sauces, to make a shorter texture in biscuits and cakes, and in custard. It's not, however, gluten-free, so is unsuitable for coeliacs.

Real cornflour (sometimes called cornstarch or maize starch, or pure maize cornflour) is made from the centre of corn. Like wheaten cornflour, it's also a fine, white powder that is good for thickening and in baking. Luckily these similarities outweigh the differences so, for most practical purposes, just substitute one for the other.

TIPO 00 (TYPE 00) FLOUR This is the typical Italian wheat flour recommended for pasta and for pizza. There's a lot of confusion about what 00 flour is, with many (including myself at one time) believing it was a soft (low-gluten) flour.

That's actually a fallacy. The term tipo 00, or doppio (double) zero, refers to how finely the flour is ground — so a hard wheat can be ground to 00 in just the same way that a soft wheat can. Gluten or protein content doesn't enter into it. The confusion probably comes about from the fact the flour feels 'soft' to the touch compared to 0 or 1, which are other grades of flour.

So, for pizza, a hard wheat 00 is suitable, and for fresh pasta a softer wheat 00 — though it differs from pasta to pasta, with hard wheat being preferred in Italy's south for their dried pasta. For all those uses I just use plain (all-purpose) flour if that's all I have, with close to perfect results. (See What Flour Makes the Best Pasta on pages 132–33.)

In some cases the fine ground flour made from durum wheat (which is high-gluten) is called continental flour.

GLUTEN FLOUR An extremely high-protein (gluten) wheat flour that is useful for adding to plain (all-purpose) flour to make bread. Gluten is the thing that gives bread a good bite and allows it to stay risen when baked. You usually wouldn't use this flour on its own, as it should be at least 75 per cent gluten. In fact, it probably shouldn't be called flour. Sometimes sold just as 'gluten' or 'vital wheat gluten', gluten flour should not be confused with 'high-gluten flour', which is a more balanced flour that is suitable for baking without mixing with ordinary flour.

BAKER'S FLOUR A high-gluten (12–14 per cent) wheat flour favoured by bakers. Also called hard flour or high-gluten flour.

CAKE FLOUR A low-gluten (6–8 per cent) wheat flour, which is good for cakes. Also called soft flour.

PASTRY FLOUR A moderate-gluten (7–9 per cent) wheat flour, which is ideal for making pastries, such as danishes and croissants.

UNBLEACHED FLOUR Most flour is bleached in Australia. This bleaching, usually done using a peroxide-based bleach, alters not only the colour of the flour, but also its chemical structure.

Unbleached flour, if fresh, doesn't make very good bread, as the gluten can't be worked up so easily. It can be aged, which usually adds a cost, to allow it to do the same rising as bleached flour. Bleached flour can make good bread, and is often favoured because it makes very good, light cakes. I tend to buy unbleached because I'd rather a firmer cake than eat some of the chemicals that are used to bleach flour.

WHOLEMEAL (WHOLE-WHEAT) FLOUR Also known as wholegrain flour, this flour is the equivalent of flour milled from the entire grain, usually of wheat. It has the bran, the germ and the endosperm in the proportions you would find them in whole wheat. Because the germ is high in fat, it does have the propensity to go rancid if stored for any length of time out of the refrigerator. It has to be ground fresh — which is why there were already seven grain windmills in Sydney just 20 years after colonisation.

Wholemeal flour has a mealier mouthfeel. Most of the time the bran is coarser than the endosperm (a result of the nature of milling), creating textural differences between the two in the finished product, sometimes akin to a nuttiness. The bran hinders the flour's ability to rise, probably due to its coarse texture at the microscopic level, meaning bread or cakes baked using 100 per cent wholemeal flour are more likely to be dense and possibly doughy. You need to allow for this when you cook with wholemeal flour, as the fine bran pops the air bubbles as they form.

STONEGROUND FLOUR The action of a stone mill has some impact on the resultant flour when compared to the more modern action of a roller mill. Some say the flour is torn rather than being squashed, meaning it absorbs moisture differently. Stoneground flour can be superfine, or coarser, depending on the mill, the grain and its operator. Some bakers insist that stoneground flour has better baking properties.

POTATO, RICE AND OTHER FLOURS Just about anything with a starch can be made into flour. Potatoes can be cooked, dried and ground to make flour. Rice can be ground into flour. Chestnut flour is an old European way of using up the common, mealy chestnut. Soya beans, in fact any beans, can usually be made into flour, too, along with tapioca, chickpeas and mung beans. Most of these other flours are particularly good for those who are coeliac as many do not contain any gluten.

WHAT FLOUR MAKES THE BEST BREAD?

Bread is one of the ultimate expressions of grain. If the grains are highly flavoured, so is the bread. If the grains are rancid, so is the bread. More than that, bread can be an expression of place, of climate, of history. That's because bread is the basis of so many cuisines, and the way it is leavened (risen) or not can make such a difference to the way it eats.

Bread is overwhelmingly made from a base of wheat flour, though potato, chestnut, rye and other grains may be heavily involved. We've seen how wheat flours differ in gluten, the all-important protein that gives bread its resilience, its chew and its ability to hold up when risen. The flours differ because of the type of wheat used, where (and how) it's grown, and the mill involved. All that can make a big difference when you use normal, commercial yeast to raise the bread. Imagine all that, with a whole bunch of wild yeasts harnessed to get the bread to rise, and you'll start to understand the vagaries, and varieties, of bread.

Bread, by its nature, relies fairly heavily on gluten. Without gluten the wholemeal Indian chapati wouldn't puff in the middle. Without gluten the Sardinian crispbread, carta di musica, wouldn't blow up like a balloon, ready to be sliced up the middle and rebaked. And without gluten it's very hard to get a nicely risen loaf to stay risen when baked. The thing is, gluten responds to acids, to mixing and to yeasts in different ways.

YEAST-RISEN BREADS

Most plain bread that comes in a packet has yeast as the raising agent. It also has about ten other ingredients that good bread shouldn't need, like preservatives and flavours.

Yeast that is used to raise most bread is a standard yeast, so it's super reliable. It's fast-acting, too, so as long as you give it what it needs — some food (sugar), some warmth, some moisture — it'll breed like mad and create little bubbles of carbon dioxide as it does so. These bubbles lift the bread. From my experience, there's little discernible difference between the fresh yeast you buy, sold in a pat like butter, compared to the dried yeast that comes in packets.

SOURDOUGH BREADS

Sourdough, the real thing, differs from yeast-risen bread in that the only ingredients needed are flour and water. The rising of the bread comes from yeasts and bacteria that are captured in a mix of flour and water that is fed for several days (see opposite). This is called a starter.

Some people use a little potato or grapes to trigger the starter when they first make it, but I've done it using nothing but flour and water. If you add some starter to a mix of flour and water and let it stand around at room temperature, the wild yeasts will raise the dough and you can make bread.

True sourdough doesn't use any added sugar or yeast, instead relying on the slow action of wild yeast and bacteria on the carbohydrate in the bread. Not only does this slow action give the bread a longer, more complex, more developed flavour, it also alters the way the gluten responds, and produces a sturdier, chewier bread. So when you make sourdough, which is achieved by harnessing the native yeasts and lactic-acid-forming bacteria in any particular location, then one sourdough isn't like the next. It's a brilliant, ancient technique that is, by definition, inconsistent, and yet produces some of the best bread on the planet.

There are examples of great breads that are made using some sourdough starter in the dough, along with the addition of cultivated yeast. In Italy this is called a 'biga', and it adds flavour and texture to the finished bread without it being a true sourdough.

WHAT IS A STARTER — AND HOW DO YOU MAKE ONE?

A sourdough starter is a living, frothy mass of wild yeast and good bacteria that replaces the factory-made yeast in bread. It can be made from scratch quite easily in many parts of the world, but the easiest way to get it going is to try and cadge a small piece from a sourdough baker and just feed it up. The starter doubles in volume every day that you feed it, which means a small amount can go a long way.

What you're trying to do is harness some helpful wild yeasts from the atmosphere, along with bacteria that create lactic acid (an acid that isn't really sour), and trying to avoid breeding up bad yeasts and bacteria. You'll have to take a risk, but if it smells good and fresh, then it should be okay. If it smells awful, or mildewy, throw it away and start again.

STARTING A STARTER Buy a good white flour, preferably unbleached and organic so it's as pure and full of good yeasts as possible, and use as pure a water as you can find. Rainwater is good if you have a clean supply (you don't want the influence of other bacteria), or use tap water that's been boiled and left to stand overnight. Mix equal quantities, by weight, of the flour and water. I start with just 40 g (1½ oz) flour and 2 tablespoons water. Some people like to add a grape, a sultana or some grated potato to help provide the yeast (these yeasts exist everywhere), and some like to add extra sugars to get it going. I've never found it necessary.

Leave the flour and water mix (with the sultana or whatever) in a non-reactive bowl (ceramic or glass is great, stainless steel is fine) in a moderate environment (about 20°C/68°F; this'll be hard to control in the tropics, easier in temperate climes). Once it is bubbling, you can cover it and refrigerate it if necessary (perhaps just during the day if it is hot, to slow it down), but this can retard its growth considerably, and the natural yeasts are unlikely to be floating around in your refrigerator.

FEEDING A STARTER Every day add a fresh batch of the same flour and water mix you originally made to feed the starter. Ideally, it's the same size as the starter. So your 80 g (2¾ oz) starter from the first day will weigh 160 g (5¾ oz) on the second, 320 g (11¼ oz) on the third and so on. I told you it grows like The Blob. (To be honest, I use a little less feed each day to cut down on the amount I end up with.)

This starter should start to bubble after about three days. It will get a nice lightly sour smell, not necessarily vinegary, but sour. You don't want any moulds growing on it, so if it goes grey or red, it's probably too warm or runny. After a week it should be a spongy mass, with a sweet, quite delicious smell, not dissimilar to yoghurt, but with a strong wheaty fragrance. Once it's made, you can freeze part of it (strongly recommended for emergencies, like when you kill the starter), and try putting some in the refrigerator to let it go to sleep. Just take it out occasionally (every few weeks) to wake it up and feed it. Professional bakers would feed theirs quite often, but they are baking a lot every day.

To use the starter, see the recipes for Rye Bread and the variation for a plain sourdough bread on page 138.

WHAT YOU NEED TO KNOW ABOUT SOURDOUGH BREAD — IN A NUTSHELL

Sourdough loaves don't have to be sour. They have a great, lingering flavour that is relatively complex and can even be slightly sweet on the palate. Inconsistency is the norm; sourdough takes a long time to rise, and the simplicity of its ingredients (flour, water, and a little salt) make it the most difficult bread to control.

Because there's no legislation in most jurisdictions to say a sourdough must be naturally leavened, dodgy bakers may just add vinegar to a standard yeast-risen dough and call it 'sour'. On the other hand, true sourdough loaves will vary by location. One area's sourdough will, by definition, taste different to another's. A proper sourdough usually has a good chew as a result of the slow rising. It is usually dense, although not always, but digests better than ordinary bread. A good indicator is the time it takes to toast. If there's any sugar added to the bread it will brown much faster than true sourdough.

Sourdough bread can come as a fairly light loaf (though nothing like the puffy bread they sell in supermarkets), or a very dense one, depending on the style of the bread, the type of flour, the maker and the oven.

PASTRY

While bread is one expression of flour, pastry is another. The difference, primarily, is in the use of fat. By using butter (or lard or suet) to coat the grains of flour, you can help prevent it getting too chewy when it's wet. This allows pastry to be very 'short', meaning it crumbles in the mouth rather than being chewy.

Good pastry, therefore, has a stage where the flour is mixed with butter, usually before any water/yoghurt or other moisture is added. The more you knead a pastry, in most instances, the worse it becomes. The hotter it gets, too, the more rubbery it becomes, which is why you start with chilled butter for some pastries. For very flaky pastry, some flecks of butter in a coarsely mixed dough is usually a very good thing. To make a really short pastry, some recipes use extra butter, or substitute part of the flour content with cornflour (cornstarch).

WHAT FLOUR MAKES THE BEST PASTA?

The best flour for pasta differs on what style of pasta you want. There's the soft, yielding, fresh pasta, usually made with egg, that originated in Italy's north. And then there's the resilient textured dried pasta from the country's south. The best for each can differ slightly, though both should be made using a very fine ground (tipo 00) wheat flour. In its absence, I just use plain (all-purpose) flour.

Fresh pasta can be made with a medium strength (moderate-gluten content) wheat flour without a problem, and in most cases it should have fresh eggs in it and be sold fresh (or made at home). But dried pasta is so much better made with durum wheat flour (sometimes called semolina flour). Durum wheat grows in hotter climates and has a really high protein content. This flour makes for the best *al dente* pasta, meaning it still has some bite in the centre when cooked. When buying it, a pasta with a protein content above 13 per cent is ideal. It not only stays resilient when cooked, it also prevents the pasta from overcooking.

Another thing to watch with pasta is the way it is rolled. Hand-rolled pasta, using a rolling pin and a wooden board, has a better texture. You won't be able to buy pasta like that. Machine-made pasta, however, also varies. Pasta extruded through brass dyes has a coarser outside, allowing it to absorb more sauce. Slow-dried pasta also has a better texture.

Chinese noodles are often made by stretching dough, not rolling it. They can be made using mung bean flour, rice flour or wheat flour. Most of the time it's easier, and better, to buy Chinese noodles (or Japanese for that matter) rather than trying to make them yourself.

HOW TO COOK PASTA

The best way for a novice to cook pasta is usually to measure the liquid volume in multiples of the weight of the pasta to be cooked. For instance, 100 g (3 1/2 oz) pasta can be cooked in 1 litre (35 fl oz/4 cups) water (ten times as much water as pasta) with 10 g (1/4 oz/2 1/4 teaspoons) salt ('as salty as the Adriatic Sea', my Italian friends suggest). This makes for a nicely salty pasta, while the volume of water allows the pasta to swell and jiggle and makes it unlikely to stick. Homemade fresh pasta will cook in the time it takes this water to come back to the boil, if it's rolled very thin. I find that most pasta packets have a fairly accurate cooking time on the side, but by trial and error the most accurate of all the very common brands that I've discovered is the Italian Barilla.

You can cook in less water (and therefore use less salt), so long as you stir the pasta fairly regularly. Really short shapes of pasta can even be cooked in a pan with just the sauce they will be served with (careful not to make the sauce too thick or strong flavoured, as it will reduce when cooked). Simply treat the dish like risotto, stirring constantly as it simmers, adding a fresh ladleful of sauce each time the pasta absorbs it.

Finally, when cooking your pasta, never, ever rinse it. Cook it at the last minute, simply drain and retain some of the cooking water. This starchy water carries a good whack of the flavour of the freshly cooked pasta, and it's useful to add a couple of tablespoons back to the pasta if it needs it. For some reason freshly drained pasta gets thirsty for a little water straight after it's drained. Some people like to lift long shapes (spaghetti, linguini) from the undrained cooking pot straight into the sauce rather than draining it, retaining some of that pasta water on the strands — see the recipe for Simple Tomato Ragu on page 386.

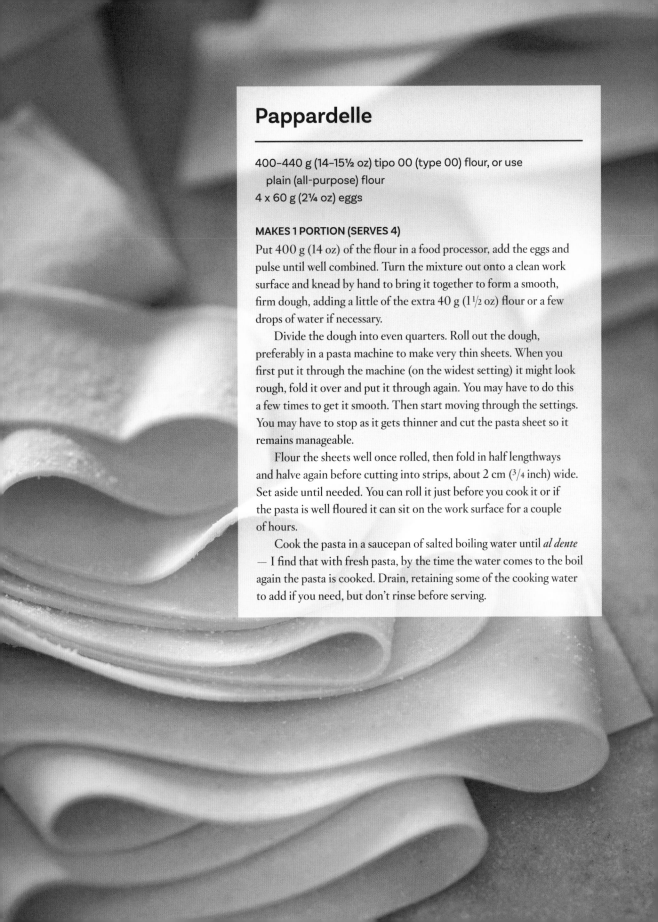

Pappardelle

400–440 g (14–15½ oz) tipo 00 (type 00) flour, or use
   plain (all-purpose) flour
4 x 60 g (2¼ oz) eggs

MAKES 1 PORTION (SERVES 4)

Put 400 g (14 oz) of the flour in a food processor, add the eggs and
pulse until well combined. Turn the mixture out onto a clean work
surface and knead by hand to bring it together to form a smooth,
firm dough, adding a little of the extra 40 g (1½ oz) flour or a few
drops of water if necessary.

Divide the dough into even quarters. Roll out the dough,
preferably in a pasta machine to make very thin sheets. When you
first put it through the machine (on the widest setting) it might look
rough, fold it over and put it through again. You may have to do this
a few times to get it smooth. Then start moving through the settings.
You may have to stop as it gets thinner and cut the pasta sheet so it
remains manageable.

Flour the sheets well once rolled, then fold in half lengthways
and halve again before cutting into strips, about 2 cm (³/4 inch) wide.
Set aside until needed. You can roll it just before you cook it or if
the pasta is well floured it can sit on the work surface for a couple
of hours.

Cook the pasta in a saucepan of salted boiling water until *al dente*
— I find that with fresh pasta, by the time the water comes to the boil
again the pasta is cooked. Drain, retaining some of the cooking water
to add if you need, but don't rinse before serving.

200 g (7 oz) sultanas (golden raisins)
100 g (3½ oz) candied orange and/or
    lemon peel (see page 468), chopped
2 tablespoons brandy
14 g (½ oz/2 sachets) dried yeast
1 teaspoon caster (superfine) sugar,
    plus 2 tablespoons extra
500 g (1 lb 2 oz/3⅓ cups) plain
    (all-purpose) flour

1 tablespoon ground nutmeg
1 tablespoon ground cinnamon
1 pinch of ground cloves
1 teaspoon salt
80 g (2¾ oz) marzipan
3 tablespoons honey, warmed for
    brushing (optional)

Hot cross buns

*In more pious times, after they had risen, Easter buns were marked with
a cross to let the devil out. Now, most bought buns use an evil flour and
water paste that is baked on right from the start. After following the
advice of friend and chef, Alan Kelly, I think marzipan works better.
Omit the marzipan cross to make fruit buns that are suitable to serve
at any time of year.*

MAKES 16

Mix the sultanas, candied peel and brandy
and set aside overnight if possible; otherwise,
warm slightly to plump the fruit. Cool
before using.

Preheat the oven to 230°C (450°F/
Gas 8). Dissolve the yeast and caster sugar
in 2 tablespoons of tepid water.

Combine the flour, spices, extra sugar and
salt in a large bowl. Make a well in the centre
and add the yeast mixture and 300 ml
(10½ fl oz) tepid water. Knead to a dough,
adding more flour if required, then place in a
lightly greased bowl and cover with a damp tea
towel (dish towel) or plastic wrap. Allow to rise
in a warm place for 1 hour, or until doubled in
size. Hit the dough to expel the air and knead
again for 10 minutes. Knead in the fruit.

Divide the dough into 16 even-sized
portions and roll into balls. Place on a baking
tray. Using scissors, cut a nick in the top of
each bun, and then another at right angles
to the first. This will be the place where the

cross sits. Cover with a damp tea towel that
doesn't touch the buns, and allow to rise in
a warm place for 30–45 minutes, or until
doubled in volume.

Divide the marzipan into 16 pieces.
Using your hands, roll the marzipan pieces
into thin logs about 12 cm (4½ inches) long
and cut into two 6 cm (2½ inch) lengths.
Press these into the cuts in the buns, to make
the crosses.

Bake the buns for about 10–15 minutes,
or until they are well browned on top and
bottom, taking care not to burn the tops.
Allow to cool, then serve warm or toasted
with lashings of cultured butter.

To give the buns a sticky, glazed look,
brush the tops with warmed honey just as
they are removed from the oven.

Hot cross buns are best eaten within
2 days. Store them in a paper bag in the
bread box or on the bench.

330 g (11¾ oz) plain (all-purpose) flour
150 g (5½ oz) sourdough starter
   (see page 131)

110 g (3¾ oz) rye flour
2 teaspoons salt

Rye bread

This rye bread uses a sourdough starter, which takes about a week to get going (see page 131). The starter acts like a yeast and is the rising agent for the bread. It is what differentiates sourdough from normal bread. By substituting the flours in this recipe, you can also make a plain sourdough loaf (see variation below).

The quantities of flour to water needed in this recipe can vary with the weather, the seasons and the type of flour used (see flours on pages 126–29), so adjust according to how the bread feels in the hand when you knead it. A woodfired oven is ideal for baking this kind of bread, but I've given instructions for using a conventional oven for all us mere mortals. The bread needs to prove for 12–18 hours, so make sure you prepare it at least a day before you wish to bake and eat it.

MAKES 1 SMALL LOAF

Mix all the ingredients together in a bowl with 300 ml (10½ fl oz) water until it comes together. Use an electric mixer with a dough hook attachment to knead for 3–4 minutes. If you don't have a mixer, tip it out onto a clean work surface, lightly dusted with flour, and knead well for about 5–10 minutes — the dough should be easily shaped and not too sticky when pinched.

Sit the dough in a large bowl, cover with a clean tea towel (dish towel) and set aside in a moderately warm environment — about 25°C (77°F) is good, but go lower rather than higher if in doubt — for 12–18 hours for the dough to rise (it should double in size). If you are in a warm climate you could place it in the refrigerator overnight then take it out early in the morning.

Turn the dough out of the bowl and shape the loaf without too much kneading. I aim for a log shape, by gently stretching (but not

tearing) it with my fingertips into a rectangle then rolling up. Once the loaf has been shaped, set aside for a further 30 minutes or so, until the dough is light and puffy, putting it on the tray you will bake it on. You don't have to wait for the dough to double in size like most bread recipes. Preheat the oven to 230°C (450°F/Gas 8), ideally with a pizza stone or similar in it.

If using a stone, you can try to shimmy the dough directly onto the stone. Otherwise bake towards the top of the oven for about 40 minutes, or until it sounds hollow when tapped on the base.

Variation: To make a plain sourdough loaf follow the above recipe but substitute the two flours with 440 g (15½ oz) wheat flour, preferably baker's flour or another high-gluten flour, but plain (all-purpose) flour will do.

- 2 tablespoons extra virgin olive oil, plus extra for drizzling
- 1 onion, diced
- 2 garlic cloves, crushed
- 500 g (17 oz/2 cups) tomato passata (puréed tomatoes) or 500 g (9 oz/2 cups) tinned tomatoes, puréed
- 3 basil leaves, torn
- 375 g (13 oz/about ½ loaf) rustic stale sourdough bread
- 300 g (10½ oz) buffalo mozzarella cheese
- 50 g (1¾ oz/½ cup) grated Italian parmesan cheese (Parmigiano Reggiano or Grana Padano)

Tomato & buffalo mozzarella bread 'lasagne'

This magical, lasagne-style dish is a great way to use up stale crusty bread, the slices filling in for the pasta sheets of traditional lasagne. I make it with whatever cheese I have to hand. Sometimes goat's curd, sometimes a fresh, sweet cow's ricotta — but always with good bread, oil and tomatoes.

SERVES 4

Preheat the oven to 180°C (350°F/Gas 4). Grease a round 2½ litre (87 fl oz/10 cup) capacity baking dish with a 25 cm (10 inch) diameter.

Heat the oil in a saucepan over medium heat and fry the onion for about 5 minutes, or until soft. Add the garlic and cook for 2–3 minutes, then stir in the tomato passata and bring to the boil. Reduce the heat and simmer for 10 minutes, then add the basil and season with salt.

Cut the bread into 1 cm (½ inch) thick, long slices. Arrange one-third of the bread slices in an even layer in the base of the dish. Spoon over one-third of the tomato sauce to cover the bread. Tear the mozzarella into small pieces and dot over the top using about one-third of the pieces. Season well with salt and freshly milled black pepper and perhaps add a drizzle more oil.

Repeat this layering another two times to use up the remaining bread, sauce and cheese. You could make more layers, but you really want to make sure there's enough tomato left to moisten the top and enough mozzarella left to scatter on top as well.

Sprinkle the parmesan over the top of the lasagne and bake for 20–30 minutes, or until the top is nicely browned.

Cut into portions and serve with a mixed green leaf salad on the side.

- 150 g (5½ oz/about ⅕ loaf) rustic white bread, crust removed, cut into chunks
- 80 ml (2½ fl oz/⅓ cup) extra virgin olive oil
- 1 carrot, finely diced
- 1 celery stick, finely diced
- 1 red onion, finely diced
- 800 g (1 lb 12 oz) ripe tomatoes, peeled (see page 378) and puréed, or use tinned
- 1 small dried red chilli, finely chopped (optional)
- 1 teaspoon salt
- 3 garlic cloves, crushed
- 15 basil leaves, finely shredded

Pappa al pomodoro

This is a very thick bread 'soup' (almost like a paste) and is perfect for making during tomato season, which peaks in late summer. While the bread may not be the major ingredient, it is one of the most important, because without it you've just got a tomato slurry. With it you've got a spoonful of Italy.

SERVES 4

Soak the bread in a bowl of cold water to completely soften.

Heat 2 tablespoons of the oil in a saucepan over medium heat and fry the carrot, celery and onion until golden but not brown. Add the tomato and chilli and continue cooking over low heat for about 15 minutes. Add the salt.

Squeeze out the bread to remove any excess moisture and mash a bit between your fingers to break it up — the water softens the crust and crumb, turning the bread into a wonderful thickener for the soup. Add to the soup and cook for a further 10 minutes, stirring occasionally. If it becomes too thick, add a little extra water.

Toss in the garlic and basil, stirring to combine and remove the pan from the heat. Season with salt and freshly milled black pepper, and add 1 tablespoon of the remaining extra virgin olive oil. Stir and let sit for a few minutes.

Serve warm (not hot) with the remaining oil drizzled over the top.

- 3 large roma (plum) tomatoes, cored and roughly chopped
- 1 tablespoon lemon juice
- 2 teaspoons ground sumac
- a pinch of salt
- ½ teaspoon freshly milled black pepper
- 1 pitta bread
- 3 tablespoons extra virgin olive oil
- ½ cup mint leaves, torn
- ½ cup flat-leaf (Italian) parsley leaves, chopped
- ½ cup coriander (cilantro) leaves, chopped
- 3 Lebanese (small) cucumbers, chopped

Fattoush

This Middle-Eastern bread salad has a really nice piquancy, thanks to the use of sumac — the ground form of a dried red berry native to the Mediterranean and the Levant. Sumac is available in good specialty stores, but if you can't find it, just use a bit more lemon juice instead.

SERVES 4

Put the tomatoes in a bowl and sprinkle with the lemon juice, sumac, salt and pepper. Set aside for at least 30 minutes to steep. The flavours will meld, and the juice will run from the tomatoes, which is just what you want.

Preheat the oven to 180°C (350°F/ Gas 4). Divide the pitta bread into halves through the middle and lay each piece on a flat baking tray. Cook in the oven for about 5–10 minutes, or until crisp — you may like to brush or spray the pitta with a little oil and sprinkle over a little salt and freshly milled black pepper before baking to give it a richer flavour. Remove from the oven and allow to cool.

When ready to serve, add the oil, mint, parsley, coriander and cucumber to the tomatoes and toss well to combine. Break the bread up into smallish pieces and toss through the salad to mix it all up well.

Serve immediately on its own for lunch, or with some lightly grilled lamb chops or chicken kebabs.

375 g (13¾ oz/about ½ loaf) rustic crusty white bread, cut into slices (or let the kids use sliced white bread)

80 g (2¾ oz) butter, softened

100 g (3½ oz/⅓ cup) marmalade

100 g (3½ oz) sultanas (golden raisins) or currants (try plumping them in 2 tablespoons of grog if it's for grown-ups)

8 eggs

500 ml (17 fl oz/2 cups) full-cream (whole) milk

200 g (7 oz) caster (superfine) sugar, plus extra for sprinkling

1 teaspoon natural vanilla extract (optional)

Bread & butter pudding

For a long time, I used croissants to make this bread and butter pudding, giving a very indulgent result (made even richer by also substituting cream for half the milk). I have also used panettone or fruit bread, and omitted the additional fruit. But in more recent times I've returned to making a basic bread and butter pudding — with its crunchy top and creamy middle it's hard to beat. If only I had more left-over bread ...

SERVES 5–6

Preheat the oven to 180°C (350°F/Gas 4). Grease a 2 litre (70 fl oz/8 cup) casserole dish. Cut the bread slices in half. Generously butter each piece of bread, smearing every second piece with marmalade. Arrange the bread in the base of the dish, overlapping each piece to create an even layer. Sprinkle some of the sultanas over the top, then continue to create these layers with the bread and sultanas until it is all used. I like to have the crust side up where the bread overlaps at the end, so that it pokes up and bakes crisp on top.

To make the custard, whisk the eggs, milk and sugar together in a bowl; the amount you will need may vary with the type and quantity of bread. Add the vanilla if you like. Pour the custard over the bread in the dish to completely cover — you want all of the bread soaked in custard, but not so wet that it's soupy. Let it stand a few minutes to soak up the custard (up to 1 hour is preferable if you are using firm bread); the ideal level of the custard after a few minutes is just below the top of the bread.

Sprinkle the extra sugar generously over the top and bake for about 30–40 minutes, or until the custard is firm in the centre.

Serve warm or at room temperature. It doesn't really need anything to accompany it, but you may want to serve it with vanilla ice cream.

Hot water pastry

This sturdy pastry is great for pork pies, and pies with heavy or wet savoury fillings. It is delicious cold, and the resilient texture comes from the fact the hot water cooks the flour a bit prior to baking.

50 g (1¾ oz) pork lard
50 g (1¾ oz) goose or duck fat
100 g (3½ oz) butter, softened
600 g (1 lb 5 oz/4 cups) plain (all-purpose) flour
1½ teaspoons salt
2 eggs, beaten

MAKES 900 G (2 LB)

Put the lard, goose fat, butter and 250 ml (9 fl oz/1 cup) water in a saucepan over medium heat and cook just until the fats have melted. Don't boil it.

Put the flour and salt in a large bowl, make a well in the centre and tip in the eggs, stirring to combine. Re-create the well and pour in the hot water and fat mixture, using a knife to stir well until it's too hard to mix, then get your hands in and make the dough into a nice, even ball. Wrap in plastic wrap or cover with a wet tea towel (dish cloth) and rest in the refrigerator for 30 minutes or so before rolling.

200 g (7 oz) butter, chilled and cubed
300 g (10½ oz/2 cups) plain (all-purpose)
    flour, chilled
½ teaspoon salt

150 g (5½ oz) natural yoghurt, chilled
50 ml (1¾ fl oz) pouring (whipping)
    cream (35% fat), chilled

Yoghurt cream pastry

This is an excellent short, savoury pastry that is perfect for pies, such as a Steak and Kidney Pie (see page 225), or any pie, really. A teaspoon of sugar added would make it suitable for sweet pies, too.

MAKES 700 G (1 LB 9 OZ)

Rub the butter into the flour and salt (or pulse in a food processor) until the mixture is crumbly. Stir or pulse in the yoghurt and cream until the mixture is just combined.

Form into a ball, cover with plastic wrap and refrigerate for 1–2 hours before rolling.

Roll the pastry between sheets of baking paper (as it's quite sticky), to about 3–5 mm ($1/8$–$1/4$ inch) thick. If possible, rest the pastry (still in the paper) on a tray in the fridge for 30 minutes, or 10 minutes in the freezer, to firm up again before lining your tin.

150 g (5½ oz) butter, chilled and cubed
250 g (9 oz/1⅔ cups) plain (all-purpose)
    flour

a pinch of salt
1–2 tablespoons ice-cold water

Pâte brisée (flaky pastry)

A good all-rounder, this pastry can just as easily be used for pies, flans or a tarte tatin.

MAKES 400 G (14 OZ)

Use your fingertips to rub the butter into the flour and salt, or pulse in a food processor until the texture resembles fine breadcrumbs. Add just enough water to make a pliable dough, being careful not to overmix.

Bring together into a ball and wrap in plastic wrap. Set aside, refrigerated if it's warm, to rest for at least 30 minutes before rolling.

125 g (4½ oz) butter, chilled and cubed
125 g (4½ oz) lard, chilled
500 g (1 lb 2 oz) plain (all-purpose) flour

a pinch of salt
1–2 tablespoons ice-cold water

Easy lard shortcrust pastry

This pastry works well for both savoury dishes and sweet fruit pies. The lard gives it a wonderful flaky texture that butter alone can't achieve.

MAKES 650 G (1 LB 7 OZ)

Rub the butter and lard into the flour and salt until evenly combined — it should resemble breadcrumbs. You can do this quickly and efficiently in a food processor — chill the bowl and blade for best results.

Add just enough water to make a dough. Barely knead until the dough is fairly even, then cover with plastic wrap and refrigerate for about 30 minutes before rolling out on a well-floured work surface.

200 g (7 oz) unsalted butter, cubed
   and softened
200 g (7 oz) caster (superfine) sugar
4 eggs

¼ teaspoon baking powder
400 g (14 oz/2⅔ cups) plain (all-purpose)
   flour, sifted

Shortcake pastry

Tricky to work, this pastry is very short (meaning it virtually melts in the mouth). It can also melt in the hands, so fast and minimal working makes for an easier time of it, and the results will speak for themselves.

MAKES 1 KG (2 LB 4 OZ)

Cream the butter and sugar together in a bowl until light and creamy. Add the eggs one at a time and beat each one in well. It may look a little curdled or split when you stop beating, but there's nothing to worry about. It'll all come together in a minute.

Sift together the baking powder and flour in a separate bowl and add to the butter mixture, stirring until just combined. Bring

together into a ball, wrap in plastic wrap and refrigerate for 4 hours, or until firm.

Roll the pastry between sheets of baking paper (as it's quite sticky), to about 3–5 mm (¹/₈–¹/₄ inch) thick. If possible, rest the pastry (still in the paper) on a tray in the fridge for 30 minutes, or 10 minutes in the freezer, to firm up again before lining your tin.

160 g (5¾ oz) butter, softened slightly
125 g (4½ oz/1 cup) icing (confectioners')
   sugar, sifted
1 teaspoon natural vanilla extract

250 g (9 oz/1⅔ cups) plain (all-purpose)
   flour, sifted
2 egg yolks

Sweet shortcrust pastry

*A good sweet pastry marries perfectly with moderately sweet pies,
or can even double as a base for a flan.*

MAKES 550 G (1 LB 4 OZ)

Put the butter, icing sugar and vanilla in a
food processor and process until the sugar is
dissolved. Pulse in the flour until the mixture
is crumbly, then pulse in the egg yolks. Tip
the mixture onto a clean work surface and
knead just until it makes a dough.

   Shape into a ball, wrap in plastic wrap
and refrigerate for 30 minutes.

Roll the pastry between sheets of baking
paper (as it's quite sticky), to about 3–5 mm
($^1/_8$–$^1/_4$ inch) thick. If possible, rest the pastry
(still in the paper) on a tray in the fridge for
30 minutes, or 10 minutes in the freezer, to
firm up again before lining your tin.

100 g (3½ oz) unsalted butter,
   cubed and softened
50 g (1¾ oz) icing (confectioners')
   sugar, sifted
1 egg yolk

½ teaspoon natural vanilla extract
135 g (4¾ oz) plain (all-purpose) flour
1 teaspoon finely grated lemon zest

Very short sweet shortcrust pastry

*My version of very sweet pastry is almost akin to a biscuit (cookie),
and could even be baked as rounds to add a textural crunch to desserts,
or to dip in clotted cream (with or without strawberry jam).*

MAKES 300 G (10½ OZ)

Beat the butter with the icing sugar in a bowl
until well combined. Beat in the egg yolk and
vanilla to combine. Fold through the flour
and lemon zest until just combined and
shape into a ball. Wrap in plastic wrap
and refrigerate for 1 hour before rolling.

Roll the pastry between sheets of baking
paper (as it's quite sticky), to about 3–5 mm
($^1/_8$–$^1/_4$ inch) thick. If possible, rest the pastry
(still in the paper) on a tray in the fridge for
30 minutes, or 10 minutes in the freezer, to
firm up again before lining your tin.

Chapter 3

POULTRY & EGGS

POULTRY & EGGS

Which came first? Great chickens or great eggs? Both, at their best, are wonderful. If I had to choose my last meal on earth, it would probably be roast chicken, with my mum's gravy. No one makes gravy like the one my mum made while I was growing up. Or like your mum, most likely. And few things in life are as good as the simplest roast bird, a great-tasting chicken with a burnished, salt-laced skin under which butter was pushed onto the breast. Of all the great restaurant meals I've had, the one at Georges Blanc in rural France, where he served a simple, incredible roast chicken that he learnt from his grandma, is a standout of elegant simplicity. The secret? The famed Bresse chicken, killed fresh, so fresh that it was never refrigerated, and it was roasted, like at home, just for me. This, in one of the world's most expensive and posh fine diners.

More recently than roasted chicken, I discovered duck. How great it tastes. How versatile it is. I even have a vegetarian friend who eats no meat at all, except for her duck exemption. It was duck, along with pork, that tempted me from my brief flirtation with vegetarian food in the 1990s. Duck confit. Roast duck legs. Crisped duck skin. Duck fat!

Meanwhile, eggs, gifted to us by chickens and ducks, are virtually irreplaceable in the cooking world. It's hard to keep a cake together without them. At their best, when soft-boiled and eaten with nothing more than buttered toast 'soldiers', they're as bright as a sunny day and a revelation of flavour.

CHICKENS

I watch, fascinated, as a Plymouth rock, a decent meat breed chicken with gorgeous white and black plumage, gathers her chicks and struts off. This is chicken as landscape; a stunning fine-laced chook, with fluffy, penguin-coloured offspring in an idyllic farmhouse setting. Any of her chicks that turn out to be roosters will be fattened for four or five months before being culled; throats slit, the feathers plucked on the farm, the carcasses left to dry by being hung on a fence while they cool. It's a quick end for a chicken that has spent most of its days purging the garden of snails and scratching around for worms.

This, however, isn't the way that chicken most people buy will be reared or killed. Most chickens are bred using strict genetics to produce a hybrid chicken that will be fattened in a shed, fed antibiotics, perhaps have its beak and wings clipped, and will live for less than six weeks before being sent to slaughter with a whole barn full of chickens the same age, only to be dipped in bleach to whiten the flesh. I'm at a farmhouse, and most people are in the city short of cash, and therein lies the problem of chicken production: factory farming is a way of producing massive amounts of very cheap meat.

The truth is, if factory farming — possible because of advances in technology over the better part of a century — has done anything, it's certainly revolutionised the production of chicken meat. What was once a luxury item is now one of the cheapest meats around.

Did we rush to get some of this new cheap meat? Just look at the figures. According to the Australian Chicken Meat Federation, demand jumped by seven times, that's 700 per cent, in the 1950s. It went up again by 500 per cent in the 1960s. In a twelve-month period after the arrival of Kentucky Fried Chicken in Australia in the 1970s, chicken production increased 38 per cent, part of a doubling of chicken sales that decade. The huge rise in demand has slowed, but steadily increased every decade since intensive farming was introduced. And the main explanation is a decrease in cost to the consumer.

What started out costing a similar amount to beef in 1971 is today less than half the cost (closer, in fact, to one-third). According to one estimate, a chicken in the 1930s would cost a day's wages for a labourer. Today it would cost about 6 minutes worth of pay. In the book *Myths of Rich & Poor*, authors W. Michael Cox and Richard Alm calculated the cost of a 1.5 kg (3 lb 5 oz) chicken as 2 hours and 40 minutes of a worker's wage in 1900, compared to 14 minutes in 1999.

But does this factory-style production, from the growing of the birds to their ultimate demise, come at an unknown cost? Experience tells us yes. While there's been little done to check the way chickens are handled and killed in Australia (as a journalist, I've been denied access to more than one chicken farm and abattoir), the evidence from the US is pretty scary. Animal rights groups have obtained footage of workers throwing chickens that didn't get stunned, pulling heads off chickens that didn't get their throats cut, and dipping chickens that are neither dead nor stunned in boiling water before plucking. With all the reports from the UK and the US about animal cruelty, it's hard to know where to start with chooks. Even if they're not mishandled, about 620 million of them die to grace Australian dining tables every year.

CHICKEN MEAT BREEDS

While all modern-day chickens originated from the wild chicken of India, the breeds have diverged. Some are good as layers, some just look great and attract the attention of chicken fanciers (arguably the most curious breed of human), and some are good dual-purpose breeds. One strain of chicken, bred specifically for meat, also comes from the same Indian origins, but has been selectively bred to be a specialist meat bird in Cornwall, England. In the UK, this Cornish hen is called the Indian game hen, and in the US the Cornish game hen, yet it's not a game bird anymore, rather a bird that produces relatively vast amounts of meat and boasts the same body shape for males and females. The meat qualities of the bird were enhanced even more in the 1950s when American breeders focused on a short-legged, really big-breasted bird that could be eaten very young.

Meat chickens these days, then, are nearly always descendants of the Cornish hen. Today, Cornish descendants are famed for being fast-growing birds that convert heaps of their feed to meat and are bred to have all-white meat. Cornish game hens and their cross-breeds tend to be the origins of the only real, viable breeding stock for commercial operators. And most are such a strange shape that they have to be fertilised by human intervention, as they can no longer mate naturally.

Despite what you think, the brown meat from a shop-bought chicken is nothing like the brown meat from most hens. Commercial varieties of broiler chickens, as the meat birds are known, are almost invariably white feathered, so there are no dark marks left on the skin after plucking. They're cross-breeds derived, in Australia at least, from great-grandparent stock that is brought in mostly from the US or Ireland.

While some alternative European breeds exist, such as gris barre chickens (usually named after the companies that bred them), they're very much the minority. Even those birds are virtually always a cross, the result of highly selective breeding, with factors like feed conversion, disease tolerance and breast-meat yield high on the list of priorities. Flavour, from all I can find out, isn't. You know you're dealing with commercial imperatives when you read of a breed dubbed 'meat king'.

HANDLING

Bred within an inch of its life, the modern meat chicken is a specialty bird that can go from the egg to the pot in less than six weeks. If you've ever raised chickens yourself, you'll know this is a remarkable achievement. They usually get fed antibiotics, which act as growth promotants. Lights are turned on and off to stimulate the pituitary gland, increasing the release of natural growth hormones — a way to enhance what happens in normal diurnal patterns. Some have lights on for 23–24 hours a day; sometimes they get an hour of light, two hours of dark, in endless cycles. They aren't kept in cages like battery laying birds, but they do often sit, idle, as food is given to them, so they don't waste any energy on foraging, because this, in some farmers' terms, is a waste of feed.

What we get is a pale, insipid, watery-tasting piece of meat that is kind of like cardboard, without the texture. So much so that if you give a slice of roasted real chook to a person who's never had real chicken before, they are often surprised, and sometimes overwhelmed, by its flavour.

It doesn't have to be this way. There are good chickens, great chickens, still for sale in the markets in Florence, in the south of France, and even (though it's frightening to have one killed in front of you) at the wet markets in China. There are delicious breeds of chicken, and more pasture-raised chickens with greater inherent flavour, now available in Australia, too.

So what goes wrong with the stuff that most of us are offered, even those with deep pockets and a passion for the product? Is it the breed, or is it the way the breed has been handled? Mostly, I'd suggest the latter. A factory bird can be ready for the table in 35 days. Some say in 28 days. Apart from the way they're fattened, many commercially reared birds are dipped in iced water, a technique known to increase the weight of the bird post slaughter. Good processing plants blast chill to create a dry bird (you can tell the difference from the water in the bottom of the bag you buy it in). Both methods chill the bird quickly, but one is a way of selling you water for the price of chicken.

The reality is that the broiler chickens we breed today could be, arguably, as good as any meat birds we've ever bred. A fine-textured, well-rounded, tender bird is not a bad thing to eat in my view. The specialist breeding programs, however, have favoured docile natures, big breasts, white meat and quick growth rates over flavour. They simply haven't given too much thought to taste. They've bred a bird that is good for factory farming to the exclusion of all else. If we took birds that grew a decent breast, but could still walk and forage, that had legs long enough to still mate naturally, birds that gained weight in a slightly longer time, they'd probably taste better.

ANTIBIOTICS: THE PRODUCER'S VIEW AND A REBUTTAL

You wouldn't let a child get sick, poultry producers argue, if there was an antibiotic you could use to cure it. And they're right. It's inhumane to let an animal suffer, and antibiotics are a fabulous tool in the armoury against disease and suffering. To a grower, particularly the intensive producer, the use of antibiotics helps to ensure a healthy, and therefore happier, flock. They argue that the use of antibiotics, particularly those that aren't used to treat humans, won't create antibiotic-resistant superbugs that affect humans, and that a withholding period means no chicken meat that is sold to the public contains the antibiotics. Free-range chickens, it can be rightly argued, are exposed to diseases from wild birds and other animals that can lead to a potential infection and painful death of the whole flock.

The problem comes with routine use. Or the overuse of those antibiotics also used in humans. Antibiotic-resistant microbes are being found more often than before. We know overuse of antibiotics is a big part of the problem. Some argue that routine use of antibiotics as a preventative rather than a cure will one day have catastrophic consequences.

Intensive, factory-style farming creates the perfect environment for bugs to breed. They're the slums and open sewers of the chicken world, the type of conditions that helped create human disease outbreaks in congested cities before we understood the germ theory. They're breeding grounds for dangerous nasties, and it's nature's warning sign that all isn't right if we need to use antibiotics as a preventative rather than a cure.

While some antibiotics are well recognised for their ability to increase growth rates, chicken and poultry breeders aren't supposed to consider this when deciding whether to feed antibiotics or not. Commercial reality, however, could encourage them to do so.

HOW TO TELL GOOD CHICKEN MEAT

Good chicken meat has well-developed colour from a mix of feed and exercise. The flesh is not white, but could in fact be a creamy colour. While corn-fed chickens are also yellow, a golden-coloured fat is an indication that the bird has been eating grass, and the beta-carotene in the grass has given them their lovely hue.

Good chickens have a large vein down the centre of each leg that has developed because it's allowed to walk a lot. This is a positive sign, though scary when you first see it on the top leg joint of a roast free-range bird.

The best-tasting chicken meat is grown slowly. This means the texture is firmer, the meat displays more nuances, and it tends to be more expensive than factory birds.

Unfortunately good chicken meat has, for the most part, gone from shelves. It's exceptionally hard in Australia, the US, the UK and New Zealand to find slow-fattened, pasture-reared chickens of the same quality available in most butcher shops and many markets in France or Italy. Simply put, they're willing to pay more for their chickens. A good bird in France cost me forty-two dollars, while in Australia the most expensive bird of the same size would've cost twenty-five dollars.

Good poultry is always free range. It could well be organic. If you don't have anything else to go by, use these two criteria to get the best bird wherever you choose to shop. If you're lucky they may sell them at your local farmers' market, otherwise try to frequent a butcher whose chickens you can trust.

1 tablespoon salt
2 leeks, white part only, rinsed
1.6 kg (3 lb 8 oz) whole free-range chicken

Homemade chicken stock
& poached chicken

The quantities of water and chicken, as well as the cooking temperature, are all important aspects in this recipe. Bigger chickens will take longer to cook and will require more water; don't take the chicken out of the pan for at least an hour after the heat is turned off, or the chicken may not be cooked through. You could also toss in a carrot and some parsley stalks if you have them.

MAKES 4 LITRES (140 FL OZ/16 CUPS)

Put 4 litres (140 fl oz/16 cups) water in a very large saucepan or stockpot over high heat. Add the leek and salt, bring to the boil, then reduce the heat and simmer for about 10 minutes.

Add the whole chicken to the pan, bring back to the boil, then reduce the heat and simmer for 15 minutes. Cover the pan, turn off the heat and let the chicken cool in the stock for 1 hour.

Strain the liquid off and use for stock. It should keep well in the refrigerator for 1 week, and stored in an airtight container in the freezer for 3–4 months. Store the poached chicken in the refrigerator for up to 4 days to use in soups, sandwiches, salads or for a light lunch.

Variation: I like to use two cobs of sweetcorn, the well washed stems and roots from a bunch of fresh coriander (cilantro) and the tops of a bunch of green spring onions (scallions) in this for a sweeter, more aromatic end result. You can also eat the corn, or use it in the stock to make soup.

Note: If you don't have homemade chicken stock, I'd rather, in most recipes that call for it, use water rather than anything else. If you've got good, pure, fresh ingredients in a dish, a bought stock — with all its strange additives and not very natural flavour — will compromise these flavours. I often make a very quick stock from onion peelings, a bay leaf and thyme simmered for 20 minutes, rather than use bought stock.

250 g (9 oz) Queensland blue or other good roasting pumpkin, peeled and chopped
2 tablespoons olive oil
1 teaspoon salt
200 g (7 oz) skinless, boneless chicken breasts

½ tablespoon chopped sage
1 tablespoon mayonnaise (see page 201)
1 teaspoon wholegrain mustard
½ tablespoon white wine vinegar
2 tablespoons extra virgin olive oil

Chicken & pumpkin salad

Below is a version of a delicious chicken and pumpkin salad made from scratch, but you could easily just use left-over roast pumpkin and roast chicken, or the poached chicken from the stock on page 163. If you prefer a lighter dressing, omit the mayonnaise and white wine vinegar and use balsamic vinegar instead.

SERVES 4

Preheat the oven to 220°C (425°F/Gas 7).

Toss the pumpkin in a baking tray, drizzle with the oil and sprinkle with some salt and freshly milled black pepper. Roast towards the top of the oven for about 40 minutes, turning the pieces occasionally, until they are starting to brown well on all sides. Remove from the oven and allow to cool.

Put 750 ml (26 fl oz/3 cups) water in a small saucepan over high heat and add half the salt. Bring to the boil.

Separate the fillets (tenderloins) from under the chicken breasts, and when the water is boiling, add all the chicken pieces.

Bring back to the boil, then turn off the heat and allow the chicken to cook in the water as it cools — about 30 minutes.

When the water has cooled, cut the chicken into slices. (You can reserve the cooking water to use as a weak chicken stock, if desired.) Place the chicken in a large bowl with the pumpkin and sage.

In a small mixing bowl, whisk together the mayonnaise, mustard and vinegar. Add the oil and remaining salt. Pour over the salad and toss to combine, just before serving.

375 g (13 oz/1½ cups) red lentils

1 x 800 g (1 lb 12 oz) good-quality whole smoked chicken

1 onion, roughly chopped, plus 1 small onion, extra, finely chopped

2 button mushrooms

1 carrot, chopped

1 celery stick, chopped

1 bay leaf

10 black peppercorns

20 g (¾ oz) butter

1 leek, white part only, rinsed and finely chopped

2 tablespoons chopped flat-leaf (Italian) parsley, to serve

Smoked chicken & red lentil soup

This is a lighter soup based on a pea and ham soup recipe. I make a stock with a smoked chicken and use the meat in with the red lentils. If you can't get a good smoked chicken, feel free to use a roast chicken in its place — though you may want to add a slice of bacon for a smoky hint.

SERVES 6

Put the lentils in a bowl and pour in enough water to cover. Set aside to soak while you get the other things together. It's not really necessary to soak the lentils, but does speed up the soup later.

Pull the meat from the chicken, reserving the carcass, and chop into bite-sized pieces.

Place the carcass, onion, mushrooms, carrot, celery, bay leaf and peppercorns in a saucepan. Pour in 2 litres (70 fl oz/8 cups) water (or enough to cover), and bring to a boil over high heat. Turn down to a simmer. Skim the surface to remove any scum that forms and simmer gently for 2 hours. Strain the stock through a fine sieve, discarding the bones and vegetables.

Heat the butter in a saucepan over a low–medium heat and fry the leek and extra onion for about 5 minutes, or until soft and translucent. Add the drained lentils and 1.5 litres (52 fl oz/6 cups) of the chicken stock — top up with water if you need more stock.

Simmer the soup gently for about 45 minutes, or until the lentils are very soft, and the soup has the consistency of really runny porridge.

Add the chicken meat and simmer for 2 minutes to heat through. Season with salt and freshly milled black pepper, to taste, and garnish with parsley to serve.

2 tablespoons extra virgin olive oil,
  plus extra, for drizzling
1 large red onion, diced
4 garlic cloves
1 kg (2 lb 4 oz) free-range skinless
  chicken thigh meat, cut into 2.5 cm
  (1 inch) dice
1 tomato, diced

400 g (14 oz/2½ cups) fresh or frozen
  peas
200 g (7 oz) artichoke hearts, preferably
  fresh (see page 398)
1 bay leaf
1 teaspoon salt

Braised chicken thigh with peas & artichokes

This is a great way to cook chicken in one pot, and end up with plenty of sauce for dipping your bread into. Peas and artichokes are one of those brilliant spring combinations that make for a very satisfying but beautifully light dish.

SERVES 5–6

Heat the oil in a large saucepan over low heat and fry the onion for at least 5 minutes, or until it softens. Add the garlic and cook for 1–2 minutes, then add the chicken and try to give it some colour, but don't worry if it doesn't.

Add the tomato, peas, artichokes, bay leaf, salt and freshly milled black pepper, to taste. Pour in enough water to half cover the meat. Cover the pan and simmer, stirring once, for about 30–40 minutes, or until the meat is tender.

Serve with a drizzle of extra virgin olive oil on the top. It tastes great with rice or bread on the side for mopping up the juices.

80 g (2¾ oz) butter

1.8 kg (4 lb) free-range chicken, cut into
  10 pieces (see note)

80 g (2¾ oz) piece prosciutto or jamón or
  unsmoked bacon, cut into short strips

2 large onions, diced

2 garlic cloves, bruised

2 tablespoons brandy

1½ tablespoons plain (all-purpose) flour

500 ml (17 fl oz/2 cups) dry white wine
  (or red, or a mix if you prefer)

10 thyme sprigs

300 ml (10½ fl oz) homemade chicken
  stock (see page 163) or water

2 carrots, cut in half lengthways

2 celery sticks, cut in half lengthways

250 g (9 oz) small button mushrooms

150 g (5½ oz) small onions (optional),
  peeled leaving the root intact

Coq au vin

The 'vin' in this dish is wine, and while most Anglicised recipes use red, I prefer white. According to The Art of Eating, *an insightful quarterly publication from the US, the French actually use their local wine for this dish — so in Alsace, for example, it would be coq au riesling. Australian chardonnay and semillon can be a bit too woody, so use lighter examples or riesling.*

SERVES 4

Heat half of the butter in a large deep frying pan over medium heat and fry the chicken pieces until well browned on all sides — you may need to do it in two batches. Add the prosciutto and cook for 1–2 minutes, then remove all the meat to a plate until needed.

In the same pan, fry the onion and garlic gently for about 10 minutes. Add the brandy and cook until the liquid has reduced. Stir in the flour and cook over medium heat for 2 minutes. Stir in the wine and thyme and continue to simmer for as long as it takes to reduce to about one-third of the original volume, then add the stock.

Return the chicken to the pan, placing the carrot and celery on one side under the liquid. The liquid should cover the chicken (add more water if necessary). Season with salt and freshly milled black pepper, to taste.

Return to a gentle simmer, cover, and cook for 15 minutes. Remove the breast meat from the pan and reserve.

Fry the mushrooms and onions in the remaining butter to moisten and let them colour. Drain on paper towel and leave to one side. After cooking the chicken a further 30 minutes, add the mushrooms, and onions if using. Keep covered and cook for about 30 minutes more, or until the meat is tender. Return the breast meat and prosciutto to the pan. Remove the thyme stalks, carrot and celery before serving.

Note: Jointing a chicken into 10 pieces is an easily learnt art — get your butcher to show you how it is done.

1.8 kg (4 lb) free-range chicken
50 g (1¾ oz) butter, diced, plus extra,
   melted, for glazing

Broad bean paste
2 tablespoons extra virgin olive oil
3 garlic cloves, crushed
1.5 kg (3 lb 5 oz) broad (fava) beans,
   double peeled (see page 391)
   (about 300 g/ 10½ oz shelled beans)
½ teaspoon salt

Sweet-breasted chicken with broad bean paste

Using butter under the skin is one of the ways you can make any chicken taste better. The skin goes fabulously golden and the breast meat stays moist and sweet. If you can't get broad beans, try using peas instead.

SERVES 4

Preheat the oven to 250°C (500°F/Gas 9).

Rinse the chicken inside and out and pat dry with paper towel. Gently loosen the skin from the flesh near the cavity and place pieces of butter underneath the skin, onto each breast and a little on the legs. Brush the outside with a little extra melted butter and sprinkle salt and freshly milled black pepper all over.

Roast for 10 minutes, then reduce the oven temperature to 180°C (350°F/ Gas 4) and cook for a further 1 hour, basting the chicken occasionally with extra butter or even better, with the pan juices (it's not essential), until it is just cooked through.

Meanwhile, make the broad bean paste. Heat 1 tablespoon of the oil in a frying pan over medium heat. Add the garlic and fry for 30 seconds, then stir in the broad beans. Add 125 ml (4 fl oz/^{1}/$_2$ cup) water and the salt and cook, stirring regularly, until the beans have softened. Remove from the heat, and mash with a fork until broken up, but still a bit chunky. Keep warm.

Just before you are ready to serve, stir the remaining oil into the broad bean paste (and perhaps some of the chicken cooking juices) and serve alongside the roast chicken.

3 tablespoons vegetable or peanut oil

1 large onion, finely sliced

500 g (1 lb 2 oz) free-range skinless chicken thighs, cut into 2 cm (¾ inch) dice

450 g (1 lb) roma (plum) tomatoes, peeled, seeded (see page 378) and chopped roughly

2 teaspoons freshly milled black pepper

12 fresh curry leaves

150 g (5½ oz) snow peas (mangetout), trimmed

1 teaspoon lime or lemon juice

Stir-fried chicken thigh with black pepper & curry leaf

Chicken thighs have more flavour than the breast meat, and will survive cooking at higher temperatures.

SERVES 3–4

Heat 1 tablespoon of the oil in a large wok or large heavy-based frying pan over high heat and fry the onion for 3–4 minutes, or until brown. Remove the onion from the wok, drain off the oil on paper towel and set aside.

In the same wok, add the remaining oil and fry the chicken thighs for 2–3 minutes over high heat, turning often, until brown on all sides.

Remove the chicken from the wok, drain off the oil on paper towel and return the chicken to the wok. Add the tomatoes and toss to combine. Cook for about 2 minutes, then add the pepper and 8 of the curry leaves and, when the chicken is nearly cooked, add the snow peas. Keep tossing until the chicken is cooked through — about 1 minute.

Add the lime juice and remaining curry leaves to the pan and season with salt (and perhaps sugar depending on the sweetness of the tomatoes) then remove from the heat.

Serve the chicken thighs crowned with the fried onion, along with some naan bread or steamed jasmine rice and maybe even some natural yoghurt.

1.6 kg (3 lb 8 oz) whole free-range chicken

1 red onion, chopped

1 teaspoon salt

4 garlic cloves, crushed

5 cm (2 inch) piece fresh ginger, grated

1 tablespoon vegetable oil

finely grated zest of ½ lime

juice from ½ lime

1 teaspoon cumin seeds, ground

1 teaspoon coriander seeds, ground

1 teaspoon garam masala

200 g (7 oz) natural yoghurt

Yoghurt roast chicken

A covering of yoghurt, particularly if you have the time to marinate the chicken for a while, keeps the flesh moist. I like to use strong spices, but if you prefer, you can keep it simple and just use paprika, which will allow the chicken flavour to shine more brightly. This marinade is brilliant for lamb legs, too.

SERVES 4

Rinse the chicken inside and out and pat dry with paper towel.

Put the onion and salt in a food processor and blend to a purée. Add the garlic and ginger and keep processing until smooth, or at least a good paste-like consistency.

Heat the oil in a frying pan over low–medium heat and add the onion mixture (you may need to add a touch more oil if it's impossibly dry). Cook for 10 minutes, or until the raw smell of the onion dissipates. The trick is to try to find when the heat of the onion is replaced by a sweet smell. Longer frying creates a better result than quick frying.

Remove from the heat and allow to cool slightly before stirring in the lime zest, lime juice, spices and yoghurt, and combine well.

Smear the yoghurt mixture all over the chicken and inside the cavity, until well covered. Set aside in the refrigerator for 30 minutes, or overnight if you're organised.

Preheat the oven to 200°C (400°F/ Gas 6). Roast the chicken, preferably raised on a trivet, for 1 hour or until cooked through. Serve with steamed rice, naan bread or lentils.

DUCKS & OTHER BIRDS

By far the most common meat bird after chicken in most societies is the duck, but there are also quail, geese, guinea fowl, pigeon (and squab), pheasant and turkey.

All these birds differ from chicken in that they are usually the progeny of very specific breeds that we eat, rather than the descendants of a single recent variety. All of them usually offer more variety in flavour, texture and conformation of the meat than commercial chicken. For instance the pekin duck, also known in the US as the Long Island duck, differs from the Aylesbury or the Rouen or the muscovy in that it has a very fine-textured but skinny breast. The muscovy is a huge bird, with an enormous fat breast. None of these ducks are hybrids (unable to mate). All, except the muscovy, of American origin, are descended from the wild European mallard. So breed plays a fairly big part in ducks, despite there not being anywhere near as many varieties as there are chickens.

Breed plays a fairly big part in the eating quality of turkeys, too, with the rare bronze wing turkey being highly prized for meat, but rarely reared for food because of its low feed conversion rate (the amount of weight it puts on per kilogram of feed). Sadly, however, commercial turkeys are bred to be big breasted and white feathered, and to fatten up quickly. They're like chickens, really, with the similar problem of breast meat that dries out markedly, and a distinct lack of character in the meat. And just like with chicken, it's in the handling that much goes wrong. I know this because I've dispatched and eaten turkeys, of unknown variety, on my farm.

FOIE GRAS

Hybridisation, the cross-breeding that results in a sterile offspring, is common in other birds besides chickens. In turkeys, for instance, it's the norm, as it is with the muscovy duck cross used to make foie gras, the fattened liver of ducks in France.

Fans of foie gras love the rich, fatty liver, with its nutty flavour and buttery texture. There are even food tourists who make a point of visiting foie gras farms in the south of France.

Animal rights campaigners believe that the force feeding of ducks (and, decreasingly, geese) is cruel, and want the practice banned. I've been to foie gras farms and seen the ducks waddle as fast as they can up to the handlers, desperate to be fed. I've watched the handlers massage the birds' throats, pouring grain through a funnel into their crop. Lacking a gag reflex, the birds are literally filled with food and can barely walk once fed. These were free-range birds, with trees and grass and water to play in, which is more than can be said for many ducks reared where I live. I'm sure there are factory foie gras farms where the process is harsh and cruel. But what I saw was just odd, really.

Foie gras originated when farmers watched ducks and geese gorge themselves on grain before migrating south for winter. When killed, they found the bird had an engorged liver. It is this liver, considered a diseased liver, that is so famed as foie gras. As usual with man's intervention, what we have now is probably an extreme of what was observed in nature.

Apologists for foie gras say that if you stop force feeding a bird, they make a complete recovery, and argue that this, along with the fact the birds are mad keen on being heavily fed, implies foie gras is no crueller than any other kind of animal farming. I have conflicted views on the subject, and because all the foie gras imported into Australia is pasteurised anyway (and hence nowhere near as interesting as the fresh stuff), I choose not to eat it most of the time.

WHAT TO LOOK FOR IN DUCKS AND OTHER BIRDS

Good poultry hasn't been frozen. It's relatively dry-looking, rather than sloppy and wet in a bag, and has good depth of breast (except, perhaps, for pekin ducks).

A good turkey, like a good chicken, has ranged free. It should have some colour to the fat, from eating grass.

Good duck should also range. Duck, if it's healthy, should have a generous amount of fat covering the body. This fat is very high in flavour and is brilliant in cooking, so don't be afraid to use it.

Quail, guinea fowl and pheasant are all available in small numbers. Farmed, they should be relatively pale, fresh and plump. Wild, they can be darker in flesh, and should be (if where you live it's allowed) hung on the feather until high (see page 290), or for a few days to let the flesh tenderise.

1 tablespoon olive oil

1.6 kg (3 lb 8 oz) whole fresh duck, rinsed and patted dry, cut into four (see note)

1 onion, roughly chopped

125 ml (4 fl oz/½ cup) red wine

100 g (3½ oz) carrot, diced

4 thyme sprigs

30 g (1 oz) butter

2 tablespoons chopped flat-leaf (Italian) parsley

1 portion pappardelle (see page 134)

100g (3½ oz/1 cup) finely grated Italian parmesan cheese (Parmigiano Reggiano or Grana Padano)

Duck ragu with pappardelle

You can cook this recipe using dried pappardelle pasta, but if you have the time, fresh is better (see page 134). I've done a classic Italian version, using a small amount of flavoursome meat over pasta. Double the duck quantities if you want more meat.

SERVES 4

Preheat the oven to 150°C (300°F/Gas 2).

Heat the oil in a flameproof casserole dish over medium heat and fry the duck pieces until brown — you may find it easiest to work in two batches. Remove the duck from the dish, drain the excess oil, add the onion and cook until golden. Add the wine and boil for 2 minutes, stirring to get all the yummy bits from the bottom of the dish.

Add the carrot, thyme and 250 ml (9 fl oz/1 cup) water, return the duck to the dish, cover and cook in the oven for about 2 hours, or until tender.

Drain the cooking liquid through a sieve and reserve. When the duck has cooled slightly, pull all of the meat from the bones and tear into bite-sized pieces, discarding the fat.

Skim and discard half the fat from the reserved cooking juices. Place the juices in a saucepan over high heat and cook for 5 minutes, or until the liquid reduces and you are left with a thick sauce. Stir the duck back into the sauce with the butter and parsley.

Meanwhile, cook the pasta following the directions on page 134.

Toss the duck ragu and parmesan through the pappardelle. Season with salt and freshly milled black pepper, to taste. Serve immediately.

Note: Because you're braising the duck, there's no need to be neat. Simply cleave the bird in half and halve again, avoiding the hard breast ridge and leg bones.

1 tight-hearted iceberg lettuce
1.4 kg (3 lb 2 oz) whole cantonese roast
   duck or other roast duck
1 tablespoon peanut oil
3 cm (1¼ inch) piece young ginger,
   finely chopped
2 young celery sticks, finely chopped
100 g (3½ oz) shiitake mushrooms, stems
   removed and caps finely chopped

4 spring onions (scallions), finely sliced
14 water chestnuts, finely chopped
a pinch of chinese five spice
2 tablespoons shaoxing rice wine
2 tablespoons hoisin sauce

Duck & shiitake sang choi bau

*There are plenty of versions of this southern Chinese classic —
apparently the original has pigeon in it — and this one has no dibs
on authenticity. The joy is in the marvellously hot filling of local duck
wrapped in cups of crisp, cool iceberg lettuce. The shaoxing rice wine isn't
essential, but it's cheap and readily available at Asian food stores and
brilliant for cooking with. You could even use a hint of brandy instead.*

SERVES 6–8

Hit the core of the lettuce firmly against the work surface and twist to remove. Slice 1 cm (½ inch) off the lettuce at the opening. Under running water, gently separate the leaves, one at a time, keeping them whole to use as lettuce 'cups'. Soak the leaves in cold water to crisp. Drain and pat dry with paper towel.

With your hands, remove the duck meat and skin, discarding any fat and bones. Finely chop the meat and skin.

Heat the oil in a frying pan or wok over high heat and fry the ginger for 30 seconds. Add the celery and stir to heat through. Toss in all the other ingredients, including the duck, adding the hoisin sauce, to taste.

When everything has heated through, serve lettuce cups at the table and allow guests to spoon some of the duck mixture into each, then fold over and hook in.

2 x 200 g (7 oz) duck marylands

olive oil, for drizzling

¼ small red onion, finely sliced

2–3 radishes, finely sliced

1 large handful mizuna leaves (or use other soft, mild lettuce leaves)

1 small handful young radicchio leaves, torn

1 tablespoon balsamic vinegar

2 tablespoons walnut or olive oil

¼ teaspoon salt

Shredded duck salad

Instead of turning the oven on just to make a salad, I like to roast a whole heap of duck marylands one day for dinner and then use the leftovers in this dish. The skin can be cut, salted and crisped in a pan and added to the salad at the last minute. It's kind of like duck crackling — delicious!

SERVES 4 AS AN ENTRÉE

Preheat the oven to 150°C (300°F/Gas 2).

Place the duck legs in a baking tray and drizzle with barely enough olive oil to just make the skin glisten when rubbed over with your hands. Season liberally with some salt and freshly milled black pepper and cook, skin side up, for about 90 minutes, or until the meat is falling from the bones.

When they're cool enough to handle, pull the meat and crisp skin from the bone. Shred the meat with your fingers.

Mix together the duck, onion and radish in a bowl and toss to combine, then mix with the lettuce and raddicchio leaves and gently distribute with your fingers.

Whisk together the balsamic vinegar, walnut oil, salt and a little freshly milled black pepper until well combined.

Dress the salad with the oil mixture, toss with your fingertips and serve immediately.

10 duck marylands (about 2.3 kg/
    5 lb 2 oz)
115 g (4 oz) rock salt
8–12 garlic cloves
5 thyme sprigs

20 peppercorns
2 bay leaves, crushed
1–1.5 litres (35–52 fl oz/4–6 cups) duck
    or goose fat (see note)

Duck confit

*This salty, preserved duck meat gains in complexity as it matures under
its thick, pale blanket of fat. The amount of salt recommended works only
if it's coarse rock salt (use much less if it's fine salt). You'll need to start
the day before so the duck has time to cure properly. If your marylands
are a different weight to the recipe, use 50 g (1 3/4 oz) rock salt per
kilogram of meat.*

SERVES 10

Weigh the duck marylands to ensure the
weight of salt is correct (see intro). Rinse the
duck and pat dry with paper towel. Sprinkle
the salt evenly over the duck, rubbing to press
into all the crevices and the skin. Arrange in a
deep roasting tray, sprinkling over any salt that
has fallen off. Scatter over the garlic, thyme
and half the peppercorns. Cover with plastic
wrap and refrigerate for 24 hours.

Rinse off the excess salt and pat dry, keeping
the garlic and thyme. Discard the peppercorns.
Preheat the oven to 130°C (250°F/Gas 1), or
lower if your oven can handle it.

Pack the duck pieces tightly back into the
clean tray, adding the remaining peppercorns,
bay leaves and the reserved garlic and thyme.
Gently heat 1 litre (35 fl oz/4 cups) of the duck
fat until liquid and pour over the duck to cover
— you may need to add some extra duck fat.

Cook in the oven for about 3–4 hours —
the oil should barely simmer and the meat
should be just about leaping off the bone
when cooked. Remove from the oven and
allow to cool to room temperature in the fat.

To store, remove the duck with tongs and
place in a sterilised airtight container. Gently
pour off the fat through a sieve, leaving
behind any herbs and liquid in the bottom of

the tray. Pour the strained fat over the duck
to cover. Discard the herbs and liquid. Store
in the refrigerator for up to 1 month.

Preheat the oven to 220°C (425°F/
Gas 7). Remove the duck legs from the fat,
scraping off any excess.

Heat an ovenproof frying pan over
medium-high heat, fry the duck, skin side
down, until the skin colours, then turn the
duck and transfer to the oven to cook for
5–10 minutes, until the meat has warmed
through and the skin is golden. Drain off any
liquid fat before you serve. If the meat is too
salty, you can add a little stock to the pan as
they reheat, to dilute the intense flavour.

Variation: You can make a chicken confit
using the method above and substituting
olive oil for the duck or goose fat. Make
sure you weigh the chicken marylands and
calculate the amount of salt required as many
will be heavier than duck marylands.

Note: The quantity of duck fat you use will
vary depending on the size and shape of the
baking tray you cook the duck in. Duck
fat is sold in tins and available from most
good delicatessens.

1 tablespoon butter, duck fat
(see note, page 181) or oil
3 large onions, chopped
6–8 large fresh bay leaves
1 large garlic clove, crushed
3 large desiree potatoes, peeled
and diced
1 kg (2 lb 4 oz/about 8) beetroot (beets),
peeled and diced

2 litres (70 fl oz/8 cups) homemade
duck stock (see variation page 224) or
chicken stock (see page 163)
2–3 teaspoons salt
3–4 duck confit marylands (see page 181)
fresh horseradish, to serve
crème fraîche or sour cream (optional)

Duck, beetroot & bay leaf soup

This soup pinks and warms the mood. You can use the bones from duck confit to make the stock, and the flesh to flavour the soup, or equally make this with duck that has simply been thrown in the oven and roasted for 90 minutes (see the Shredded Duck Salad on page 179).

SERVES 8–10

Heat the butter in a large heavy-based saucepan over medium heat and fry the onion with the bay leaves for 5–10 minutes, or until the onion is just starting colour a little. Add the garlic and cook for about 30 seconds longer.

Add the potatoes and beetroot to the pan, then pour in the stock and bring to the boil. Reduce the heat and simmer for about 30 minutes, then add the salt and some freshly milled black pepper, to taste.

Flake or chop the duck meat into bite-sized pieces, discarding the skin, and add to the broth. Continue cooking for a further 10 minutes then test the beetroot — it should be very tender.

Season to taste, and serve hot with the horseradish on the table and an optional small dollop of crème fraîche on top. And remind your guests not to eat the bay leaves.

100 g (3½ oz/1¼ cups) fresh
  breadcrumbs
10 sage leaves, chopped
30 g (1 oz) butter, melted
80 g (2¾ oz) whole chestnuts, roasted,
  peeled (see page 506) and finely
  chopped (or use tinned chestnuts or
  unsweetened purée)

50 g (1¾ oz) pancetta, diced
1 large turkey breast, butterflied
  (ask your butcher to do this)
olive oil, for rubbing

Roasted rolled turkey breast with chestnuts

*A good turkey is a rare and beautiful thing. Until I grew my own,
I hadn't realised the depth of flavour, the moist texture or the lovely
aroma that turkey can have. Old-breed organic turkeys are the best
flavoured of any that I've found.*

SERVES 8

Fire up a kettle-style barbecue an hour before you intend to cook. Alternatively, you can preheat the oven to 220°C (425°F/ Gas 7).

Put the breadcrumbs, sage, butter and chestnuts in a bowl and mash to a paste, then stir through the pancetta to combine and season well with sea salt and freshly milled black pepper.

Lay the turkey breast, skin side down, on a clean work surface and top with the paste. Roll up, tying tightly with kitchen string at regular intervals. Rub with a tiny bit of oil and season well.

When the coals are heated through, place them on either side of the centre (so you don't burn the bottom of the turkey), and roast the meat for 60–90 minutes with the lid on. If you are cooking the bird in the oven, place the turkey in a baking tray and reduce the temperature to 180°C (350°F/ Gas 4) after 10 minutes, and continue cooking for a further 50 minutes or so.

Check to see if the turkey is cooked by cutting into the centre and looking for clear juices. Allow to rest under foil for 10 minutes before carving. Cut into slices and serve with salads and boiled, buttered new potatoes.

Quails with lemon, bay leaf & olive oil

This meal is a lovely, simple way to taste the best farmed quail.

8 quails, butterflied (ask your butcher to do this)
100 ml (3½ fl oz) white wine
2–3 tablespoons lemon juice
8 fresh bay leaves
100 ml (3½ fl oz) olive oil

SERVES 8

Put the quail in a non-reactive baking tray and pour in all the other ingredients to coat; season with sea salt and freshly milled black pepper. Leave to marinate overnight.

Preheat the oven to 230°C (450°F/Gas 8). Drain off most of the marinade, making sure the quail is in an even layer and roast for about 15 minutes. Rest for a few minutes before serving.

EGGS

Most modern chicken eggs, as many people know, are produced by hens that spend no time outdoors, that can't forage, that sit in a cage and will never know the feeling of the sun on their backs, the wind in their faces, or the joy of chasing a grub around the yard. Cage eggs, they're known as where I live — or battery hen eggs, if you want the now outdated but more emotive term.

And all that, really, could be considered just emotional twiddle-twaddle. But the fact is that a happy chicken produces a better egg. Anybody who has kept chickens, arguably the easiest livestock to own, can tell you that.

Sure, the yolks from home-laid eggs vary in colour. The chickens moult in autumn, which stops them laying for a bit, and there's some maintenance work involved, but real, proper free-range birds that are bred to forage, and that enjoy the outdoors, produce eggs of incomparable quality. The yolks aren't just vividly orange (you can simply put additives in the feed to deepen the colour); the flavour is far deeper, richer and vibrant on the palate. The whites are also firmer.

So what are your options if you don't want to, or can't, have your own chooks?

There are cage eggs, laid by birds that live in a wire cage about the size of an A4 piece of paper. There are barn-laid eggs, where the chickens can walk around a little, free from cages, in big sheds. And there are free-range eggs, where the chickens have access to the outside for a few hours each day — though free-range, in a commercial sense, means that the chickens may not want to wander out of doors, because there may be no food there, no fresh pasture, no shelter. And many commercial layers are pretty lazy eaters and have very little instinct for foraging.

What we should add to this list are pastured chickens. Chickens that not only have access to pasture and daylight, but are actively encouraged (and bred) to use it. Even these won't be quite as good as home grown. If you know someone with backyard chickens, angle for a dozen eggs every now and then.

CHICKEN EGG BREEDS

For some time, the hybrid factory-laying birds of choice have been the French-developed Isa Brown and the almost identical US breed Hyline, which produce consistently for a year, but are relatively useless at ranging. Very similar to the Isa Brown are the Dutch-breed Hisex Brown hens, which can be sexed much more easily at day one (apparently it's a very hard task, normally), so you don't have to worry about breeding up too many roosters. (Baby roosters from egg-laying flocks are killed at one day old because they're just a waste of feed.) Other breeds such as the old Dutch barnevelder, the Plymouth rock, the light Sussex and many other so-called utility breeds (such as Australia's own Australorp) are pretty good at laying and pretty good for eating, but not absolutely brilliant at either. In reality, cross-breeds usually make better layers, even for home production, and truth be known, the breed of chicken is only relevant to breeders or small farmholders, because every situation may differ, and the reality is that an egg is an egg. It's how the bird forages and eats that matters to the customer who is not just going to buy the egg, but put it in their mouth and eat it. Australian consumers love brown eggs – hence the ubiquitously brown eggs produced by commercial farms, but in the US, customers generally prefer their eggs to be white.

STORING EGGS
The simple rule with eggs is that a day on the bench, out of the refrigerator, is like a week in the refrigerator. Keep eggs in the carton (they're a brilliant design for retaining egg moisture and quality), with the pointy end down, and in the fridge. While you should store your eggs in the fridge, for most dishes they are generally much better if brought to room temperature before using. Cracked shells can let in bacteria, so any damaged eggs are best discarded, as they are more likely to make you ill.

HOW CAN I CLEAN DIRTY EGGS?
If you get eggs from your own chookhouse or a farmer and they have some straw or muck on them (is it mud or poo?), don't wash them ahead of using them. That's right, the egg has a beautiful natural protective layer on the outside, a bloom that helps protect the egg from attack by microbes. Washing destroys the eggs' natural protection, so just brush off anything loose, then store them in the refrigerator until you're ready to use them.

You should, however, try to use these eggs immediately after gently rubbing, sponging, or at worst washing or rinsing the shells, to help prevent contamination. Use them only for cooked products — not raw in mayonnaise and the like.

For many people, some muck on an egg shell is a sign that this is the real deal, an egg of excellent quality, though health authorities rightly frown on dirty eggs.

DUCK EGGS
Compared to chicken eggs, duck eggs are usually a little bigger, and have a huge yolk. The yolk is also richer, more flavoursome and brighter in colour. For this reason duck eggs are perfect in baking, particularly in the classic sponge cake (see Duck Egg Sponge, page 198). Duck eggs are also great in quiches, and make the finest crème brûlée.

A GOOD EGG?

Good eggs come from birds that not only have access to the outdoors, but are actively encouraged to feed on fresh pasture. As with most animals, a varied diet means a better-flavoured end result.

The variety of chicken plays little part in the eating quality of a chicken egg. Good eggs can come from almost any breed, though some do look better, and are bigger, than others.

A fresh egg is best for just about any cooking and all eating, and can be either brown or white. Darker eggs tend to come from the darker-coloured birds, and the hue of the shell has no influence on the flavour.

2 bunches (about 400 g/14 oz) asparagus
white vinegar, for poaching
4 eggs

100 g (3¼ oz) good-quality, cloth-bound
cheddar cheese or similar hard cheese,
shaved

Asparagus with poached egg & cheddar

The most perfect use of asparagus is usually the simplest. Much green asparagus can be so tender you can eat it raw if it's really fresh, so a bare grilling or steaming is enough. I love to chargrill it on a barbecue, but a ridged pan in the kitchen is just as good. If you use white asparagus, use a little of the cooking liquid on the plate to lift the flavours. This dish makes a great entrée or light lunch.

SERVES 4

Snap the woody ends off the asparagus and discard — these can be used to flavour stocks for asparagus risotto if you like. Place the asparagus spears in a frying pan with a dribble of boiling water, cover with a lid and cook for 2–3 minutes.

In the meantime, heat a deep frying pan with water and about 5–10 per cent vinegar (that's about a tablespoon of vinegar per cup of water) and poach the eggs to your liking. Three minutes is usually enough for a classic poached egg where the yolk is runny and the white set.

Drain the asparagus spears and divide evenly between four serving plates. Place a poached egg on top, season with sea salt and freshly milled black pepper and scatter over the cheddar cheese, to serve.

400 g (14 oz/1⅔ cups) tinned
    chopped tomatoes
1 tablespoon vegetable oil
1 small onion, finely chopped
1 long green chilli, seeded and
    finely sliced

½ teaspoon green cardamom seeds
15 fresh curry leaves
12 hard-boiled eggs, peeled
a pinch of sugar
lime juice, to taste

Hard-boiled eggs with curry leaves

*Curry leaves are a specialty ingredient available at good greengrocers,
Asian food stores, or cadged from South Indian restaurants (as I've often
done). They are becoming more widely available and grow in warmer
climes quite well. You can substitute fresh coriander (cilantro) leaves for
a different but equally lovely result, but don't use dried curry leaves as
they taste like mildew. For best results, you will need to prepare this dish
a day in advance.*

SERVES 6

Lightly blend the tomatoes in a blender and
set aside until needed.

Heat the oil in a frying pan over medium
heat. Add the onion and a pinch of salt and
fry until the onion starts to brown. Stir in the
chilli, cardamom and curry leaves and fry for
about 30 seconds, then add the tomatoes.

Reduce the heat and simmer for about
10 minutes. Add the whole eggs and sugar,
stir, and simmer for 5 minutes longer, turning
to coat the eggs in the sauce.

Remove the pan from the heat, cool and
allow to stand in the refrigerator, overnight if
possible, or serve immediately with a squeeze
of lime juice and steamed rice. It's good as
part of a curry meal — try serving with Raita
(see page 52), Taxi Driver's Lamb Curry
(see page 254) and some lentils.

If serving the next day, gently reheat
in a saucepan over medium heat.

2 tablespoons olive oil

1 tablespoon chopped flat-leaf (Italian) parsley

1 onion, chopped

1 red capsicum (pepper) seeded, membrane removed and chopped

1 green capsicum (pepper), seeded, membrane removed and chopped

400 g (14 oz/1⅔ cups) tinned chopped tomatoes

1 tablespoon chopped oregano

2 eggs, lightly whisked

Piperade

Piperade is sort of like stewed capsicum with egg through it. In a very loose way, mine is based on the dish that originated in the Basque region of Spain. It's a nice way to start the day, or end it, but a little chorizo cooked with the capsicum is perfect for dinner.

SERVES 2

Heat the oil in a frying pan over low–medium heat and fry the parsley with the onion for about 5 minutes, or until the onion is soft. Add the capsicum and fry for a further 15 minutes, or until lightly coloured.

Add the tomato, cover, and simmer for about 15 minutes. Stir in the oregano, cook for 1–2 minutes longer, then pour in the eggs, removing the pan from the heat and stirring as you do so. The sauce should thicken slightly; if it re-boils it will curdle.

You can make a similar dish by poaching the eggs in the sauce instead — crack them into the centre of the pan rather than lightly whisking, and cook with the lid on until the egg whites are set.

Serve the piperade on slices of crusty bread that has first been grilled and drizzled with a touch of olive oil.

4 egg yolks
50 g (1¾ oz) caster (superfine) sugar
180 ml (6 fl oz) red wine, such as
pinot noir

Zabaglione

Zabaglione is a luscious Italian whipped-egg dessert that is traditionally made with Marsala, but here I've used red wine instead. The difference is a more vibrant flavour – and let's be honest, you're more likely to have red wine in the house.

SERVES 4

In a large, heatproof (preferably stainless steel) bowl, whip the egg yolks and sugar together until pale and light. Add the wine, then place the bowl over a saucepan of gently simmering water and continue whisking vigorously as the mixture warms. Move the whisk around all parts of the egg mixture to avoid it cooking hard in any one place.

As they cook, the eggs will foam up and increase in volume. When the mixture has a rich, dense look and retains the shape of the whisk for a few seconds, it is done; this should take between 5 and 10 minutes. (If, as you whisk, you see any lumps or feel the bottom hardening, remove from the heat for a few seconds.)

Serve the zabaglione warm or cold. It tastes particularly nice served with fruit, such as Baked Quinces (see page 425). Don't keep the zabaglione more than a few hours, as it's made with only semi-cooked eggs.

finely grated zest of 6 lemons

8 eggs, lightly beaten

200 g (7 oz) unsalted butter, cubed,
    softened

juice of 6 lemons, strained

400 g (14 oz/1¾ cups) caster
    (superfine) sugar

Lemon curd

*A gorgeous use for excess lemons, this is my family's recipe for lemon
curd — it is sharp, rich and sweet, and melts dreamily into toast.
Are you like me, imagining breakfast? This lemon curd can also be
used to fill tarts, or be eaten with sharp fruits, such as raspberries
and stewed rhubarb. It's also amazing on pavlova.*

MAKES 1 LITRE (35 FL OZ/4 CUPS)

Sit a large stainless steel bowl over a saucepan of boiling water. Add all the ingredients, stirring occasionally with a wooden spoon until melted. Continue stirring for about 10 minutes, or until the mixture thickens slightly, scraping the bottom as you stir. Don't worry if there are lumps — this just proves it's homemade. The lemon curd will continue to thicken as it cools.

Transfer the mixture to sterilised airtight jars and once completely cool store in the refrigerator. Serve on slices of toasted sourdough. The lemon curd will keep for up to 2 weeks.

2 x 90 g (3¼ oz) duck eggs or 3 x 60 g
   (2¼ oz) chicken eggs, separated
1 teaspoon natural vanilla extract
70 g (2½ oz) caster (superfine) sugar

100 g (3½ oz) cornflour (cornstarch)
1 teaspoon baking powder
jam and whipped cream, to serve

Duck egg sponge

There are as many sponge cake recipes as there are members of the Country Women's Association – in fact, probably a whole lot more. This is my version which, like most, suggests sifting the flour multiple times to ensure a very light and airy cake. Many recipes use custard powder, which is just expensive cornflour (cornstarch) with the addition of yellow food colouring and vanilla flavour. If you can get your hands on duck eggs, this sponge looks and tastes its best.

SERVES 8

Preheat the oven to 190°C (375°F/Gas 5). Lightly grease a 22 cm (8½ inch) round spring-form cake tin and line the base and side with baking paper.

Whisk the egg whites in a large bowl with the vanilla until soft peaks start to form, then continue whisking as you pour in the sugar — it should look like meringue at this stage. Keep beating as you pour in the egg yolks, then stop beating as soon as the mixture is evenly coloured.

Sift the cornflour and baking powder together three times, then fold into the egg mixture — do this very gently using a spatula and a gentle motion, until the flour is just incorporated. Pour the mixture carefully

into the prepared tin and bake in the centre of the oven (preferably not on a fan-forced setting) for about 20 minutes, or until a skewer comes out clean when inserted into the centre of the cake.

Rest the tin on a wire rack to cool for 10 minutes, before removing the base. When completely cool, cut the sponge in half and fill generously with jam and whipped cream.

This sponge cake is best eaten on the day it is made.

250 ml (9 fl oz/1 cup) full-cream
   (whole) milk
1 tablespoon caster (superfine) sugar
2 eggs
¼ teaspoon salt
90 g (3¼ oz) plain (all-purpose)
   flour, sifted

20 g (¾ oz) butter, melted, plus extra
   for cooking
2 teaspoons finely grated lemon zest

Crepes

'There's only one place to toss a crepe thick enough to be tossed,' said 1950s British food writer Fanny Cradock: 'into the bin.' I agree, because a thick crepe is a pancake, while a thin crepe is a work of art. If you are just starting out, however, thicker crepes are easier to master. On your first attempt you may want to add a little extra flour (about 1–2 tablespoons), as this recipe makes beautifully delicate crepes, but they can be tricky to turn for the novice. Once you're in the groove, it's much quicker to pump them out if you have two hot pans on the go at the same time.

SERVES 4 (MAKES 1 PORTION)

Put the milk, sugar, eggs and salt in a food processor and blend to combine. With the motor running, add the flour, one tablespoon at a time, until the mixture is just smooth. Pulse in the melted butter, then pour this mixture through a sieve into a bowl. Stir through the lemon zest and set aside in the refrigerator for 30 minutes.

Heat a crepe pan or non-stick frying pan over medium heat, brush with a hint of melted butter, and ladle just enough of the crepe batter into the pan to thinly coat the base — in an ideal world, you should make a circle with an 18 cm (7 inch) diameter but it will depend on your pan.

Twist your wrist to swirl the mixture just once around the pan as you pour in the batter. When the base is a light brown colour use a spatula to flip the crepe over and cook

the other side. As a rule, the first crepe will stick to the pan and be ruined — it will look messy but is a bonus one for the cook. Remove to a plate, cover and keep warm in a low oven. Repeat with the remaining batter until it is all used.

I like to eat these crepes with just a sprinkle of caster sugar and a squeeze of lemon, or spread them with jam, roll them up and scoff them like a greedy schoolkid. Or use them in the Tangelo and Cumquat Crêpes Suzette (see page 467).

Variation: To make a savoury crepe, omit the sugar and lemon zest from the recipe.

Mayonnaise

Real, homemade mayonnaise is a wondrous thing. It's really just a lush egg and oil emulsion that makes bought mayonnaise look awful.

2 egg yolks
1–2 teaspoons dijon mustard
1–2 teaspoons white wine vinegar
250 ml (9 fl oz/1 cup) vegetable oil, such as sunflower
1–2 teaspoons lemon juice

MAKES 300 G (10½ OZ)

Place a cloth, such as a tea towel (dish towel) over the top of an empty saucepan. Sit a large bowl over the top (the cloth prevents the bowl from spinning as you whisk). Or better still, get a friend to hold the bowl.

Put the egg yolks in the bowl and whisk together with the mustard and vinegar to combine. Pour the oil in a thin stream, whisking continuously. Adjust to taste with salt, freshly milled black pepper and lemon juice, as required. It's as simple as that.

Any left-over mayonnaise can be covered in plastic wrap and stored in the refrigerator for up to 1 week.

Variations: To make a cocktail sauce that goes wonderfully well with shellfish, you can flavour the mayonnaise with tomato sauce, Worcestershire sauce, a hint of Tabasco and some cognac or brandy.

You can also make a roasted garlic aioli by roasting 4 unpeeled garlic cloves in foil in a preheated 180°C (350°F/Gas 4) oven for 25 minutes, or until soft. Squeeze the garlic from its skin and whisk into the mayonnaise with the mustard and wine vinegar. You will need to replace 50 ml (1³/4 fl oz) vegetable oil with olive oil.

Chapter 4

MEAT

MEAT

Forget Old McDonald's Farm. The small farmhouse with a few chooks scurrying around the house garden, a couple of cows idly chewing their cuds in pea-green paddocks, black-faced sheep rugged up against the cold, and a couple of droopy-eared pigs wallowing around in the mud — well this model has nearly ceased to exist as a commercial farm. It does continue to exist as a hobby farm, especially with increasingly self-sufficient smallholders, and it does describe our farm, but the production of meat for the general population is very much an industry.

While some meat may still be produced in that rural idyll we have in our heads (I'm doing some myself), mostly it's mass produced at places that would shock most city dwellers. The stench of a feedlot, the suffocating ammonia of a chook shed, the bathtub-sized stall filled with the entire length and breadth of a sow — these are the striking realities of modern farming. Even when animals are well cared for, their instincts allowed to surface, the only way to make a viable business out of most meat production is to do it intensively.

Farming is a business, and to make money, cattle and sheep farmers focus on what they know. Flavour isn't high on their list of priorities when there's a drought on, wool to be sold, and the demand for low-quality meat that can be minced or turned into pies.

All this is relatively recent. Before 1900 factory farming was unheard of. Just about all agriculture was pretty much organic by necessity. But with new technology came new, modern confinement methods, and newer breeds that could cope with the realities of life indoors. What we lost, I suggest, is the flavour and texture of real meat.

On the other hand, what we have today can surpass times gone past. If we use our increased technology, our ability to breed faster and more efficiently, if we use our incredible information age and ready transport, the animals we can breed, and their eating quality, can improve upon anything that we've seen in the past.

The problem is, it will cost. If we don't change the way we do things, however, it will cost our children, and the land that will feed them.

BREEDS

Old breed: for some it translates to old-fashioned, in a bad way, like polio or smallpox. The term old breed can make people think of skinny chickens and tough old mutton that you eat when times get hard. For others it signifies nostalgia, a time that may or may not have existed when life was simpler, meat was more flavoursome and animals weren't reared in cramped conditions using growth promotants. For me, old breed has all those meanings and more.

For thousands of years we've bred animals to suit our needs. We've spent 9000 years domesticating the pig, during which time their more flighty characteristics and much of their aggressive behaviour have been bred out. Old breed doesn't necessarily mean better. But it can.

The good news about breeding is that we've done so much of the hard work — arguably all the hard work — already. If you can imagine a farmhouse in the 1600s where the cow was used predominantly for milk, the sheep for wool and the only animals that were eaten died of old age or disease, it is not hard to understand why these breeds may not suit our needs today.

There came a time when some cows were bred for meat, as distinct from those bred for milk. Pigs were developed to produce bacon, or back fat (to make lard and more), and others for roast meat. Chickens were differentiated into meat birds and egg birds (though there have always been dual-purpose birds, which are currently making a comeback among smallholders because they suit backyards and small farms). Sheep were selected to be meat breeds or wool breeds. Hundreds if not thousands of years worth of breeding led to the domestic livestock we know today, all with characteristics chosen, more often than not, with the end use in mind — with flavour and texture as priorities. All we need to do these days, it would seem, is to fine-tune those breeds.

All that breeding, the herd books, the chicken shows, all that excellence in the quality of meat breeds, however, was before the 1900s. During the twentieth century we learnt that we could farm animals far more intensively than before. The same industrial revolution that allowed the creation of cotton mills and foundries eventually meant that we discovered that you can cram chickens into cages and pigs into pens, thereby increasing the output of farms substantially.

The yields were enormous, and the benefits to consumers, in terms of *cheaper* meat, incredible. However, this technology required animals to have different characteristics. A barnevelder hen, for instance, isn't really good for battery hen farming, as it's a rugged, flighty bird that just loves to scratch and only gives a bit over two hundred eggs each year. An Isa Brown, on the other hand, can lay just about every day of the year (though she's as likely as not to get 'egg-bound' in the following year and die an awful, painful death). A Wessex saddleback pig has predominantly black skin and can wander about in the sun, even the brutal Australian sun, as long as it has shade and a wallow, so as not to get sunburnt, but they don't thrive in sow stalls. Breeds in the past one hundred years have been developed to suit modern animal husbandry, with only secondary thought for flavour, and virtually none for how things are actually cooked. Add this technology to the paucity of knowledge of how to choose, buy and cook meat, coupled with a lack of choice and falling relative prices of meat, and old breeds fell out of favour.

The good news is that many old breeds do still exist. The Rare Breeds Trust and similar organisations are championing breeders who are keeping the genetic variation in meat, and helping to preserve and revere the work our forebears put in.

HANDLING

All meat, we now know, gets tougher if the animal it comes from is stressed. The 'fight or flight' reaction, the increased levels of adrenaline in a frightened animal or bird, cause it to burn muscle glucose, which in turn causes unwanted reactions in the resultant meat.

Because of this, and also because you could argue it is more humane, it's important that animals die a good, quick, painless death.

But changes to the quality of meat can happen before an animal is killed. An animal that is free to range, to move freely, has different textured muscle to one that is confined. A bird that can walk and flap its wings will have a sturdier-textured meat. It could get tough, but without exercise the meat can be sloppy and unattractive. Animals fed in feedlots (the bovine equivalent to a factory farm) eat grain that they could never access if they were free to wander, leading to unwanted intestinal troubles. They constantly stand in their own faeces, when they would never do that on the range. Sure, the meat can be more tender, but tenderness is just one, minor, characteristic. Proper handling of meat, from the abattoir to the butcher to the home cook, can cope with textured meat. If you ask me, I'd rather chew a good steak than gum it, while I still have the teeth to do so. We are omnivores, and we are meant to chew. Gnawing a bone, some resilience in meat, these are some of the joys of eating.

But more than this, the way an animal is treated, how it has lived its life, probably has an impact on how it eats. A happier cow is a happier diner, generally. The more the animal has been able to express its instincts, the more likely it has been comfortable, free from danger and disease, the more likely it is going to be good in the pot. We have a responsibility to treat animals humanely — not just because it's the right thing to do, which is actually more important, but also because good handling leads to better meat. And better meat means we need less of it, so we can afford to pay more per kilogram. More per kilogram means there's the all-important extra reward for the farmer.

FEED

Most meat reflects the feed that an animal consumes, particularly during the last few weeks of its life. Some pigs are fattened on corn to sweeten the meat, chickens can be finished on a milky mash to help alter their taste, and cows are often grain-fed for the last weeks and months of life.

There is great conjecture about the role of pasture, such as fresh grass and clovers, in the flavour of meat, but most say a complex pasture creates a complex meat. University tests from the UK show that grass-fed lamb is perceived to have a more true, meatier flavour than grain-fed. Pigs are virtually always fed grain, but true farmhouse pigs may get to forage for roots, and graze on grass, or be fed fresh milk or whey, and their flavour reflects this. Most tasting notes of beef show a more intense, beefy flavour when fed grass compared to grain. A diet high in grains also affects the fat profile, with the resultant meat higher in less desirable omega-6s and lower in omega-3s.

Some people, however, prefer the taste and texture of grain-fed meat. Grain-fed beef and lamb can have more flavour, but this is usually a simpler, fattier flavour, which is very dependent on breed and the grains used. It is a one-dimensional flavour, though it can have an immediate, satisfying effect on the palate, like all simple fats. Grain feeding, along with feedlotting, means the flesh is also less likely to be tough, which allows for easier grading of the meat post slaughter. Tough stuff usually goes to hamburgers, the more tender to steak.

ORGANICS

Certified organic meat, by nature, means that animals have probably led a better life than those on intensive farms, and their diet has been organically based. From my experience, given the same genetics and the same handling, the organic meat will probably taste better. We know there will be less chemical residue in the meat, and that the animals can't be fed in feedlots, so they will be able to use their muscles pretty much as nature intended, allowing them to develop a natural texture.

Animals that have been reared on organic farms are probably more humanely handled, and therefore, if for no other reason, taste better (and make you feel better about the world when you eat). From a diner's point of view, however, buying organic comes second to good breeds, good handling, good ageing of meat and good feed. If you get all of that, and it's organic as well, you're probably onto a winner (and probably a few dollars poorer in the process).

WHAT IS REGENERATIVE AGRICULTURE, AND DOES IT MAKE MEAT BETTER?

Regenerative agriculture is a modern wave of farming (usually including livestock) that is trying to restore degraded ecosystems, including the most important ecosystem of all, that of topsoil. Meat from regenerative farms can come from various grazing methods, but usually animals are moved regularly, and often they have low or no chemical inputs (such as routine worming and artificial fertiliser). Evidence for an increase in nutrient density directly from regenerative agriculture is sparse, but does tend to show that farms that concentrate on biodiversity and regenerating ecosystems benefit from healthier soil, plants and animals. And this health is more likely to be present in the quality and flavour of the meat.

CUTS

The front end of animals that work on four legs is tougher than the back end. So the cuts that are best for roasting are pork and lamb legs (which come from the back). The best-flavoured cuts, which suit braising, are usually from the front (forequarter, shoulder), and the most tender are those that run along the back (the fillet and loin or sirloin). There are exceptions, particularly with younger animals where the whole animal is quite tender, and with pork neck, which makes a spectacular roast (though it often comes without the requisite crackling).

THE BUTCHER

My advice to you is to give your butcher a hard time. Quiz them on breed and on where their meat comes from. Tell them what you liked about the meat you bought last time, and complain if it doesn't perform like it should. Nurture your relationship with your butcher and don't let them intimidate you, because when it comes down to it, you could well know as much about the preparing, cooking and eating of meat as they do.

If you can find a good butcher, it will save you hours in the kitchen and enhance your life. They will explain the meat as they cut it for you. They can tell you all about the different cuts, and they should understand the rearing, handling and cooking of meat. Most of all, a good butcher will make you a better and happier cook.

BEEF & VEAL

When I first moved to Tasmania, I met a local beef farmer, Gerard Crochon, who didn't force his cows to wean. His hereford–friesian cross calves would stay on their mother's milk for nine or ten months, with a month or two more feeding on lush green grass — and only then would Gerard send them to market. The reason? He wanted the sweet, mild-tasting meat from a young animal. The long weaning came from his organic principles; he didn't like to interfere too much with nature. What I got from talking to Gerard is that nothing on his farm happened by accident.

Like Crochon, I am now a convert to the yellow fat of pastured beef. This goes against most conventional wisdom these days, which suggests the fat should be white. 'It tells me that they've been eating a lot of grass. The yellower the better,' Crochon argued, saying that the fat of a grass-fed animal develops more of a golden hue as the cow ages. 'That shows it's got a lot of beta-carotene.'

The beef we eat on our farm is informed by the same principles Gerard taught me over a decade ago. It all happens not by accident, but by design. We choose the breed, the diet, the age and the conditioning of the cattle we take to the cutting shop. What we do on our farm is all about *eating* the meat, not just selling it. It's not just what's good for the farmer, it's what's good for the cattle, too, and importantly, the customer. It's important for those who eat the meat, including those of us who grew the animal in the first place.

The aim on our farm, and we're by no means alone in this, is diversity in the grasses, to get a healthy diet for the animal, and many micronutrients in the resultant beef. Our pasture is a mix of rye, plantain, cock's foot, clover and so-called 'weeds', such as dock, buttercups and dandelion. The weeds offer an indication of the health of the soil, but also provide elements like tannins and phytochemicals that are important in a healthy diet. About forty different species of plant dot the landscape where the cows graze.

Contrast the age of Crochon's barely 12-month-old cattle with Rob Lennon's, whose wagyu–angus cross-breed are fattened, like ours, for up to three years, to get maximum flavour. They're grown out for as long as possible on organic pasture (without feedlotting, because he's organic and that goes against organic principles), then slaughtered when they're nearly three times older than most commercial cattle. The reason? The older the cow, like any animal, the more flavour it has. And unlike some animals, where a robust, full-grown meaty flavour may be considered overtly strong, beef doesn't suffer from this complaint. If anything, the handling, maturing and cooking of some of the best beef is all about concentrating flavour. Another benefit of letting the animals age is that you get marbling (that fine lattice of fat through the meat).

While it may seem that people who raise grazing animals do little besides letting cattle eat grass, turning the indigestible (to us) cellulose in grass into high-quality protein, the thing about good red meat is attention to detail: the fact that a farmer cares about quality, not just of the live animal, but of the way the resultant food will taste.

Good farmers rear animals so that they have heaps of flavour, and are good for the land that grows them. It's a simple leap from the paddock to the dining tables of the nation, but one that only intelligent, careful farming really nails.

'I don't know how to calibrate a spraying machine,' Crochon once told me. 'But I do know my cows are in good health. I know my soil, my pastures. It comes down to what's on the plate. My customers know.'

I know it too, now that I rear my own animals for the pot. You'll know it as well, when you find exceptional quality meat that makes cooking easier, and eating a dream.

WHAT IS GOOD BEEF?

Good beef comes in many guises. Some like the heavy marbling that comes with a wagyu-style beast, fed in feedlots on grain. Rob Lennon's organic cows, also a wagyu cross but grass-fed, never achieve the same quantity of marbling, but what the meat does have is enough marbling to make it tender and flavoursome without being fatty.

In my view, good beef is raised on lush, complex pasture. It's close to three years old when it is sent to market, and the meat is then dry-aged for at least two weeks — preferably four weeks and ideally six.

Good beef is boldly red in colour, like a good red wine stain. It may be deeper, more burgundy-coloured towards the outside if it has been aged (the loss of moisture intensifies the look of the meat), and it should, if it's had plenty of grass and is old enough, have marbling through the eye of the meat.

Good, proper beef has some texture to it. It's not like eating butter, or veal, or chicken breast. It needs chewing, but the top-end cuts (sirloin, rump and rib-eye) needn't be chewy as such, just nicely resilient in the mouth. Achieving this effect comes down partly to breed, partly to feed, and a lot to handling.

WHAT IS GOOD VEAL?

In most of the world, veal is defined as being from a cow that is under one year of age. Good veal is pale. Australia and similar countries have outlawed the practice of keeping vealers anaemic, so the meat is unlikely to be the true white veal, but more often will have a rose-coloured flesh, because the animal has been able to eat some grass and is allowed to walk freely rather than being kept in stalls. Obviously the flavour, texture, colour and also the cooking of the meat will vary a lot depending on whether the cow is four months or eleven months old. To me, the best veal is pale with a blush. I like it under six months old so it's tender, and I really like it if part of its diet is still from milk.

ISN'T VEAL CRUEL?

Yes and no. By definition, veal is a young cow, and if you don't like the idea of killing young things, even if they've led a good life and are slaughtered humanely, then you'd better stop eating chicken as well as veal. But if young isn't a problem, then you can definitely eat veal.

Some veal is reared in what is arguably an inhumane fashion. In these cases the calf is wrenched from its mother at one day old and fed formula, then kept in isolation in 'veal crates' without enough room to lie down or turn around, and not allowed to socialise. These cows are fed a diet that makes them anaemic so the resultant meat is nearly pure white, and not pink or red.

But veal can also come from a healthy calf, one that was allowed to walk and socialise and drink from its mother at least for a time. It may be fed on a milk powder, instead, as a supplement, but has access to grass, which it will start to eat not long after being born.

The reality of veal is that it is a by-product of the dairy industry. A milking cow will only really give up its milk for one year before it needs to be put in calf again. That means getting it pregnant again. And when the young calf is born, if it's a male, then it has no use to the farmer. Farming is a business, and you can't rear animals just because they have soft eyes and a cute face. If you don't eat veal, but you still want to eat cheese or drink milk, then this male calf will more than likely have a bullet put through its head as soon as it is born. But if someone wants veal, the young calf can be reared for a few weeks or months before being sent to market. It may be a short life, but at least it is some life. If you don't want to eat an animal before it matures, sorry to tell you this, but you should also stop eating chickens, turkey, lamb and pork, not to mention duck, pigeon and salmon.

The good news for those concerned about animal welfare is that veal crates — isolation crates in which a calf has no room to turn around — have been banned in the UK since the mid 1990s, and in the rest of the European Union (EU) since 2007. Veal crates are not allowed in Australia and have been phased out in the US. Intensive housing continues in the US, however, somewhat tainting the industry's reputation.

WHAT IS BOBBY VEAL?

Bobby veal is the term used to describe veal that is a few days to a couple of weeks old — three weeks at the most. At its best, it is the most sublime expression of veal as it is very young and sweet (though with loose texture because of virtually no muscle development), but inconsistency in handling means it varies markedly. Because most dairy farmers aren't meat farmers, bobby veal typically comes from a variety of herds, breeds, sources and handlers, and your butcher is at the mercy of them all. Using bobby veal makes use of what the RSPCA estimates are 600,000 male calves born into the Australian dairy industry each year.

WHAT IS ROSE VEAL?

Rose veal is from milk- and grass-fed free-range young steers and heifers, which can be meat breed or dairy breed, or a mix. It takes its name from the pink rather than white flesh, a natural transition as the diet moves towards more grass, and the animal's body has more haemoglobin, adding a reddish tinge.

WHAT IS WHITE VEAL?

Banned in Australia, but common in Europe, calves up to eight months of age are fed a low-iron diet, mostly of milk powder or substitute. This keeps the calf anaemic and produces very pale meat.

WHAT IS 'YEARLING'?

Yearling is the most common meat sold in Australia and the US. At about one year old, or more precisely about 14 months, many cows have been through their biggest growth spurt, and weight increase slows down markedly. This is the best time for a farmer to sell because of the law of diminishing returns.

However, as we've seen with most ingredients, while this may suit the farmer, it doesn't necessarily mean it's the best time to eat the meat. The best time to eat most beef is when the taste has intensified, when the meat has firmed up more. Yearling is more likely to be tender, but also more likely to taste of little compared to beef reared for three years on grass.

WHAT IS MARBLING?

Marbling refers to the fine, lacy, roadmap-like filaments of fat that course through the centre of a cut of meat, as opposed to on the outside of the cut. This fat keeps the meat moist while it cooks, helps to keep it tender, and adds a lot of extra flavour to the meat. Marbling arises as a result of the breed of animal, its handling and its age. Older cattle (and pigs and sheep) are more likely to have marbling. Grain-feeding can increase marbling, as can the right genetics, hence the popularity of crossing with wagyu, a heavily marbled beef breed from Japan.

The more marbling, the more flavour (a fatty flavour), and the juicier the meat will be once cooked. Meat with no marbling is more likely to be dry and lighter in flavour. Heavy marbling, however, means you must cook the meat past blue. External fat on the outside of the cut isn't a bad thing, either. Meat, particularly when roasted, cooks better and stays juicier with a nice band of external fat on it.

WHAT IS GRASS-FED BEEF?

Grass-fed beef is probably what you think you're buying: from a handsome cow chewing its cud in a paddock of emerald green. University studies and apocryphal tales alike have shown that grass-fed meat is typically more complex in flavour, thanks to the varied diet of the animal. It is also usually sturdier in texture (which can mean chewier, less tender meat), as the animals have walked more to find food and socialise. This dries out the meat and toughens the muscles to some extent. Grass-fed meat benefits greatly from ageing, particularly dry-ageing, and typically takes about three-quarters of the time to cook as grain-fed meat, because it has a lower moisture content even before it is dry-aged. (See cooking times in How to Roast Beef, page 222.)

WHAT ABOUT GRAIN-FED BEEF?

Some cattle are fed grain to boost their feed. Most don't get grain as a supplement, but rather as their entire diet in a feedlot system. Animal rights activists consider the intensive feedlot system of cattle, where they stand in their own poo side by side and eat from troughs, to be the bovine equivalent of battery hens. However, the cattle are free to move around, within a crowded enclosure, so a better comparison is probably barn-reared hens rather than battery hens. Proponents of the feedlot technique like to talk about cows fattened on a scientifically balanced diet of grains and roughage.

Grain-fed meat is typically more tender than grass-fed because the animals don't walk much and their diet can be strictly controlled. They put on more weight more quickly, thanks to the lack of exercise and a high-energy diet, and the meat retains more moisture. Most feedlot cattle are given growth promotants at some point, and their feed is laced with antibiotics to prevent disease (though public pressure means feedlots are attempting to use less or none at all).

Grain-feeding is common with animals reared on marginal country (think of the arid, seemingly grassless vision of western Queensland or the arid southern US), and with breeds that are tick resistant but typically more lean, such as brahman cattle. This is of great benefit in a country like Australia where rainfall is sporadic, and cattle can be grazed on enormous properties and finished in feedlots. Grain-feeding allows a grower to more readily guarantee the meat from their animals is tender. Wagyu is typically grain-fed to increase the marbling — intramuscular fat — in the meat (see What Is Marbling, page 215). If an animal is said to be '200 days, grain-fed', then it is arguably more tender and consistent in flavour than '120 days, grain-fed'.

The flavour of grain-fed meat is typically not as beefy, and arguably more fatty than grass-fed meat.

CATTLE BREEDS

Unlike chicken and pork, beef breeds haven't been so debased in the past hundred years. Good-quality, old-fashioned meat breeds have flourished, probably because there has been little intensive farming, and cattle have traditionally been able to graze on pasture. Easy transport, combined with the advent of artificial insemination, have led to quicker, easier breeding for certain traits.

For many, the British breeds offer the best flavour. After all, even the French considered the Brits kings of beef, nicknaming them Les Rosbif (The Roast Beefs). Breeds such as Aberdeen angus (shortened almost always to a more apt, modern angus), hereford, dexter, Galloway and the shaggy highland cattle are among the most common. For every climate there are breeds that are better suited, though it does seem that cool-climate cattle produce better-tasting meat.

The French breeds that are bred outside their homeland, mostly charolais and Limousin cows, are quite different in texture, being a firmer-fleshed animal when eaten, from my experience. They are horned in France, but sometimes bred to be polled, as are hereford and others, or have their horns cut off. Polled simply means that they have been bred to grow without horns, which, as you can imagine with several hundred kilograms of meat on four legs coming at you in a pen, is important for the safety of workers and other cattle, particularly when being shipped, moved or feedlotted.

Brahman are an American breed developed from Indian cattle to be tick resistant (along with their crosses). They can survive on lower-quality feed, and are particularly hardy, which makes them a good tropical or warm-weather breed, not noted for excellent eating. These days most brahman are finished on feedlots and used for manufacturing or to make mince. The Texas longhorn, the classic, iconic breed from the Americas, is also a hardy breed, often used to cross-breed with other cattle.

As with many animals, cross-breeds are often used to get the right characteristics. This is particularly true of the Japanese wagyu, because of the high cost of genetics, as the Japanese don't let many bloodlines out of the country, and cross-breeds avoid any problems with in-breeding. It also means the characteristics of wagyu can be used in conjunction with cattle that are more likely to range freely and suit other climates.

WHAT IS WAGYU — AND WHY IS IT SO EXPENSIVE?

Wagyu is the name for beef cattle from Japan, and implies a Japanese breed favoured for its marbling. Good wagyu can be almost white in colour from the fat. Some argue that the feedlot system required to produce wagyu is cruel, while some organic growers use wagyu cross-breeds fed on grass to get better marbling in their meat.

The original breeds are used to being quite confined, often to a small farmhouse, and there is much conjecture about them being fed beer and getting a massage and listening to Mozart. Most of that, from my research, is just gumpf.

Most wagyu bought outside of Japan (and much of the beef in Japan) is the result of wagyu–angus cross-breeds, or more recently wagyu–friesian cross-breeds, which are a by-product of the dairy industry. They may offer increased marbling and tenderness, but the real, purebred thing will cost hundreds of dollars per kilogram and is out of the reach of most ordinary people.

Export-grade wagyu destined for the Japanese market, unlike many feedlot cattle, are free of antibiotics and aren't given growth promotants.

WHAT ABOUT GROWTH PROMOTANTS?

I was once in a paddock near Parkes in the arid west of NSW and noticed the cows had tags on both ears. One is to identify them, I was told by the station manager; the other to locate the hormone insert that helps them grow. I was shocked to find most cattle in Australia tend to be grown out using implanted growth hormones. I was told that the cattle on this property, which were destined for Australian supermarkets, wouldn't come back to the property as food for the workers. If the people who rear the cows won't eat the ones with growth promotants, it makes you wonder, really, just why we use them at all.

Growth hormones are used as a matter of course in the US, and the only state in Australia that bans their use (usually administered via a pellet in the cow's ear) is Tasmania. This hormone mix (the equivalent of bovine anabolic steroids) can accelerate the growth of the animal by around 1 kg (2 lb 4 oz) a week (with wide variation), which means big money to a farmer.

According to Meat and Livestock Australia, the use of growth promotants can lead to tougher meat and less marbling. To overcome this, they recommend longer ageing after the animals are slaughtered. One scientific paper I read stated that there were no major research reports indicating that growth promotants improved meat quality — but they do, undeniably, increase the weight of the carcass.

Defenders of growth promotants point out that while they lead to an increase in the hormonal content of beef (and all beef contains some hormones), it is negligible compared to other commonly consumed foodstuffs (such as cabbage, soya bean oil and milk), and it makes economic sense to use them. The EU has banned the use of growth promotants in their beef and any beef imported into the EU.

WHAT IS DRY-AGEING?

Dry-aged meat is an old-fashioned way of increasing tenderness and promoting flavour by hanging whole carcasses or large cuts for weeks at a time in a temperature- and humidity-controlled environment.

While most people think of meat as a fresh product that will go off in a few days, larger cuts of meat can be left for several weeks without spoiling. Sure, it may get some mould on the outside. Yes, the meat will darken, and the outer surface become leathery and unappetising to look at, but it will also alter in character. Enzymes within the meat will break it down, making more complex flavours in the process, an giving an increase in 'umami', that all-important mouthwatering taste. The meat will also become more tender and better to eat.

The tragedy is that only good butchers bother to dry-age meat these days due to the costs involved.

When you hang meat you must have a room. A big room. And the room needs a motor and lights, which of course costs money. You will also have some capital tied up in meat — a decent sized butcher could have A$60,000 worth of meat sitting in a hanging room at any one time.

But the biggest factor in cost is that as the meat hangs, it dries out. Meat can lose 20 per cent of its weight in moisture loss alone. (The good thing, as a beef eater, is that this loss is just water — when you buy dry-aged meat, you're not buying water at the price of beef.) On top of this, dry-aged meat must be trimmed of the leathery outside, so you lose up to another 20 per cent of the meat this way.

Beef is dry-aged for up to six or eight weeks for large animals. Lamb is dry-aged for one week for small animals, or two to four weeks for bigger, older beasts like mutton. Pork is usually dry-aged for one week, or up to three weeks for large, fat animals.

WHAT, THEN, IS WET-AGED MEAT?

This is a term for vacuum-packed meat, the technology known as cryovac in some places. The meat is sealed in plastic bags in smaller cuts than are used for dry-ageing (a fillet or a sirloin, for example, rather than a side), and the same enzymes that tenderise the meat in dry-aging work in this oxygen-depleted environment. Wet-aged meat doesn't shrink at all and is much cheaper to produce. Critics of wet-aged meat point to the smell (a funky, corpse-like aroma when you first open the bag, and which inveigles the meat) and the sloppy texture. Some of the flavour in wet-aged meat will be missing, as wet-ageing favours tenderness over complexity of flavour.

WHICH CUTS TASTE BEST?

The better-tasting cuts of beef usually have a coarser texture: an animal's rump tastes better than its sirloin, sirloin tastes better than fillet. But fillet is more tender than sirloin, and sirloin is more tender than rump, so it's a trade-off. Great-tasting chuck and blade is so chewy it should be stewed or braised. Generally, as with most animals, the forequarter is the toughest, the bits along the back the most tender, and the hind legs somewhere in between. For me, the best-tasting meat for braising and curries is shin, sometimes cut as osso buco, through the bone, but just as often sold as boneless meat. To me, the single most flavoursome cut is brisket, from the area of chest between the legs.

HOW CAN I TELL A STEAK IS COOKED?

Gently touch your index finger to your thumb. Now feel that fleshy bit at the base of your thumb? Imagine that's your fillet steak. As it cooks, you gently press a steak to see how it has firmed up. A medium-rare fillet relates to the index finger and thumb. Now touch your middle finger to your thumb. The fleshy bit at the base of the thumb is firmer — an indication of a medium fillet. The third finger is medium to well done; the little finger well done. Of course it depends on the texture of the meat when raw (some steak is softer than others). For sirloin, press your chin for medium–rare, your nose for medium and your forehead for well done. Again it will vary with the meat you're buying.

When blood comes to the surface of a steak as it sears, it means the meat is about medium on that side. The biggest problem is usually overcooking, so err on the side of caution. Always rest the meat on the edge of the barbecue or covered with foil in a warm place for a few minutes before serving.

HOW TO ROAST BEEF

Good beef has a resilient texture and some marbling. It's best if dry-aged, which can look a bit daunting at first, with dried-out bits on the edges. Meat cooked on the bone has more flavour than meat cooked off the bone, and a wing rib has a remarkably good flavour simply because of the cut of meat. As a general rule, buy a cut with a good layering of fat on the outside. It will be less likely to dry out, and the fat carries a lot of flavour. You can cut it off once the meat is cooked (though I often savour eating some of the fat). Season any cut well with salt and freshly milled black pepper, using a little oil to help the seasoning stick as needed. Depending on the size of your oven, roast the rib standing upright, or with the fat facing heaven, to let gravity do the basting for you.

Grass-fed beef is generally more resilient than grain-fed beef, and could be considered tougher if it weren't for proper handling. Dry-ageing will make the meat more tender. Grain-fed beef is wetter, because the animal has stood around and not walked as much, and is likely to have more marbling if grain-fed for some time. Its flavour isn't anywhere near as complex as that of grass-fed beef, but in place of flavour you get more consistent juiciness and tenderness.

Cook grain-fed meat for about one-third longer than a similar grass-fed cut (so, instead of 45 minutes, it would take 1 hour). The lower moisture content of grass-fed meat means it heats through more quickly, and hence cooks more quickly. A shorter cooking time will leave it juicier.

You'll need about 150–200 g (5½–7 oz) of raw meat per person, excluding any substantial outside fat and bone. It's worth considering this, because while a sirloin is just about entirely edible, on a wing rib of beef you can't eat about one-third of the cut because of the fat and bone. Every cut is different, and every meat needs its own cooking timetable, but on the opposite page is a rough indication of how long you should roast your meats. These cooking times relate most to grass-fed beef and lamb.

ROASTING TIMES

Start with a hot fan-forced 250°C (500°F/ Gas 9) oven for the first 15–20 minutes — a hot start gives the meat its colour. (Colour means you've activated the 'Maillard reaction', a caramelisation that essentially adds more flavour to the meat.) After the hot start, reduce the oven temperature to 160°C (315°F/Gas 2–3), so the meat doesn't shrink too much — the faster it's cooked, the more moisture is forced out of the meat. Then, cook as follows:

FOR RARE — an additional 20 minutes per kilogram; a meat thermometer pushed into the centre should read 45–50°C (113–122°F).

FOR MEDIUM — an additional 30 minutes per kilogram; a meat thermometer pushed into the centre should read 60°C (140°F).

FOR WELL DONE — an additional 35–40 minutes per kilogram; a meat thermometer pushed into the centre should read 70°C (158°F).

2 kg (4 lb 8 oz) beef or veal bones
2 onions, halved
2 carrots
2 celery sticks, halved

2 bay leaves
2 thyme sprigs
1 tablespoon white wine vinegar

Homemade beef stock

A good stock is a thing of beauty. It needn't be too fancy, and it's best to make as much as you can in one go because it will always find a use, be it in soup, sauces or stews. As it's unseasoned, it will need salt regardless of the end use you put it to. The quantity you get varies with evaporation, but it's easy to adjust the volume with water. Veal bones make a stickier, paler, and much more elegant beef stock, but they can be harder to find. I have also included variations for brown stock and duck stock below.

MAKES 3 LITRES (105 FL OZ/12 CUPS)

Place everything in a large stockpot with 4 litres (140 fl oz/16 cups) water, making sure the water covers all the ingredients. Place over high heat and bring to the boil. Just as it comes to a boil is the best time to skim it, running a ladle around the edges to scoop off any scum. The vinegar helps clarify the stock, but skimming is great, too.

Reduce the heat as soon as it boils, and simmer for 4–6 hours, depending on your patience. You may need to top up the water during this time to keep all the bones and vegetables covered, as the stock is constantly evaporating. Strain and discard all the bones and vegetables.

This stock keeps well for up to 1 week in the refrigerator (reboiling extends its life), or 3 months in the freezer.

Variations: For a brown stock, smear the beef or veal bones with 1 tablespoon tomato paste and then roast them with the onion and carrot in a 200°C (400°F/Gas 6) oven for 1 hour, or until brown before using as above. Brown stock has a stronger flavour and is good for gravy and bold-flavoured soups.

For duck stock, make half the amount, replacing the beef bones with duck bones and only cook for 2 hours. I like to use the bones from roast duck, or duck confit, rather than try to find bones or use a whole bird. Substitute duck stock with chicken stock (see page 163) as the next best option.

40 g (1½ oz) lard or butter

1 kg (2 lb 4 oz) beef shin or skirt, cut into 2 cm (¾ inch) dice

2–3 tablespoons plain (all-purpose) flour

150 g (5½ oz) beef or pork kidneys, cut into 1 cm (½ inch) dice

80 ml (2½ fl oz/⅓ cup) tomato passata (tomato purée) or sauce (ketchup)

250 ml (9 fl oz/1 cup) dry red wine

750 ml (26 fl oz/3 cups) homemade beef stock (see page 224) or chicken stock (see page 163) or water

1 tablespoon worcestershire sauce

2 teaspoons dijon mustard

2 bay leaves

700 g (1 lb 9 oz) yoghurt cream pastry (see page 148)

Steak & kidney pie

You can make a suet pastry, using a little suet to replace some of the lard in the Easy Lard Shortcrust Pastry on page 149, but I think the Yoghurt Cream Pastry works well, albeit being a little crumbly.

SERVES 6

Heat the lard in a large saucepan over medium heat. Dust the beef with the flour and fry, in batches, to brown on all sides — rubbing the yummy stuck-on bits from the bottom of the pan as you go. You may need some more fat to fry it in. Remove the meat from the pan and set aside.

Dust the kidneys in flour and fry to brown on all sides, then remove to the plate with the beef.

In the same pan, fry the tomato passata just until it starts to colour, then add the wine, increase the heat, and boil vigorously, rubbing the base of the pan with a wooden spoon to loosen the stuck-on flour and paste. Return the meat to the pan with the stock, worcestershire, mustard and bay leaves.

Bring to the boil, then reduce the heat and simmer, stirring often, for about 90 minutes, or until the meat is tender; season with salt. If the sauce is getting gluggy, add 1–2 tablespoons of water as it cooks, or cover with a lid. It's best if this mix isn't too hot when you fill the pie; be sure to remove the bay leaves.

Preheat the oven to 200°C (400°F/ Gas 6). Lightly grease a 25 cm (10 inch) round pie dish.

Roll out two-thirds of the pastry to 5 mm (¼ inch) thick all over and use it to line the base and side of the dish, leaving a 1 cm (½ inch) overhang around the edge. Fill with the meat mixture, which should now be coated in a rich, thick sauce. Roll out the remaining pastry to make the lid. Place over the mixture and crimp the edges together to seal. Cut a slit in the top to let steam escape.

Bake the pie towards the bottom of the oven for about 45 minutes, or until the pastry is a deep brown.

Serve hot with lots of mustard, steamed carrots and green vegetables.

2 kg (4 lb 8 oz) beef shin meat, trimmed
    and cut into big unfussy chunks
1 small pork hock
2 bay leaves
2 thyme sprigs
3 cm (1¼ inch) strip orange peel
2 star anise
10 juniper berries
3 celery sticks, cut into thirds
3 carrots, cut into 3 cm (1¼ inch) chunks

3 onions, halved
5 garlic cloves
400 g (14 oz/1⅔ cups) tinned chopped
    tomatoes
375–560 ml (13 fl oz–19 1/4 fl oz/
    1½–2¼ cups) red wine, or red and
    white wine mix

Beef shin daube

*There are as many types of daube as there are French cooks, because
a daube is really just a French casserole, but a noble casserole for sure.
A proper slow-cooked daube requires the patience of Buddha. Start
it on a Saturday to eat on Thursday, or at best to eat the next day.
Marinating the meat in the wine for a day prior to cooking adds yet
another layer of complexity to both the dish, and the making of it, but
really, it's fine to just throw stuff together and let the oven and the
ingredients do all the work. I use up any opened wine I've failed to
drink, so long as it is at least half red. Pork is a really important
addition. If you can't get a hock, use bacon or a good-sized chunk
of pork skin.*

SERVES 8–10

Preheat the oven to 150°C (300°F/Gas 2).

Put all the ingredients except the wine
into a large cast-iron pot or large ovenproof
saucepan, casserole dish or stockpot. Pour in
enough wine so it comes three-quarters of
the way up the other ingredients. Cover with
a tight-fitting lid and place in the oven.

Reduce the oven temperature to about
100°C (200°F/Gas ½). The broth should
simmer so slowly that evaporation isn't an
issue. Check to see if it is just simmering
after 1 hour. If not, use a higher temperature
and cook the daube for a shorter time.

Cook the daube for about 8 hours
(it's best to do this overnight, or on a cold

day when you want to warm the kitchen).
Make sure it is simmering when you turn
it off; the shin should be tender. Adjust the
salt and freshly milled black pepper, to taste.
Cool, then, ideally, let it sit in the refrigerator
for a couple of days.

When you want to eat the daube, skim
off some, but not all of the fat on the surface,
reheat on the stovetop or in the oven. Serve
the beef chunks, vegetables and sauce with
baked potatoes. You can also get the meat
from the hock and gobble that up too. Freeze
any leftovers for another winter's day.

1 tablespoon vegetable oil

2 onions, diced

2 carrots, diced

2 cm (¾ inch) piece ginger

1 garlic clove, peeled

1 lemongrass stem, bruised with the back of a knife

2 kg (4 lb 8 oz) beef cheeks (or beef shank or oxtail), trimmed

375 ml (13 fl oz/1½ cups) red wine (shiraz is good)

375 ml (13 fl oz/1½ cups) unwooded white wine (riesling or gewürztraminer are good)

2–3 kaffir lime leaves

2 teaspoons salt

Braised beef cheeks with ginger & lemongrass

Winter is the perfect time to cook sticky, gelatinous beef cheeks. In this recipe they're flavoured with a few Asian ingredients, which add more aroma and zing than most European versions. If you don't have lime leaves, try a few cumquat or lemon leaves (well washed, and pesticide free, of course) instead.

SERVES 8

Heat the oil in a large saucepan or stockpot over medium heat and fry the onion and carrot for 5 minutes, or until slightly browned (the onion will darken first, so don't overdo it). Add the ginger, garlic, lemongrass (maybe cut in half so it fits in the pan) and beef cheeks. Pour in the wine and bring to the boil. Skim off any scum that rises to the surface.

Reduce the heat to low, add the lime leaves, salt and some freshly milled black pepper. Cover with a tight-fitting lid and simmer for about 3 hours (you can do this in a low oven if you prefer), or until the meat is so tender you could cut it with a deep sigh.

At this stage you may want to reduce the sauce so that it thickens more. To do this, take the meat from the pan and simmer the sauce rapidly on the stovetop, uncovered. The sauce will reduce more quickly in a pan with a wider base.

Discard the ginger, lemongrass and lime leaves and serve the cheeks with mashed potatoes or steamed rice.

Variation: To make a thicker sauce, before reducing the liquid, pull the meat, lemongrass, ginger and lime leaves from the pan, and purée the onion and carrot into the sauce.

45 g (1¾ oz/½ cup) desiccated coconut

2–3 tablespoons vegetable or peanut oil

1.5 kg (3 lb 5 oz) beef shin, sliced osso buco style

1 large red onion, roughly chopped

5 cm (2 inch) piece ginger, roughly chopped

5 garlic cloves, peeled

½ teaspoon salt

8 kaffir lime leaves

1 cinnamon stick

2 teaspoons ground coriander

1 star anise

400 g (14 oz/1⅔ cups) coconut cream

2 tablespoons lime juice (or tamarind or lemon juice)

Beef, coconut & lime leaf curry

Loosely based on a rendang, but nowhere near as complex (or time-consuming) to make, this curry can be adapted to suit your spice cupboard. Feel free to add a dried chilli or two, some cumin or cardamom, or substitute turmeric for the star anise, or cassia for the cinnamon. I like to cook the curry in a 130°C (250°F/Gas 1) oven for three hours, but below I've given a quicker stovetop method. Ask your butcher to slice the beef shin for you, osso buco style; most meat sold as osso bucco is actually beef these days, not veal, by the way.

SERVES 4–6

Dry-fry the coconut in a small frying pan over low heat, stirring constantly until it colours well but doesn't blacken. If you have a mortar, pound the hot coconut in it until the oil comes out. If not, you'll just have a flecked curry.

Heat the oil in a large heavy-based frying pan over medium heat and fry the beef, in batches, for 4–5 minutes on both sides, or until well browned. Remove the beef from the pan and set aside.

Put the onion, ginger and garlic in a food processor and blend to combine to make a paste, adding the salt once it's fine. In the same pan, fry the onion mixture until it starts to dry out and colour. Use a flat-bottomed wooden spatula to stir and scrape the base of the pan so the mixture doesn't stick.

Return the meat to the pan with the fried coconut, lime leaves, spices, coconut cream and 250 ml (9 fl oz/1 cup) water. Cover and simmer gently for about 90 minutes, or until the meat is tender. Remove the lid from the pan and adjust the seasoning to taste.

If you want a thicker sauce, increase the heat and allow it to evaporate, stirring regularly. When you're ready to eat, add the lime juice (and add some sugar if you like sweet curries). You could even use fish sauce to add a salty tang.

Serve the curry with steamed jasmine rice and a light vegetable dish on the side.

- 100 g (3½ oz) butter
- 2 onions, finely chopped
- 2 tablespoons chopped flat-leaf (Italian) parsley
- 5 celery sticks, finely diced
- 2 carrots, finely diced
- 2 bay leaves
- 750 g (1 lb 10 oz) minced (ground) veal (preferably neck)
- 500 g (1 lb 2 oz) minced (ground) pork (preferably neck)
- 1 teaspoon salt
- 500 ml (17 fl oz/2 cups) full-cream (whole) milk
- ½ teaspoon ground nutmeg
- 500 ml (17 fl oz/2 cups) dry white wine
- 880 g (1 lb 15 oz/3½ cups) tinned chopped tomatoes
- freshly cooked pasta, to serve
- butter and grated Italian parmesan cheese (Parmigiano Reggiano or Grano Padano), to serve

Real Italian bolognese

A real Italian bolognese (what they call a ragu) is an amazing thing to taste. It takes ages to cook, but ends up warming the house, making it smell like the home you wish you'd grown up in. Luckily the stove does most of the work while you write your great literary masterpiece. I've used minced veal here, but you can also use beef mince or veal meat diced into 5 mm (¼ inch) cubes. If you can't hang around the house, you could, at a pinch, hurry things along in a pressure cooker. This recipe makes such a quantity that you can freeze it in small batches for quick meals later.

MAKES ABOUT 2 KG (4 LB 8 OZ)

Heat the butter in a large heavy-based saucepan over medium heat and fry the onion and parsley until translucent. Add the celery, carrot and bay leaves, and continue to fry for 2 minutes. Increase the heat, add the veal and pork minces, the salt and some freshly milled black pepper, to taste, breaking up the meat as it fries. Cook the mince until the liquid has evaporated. This could take ages, depending on how wide the top of your pan is.

Stir the milk into the pan and reduce the heat. Simmer, stirring occasionally, until the milk has evaporated. Add the nutmeg and wine, stirring, until it has evaporated too, then add the tomatoes and 500 ml (17 fl oz/ 2 cups) water. Reduce the heat to low and barely simmer for 2–3 hours, stirring from time to time, adding 125 ml (4 fl oz/½ cup) water as needed. The bolognese should be fairly rich and not watery by the end.

Adjust the seasoning, to taste, and serve with your favourite pasta. Remember to toss a little bolognese through the pasta rather than dolloping a spoonful on top. Enrich it with about 1 teaspoon butter per serve, and serve with grated parmesan cheese.

Note: If you like, you can finish cooking the pasta for the last couple of minutes with the bolognese: use about 50 g (1¾ oz) ragu per 100 g (3½ oz) dried pasta for one modest serve — you will need to add at least a couple of tablespoons of the pasta cooking water, which will be absorbed as you stir.

4 x 200 g (7 oz) veal cutlets, batted
    out a little
1 tablespoon olive oil
20 g (¾ oz) butter, plus 20 g (¾ oz)
    extra, melted (optional)

20 sage leaves
4 thin slices prosciutto

Veal cutlet saltimbocca

*To make a variation on Rome's original, I often use just a whisper of
fresh mozzarella on top with the sage, to add a milky hint. You can also
use quail, spatchcock or lamb cutlets with great results.*

SERVES 4

Preheat a grill (broiler) to high. Season the
veal with a little salt and freshly milled black
pepper if desired. Don't overdo it, as the
prosciutto is salty.

Heat the oil and butter in a frying pan
or chargrill pan over high heat and sear the
veal on each side as desired, about 2 minutes
each side for medium, but it will depend a lot
on the thickness and age of the veal.

Remove the veal cutlets to a baking tray
and top with the sage leaves. Lay a prosciutto
slice over each cutlet and place under the
grill for as long as it takes for the prosciutto
to crisp a little on the edges. We're talking
1–2 minutes if your grill is hot. Brush with
melted butter, if using, and serve with a salad,
roasted baby potatoes and some chargrilled
eggplant (aubergine) or roasted fennel.

Oregano gremolata

Finely grated zest of 1 lemon

½ teaspoon lemon juice

1 garlic clove, crushed

1½ tablespoons chopped flat-leaf (Italian) parsley

½ tablespoon oregano leaves, chopped

2 tablespoons extra virgin olive oil, plus extra for drizzling

4 x 140 g (5 oz) veal steaks, preferably butterflied from the striploin

3 ripe tomatoes, diced (or use tinned if you must)

2–4 anchovy fillets, chopped

a pinch of sugar (optional)

Veal with tomatoes & oregano gremolata

The essence of some recipes lies in simple yet seasonal ingredients. Tomatoes actually taste like tomatoes in summer, if you buy them ripe. Bottled anchovies usually taste less salty and more like fish than tinned ones, and fresh herbs are a must-have to make this dish really shine.

SERVES 4

To make the oregano gremolata mix together the lemon zest and juice, garlic, parsley and oregano and stir to combine. Set aside until needed.

Heat 1 tablespoon of the oil in a heavy-based frying pan over high heat and quickly seal the veal for about 1 minute on each side. Remove to a plate.

Reduce the heat, add the remaining oil and fry the tomatoes for a couple of minutes until they are just breaking down. Add the anchovies and stir to combine. Depending on the flavour of your tomatoes, they may need a little sugar to bring out their true beauty. Taste for salt (the anchovies add a bit) and freshly milled black pepper. Stir in the gremolata and simmer for 1 minute longer.

Return the veal to the pan for a few seconds, turning to coat in the sauce and heat through. Serve the veal topped with the tomato pieces, which should still be moist enough to act as a kind of sauce, and drizzle about 1 tablespoon extra virgin olive oil over each serving.

234

heart from 1 bunch celery, chopped

2 tablespoons flat-leaf (Italian) parsley, torn

80 ml (2½ fl oz/⅓ cup) extra virgin olive oil

2 tablespoons raspberry vinegar, or substitute a good red wine vinegar

½ teaspoon finely grated lemon zest

½ cup walnuts, lightly crushed

2 hard-boiled eggs, peeled and cut into quarters

1–2 tablespoons olive oil

4 x 150 g (5½ oz) veal leg steaks

Veal & celery heart salad

Celery heart is the sweet, tender, pale-green inner stems of the celery. It's the bit that tastes the best eaten raw, while the darker outer stalks tend to be better in cooking. This dish matches that fresh, crisp heart with the mildness of young veal.

SERVES 4

To make the salad, place the celery in a bowl. Sprinkle in the parsley, toss very gently and season to taste with salt and freshly milled black pepper. Whisk the olive oil, vinegar and lemon zest together in a bowl and add to the celery mixture, stirring just a little to coat. When ready to serve, lightly toss the walnuts and eggs through the salad.

Rub the oil into the veal and season to taste. Heat a frying pan, ridged pan or grill plate on a barbecue to high and sear the veal well on each side until lightly coloured and cooked to your liking — more than 1 minute on each side can often cook thin pieces of veal right through.

Serve the warm veal with any pan juices drizzled over, and the salad on top, perhaps with boiled, buttered new potatoes or crusty bread on the side.

3 tablespoons olive oil

2 kg (4 lb 8 oz) osso buco, preferably
   young veal

plain (all-purpose) flour, for dusting

2 large onions, diced

3 celery sticks, diced

3 carrots, diced

2 bay leaves

250 ml (9 fl oz/1 cup) dry white wine

400 g (14 oz/1⅔ cups) tinned chopped
   tomatoes

Gremolata

2 garlic cloves, crushed

finely grated zest of 1 lemon

juice from ½ lemon

2 tablespoons chopped flat-leaf (Italian)
   parsley

Osso buco with gremolata

*Osso buco, which means literally 'bone hole', takes its name from the cut
of veal used to make it — slices from the shank that have marrow in the
middle. This version is fairly classic.*

SERVES 4–6

Heat the oil in a large saucepan over
medium–high heat. Dust the osso buco
with flour to coat both sides and shake to
remove any excess. Fry for 3–4 minutes to
brown on both sides — you may need to do
this in two batches, using a wooden spatula
to scrape all the stuck-on bits from the base
of the pan as you go so they don't burn.
These will help the osso buco taste fantastic.
Remove the meat from the pan and set aside.

In the same pan, fry the onion, celery and
carrots for about 10 minutes over low heat,
or until the onion is very soft. Return the
meat to the pan, add the bay leaves and wine
and simmer for 2 minutes.

Add the tomatoes and 400 ml (14 fl oz)
water, cover, and simmer for about 1 hour.

Add salt and freshly milled black pepper
to taste and simmer for another 20 minutes,
or until the meat is very tender. The older
the veal, the longer it will take to cook.

To make the gremolata, mix together
all the ingredients and stir to combine.
Sprinkle half into the sauce, stir well, and
bring back to the boil.

Serve the braised meat with the
remaining gremolata sprinkled over the top.

1 kg (2 lb 4 oz) milk-fed veal loin
9 anchovy fillets
185 g (6½ oz) tinned tuna in oil
2 egg yolks
250 ml (9 fl oz/1 cup) canola or
    sunflower oil

1½ tablespoons lemon juice
2 tablespoons salted capers, rinsed
    and well drained

Vitello tonnato

*Vitello tonnato is, classically, poached veal topped with a tuna sauce.
It's light and bright, and in Italy they would cook the veal for well over
an hour; I prefer it still pink. You can flavour the poaching water with
celery, parsley, carrot and peppercorns, or use stock if you wish. Or, you
can roast the veal if you don't want to poach it. Some people even like to
use chicken or pork instead of veal.*

SERVES 8

Use a sharp knife to make twelve narrow
holes in the veal. Cut six of the anchovies
in half and push a piece into each hole
in the veal.

Place the veal in a saucepan and pour
over enough boiling salted water to cover
the meat. Cook over high heat until nearly
boiling. Turn down and barely simmer for
10 minutes. Allow the meat to cool in
the water, then remove the veal and keep the
cooking liquid for stock (it's great in risotto).

Drain the tuna, reserving the oil. In a
food processor, blend the tuna, remaining
3 anchovies and the egg yolks until smooth.

With the motor running, add the canola
or sunflower oil in a thin stream until well
incorporated. Add the reserved tuna oil and
the lemon juice, also with the motor running.
Season with salt and freshly milled black
pepper, to taste.

Thinly slice the veal and serve with the
sauce smothered over and a scattering of
capers on top.

Fennel coleslaw

300 g (10½ oz) red cabbage, cored
    and finely shredded
2 fennel bulbs, finely sliced
1 teaspoon salt
¼ teaspoon freshly milled black pepper
1 teaspoon black mustard seeds
1 tablespoon grated fresh or bottled
    horseradish
2–3 tablespoons extra virgin olive oil
2–3 teaspoons lemon juice or either
    red or white wine vinegar
100 g (3½ oz/1 cup) dry breadcrumbs

30 g (1 oz) finely grated Italian parmesan
    cheese (Parmigiano Reggiano or Grana
    Padano)
4 x 120 g (4¼ oz) veal schnitzel, beaten
    until thin
plain (all-purpose) flour, for dusting
1 egg, beaten
1–2 tablespoons butter or olive oil,
    or a mix of both
lemon wedges, to serve

Parmesan-crumbed veal with fennel coleslaw

The milky sweetness of good Italian parmesan cheese adds a sexy hint to a veal schnitzel, while the slaw acts as a bright, lively counterpoint.

SERVES 4

To make the fennel coleslaw, mix the cabbage, fennel, salt, pepper, mustard seeds, horseradish, oil and lemon juice together in a bowl until well combined and ideally allow to settle for 1–2 hours, covered, but out of the refrigerator in moderate climates, before serving.

To make the veal, mix the breadcrumbs and parmesan together in a bowl. Dust each piece of veal first with flour, then dip into the egg and roll in the breadcrumb mixture to coat on both sides. (I like to do this last step in a plastic bag.)

Heat the butter in a large frying pan over medium heat. When it is just starting to change colour, add the veal pieces, you may need to cook them in two batches, frying for 2 minutes on each side, or until golden, adding more butter if necessary.

Serve the crumbed veal with lemon wedges on the side and the fennel coleslaw.

LAMB

*'I should've shaved and combed my hair,' says Craig 'Fred' Leaman
after I drag him out of his house on Bruny Island on a wild winter's day.
But to my eyes, he's perfect. An old-variety sheep breeder should be as
shaggy as his sheep. The Leaman family breed the rare Wiltshire horn
variety, one of the original meat breeds, with descriptions in the British
Isles dating back to around 250 years ago (and possibly Roman times).
They're so specific a meat breed that they shed their fleece each year,
leaving shearers unemployed and knitters empty handed.*

Leaman's sheep have big bodies, nicely rounded, with decent chops you can almost
see through the flesh where the wool has dropped away. 'They have terrific marbling,'
says Fred, of the chops. 'There's virtually no fat on the outside; it's all in the eye
of the meat.' In other words, it's better fat for you, it makes the meat juicier, more
tender and more flavoursome, and the sheep are grass-fed, meaning they have a
more complex, interesting flavour.

In Australia, like New Zealand, most sheep are bred for wool. The flagship merino
sheep is a terrific fleece animal, even if it was stolen from the Spanish. I wear a lot of it.
But when it comes to high-quality meat, most sheep in Australia are a cross of merino
with a terminal sire, such as Hampshire down, or perhaps a white Suffolk, which has had
its black face bred out to avoid contaminating the fleece with black wool. Meat breeds,
however, have their own inherent qualities, and while the cross-breeds may suit the
grower, they don't necessarily make for better eating. Wiltshire horn is a great example
of a breed that is bred solely for meat, with no commercially viable fleece to confuse the
issue. The horns make them more difficult to handle and transport. They are, however,
almost perfectly suited to organic farming as they don't need mulesing (where the folds
of skin at the back of the sheep are removed in a painful, anaesthetic-free cut). Wiltshire
horns boast a hardiness and maternal instinct not found in many wool breeds, they don't
suffer fly strike, and with careful selection can be bred to be worm resistant. But what
matters to the eater, to us as consumers, is flavour.

Most lamb is sold without reference to breed. That's for many reasons, not least
because it's in the interests of those who have wool breeds to keep up the anonymity.
It also happens because other breeds are often run by smaller operators in very small
flocks, and their meat is hard to separate out at the abattoir. In addition to that, the
more specific meat breeds are often reared by passionate farmers who may not sell
many, except to their family and friends.

WHAT IS LAMB?

Definitions vary between countries, but in Australia lamb meat is from a sheep that is usually less than one year old and has no permanent teeth.

Milk-fed lamb is from sheep that are up to six or eight weeks old and have been fed predominantly on their mother's milk. This term can also be used for sucker lambs, which haven't been weaned, but do eat grass as well as still suckle from their mothers.

Spring lamb is from lambs that are *born* in spring. These sheep grow up on the more lush pasture of spring, as opposed to autumn lambs. You would usually buy them in autumn (not spring, despite the marketing hype at the end of each winter), when they're five or six months old.

Good lamb is pale, tender and probably small; most likely you'll be sold something older than desirable, at the high price of lamb. Good lamb needs little done to it, as its delicate flavour and gently juicy texture can be overwhelmed by strong flavours or harsh cooking.

Young lamb should be a pale pink in colour, especially really young lambs, which should be milky pink and closer to white. It should be so tender it cuts at a harsh word. The meat gets a rose tinge as the lambs move from mostly milk to a mix of more grass and milk. Roast or grill young lamb gently, or braise it if it's from the front end (shoulder, forequarter, neck) and a bit older.

WHAT IS HOGGET, OR TWO-TOOTH?

When a lamb gets no more than two permanent incisor teeth, the meat is called hogget. I like the name two-tooth as it's more attractive than hogget. Being a two-tooth tends to mean a sheep is over one year old, but not yet two, though because it's determined by dental records, it does depend on how fast they mature.

Most of what you'll buy labelled lamb is actually closer to hogget. Good hogget should be deeper in colour, and larger than lamb, with more marbling through the meat. Milder than mutton, hogget is perfect for stronger flavours such as cinnamon and cumin. Hogget shanks make great braises and soups. Hogget forequarter (shoulder) is terrific cooked slowly with olives and lemon. The leg likes to be wet-roasted, perhaps with red wine splashed in. Some of the better cuts, such as loin chops, can be cooked in the same way lamb can.

WHAT IS MUTTON?

Mutton is the meat from an older sheep, typically two years old, or even older, and it usually comes from ewes or castrated males (wethers).

Good mutton should be bred for eating, not just some old sheep the farmer wants to be rid of. It is best hung (dry-aged) for at least two weeks post slaughter, and trimmed of fat. Cook mutton with moisture to break it down if tough. It works best in curries with lots of aromatics and root vegetables (carrot, celery, parsnip, onion, garlic), and cooked with care, as it is strongly flavoured. It can carry through an Irish stew very well (use less meat to onion and potato to allow for its stronger taste), is terrific larded with green bacon (see pages 266–7) and wet-roasted for hours and hours. Mutton can add great body to a more complex stew, though it can be uncommonly flavoursome if you're not used to it. Mutton fat, for instance, is often quite strong, with a distinct lanoliny character, and is best avoided. I like to cook dishes with mutton a day ahead, refrigerate them overnight, and lift the fat off the top of them before reheating the next day.

HOW BIG SHOULD MY LAMB BE?

It depends on what you want it for. A milk-fed lamb may only weigh 6 kg (13 lb 8 oz) in total. A leg of spring lamb sold at about six months of age should weigh about 2 kg (4 lb 8 oz). Any larger than 2.5 kg (5 lb 8 oz) and it's probably getting close to two-tooth or mutton.

SHEEP BREEDS

Breed matters. Where I live in Tasmania we have a lot of meat breeds, but in much of Australia and wherever wool is sought after, the breed comes second to wool production. Meat sheep ('fat lambs' in the trade) are often a first cross of a good meat breed with a merino. This is intended to keep much of the meat breed's conformation, but isn't usually as good eating as a purebred meat sheep.

Some lesser known good meat breeds are the Wiltshire horn, wiltipoll (bred to not have horns), Hampshire down, southdown, Shropshire, Dorset downs, Dorset horn and dorper. Also, keep an eye out for saltbush lamb, which can be any breed, and is fed on stands of a rugged, saline-resistant native saltbush plant in some marginal parts of Australia, giving the lamb a complex, interesting, wonderful flavour. It's not dissimilar to the French salt marsh lamb, which is available in the UK, as well as salt meadow lamb being grown in Wales.

1.5 kg (3 lb 5 oz) spring lamb leg
500 g (1 lb 2 oz) garlic, peeled
10 anchovy fillets
oil or dripping

1 litre (35 fl oz/4 cups) boiling water
500 ml (17 fl oz/2 cups) homemade beef
    stock (see page 224) or chicken stock
    (see page 163) or water and a bay leaf

La gasconnade

From the Gascony region of France, this dish uses an intriguing combination of anchovies and garlic with lamb, traditionally cooked on a spit. And not just a few cloves of garlic, either. Even though the quantity of garlic looks like a mistake, it actually becomes mild and nutty with a delicious warmth once cooked. You can peel the garlic by blanching it first in boiling water. While roasting on a spit is a more romantic notion, the oven is reality for most of us.

SERVES 4

Preheat the oven to 180°C (350°F/Gas 4). Use a sharp knife to cut about twenty slits into the lamb flesh, about 2 cm (3/4 inch) deep. Insert 10 of the garlic cloves into half the holes and push the anchovy fillets into the remaining holes. Sit the lamb in a deep roasting tray, rub the outside of the leg with oil, and sprinkle over salt and freshly milled black pepper.

Roast the lamb in the oven for about 45 minutes, or until cooked to your liking. Cover with foil and set aside to rest in a warm place for about 10 minutes before serving.

While the lamb is cooking, pour the boiling water over the remaining garlic, and allow to steep for 2 minutes. Drain well.

Place the garlic and stock in a saucepan, bring to the boil over high heat, then reduce the heat and simmer for about 30 minutes, or until the garlic is soft.

Increase the heat, stirring constantly, and reduce the mixture to a loose, rough paste. Add some zing with the pan juices from the lamb. Season to taste and serve the carved lamb with a dollop of the garlic paste.

Variation: Alternatively, you can make a garlic and anchovy paste and smear it over the lamb before roasting.

2 tablespoons olive oil or lard

3 thin slices prosciutto, cut into strips

1.5 kg (3 lb 5 oz) young lamb (less than
6 months old) on the bone, cut
into 12 chunks

10 garlic cloves

1 rosemary sprig

15 sage leaves

2 tablespoons wine vinegar
(either colour)

L'abbacchio

L'abbacchio is a Roman dish of roasted lamb. I tend to cook it for a shorter time than the Romans do, but that's more to do with the reliable quality of lamb I can get, and personal preference. If you're using older lamb, or even full-flavoured hogget, cook it for 40 minutes before lifting the lid. You can add a mashed anchovy fillet with the vinegar, because this is what some did traditionally, but I tend to do it without.

SERVES 5–6

Preheat the oven to 160°C (315°F/ Gas 2–3).

Heat the oil in a large ovenproof saucepan over a medium–high heat and fry the prosciutto for 1 minute, or until the fat starts to melt. Add the lamb and brown on the outside. Drain the fat from the pan. Season with salt and freshly milled black pepper, then add the garlic, rosemary and sage and cover with a tight-fitting lid.

Transfer the pan to the oven and cook for about 20 minutes. Remove the lid, add the vinegar, and cook for another 5 minutes or so without the lid.

L'abbacchio is traditionally served with roast potatoes and I'd have a big dish of Wilted Kale with Garlic (see page 372) on the side.

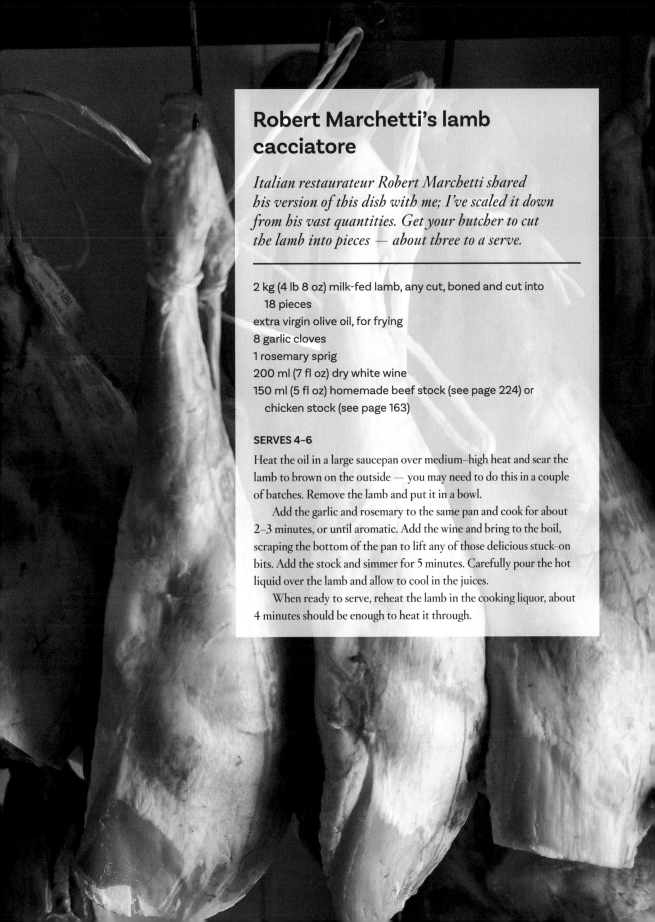

Robert Marchetti's lamb cacciatore

Italian restaurateur Robert Marchetti shared his version of this dish with me; I've scaled it down from his vast quantities. Get your butcher to cut the lamb into pieces — about three to a serve.

2 kg (4 lb 8 oz) milk-fed lamb, any cut, boned and cut into
    18 pieces
extra virgin olive oil, for frying
8 garlic cloves
1 rosemary sprig
200 ml (7 fl oz) dry white wine
150 ml (5 fl oz) homemade beef stock (see page 224) or
    chicken stock (see page 163)

SERVES 4-6

Heat the oil in a large saucepan over medium–high heat and sear the lamb to brown on the outside — you may need to do this in a couple of batches. Remove the lamb and put it in a bowl.

Add the garlic and rosemary to the same pan and cook for about 2–3 minutes, or until aromatic. Add the wine and bring to the boil, scraping the bottom of the pan to lift any of those delicious stuck-on bits. Add the stock and simmer for 5 minutes. Carefully pour the hot liquid over the lamb and allow to cool in the juices.

When ready to serve, reheat the lamb in the cooking liquor, about 4 minutes should be enough to heat it through.

1 tablespoon olive oil

3 large onions, diced

2 garlic cloves

150 g (5½ oz) green olives, rinsed

800 g (1 lb 12 oz) tinned chopped
  tomatoes

1–2 bay leaves

2 anchovy fillets

2 kg (4 lb 8 oz) lamb shoulder,
  on the bone (ask the butcher to
  leave the shank on, but bend it over)

600 g (1 lb 5 oz) starchy potatoes,
  chopped

Lamb shoulder braised with tomato & green olives

This is a pretty simple dish to prepare, but one that improves with time in the oven. Use good olives, and if they're not split or pitted or anything, lightly press them to crack open and release their flavour. Use the side of a big knife or a meat mallet to do this. I've used lamb on the bone in this recipe because it makes a rich, indulgent sauce, and I've finished it with potato, but you could add risoni or rice and adjust the cooking accordingly. Or if you prefer, you can just serve it with lots of good bread for dipping into the sauce.

SERVES 4–6

Preheat the oven to 150°C (300°F/Gas 2).

Heat the oil in a large ovenproof saucepan or stockpot over medium heat and fry the onion for 5–10 minutes, or until starting to colour. Add the garlic and fry for 1 minute, then add the olives and tomatoes, stirring to combine. Add 1 litre (35 fl oz/4 cups) water, the bay leaves and the anchovy fillets (don't worry, you won't taste the fishiness at the end). Season with salt and freshly milled black pepper, to taste.

Carefully lower the lamb into the pan — the sauce probably won't come right over the lamb and that's just fine.

Cover and bring to the boil, then transfer to the oven. Alternatively, you can reduce the heat and continue to cook at a gentle simmer on the stovetop. Cook the lamb for 1 hour, turn it over, check to make sure there's enough liquid so it doesn't burn, then cook for a further 1 hour, or until tender.

At this point, I skim the fat off the sauce (it may be easiest to try to remove the lamb, which may or may not fall off the bone, depending on how well it's cooked; either way is fine). Return the lamb to the pan, add the potatoes (checking the liquid level and adding water as needed) and simmer gently for another 20–30 minutes, or until they are well cooked.

Serve chunks of lamb with the sauce and potatoes and a suitably meaty glass of grenache.

2–3 tablespoons olive oil
1 kg (2 lb 4 oz) lamb shoulder, diced
2 large onions, finely chopped
2 carrots, finely chopped
3 celery sticks, finely chopped
2 garlic cloves, crushed
1 large handful flat-leaf (Italian) parsley, chopped, plus extra to garnish

400 g (14 oz/1⅔ cups) tinned chopped tomatoes
100 g (3½ oz) artichoke hearts (see page 398), rinsed and chopped
juice of 1 lemon
finely grated zest of 1 lemon

Stewed lamb with lemon & artichokes

Imagine who it was that first ate an artichoke and said thanks. This relative of the thistle must be one of the most inedible raw vegetables, with a coarse and chewy exterior and unappetising flesh, unless sliced wafer thin. But once cooked, if they're cooked well, they're wonderful. (I've even eaten thistles in Sicily and Sardinia, though they're less interesting than their artichoke cousins.) I've cooked this using lamb, because it's what I had at the time, but kid works wonderfully too.

SERVES 8

Heat 1 tablespoon of the oil in a large heavy-based saucepan over high heat and sear the meat until brown on all sides — you may need to do this in two batches, adding more oil if needed. Remove the meat from the pan and set aside.

Add another 1 tablespoon of the oil to the pan and gently fry the onion, carrot, celery, garlic and parsley for about 10 minutes, or until the vegetables are soft. Return the meat to the pan, add the tomatoes and enough water to just cover. Bring to the boil, cover, reduce the heat and simmer for 1 hour.

Season with salt and freshly milled black pepper to taste. Add the artichokes to the pan and simmer for a further 20 minutes, or until the meat is tender.

Add the lemon juice, mix the lemon zest with the extra parsley and add half to the pan. Adjust the seasoning, to taste, and serve with Soft Polenta (see page 106) or steamed rice, with a little more of the lemon parsley mix sprinkled over the top.

1–2 tablespoons olive oil

8 lamb shanks

plain (all-purpose) flour, for dusting

2 large onions, diced

3 carrots, diced

2 celery sticks, chopped

2 teaspoons ground coriander

1 tablespoon ground cumin

250 ml (9 fl oz/1 cup) white wine

500 g (9 oz) ripe tomatoes, chopped

1 strip orange peel

Orange gremolata

1 garlic clove, crushed

finely grated zest of ¼ orange

juice of ¼ orange

finely grated zest of ½ lemon

juice of ½ lemon

2 tablespoons chopped flat-leaf
   (Italian) parsley

Braised lamb shanks with tomato & cumin

Peeling the tomatoes for this recipe isn't essential, but please feel free to do so if you want (see method on page 378). If you can't get ripe tomatoes, it's fine to use tinned, but avoid those with any added herbs or flavourings as they will make your braise taste skanky rather than shanky.

SERVES 4

Heat 1 tablespoon of the oil over medium heat in a large saucepan or stockpot, preferably one that can be used for the whole braise when everything is added. Lightly dust the lamb shanks with flour and fry gently on each side to tan — you'll probably need to do this in two batches. Remove the shanks as they are done.

In the same pan, adding more oil if necessary, gently fry the onions for 2–3 minutes. Toss in the carrots and celery and continue frying for another 3 minutes to soften.

Reduce the heat to low, add the coriander and cumin and fry, stirring constantly, for 1 minute or less. Pour in the wine and bring to the boil. Add the tomatoes and orange peel and season with salt and freshly milled black pepper. Scrape the bottom of the pan to remove any stuck-on bits, then add 1 litre (35 fl oz/4 cups) water and return the lamb shanks to the pan.

Cover, bring to the boil, then reduce the heat and simmer for about 90 minutes. The meat should be so tender it falls from the bone when shaken. Keep cooking if necessary (I take the lid off for a bit to reduce the sauce).

To make the gremolata, at the last minute mix together all the ingredients in a bowl until well combined.

Add half the gremolata to the shanks and simmer for 1 minute further. Adjust the seasoning, to taste, and serve with couscous, or rice, or mashed potatoes with a little more gremolata sprinkled over the top.

1 tablespoon vegetable oil

2 large onions, diced

1–2 long dried red chillies

2 brown cardamom pods (the big ones)

6 green cardamom pods

1 cinnamon stick

a pinch of blade mace

2 cloves

10 peppercorns

2 teaspoons coriander seeds

1 kg (2 lb 4 oz) diced lamb shoulder

400 g (14 oz/1⅔ cups) tinned chopped tomatoes

Taxi driver's lamb curry

It was late, the taxi driver was from Pakistan, and he told me how to make a simple but effective north Asian curry. It uses whole spices, which you try not to chew as you eat, though the cloves might be nice if you've a toothache. I might have changed one or two ingredients when I cooked it, so if you drive for a living, forgive me. If you only have one type of cardamom, you can still make this curry, although the flavour won't be quite as complex. Just use ten green pods or four brown ones.

SERVES 4–6

Heat the oil in a large saucepan over medium heat and fry the onion until starting to colour. Add the spices and fry until aromatic.

Add the lamb to the pan and cook until starting to colour, but don't let the onion or spices burn.

Roughly blend the tomatoes and stir into the meat with any juice. Add 125 ml (4 fl oz/½ cup) water and season with salt, to taste. Simmer, covered, for a bit over 90 minutes, stirring regularly, until the meat is tender — you may need to add a little more water as it cooks.

Serve the curry with The Perfect Pilaff (see page 110), some Raita (see page 52) and a little Indian pickle.

1 kg (2 lb 4 oz) lamb or hogget neck chops
1.25 kg (2 lb 12 oz) starchy potatoes
2 onions, sliced

Simply delicious Irish stew

*Throw these ingredients in a dish and 2 hours later you'll find
dinner is ready. How easy is that? The quantities are obviously
going to vary according to the size of the spuds, but I recommend
keeping the amount of potato just slightly more than the meat —
a big change from the olden days when meat was scarce; back then
they would've used one chop to flavour a bucketful of spuds. Hogget
is the better option, but tricky to find sometimes, so if you can't get it,
go for decent-sized lamb neck chops when you go to the butcher.*

SERVES 5–6

Preheat the oven to 200°C (400°F/Gas 6).

Trim the chops of all fat, including the skin. Cut the potatoes roughly into 5 mm (¼ inch) thick slices. Arrange half of the potatoes in an even layer in the base of a 4 litre (140 fl oz/16 cup) casserole dish.

Scatter over half of the onion and then lay the chops over the top to form another layer. Season well with salt and freshly milled black pepper. Scatter the remaining onion over the lamb and top with the remaining potato slices; season again.

Pour in 750 ml (26 fl oz/3 cups) water, cover with a lid, and cook in the oven for 15 minutes.

Reduce the oven temperature to 150°C (300°F/Gas 2) and continue cooking the stew for about 1 hour 45 minutes. Check it after about 1 hour to see how much liquid there is; you want to have some broth, enough to cook the potatoes and meat, but not too much that it becomes soupy. You can take the lid off for the last 15 minutes of cooking to give the spuds on top a crispier, drier finish.

Serve the Irish stew with Duck Fat Brussels Sprouts (see page 371) or just dish it up with some bread and steamed carrots.

PORK

The pigs at Jen Owens' farm look spectacular. Their handsome black coats, broken by a white stole around their shoulders, create a look that is as much landscape as livestock. These terrific-looking pigs are a variety called Wessex saddleback, an old breed known for being a slow grower with intensely flavoured meat. They're also famed as being a grand producer of that miracle of the cooking world, fat.

The pigs trot eagerly when Jen calls, playfully following her into the orchard for a feed of sprouted barley and windfall apples. These porkers are not like the factory-farmed pigs that are sold off for supermarket and cheap butcher meat.

Pork is the meat that has been debased almost as much as any — only chicken has a worse reputation. True free-range pigs, allowed to walk and mature slowly, can have an intensity of flavour and an ability to enhance other dishes that makes most intensively farmed pork look insipid.

Jen's way of rearing pigs is about as far from the norm as it's possible to find. Most of the Western world's pigs will never see the outside until they are trucked to the abattoir. Most of their mothers will be stalled in pens so small they can't turn around or walk for at least some of their pregnancy. Some for their entire adult lives. Most pork meat is produced as quickly and cheaply as possible, using growth promotants, heavily formulated feeds and finely tuned intensive farming techniques. This for an animal that is intelligent, playful, very sociable and remarkably clean living, as anybody who has kept a house pig should be able to attest. As I write this, I can see ten frolicking saddleback pigs in their paddock.

A pig is a social creature. They love to wallow and play. Left to their own devices in a paddock, they'll chew the grass and plough up the earth looking for flavoursome grubs, fungi and roots. In some circles they're known as pink-snouted tractors (though Jen's would be more accurately known as black-snouted tractors). Ours like to frolic in the sun, teasing the calf in the main paddock and sleeping in a heap when their hunger has been sated.

The intensive farming practices adopted over the past sixty years, however, means this kind of farming is just about dead. Factory farming of pigs, most of which has occurred since the 1920s, has led to a change in animal behaviour. Pressed together, pigs are more likely to bite each other's tails and take a nip at each other. They'll be kept on hard floors for much of their life, drinking from drip tubes and fed a strict diet of formulated feed. They may well have their tails docked and a ring put through their nose. And they won't ever be able to walk outside, to wallow or forage. That's the way modern farming does it.

Pork meat has also suffered terribly from our 1970s and 1980s aversion to fat. Pigs can lay down a good layer of the stuff on the outside, and as the mentality of the era was that fat is bad, pigs were bred for leanness. But with that leanness came an enormous loss of flavour. Rushed from the teat to the pan, the meat became sloppy, lacking in marbling, and of dubious texture. Eating pork soon became a lesson in how dry and unappetising meat can be. When I was a chef in the 1990s, virtually nobody would cook pork in a posh restaurant, it was that bad.

The pork industry did a few things to address the problem. They started advertising lean cuts that you could cook to medium, therefore leaving some moisture in the meat. They also decided to promote a thing called 'moisture enhanced' or 'moisture infused' pork. That means that instead of reverting to better breeds and rearing practices, they pumped the meat with salty water to prevent it having the texture of sawdust when cooked. While this may be a good thing for the butcher, as salty water is much cheaper to produce than meat, in my view, it is not so great for the eater. What we get, as consumers, is more dilute, watery-tasting meat. It does keep the meat more moist, however. You can do this kind of thing at home by brining meat, though it takes longer (because commercially they have big needles), which means the pork will cure slightly in the process.

An old-breed pig often matures more slowly than a factory pig because they're not genetically bred for super-fast fattening. Any animal that is allowed to walk around uses a lot more feed and also fattens slower. And of course, just as with sheep and cattle and chickens, the more complex the food they get to eat, the more complex the flavour of the meat will become. To overcome this, pigs have been bred to be less anxious when confined. A sow is often kept in a stall the size of a bathtub in which she is unable to turn around. When she gives birth (farrows), she's put in a farrowing crate where her young are confined. They're weaned at 2–3 weeks instead of at 2 months. And they're fed growth promotants that get them fattened up in four months rather than seven.

Unfortunately, a true free-range pig that can actually forage for part of its diet isn't one you'll be able to eat very often. They're simply not financially viable. The commercial reality is that pigs (including virtually all free-range pigs) will be fattened on grain, perhaps supplemented with formulated feed pellets. Occasionally, pigs are fed milk or whey, or they may get apples or bread or potatoes. But real pork, the sort that small farmholders get to enjoy from their two pigs a year, is a treat probably reserved for those who go to the trouble of growing their own.

On the upside, some good-quality pork is now commercially available. Meat products from older-breed black free-ranging pigs are becoming more commonly seen at farmers' markets and good butchers. Customers are demanding to know if a pig was born and raised free-range. They want to know what the breed is, the gender (girls are better for most uses), what they're fed and how they've been kept. Even better, as we relearn how to cook, and how to use just about all of the pig — including its fat — we're able to use a little pork to flavour a lot of food.

PIG BREEDS

Most of what goes into making good pork is what goes into making good pigs. The genetics (breeding), the feed, the age of the animal and the animal husbandry are all factors, and none of them act in isolation.

Of roughly 650 recorded farm pig breeds, 150 have become extinct over the past hundred years. One-third of the remaining pig breeds are at risk of being lost. In Australia we no longer have Gloucester old spots. The UK has lost its Essex and Wessex saddlebacks (they just have a generic saddleback now). Most factory pigs are the progeny of very few breeds, sometimes cross-bred for certain traits.

Connoisseurs favour middle whites, large blacks, Berkshires, Tamworths, Wessex saddlebacks, British lops, and Oxford sandy and blacks. The extremely rare but fabulous-tasting Gloucester old spot is high on that list, too. The grandaddy of most factory pigs of choice these days, the landrace, is also an old breed, originally from Denmark, but selectively bred for different characteristics around the world. It's favoured for its docile nature, which means it can mentally cope with confinement, and for its fast growth rate, lean composition and long body, which is good for bacon.

FEED

As with all animals, the feed a pig is given makes a marked difference to the flavour of the meat. They are what they eat. Pigs are customarily fed grain, or a feed ration based on high-protein grains, with some vitamins and minerals added.

In the wild, pigs would eat roots as well as above-ground vegetation, while also seeking out grubs and worms. In captivity, despite pigs being omnivores, it's illegal in many places to feed them meat, mostly because of biosecurity fears (mad cow disease being the great example of a failure of biosecurity).

Well-fed pigs may be given whey, milk, windfall apples, potatoes and pears, supplemented by grain. And if they free-range, and can forage, they tend to get a more complex flavour in the meat than if they are fed grain alone. That said, feed works with genetics and the other factors to create good pork. Some growers use a large proportion of corn in the food at the end of the pig's life in order to sweeten the meat, though some suggest that this creates merely a sweet, one-dimensional flavour.

AGE

Most pigs headed for the abattoir are about four to five months old. At this age they weigh about 50–70 kg (110–155 lb) dressed weight (that is, hair removed and gutted). Uncastrated male pigs are usually killed before they sexually mature.

The age of the animal makes a difference to flavour in pork, just as it does in beef and lamb. A young animal (especially milk-fed) has a sweeter, milder flavour. Older animals get more flavour in their meat.

Free-range pigs tend to mature more slowly than those kept indoors, and many say this slow growth leads to a more complex flavoured meat — meat that is less sloppy or wet (probably due to the exercise the animal gets).

A one-year-old free-range pig will have bucketloads of flavour, but as they get older, they do start to put on more fat compared to meat. They do, however, get the best and most important fat, marbling (see below). A one-year-old pig kept in confinement will probably turn to fat, and the meat may not get the requisite exercise. That said, much of Europe's great ham, such as the famed prosciutto di Parma, comes from old, fat, factory pigs, though they've usually been fed very well (perhaps on whey) and the meat is expertly handled.

The best dry-cured ham in the world, however, is made from free-range pigs that are more than three years old and fed on acorns – the jamón ibérico de bellota from Spain. Far from being tough, the meat is as succulent as a kiss, as soft as butter and a miracle of meat.

MARBLING

Marbling, the fine threads of fat that course through the muscles, is essential in good pork. The sad thing is that most of the marbling is laid down after four months of age, when the vast majority of pigs have already been sent to market.

Marbling does three things. It keeps the meat moist as it cooks, melting down and doing the equivalent of basting the meat from the inside. As it breaks down, it also helps to keep the pork tender. The third and arguably most important thing is that this fat carries a lot of pork's flavour. Without it, you're just eating meat. With it, if it's good pork, you're experiencing one of the finest flavours in the meat eater's world.

The fat that marbles meat, by the way, is reputedly a much healthier form of fat than the stuff that lines the outside of the cut, which is also true of all other animals.

FREE-RANGE — AND REAL FREE-RANGE

The commercial pig industry hates it, but the fact is that free-range pigs do taste better than their factory-bred cousins. Yes, as a grower of some pigs myself, I *would* say that, but a pig that has matured more slowly, that has foraged, that has been able to indulge all its instincts, makes for better eating. I know, because I've fattened my own pigs, and unless you've had pork like that, you won't know what you're missing.

Critics of free-ranging pigs point to the consumer demand for cheap meat, to pigs' propensity for getting sunburnt (particularly in a climate like Australia's), and to some logistical demands to do with water quality. And they're probably right: to produce the same amount of mass-farmed pork in a free-range environment would be difficult to sustain. (Not that the factory farms are sustainable, necessarily, in the very long term.) My view is that you should eat better pork, pork with more flavour, and eat less of it.

Free-range pork fat is better for you too, containing less saturated fat and more omega-3 oils, if you're into that kind of thing.

There is another form of pork called 'bred free-range' — or, confusingly, 'Outdoor Bred, Raised Indoors on Straw' — which means the sow is free to range, but once weaned the porkers are fattened in stalls or deep-litter environments. Critics of the 'bred free-range' title, mostly those who let their animals range free their whole lives, believe it only confuses customers, but they lost a court case in Australia in 2008 to disallow the term.

Some critics of the free-range method believe that what they do is in the best interests of the animals. One example is the use of farrowing crates, metal grated cages where the piglets ('slips' in the trade) can suckle from the sow with less chance of being crushed, as it isn't uncommon for slips to be crushed by a 200 kg (440 lb) sow lying down on them in their first week after farrowing (giving birth).

Free-range pigs are subject to sunburn if not allowed a good wallow to let them coat themselves in mud (for some, a dust bath is nearly as good in colder weather). Sunburn is less of a problem with black pigs than white, but even white pigs bred in a free-range environment will grow coarser hair, will wallow in mud, and will use shade to protect themselves from sun.

Where I live, the peak pork body is very defensive of intensive systems, but in other parts of the world sow stalls and farrowing crates have been made illegal. The EU has banned sow stalls since 2013 for the entire pregnancy. The problem comes with the literal 'for their entire pregnancy' caveat: because some farmers still can't manage the pigs in early pregnancy without sow stalls, they remain in routine use for the first month of a sow's pregnancy.

WHAT TO LOOK FOR WHEN BUYING PORK

The first thing you need to ask your butcher is: 'Is the meat from free-range pigs?'. Or, even better, from 'pastured pigs', which have been given access to fresh grass their entire life. If you can find out (and a good butcher should be able to tell you), ask them about the feeding regime. It is also good to know if the meat comes from female pigs or castrated males, and to get an indication of what breed you are buying (see Pig Breeds, page 260). Is it a slow-growing breed famous for its flavour?

WHAT IS HAM?

Ham is a general term usually applied to a cured hind leg of pork, which is sometimes smoked. The exception to this is in the US, where a raw leg of pork can be called ham. These days, shoulder (picnic ham) and other cuts that are cured are also sometimes called ham.

DRY-CURED (AIR-DRIED) HAM Dry-cured ham, cured for more than one year, is a miracle of flavour. Like an aged cheese, the more it matures (up to a point, obviously), the more complex the flavour becomes.

Dry-cured ham is ham in the more European or Chinese sense than English. It's pork that is dry-salted (you put the leg in powdered salt, not a salt-water brine), and it may or may not be smoked, depending on the tradition. Think of Italian prosciutto crudo (the most famous being from Parma and San Daniele), Spanish jamón (ibérico de bellota from acorn-fed black pigs, is the most prized), Portuguese presunto, French jambon (particularly Bayonne), and the Chinese jinhua ham among many others. A very salty, sometimes smoky, version is the Virginia or 'country' ham of the southern US, which needs to be soaked before using as it's so dry and concentrated. These hams vary in how they're cured, how salty, dry, or sweet they become, and the way in which they are matured, but at their heart, they're all great hams.

Dry-cured ham retains its pink colour through a natural chemical alteration of protein in the meat, not through the addition of preservatives, although some dry-cured hams (particularly the fast-cured, mass-produced pretenders to real prosciutto that you find in cheap delis and supermarkets) are made using sodium nitrate, sodium nitrite or similar preservatives.

York ham is a variation on the English wet-cured ham; it's dry-cured, then hot-smoked over oak sawdust. When soaked and cooked it retains a texture more reminiscent of English ham than a dry-cured version from Europe, probably because it isn't hung and aged as long. It's likely that York ham was the precursor of America's country hams.

Good air-dried ham should come from a big, fat, flavoursome female pig that weighs about 100 kg (220 lb) or more, and has had a variety of interesting feed, perhaps acorns, or whey, or apples along with grain. The meat should have a good layer of external fat with prolific marbling, and be cured on the bone. The pig should be at least 12 months old, to mature the flavours, and is preferably free-range. A bloom of white mould should be growing on the outside — the same mould camembert gets, which adds more flavour. A good delicatessen should know how the ham was matured.

WET-CURED HAM Wet-cured, smoked ham is the sort developed by the English. It's cured using a brine solution, usually containing sodium nitrate or sodium nitrite to preserve the pink colour of the ham. The brine is usually pumped inside the leg using hollow needles to ensure even and fast curing, though some say the best ham is cured without pumping. At its best the ham is a moist, succulent, gorgeous combination of sweet pork overlaid with the intoxicating aroma of woodsmoke. At its worst it makes a mockery of our heritage.

Traditionally the hind legs of pigs were brined, then cooked in a slow smoker to roast them. This is what is now called a smoke-roasted ham or hot-smoked ham.

Unfortunately for eaters, the process of making ham has seen several 'improvements' over recent years. Pork legs are more often than not boned out, losing some of the flavour in the process (all meats cooked on the bone have more inherent flavour). These days, legs are often tumbled in what look like cement mixers to help soften the flesh, ensuring they absorb much more of the brine. A leg done this way is then poached rather than baked, so it doesn't lose as much moisture.

This ham, at its worst, is then flavoured with a smoke-flavoured chemical — a syrup that is poured into the poaching water. No smokehouse, no actual smoker, just a chemical you can buy in 20 litre (5 gallon) tubs. This way an 8 kg (18 lb) leg of pork can weigh as much as 12 kg (26 lb) after being tumbled in brine — that's a cool 4 kg (8 lb) of salty water — and 11 kg (24 lb) after being simmered. If you cure and smoke an 8 kg (18 lb) leg the old-fashioned way it is going to weigh about 7 kg (16 lb) when finished — two-thirds of the weight of a commercially cured ham, and well worth double the price in terms of flavour. If you factor in the cost of a slower growing, free-ranging pig, the difference is more likely to be two and a half times as much. So it costs more to produce a beautiful, full-flavoured, smoke-roasted ham, but you do get a lot more meat and real flavour for your money.

Not all wet-cured ham you'll buy is done this way. The smoking of a real, properly produced ham is a very important final step. Some like applewood, some like hickory. I used to sell ham smoked over local hardwood and its flavour is hard to beat. I tend to find that it's more important that the smoker is set up right than the composition of what is burnt to make the smoke. Because some hams are made using a lesser meat, in an effort to obtain a deeper, smokier result, some hams are double smoked — something the Germans do with aplomb.

WHY IS LEG HAM CONSIDERED SUPERIOR, AND IS IT?

Leg ham is the classic ham from the rear leg of a pig. It has less fat between muscles than shoulder ham, and is more tender. But is it better? The way most people make it, probably yes. But a good shoulder ham has more natural jelly and more flavour in the meat. Shoulder ham does run the risk of being overly fatty from an older breed or larger pig, and it could be slightly tough because of the numerous sinews that run between muscles. It is, virtually without exception, made from a boned-out shoulder rather than with the bone in. The good news is that it has a more intense, more resolute flavour than leg ham.

WHAT IS BACON?

Bacon refers to different things in different countries, but it tends to imply a cured belly. In Australia, as in much of the world, it is almost ubiquitous that it is not only cured, but also smoked.

Cured bacon is made in two ways, just like ham. It can be dry or wet-cured (see page 265). While wet-curing is likely to increase the weight of the bacon, dry-curing will undoubtedly decrease the weight of the bacon. A lot of bacon is cured with a savoury and sweet element: a salt/sugar mix or salt/honey mix. Wet-cured bacon is usually pumped in the same manner as ham, and virtually all cured bacon contains a preservative (sodium nitrate/nitrite) that fixes the pink colour. Commercially produced bacon is usually flavoured with liquid smoke while curing, or dipped in liquid smoke after curing.

Bacon made the old-fashioned way is smoked in actual smoke. It can be hot or cold-smoked. Hot-smoking means the smoke is hot and the smoker acts like an oven. Cold smoke is taken from the fire and passed along a pipe to cool as it leaves the fire, or is made under relatively low heat, before being used to smoke the bacon. So, cold-smoked bacon is cured but raw. Unlike ham, it doesn't need to be boiled if it is cold-smoked because it will be cooked later, after the customer takes it home. Hot-smoking obviously dries out the bacon more than cold-smoking, leading to a bacon that is less likely to shrink markedly when cooked. (Commercially produced bacon can shrink by up to 70 per cent when you fry it — again, they've sold you very expensive water.) A cured but cold-smoked product can be referred to as 'green' bacon, though this term usually means a cured but unsmoked bacon.

The process of pumping bacon and using inferior-grade pork for smallgoods has led to bacon being watery in texture. This bacon is likely to leach a white liquid when cooked, leading to a fishy smell, and there can also sometimes be a hormonal tang from boar taint (see below). The fishy smell can also come from fish meal in the pig's diet — a very cheap way of adding protein, but with a downside in terms of flavour.

Streaky bacon is the bit striped with fat from the belly. It crisps wonderfully and has much more flavour from the fat.

So, the best bacon is from a good, slow-grown, free-ranging pig that has been smoked in a proper smokehouse. The bacon should be fatty, because it is the fat that holds much of the flavour. It should not be so full of water that it shrivels to nothing when you cook it. Try and buy bacon sliced to order, so you can choose fat or thin slices.

BOAR TAINT

Uncastrated male pigs can get a hormonal stink called boar taint. As many as 15 per cent of the herd can show this character and, if noticed, the pigs are then used for smallgoods to try to mask the flavour. Good butchers tend to favour female pigs or castrated males, though the smell of boar taint is often found in cheaper pork and meat used in processing. It can smell funky, off, just not nice, or like fish — similar to when you fry cheap bacon.

Some commercial pigs are chemically castrated to avoid boar taint, but the meat ends up drier and stringier as a result.

1.5 kg (3 lb 5 oz) boneless pork loin, rind removed leaving the fat intact
2 large handfuls flat-leaf (Italian) parsley, chopped

4 garlic cloves, crushed
300 g (10½ oz) caul (optional) (see note)

L'astet

In the south of France, in a little medieval hilltop town called Najac, they cook a dish called pork astet, which is unheard of one train station up or down the line. It is a simple dish that tastes wonderful cold as leftovers — if you can leave any. Crank up the kettle-style barbecue for best results.

SERVES 4–6

Preheat an enclosed hot barbecue or the oven to 220°C (425°F/Gas 7).

Season the insides of the pork with salt and freshly milled black pepper. Mix together the parsley and garlic in a small bowl and spread over the meat on the inside (non-fat side) only.

Roll up the loin to form a log and tie with kitchen string to secure. Better still, experienced cooks may want to use caul (sometimes called pig's lacy) soaked in tepid water with a little lemon juice to soften it, because this adds its own flavour and richness. Place in a roasting tray.

Roast the pork in the enclosed barbecue or in the oven for 1 hour, or until just cooked. Test the meat by inserting a metal skewer and feeling how hot it is at the point that reaches the middle. It should be hot right through and any juices running out should be clear.

Rest under foil for 10 minutes while you get everything else sorted.

Serve slices of l'astet with Roasted Jerusalem Artichokes (see page 360), Fennel Braised in White Wine and Thyme (see page 400), Chunky Roasted Carrot Paste (see page 363), or Warm Potatoes with Dill Mustard Butter (page 359). You could also make a mushroom sauce using the pan juices and sautéed Swiss brown mushrooms boiled with a little reduced red wine. The scraps, as leftovers are known in my house, go well with Roasted Garlic Aïoli (see variation to Mayonnaise on page 201).

Note: Caul, sometimes called pig's lacy, is a fine lattice-like lining from a pig's gut that adds flavour and moisture, while holding things together. It is available from good butchers.

1–2 tablespoons olive oil
4 x 200 g (7 oz) pork neck or
    forequarter chops
2 large red onions, thickly sliced
3–4 large carrots or parsnips,
    cut into rounds

2 whole cloves (if using ground cloves,
    use the amount that perches on a
    pointed knife's tip)
500 ml (17 fl oz/2 cups) draught cider
1 lemon, thinly sliced

Drunken cider chops with lemon

Mass-produced Australian cider is often quite sweet, but this can be fixed with a little lemon juice or a touch of vinegar. The best frying pan to cook these chops in is one that holds them in a single layer. Shredded cabbage makes a nice adjunct, added with the carrots — just use a little extra cider to moisten.

SERVES 4

Preheat the oven to 190°C (375°F/Gas 5).

Heat the oil in a large frying pan or wide-based, flameproof casserole dish over medium heat and fry the chops until they brown wonderfully on both sides — you may want to do this in two batches.

Remove the chops to a clean plate and drain off some of the fat from the pan. In the same pan, cook the onion until it starts to colour. Add the carrot and then return the chops to the pan, spreading them out in one layer, making sure you tip any juices that have dripped from the meat back into the pan. (If you're transferring this to another dish to bake, then place it all in the fresh dish and use the cider and a little water to clean off all those glorious bits stuck on the frying pan and add to the meat.)

Add the cloves and cider and season with salt and freshly milled black pepper, to taste. Lay the lemon slices over the meat, cover, and roast for 45 minutes.

Remove the lid and cook for a further 15–20 minutes, adding a touch more cider or water if it looks like it's drying out; the meat should be tender by this stage.

Serve the pork chops with baked, boiled or mashed potatoes and some greens.

1.5 kg (3 lb 5 oz) pork belly, off the bone,
   skin on
olive oil, for rubbing

Slow-roasted pork belly

Commercial pork producers have just about bred all the flavour out of the meat, making pork chops a dry, chewy tasteless nightmare. Restaurants have learnt, however, that even factory pork belly has heaps more flavour than other cuts, though you have to take care to cook out most of the fat. This dish takes hours in the oven, but can be made a day or two in advance.

SERVES 4

Preheat the oven to 200°C (400°F/Gas 6). Oil the pork skin, lightly rubbing all over with your hands, then season the meat well, particularly the skin, with salt and freshly milled black pepper.

Place the pork belly in a deep roasting tray, skin side up, and place in the oven. After 15 minutes, reduce the oven temperature to 130°C (250°F/Gas 1) and roast for another 4 1/2 hours, checking to see that the bottom doesn't burn, though it should brown nicely.

When the time is up, remove the pork from the tray, draining off as much fat as possible, and place the pork between layers of baking paper. Put the pork on a tray (you can use the baking tray if you like to save washing up) and place another smaller tray on top to cover. Find something heavy to use as a weight to place on the tray — this will press out any extra fat. Allow to rest for 1 hour.

Drain any fat from the tray. If you want to store the pork for another day, store it now by covering and refrigerating.

When you are ready to serve the pork, preheat the oven to 220°C (425°F/Gas 7). Use a sharp knife to cut it into six pieces, from the inside of the flesh out towards the skin. Heat an ovenproof frying pan over high heat and place the pork pieces in the pan. Sear the non-skin side first, then turn over and heat the skin really well. Place in the oven to warm through (the skin tends to puff and become crisp).

Remove from the oven and press down on the pork belly to drain the excess oil onto paper towel. Serve with Braised Red Cabbage (see page 374), or Wilted Kale with Garlic (see page 372), or something lightly acidic to cut the richness, and lots of steamed vegetables.

500 g (1 lb 2 oz) whole starchy
  potatoes, peeled
100 g (3½ oz) butter
1 onion, diced
500 g (1 lb 2 oz) silverbeet (swiss chard),
  washed and shredded

85 ml (2¾ fl oz) full-cream (whole) milk
  (or milk and cream mix)
4 x 120 g (4¼ oz) slices kassler (smoked
  pork loin)
2 teaspoons olive oil

Kassler with silverbeet colcannon

Kassler is a smoked pork loin that is available from continental-style butchers (try it simmered with lentils — yum!), while colcannon is an Irish dish of mashed potato and cabbage. You can use other smoked meats or sausages; just ask for advice at a good butcher. Try cabbage or kale instead of the silverbeet if you wish. Fat slices of speck or bacon make a good alternative to the kassler.

SERVES 4

Steam or boil the potatoes until tender, about 20 minutes, depending on the size. You could cut them to speed up the cooking time.

Meanwhile, heat the butter in a large frying pan over medium heat and fry the onion until translucent. Add the silverbeet and cook for 5-10 minutes, stirring occasionally, until wilted — the stem parts should still retain some bite.

Use a fork or potato masher to coarsely crush the hot potato with the milk, until the milk is absorbed. Add to the silverbeet and season with salt and freshly milled black pepper. Keep warm.

In another frying pan, fry the kassler in a teaspoon of olive oil, or as needed, over a high heat until it is browned on both sides. Tip any of the cooking juices into the colcannon and mix through.

Serve the meat warm over the colcannon, with a few steamed vegetables on the side.

2 kg (4 lb 8 oz) pork rack (loin on the bone or standing pork rib roast)

olive oil or vegetable oil, for rubbing

Roast pork with crackling

Roast pork was the meat that converted me from vegetarianism. Well, crackling was. You don't have to cook pork all the way through these days; having it vaguely pink and moist in the middle is better than dry and overcooked — as can often happen with modern, fast-fattened pork.

SERVES 8

The secret to making unforgettable crackling is to have a good layer of skin, and to score the skin well. So-called 'new fashioned' pork can be a little lacklustre, and older breeds with a good layer of fat work and taste much better as the fat drains out of the roast into the pan. The rest of the fat you can just cut off and discard on your plate.

Take a very sharp knife (or a box cutter) and check that your butcher has scored the pork skin properly. They won't have. It's important that the scoring lines are parallel, starting at the top of the pork, go all the way down the skin, right to the edge, without gaps, and pierce the skin properly to release the fat — this helps the fat to drain and the skin to crisp. The incisions should be about 1 cm (½ inch) apart. Try not to cut right through the fat and into the flesh. Use your hands to rub the oil into the skin so that it is quite moist, then sprinkle over plenty of normal, fine table salt and freshly milled black pepper, evenly dispersing the salt over the skin — this will draw out moisture and ensure success.

Preheat the oven to 250°C (500°F/ Gas 9). Place the pork, skin side up, on a trivet over a deep roasting tray. If you don't have a trivet, use slices of onion to raise the pork from the tray base instead.

Roast the pork for 20–30 minutes, then reduce the oven temperature to 180°C (350°F/Gas 4). Baste the pork if you want by spooning the fat from the bottom of the pan evenly over the meat, then continue roasting for about 1 hour 20 minutes (as a general rule, allow about 20–25 minutes per 500 g (1 lb 2 oz) meat). To be honest, I rarely baste. The pork is ready when the juices run clear after a skewer is inserted into the middle of the meat. It's best to use a metal skewer to check if it is ready — too hot to touch the skewer and it's hot enough to eat.

Carve off the crackling and, if the crackling isn't quite crisp, place it back in the oven on high in the roasting tray to finish it off. Cover the meat with foil and allow it to sit for at least 10 minutes in a warm place — this 'resting' is just as important as the cooking to create moist, flavoursome pork.

Carve the pork either into chops or off the bone into slices and serve with Chunky Roasted Carrot Paste (see page 363), or some other root vegetables and a healthy dose of steamed greens.

50 g (1¾ oz) butter

3 onions, diced

10 thyme sprigs, chopped if tender

80 ml (2½ fl oz/⅓ cup) pork jelly, cooled, plus extra, melted, for filling (see note)

1 kg (2 lb 4 oz) pork shoulder, cut into 1 cm (½ inch) dice, and chilled

900 g (2 lb) hot water pastry (see page 147)

Ross's high-top pork pie

A great mate, Ross O'Meara, who once ran a market stall with me, makes stunning pork pies. I used to put bacon or ham in mine, but his is simpler, letting good pork (and you have to get good pork for this) do the work. If you can't get great pork, replace at least 100 g (3 ½ oz) of the shoulder meat with diced bacon or ham.

SERVES 4

Heat the butter in a large, wide saucepan over low heat and gently cook the onions and thyme until the onions start to caramelise. Allow them to cool, then add the pork jelly and pork to combine well and season with salt and freshly milled black pepper, to taste.

Preheat the oven to 200°C (400°F/ Gas 6). Roll out three-quarters of the pastry to 1 cm (¹/₂ inch) thick all over and use it to line a 20 cm (8 inch) spring-form cake tin or similar. Trim the excess pastry, leaving a 2 cm (³/₄ inch) overhang around the edge.

Spoon the pork mixture into the pastry, pressing gently to exclude any air, leaving the middle a little taller than the outside. Roll the remaining pastry to make a lid and fold the edges over, crimping well to seal, as a lot of moisture comes from the pork as it cooks. Cut a decent-sized hole in the top, about 1 cm (¹/₂ inch), to allow the steam to escape (and more jelly can be poured in the top later). Roll up a piece of foil to use as a pipe and fit it carefully into the hole.

Bake for about 90 minutes, or until the pie crust is golden; it may take up to 2 hours. Remove from the oven and rest for 20 minutes before removing the outside ring of the tin.

After an hour or so, while the pie is still warm, carefully, very carefully, pour in the jelly. This will take some patience, as it has to seep around the now shrunken, cooked pork meat. Don't hurry the process. You can do a little at a time, wait, then pour in some more. A funnel is very helpful.

Chill the pie and serve cold or at room temperature, with pickled onions.

Note: The best way to make a good pork jelly is to boil pork hocks as you would for Homemade Beef Stock (page 224). Replace the beef bones with the same amount of pork hocks, use as little water as possible, and simmer for 3 hours until the liquid reduces to about 600 ml (21 fl oz). Strain and allow to set, then skim off any fat. Season to taste. You will need to melt it again before using.

80 g (2¾ oz) glass noodles
500 ml (17 fl oz/2 cups) boiling water

Sauce
3 dried shiitake mushrooms
125 ml (4 fl oz/½ cup) boiling water
½ Chinese cabbage, cut into large
  chunks
4 cm (1½ inch) piece ginger, halved
500 ml (17 fl oz/2 cups) homemade
  chicken stock (see page 163)
150 ml (5 fl oz) dark soy sauce

Meatballs
400 g (14 oz) minced (ground) pork belly
1 tablespoon dark soy sauce
4 spring onions (scallions), chopped
40 g (1½ oz) water chestnuts, chopped
½ teaspoon sugar
1 egg white, lightly beaten
1–2 tablespoons peanut oil

Lion's head meatballs

Depending on which Chinese person you talk to, the cabbage or the
noodles in this dish are supposed to represent the lion's mane. To achieve
tender meatballs, simmer for 2 hours.

SERVES 4

To make the sauce, put the mushrooms
in a bowl with the boiling water and set
aside to soak for 1 hour, or until soft. Drain
the mushrooms, reserving the liquid too.
Discard the stems and finely chop the caps.
Place in a saucepan with the reserved soaking
water, cabbage, ginger, stock and soy sauce.
Bring to the boil, then turn off the heat until
ready to use.

To make the meatballs, put the minced
pork in a bowl and mix together with the soy
sauce, spring onion, water chestnuts, sugar
and egg white. Season with salt and freshly
milled black pepper, to taste. It's easiest and
most effective to do all this mixing with
your hands.

Divide the pork mixture into four
portions and shape into large meatballs.
Heat the oil in a frying pan over high heat
and cook the meatballs, turning regularly,
until brown all over.

Transfer the meatballs to the pan with
the sauce and simmer in the sauce over low
heat, covered, for at least 1 hour.

Put the noodles in a bowl with the boiling
water and soak for 1 minute. Drain well and
rinse in cold water. Add the noodles to the
sauce at the last minute to cook through.

Serve the meatballs with the sauce
spooned over and steamed rice on the side.

1 kg (2 lb 4 oz) dried cannellini or
    white/northern beans
500 g (1 lb 2 oz) pork belly
300 g (10½ oz) speck, pancetta or bacon
3 carrots
3 onions
2 cloves
4 garlic cloves
2 bay leaves
2 teaspoons salt

1–2 tablespoons rendered pork fat
    (see note), or use duck or goose fat,
    or olive oil
500 g (1 lb 2oz) lean pork shoulder
    or neck, diced
1 kg (2 lb 4 oz) minced (ground) pure
    thick pork sausage
250 g (9 oz/1 cup) tinned chopped
    tomatoes
150 g (5½ oz) fresh breadcrumbs

Pure pork cassoulet

*I know a man who makes cheese, who knows a man who breeds pigs that
like eating whey, who knows a bloke who wants to make sausages. That's
lucky, because I always want cassoulet in winter, and good pork sausages
are an essential component. Cassoulet is a homely bean casserole that is
a hearty peasant dish with noble aspirations. This fantastic, must-share
recipe makes a lot and is perfect for large dinner parties. You will need to
use a very large pot, or divide into two large casserole dishes and keep one
for another day. It's best to finish the final stage of cooking on the day you
want to eat it, rather than cook both dishes to the end stage and keeping it.
You will need to soak the beans overnight before you begin cooking, and
be sure to get starch-free sausages for best results.*

SERVES 4

Put the cannellini beans in a bowl and cover
with cold water. Set aside to soak for at least
5 hours, or preferably overnight. For most
recipes you can get away without soaking,
with cassoulet it will be less successful if you
don't, but you can still do it, they'll just take
longer to cook. Rinse and drain well.

Place the beans, pork belly, speck,
1 whole carrot, 1 whole onion spiked with
the cloves, 2 of the garlic cloves and the bay
leaves in a large saucepan. Add salt and pour
over enough cold water to cover. Bring to the

boil, then reduce the heat and simmer for
45 minutes, or until the beans are nearly
cooked. Drain the meat and vegetables;
reserve the cooking water and discard the
onion, carrot, bay leaves and garlic.

Meanwhile, heat ½ tablespoon of the
pork fat in a frying pan over medium–high
heat and cook the pork shoulder and sausages
in two batches for 8–10 minutes, or until
brown. Remove to a bowl. Discard the fat
from cooking. Cut the sausages into bite-
sized pieces, reserving any cooking juices.

Place the sausage and pork shoulder in a large saucepan with 2 diced carrots, 2 diced onions, 2 cloves crushed garlic, the tomato, and 1.5 litres (52 fl oz/6 cups) water. Season with salt and freshly milled black pepper, bring to the boil, then reduce the heat and simmer gently for 1 hour.

Preheat the oven to 150°C (300°F/Gas 2). Remove the skin from the pork belly and speck and dice the meat. Place the skin, fat side down, in a very large pot, or divide into two large 3 litre (105 fl oz/12 cup) casserole dishes. Add the cannellini beans, pork belly and speck, the sausage and pork shoulder and their vegetables and liquid and stir to combine. Add enough of the bean cooking liquid to just cover the other ingredients. Sprinkle with half the breadcrumbs and dot with about 1/2 tablespoon of fat (or splash on if liquid).

Cook the cassoulet in the oven for 1 hour — topping up with more bean cooking liquid if necessary and stirring occasionally. If you are cooking it in two casserole dishes and not planning on eating it all immediately, remove one from the heat and allow to cool before storing in the refrigerator for up to 3 days.

You will then need to finish off cooking it on the day you plan to eat it. Taste at this stage for salt and pepper.

Top with the remaining breadcrumbs and fat. Cook in the oven for another 2 hours, checking that the liquid doesn't fall much below the top of the beans and meat, adding more of the bean cooking liquid, or water if that runs out. It should have a golden crust on top.

Allow to stand for 30 minutes before serving. Serve with rustic white bread and a voluptuous pinot.

Note: Rendered fat is the runny fat that comes out when you cook back fat with a tiny amount of water over low heat in a covered saucepan. Lard is the commercial equivalent, which is fine for this dish.

4 tablespoons olive oil

400 g (14 oz) pure pork chipolatas

200 g (7 oz) unripe sour green grapes

Chipolatas with sour green grapes

This is the kind of dish you'd have in the vineyard when thinning out the fruit and feeding the farm workers. It doesn't work so well with sweet table grapes, but you could try them and splash over roughly one tablespoon of verjuice (unripe grape juice) instead. Just adapt the recipe to the home kitchen if you're not, sadly, in the vineyard yourself.

SERVES 4

Heat the oil in a frying pan (preferably cast-iron) over a small fire that has burnt down to coals (or medium heat). Ideally the fire is of vine trimmings. Fry the chipolatas to brown all over and when they're just cooked through, after about 5 minutes, throw in the grapes. Allow them to sizzle in the pan a little as you take it from the heat.

Serve with chargrilled bread and vegetables with a little more olive oil on the side, and a glass of something red and dusty.

GAME

It's 1996. The hills resound with gunshot. It's autumn in Umbria, central Italy's hilly, wild region where real men hunt and fish, and women cook like angels. It also happens to be mushroom season, so I keep my head down and my ears pricked when foraging for porcini. You know you're in an Italian version of the wild west when the local pasta, strangozzi, is named after the garrotte used to strangle tax collectors during the time of the papal states. Italy's wild west is still full of fishers and hunters at just about any time of the year.

Hunting is how humans first learnt to gather fresh meat. It's an ancient, primeval, perhaps questionable way of putting animals on the table. But most of the so-called game you'll find on dinner plates these days isn't actually wild, like the boars Umbrian hunters will bring home. Game also refers to former game meats that are now farmed, such as goat, camel, pheasant (and other game birds), deer (venison), boar, ostrich, buffalo and rabbit.

In Australia, game includes wallaby, kangaroo, crocodile and emu, as well as feral pig, goat, buffalo, pigeon and rabbit sold for human consumption. On the fringes lie magpie geese and mutton bird, which are less widely consumed. Australian Indigenous people also eat snake, goanna, turtle and other wild foods that they have traditional rights to.

REAL WILD GAME

Wild game is, by its nature, of indeterminate age. This means it can be really, really old, tough and full of flavour — or younger, sweeter, yet still firm in texture from its wild existence. It can be hormonal (particularly males), stringy, and is often a challenge for the novice cook. For an experienced cook, or those used to the exaggerated flavour of wild meat, it's a joy that farmed meats can only dream of delivering.

I've eaten wild pigeon cooked over coals in a Tokyo izakaya (bar) and had my world altered. For the better. I've been in the kitchen of a house in southern Wales when a mysterious knock on the door delivered poached pheasant swinging from the hunter's hand, still feathered and warm from the woods. I like kangaroo and wallaby, the sweet meat tasting like an interesting variation on beef.

Wild game often favours long, slow cooking. It usually benefits from marinades; something with acid to help break down the flesh. Truly wild game has such strong, savoury aromas that it goes far better with fruit than its domesticated brethren. It's usually leaner meat, meaning anything besides the most tender cut is best wet-roasted or braised, stewed or simmered for hours, rather than given a simple grilling (broiling).

FARMED GAME

Most game sold these days is actually meat from former game animals that are 'domesticated'. This meat is quite different to its feral counterpart. Wild venison, for instance, is nothing like farmed venison. Some might describe the meat from farmed deer as 'polite' or 'restrained' or even 'bland'. I don't, but I do think farmed game has a far more elegant, subtle and often more containable flavour that can be awful if you use a recipe designed for wild food.

The trick is to adapt the recipes you know or have read from wild meat to farmed. A farmed pheasant may only need to be roasted for 20 minutes, a wild bird for 90 minutes. Farmed goat meat is marvellous as a substitute for two-tooth or mutton, or even lamb. It's strong enough to carry good spicy flavours, but not completely feral. Properly hung farmed venison, where it has spent at least three weeks dry-ageing, has complexity and sophistication, without being so funky that it puts hair on your palms.

WHAT DOES THE EXPRESSION 'HIGH' MEAN?

Traditionally, in colder climates, game is often hung to help soften the flesh (similar to dry-ageing, see page 220). Sometimes it is hung whole — with skin or feathers on, and guts still in. They used to say you should hang a game bird by its legs, and eat it when it fell to the ground, after the flesh had decomposed enough that it broke free at the joints.

This decomposition, particularly with the guts inside, causes what's called a 'high' smell. Some would call it putrid. The meat's not quite putrid or off, but dangerously close to both. Varying degrees of this high, gamey character are sought after in countries that pride themselves on wild game, such as the UK and France. The selling of whole game animals that aren't plucked, or skinned, and drawn, along with the hanging of game with fur or feathers still on, is illegal in a commercial sense in Australia. You can, however, do it for your own consumption, but there is still the risk of food poisoning.

A WORD ON RABBITS

The difference between farmed and wild rabbits is marked. Wild, they're full-flavoured, of darker meat, usually tough and old and need quite a lot of cooking. Farmed, they are kept in cages, are invariably white furred, are fleshier, have super lean meat, and are, in my view, just a shadow of what rabbit should taste like. Their white meat can be milder than commercial chicken, and that's saying something, though the flavour is really attractive if it's not swamped by spices or other strong-tasting ingredients.

For the cook, the main difference between farmed and wild rabbits is how to approach them. Farmed rabbits are so lean that they should be gently cooked, particularly the loin, which can dry out terribly (worse than factory-farmed chicken). The legs can be braised longer than the loin, stewed with a light medley of sweet onion, root vegetables and white wine. Wild rabbits are best cooked for long, long periods, with stronger flavours; think lots of French shallots, red wine, perhaps some olives, star anise and sausages.

THE ETHICS OF WILD GAME

I used to think of hunters with some kind of distant horror. How could they want to kill things, often majestic beasts that walked free, simply to eat them? But if you compare the life of a wild beast to that of those we factory farm, it's a far better, more natural, fully instinctual life. How they die, obviously, has the potential to be more painful than their domesticated cousins if it isn't instant, but all animals must die, so that of itself is no reason to avoid game.

What worries me is that some hunters, many in fact, like to hunt for sport; a form of bloodlust that seems incongruous with modern society. People who go out and kill things just for the fun of killing them, well, that seems to show a strange attitude to the sanctity of life, and not one that I want to encourage.

If you're comfortable eating meat, and the game is shot humanely, and taken sustainably (or in the case of Australia, feral animals culled to benefit native species), then wild game is an option with just as much going for it as other ways of producing meat.

BUYING WILD GAME

You can hardly buy wild game legally in Australia. There are mutton birds from the south of the country, rabbits from all over, plus wallaby and kangaroo in most jurisdictions. Wild deer, wild duck and wild pheasant, however, and other wild animals are usually not available commercially, or hard to find. Sometimes wild goat and wild boar are available at markets. Most of Australia's wild harvest of goats and pigs is exported.

In the UK there are game specialists and good butchers who can source game in the season. In the US you can buy wild elk, boar, rabbit and turkey from specialty suppliers.

If you're buying game, older birds will have pin feathers that are almost impossible to remove, and firm-feeling breast meat. The presence of pin feathers will give an indication of age. Old game meats will be darker than young game meats, but it's best to assume all game will need extended cooking.

If you're worried about sustainable game, only eat feral species or species that you've done the research on and feel comfortable eating.

ARE WE OVERHUNTING?

Yes. Not everywhere, but in many places, yes. There are many examples, worldwide, of species lost or endangered due to overhunting. Here are two. In just four days in 2000, the southern Chinese regional government of Guangdong confiscated 17,582 protected wild animals from food markets and restaurants.

Those Umbrian boars that the rough-faced Italians hunt these days aren't the native pig anymore. Those were wiped from the landscape thanks to overhunting in the 1950s. Modern pigs have been brought in from Croatia and other eastern European states to replenish stocks and keep an age-old custom alive.

In southern French markets, the wild boar saucisson (dry-cured sausage) is often made with Australian feral pig, thanks to the paucity of a local option.

2-3 tablespoons duck fat or lard

1 leek, white part only, rinsed and
　chopped

4 garlic cloves, chopped

1.5-2 kg (3 lb 5 oz-4 lb 8 oz) whole rabbit
　or duck

2 x 4 cm (1½ inch) strips mandarin
　or orange peel

1 cinnamon stick

1-2 whole star anise

20 whole black peppercorns

1 teaspoon salt

lard or butter, for sealing

Rabbit rillettes

*Rillettes are a wonderful pasty, meaty concoction, kind of like a cross
between a pâté and a terrine. They're best served at room temperature,
with good tiny pickled gherkins (cornichons), pickled onions or even
homemade Pickled Cucumber (see page 384). Rillettes are not for the
faint-hearted, as they are a bit rich — though you can reduce the fat
and leave them more moist at the end). You can also make this recipe
using duck instead of rabbit.*

SERVES 10

Heat 1 tablespoon of the duck fat in a heavy-based saucepan over low heat and gently fry the leek and garlic for 5 minutes, or until soft. Remove with a slotted spoon.

Joint the rabbit or duck into 10 pieces (see note), pulling away any loose fat and discarding any liver or kidneys for another use. Fry the loose fat in the same pan you cooked the leek, for a couple of minutes. Add the meat in two batches and fry over a medium heat until well browned. Return the first batch to the pan.

Return the leek and garlic to the pan. Add the mandarin peel, spices, salt and 500 ml (17 fl oz/2 cups) water. Cover, bring to the boil, then reduce the heat to a gentle simmer. Cook for 2-3 hours, or until the meat is falling off the bone, adding more water if it starts to dry out, and checking the meat isn't sticking to the bottom. (You can also cook it in a low oven or a pressure cooker.)

Remove the meat with tongs and allow to cool. Pour the cooking liquid through a fine sieve, discarding the solids. Shred the meat finely with your fingertips, checking very carefully for bones. If you have a mortar and pestle, pound it in small amounts, just until it starts to clump together. (You can pulse it in a food processor if you prefer.)

Place the meat with the strained cooking liquid in a saucepan and simmer to form a dryish paste. Stir through the remaining duck fat and taste for salt and freshly milled black pepper. Press into 250 ml (9 fl oz/1 cup) ceramic dishes.

If you want to keep it for a few days, melt some lard or butter and pour over to seal.

Note: You can cut the rabbit roughly into pieces to help them brown. Avoid the hard leg bones though, or get your butcher to do it.

2 tablespoons vegetable oil

5–6 small dried red chillies

8 whole green cardamom pods

1.2 kg (2 lb 10 oz) diced goat shin or shoulder

2 large onions, chopped

5 cm (2 inch) piece ginger, thinly sliced

1 teaspoon salt

1 teaspoon cumin seeds

2 teaspoons coriander seeds

¼ teaspoon green cardamom seeds

2 tablespoons pouring (whipping) cream (35% fat)

1 teaspoon garam masala

Goat shin curry

Most of the 'mutton' used in India to make a meat curry is actually goat. The flavour is wonderful, but you could try lamb, hogget or mutton instead.

SERVES 4

Heat the oil in a large, heavy-based frying pan over high heat and add the chillies and cardamom pods. When they start to crackle, add half the goat and brown it on all sides. Remove the meat with a spoon, leaving behind the spices, then fry the remaining goat. Remove the meat and spices with a slotted spoon and set to one side.

In the same pan, fry the onion and ginger with the salt until well browned. Remove from the heat and keep to one side.

Roast the seeds very gently in a clean, dry frying pan for 2 minutes, or until aromatic but not dark.

Place the dry-fried spices (if you're using a food processor, the spices should be ground separately first), onion and ginger in a blender or food processor and blend to a paste. Add 125 ml (4 fl oz/½ cup) water to moisten if necessary.

Return the meat and spices to the pan with the paste and add 250 ml (9 fl oz/1 cup) water. Cover and simmer for 2 hours, or until tender — checking occasionally to ensure it doesn't dry out.

Stir through the cream and garam masala. Serve the curry with steamed basmati rice.

1–2 tablespoons vegetable oil or ghee

1 kg (2 lb 4 oz) venison or beef shanks, sliced osso buco-style (ask your butcher to do this)

2 large onions, finely sliced

5 cm (2 inch) piece ginger, grated

3 garlic cloves, crushed

1 cinnamon stick

1–2 small dried red chillies

5 brown cardamom pods (or use about 20 smaller green ones)

1 teaspoon ground cumin

½ teaspoon ground coriander

1 large tomato, chopped, or use 200 g (7 oz) tinned chopped tomatoes

Dark curry of venison with cardamom

The trick to a good curry often lies with the flavourings — especially fresh 'herbs', such as onion, ginger and garlic. In this curry they have to be gently browned by slow cooking. Faster cooking can also brown the onion, giving an okay but less persistent flavour, so the longer and slower you can cook it, the better. This Indian-style curry uses big brown cardamom pods to give the meat a tremendously aromatic note. South-East Asian green cardamom pods are an alright substitute. Try it with beef, mutton or goat if you want, or even use the shin meat off the bone. As usual with curry, it's best the next day.

SERVES 4–5

Heat 1 tablespoon of the oil in a large saucepan over medium heat and fry the meat for about 5 minutes, turning over when each side turns a good tan colour. You may need to do this in two batches. Remove the meat and keep to one side.

In the same pan, possibly adding more oil to ensure it cooks properly, fry the onion very slowly until it softens and starts to colour. I like to add a pinch of salt while it fries to draw out moisture. Add the ginger and garlic and keep frying, stirring often, until it all goes a nice light brown colour. It may stick a bit, which is fine, but try to scrape the base of the pan with a wooden spatula if it looks like it may burn.

Add the cinnamon, chillies and cardamom pods and stir until fragrant, about another 2 minutes. Stir in the cumin and coriander and fry for 30 seconds. Add the tomato and about 500 ml (17 fl oz/2 cups) water, or enough to barely cover. Stir to rub off any bits stuck to the base of the pan.

Return the meat to the pan. Season with salt and freshly milled black pepper, to taste. Cover and cook for 90 minutes, or until the meat falls from the bone. You can do this in a 150°C (300°F/Gas 2) oven if you like, but if cooking it on the stove, stir occasionally to stop it scorching on the bottom.

Serve the curry with steamed basmati rice, pappadums and Raita (see page 52).

Rabbit cacciatore with potato & rosemary

This recipe is designed for farmed rabbit. Wild rabbit, being tougher and of indeterminate age, needs a much longer cooking time, usually a couple of hours or more. The subtle use of wine makes a delicate sauce, as farmed rabbit can be fairly light-on for flavour.

1.2 kg (2 lb 10 oz) whole rabbit, though jointed by the butcher is probably easier to manage
2 tablespoons extra virgin olive oil
1 small red onion, cut into wedges
6 garlic cloves
1 rosemary sprig
250 ml (9 fl oz/1 cup) dry white wine
500 g (1 lb 2 oz) baby pink eye, nicola or dutch cream potatoes

SERVES 4

Preheat the oven to 180°C (350°F/Gas 4). Place the rabbit and all the other ingredients in a casserole dish or large ovenproof saucepan, season well with salt and freshly milled black pepper, and cover. Bake for about 1 hour, or until the meat is tender. Serve the rabbit with the sauce around and the potatoes for crushing into the sauce.

Note: Add a diced tomato or two if you feel the dish needs more depth.

Chapter 5

SEAFOOD

SEAFOOD

Morrie Wolf has lived a few lives. Four hip operations, a chance meeting with God that led to a religious conversion, and fifty years after first putting out to sea, Morrie no longer has the ability to fish for southern rock lobsters (crayfish). Instead, he now drops lines and nets for fish, and takes recreational anglers out off the southern coast of Australia in an attempt to hook tuna, or striped trumpeter, or trevalla.

The fish that Morrie catches could be served in the finest restaurants in the world. It's immaculate fish that tastes as good as you'll find anywhere. But all that is coming to a close. What our descendants will get to eat in the future may not include the majestic seafood I've been fortunate enough to enjoy in my lifetime. And it may include few wild fish at all, unless you earn a fortune.

There will be far fewer Morrie Wolfs in years to come, thanks to overfishing and a scramble to buy back licences worldwide. It's estimated that there's been a 40 per cent drop in biodiversity around the world's coastlines since 1800, and that about one-third of all commercial fisheries are now practically defunct. I've been alive while much of it has happened, and not even realised. To my shame I probably ate as much critically endangered tuna during the five years I worked as a restaurant reviewer as my child is likely to see in his hopefully long life.

I should've seen what was coming when, in the year 2000, I stood with Ari, a Finnish salmon and herring fisherman, at his home on an island in Helsinki Harbour. He looked crushed, this being yet another day when he came back from sea without a single salmon from a morning's work. This is not a specific case. You can see the loss of wild fish in the catches brought back by picturesque blue fishing boats as they arrive next to the markets at Trani in southern Italy; paltry catches of mostly small fish, perhaps too small to have bred yet. There's so little southern bluefin tuna caught these days where it used to be fished on the NSW coast near where I grew up that the line-caught fishery has all but closed. Around the world, fishing is in crisis.

It's a sad combination of factors that has led to this condition, and many people now place their hope in fish farming to provide good seafood into the future.

WHY FARMED ISN'T NECESSARILY BETTER

According to sustainable fisheries advocate, the Australian Marine Conservation Society (AMCS), it can take up to 2–4 kg (4 lb 8 oz–8 lb) of wild fish turned into feed to produce 1 kg (2 lb 4 oz) of farmed salmon, and up to 12 kg (26 lb) to produce 1 kg (2 lb 4 oz) of tuna. This fish meal is taken from wild stocks, which must have some, probably as yet undocumented, impact on ocean ecology. And did you know that the impact of intensive fish farms on the ocean floor could have tragic consequences for the wild populations and the environment? Fish farming is an industry that has a chequered history in environmental terms, all around the globe.

Nobody talks about it much where I live, as farmed fish takes on a 'clean, green' profile thanks to the undeveloped waterways used to fatten them. It's a huge industry that provides plenty of well-needed jobs, too. But sea-cage aquaculture doesn't yet get a sustainability tick from the AMCS. Inland-farmed fish, such as trout and Murray cod, and even freshwater-reared salmon, may well have better environmental outcomes, though the food issue is still a problem.

WHAT ELSE WAS IN THE NET?

Some people may remember the campaign waged against the manufacturers of tuna, and how it had an impact. When you buy seafood, think of what other things may get caught in the net. Some fisheries ensnare seals, dolphins, turtles and more. Some prawn (shrimp) fisheries have a bycatch of unwanted species in the ratio of ten to one — ten times as much bycatch as prawns. Think sustainable: line caught is better than net caught, and some nets are worse than others. Scallop dredging can decimate sponge gardens and the sea floor. Concerned consumers can encourage fisheries to be more responsible.

WHAT NOT TO BUY

It will depend on where you live, because of the vast number of fish species worldwide. Check out your local marine conservation agencies for the most relevant and up-to-date information.

In Australia, according to the AMCS, southern bluefin tuna should be off the menu entirely until stocks replenish. Goodbye swordfish, eastern gemfish (hake), redfish and anything from sea-cage aquaculture (ocean trout, salmon, some kingfish, barramundi and yellowtail). But it's hello to trevalla, hand-dived scallops, leatherjacket and western rock lobsters.

The AMCS publishes Australia's Sustainable Seafood Guide, an app and website designed to help you decide what's not so good to buy, what's good to buy and what to say no to; visit www.amcs.org.au. Another Australian resource, one that uses various measures of sustainability, is www.goodfishbadfish.com.au.

For international fisheries there are various organisations. One, the prestigious international Marine Stewardship Council, also certifies fisheries as sustainable. See www.msc.org.

THE END OF WILD FISH IN OUR LIFETIME

Strange as it may seem, the ecology of our oceans and the total breeding cycle of some fish are still something of a mystery. A lack of research, combined with overfishing in the past and the unknown effects of global warming, mean the future of what we'll eat from the sea is in question.

Fisheries management is now cracking down on unsustainability, but the number of local species classified as overfished in Australia (where, according to the United Nations, we've got a great reputation for more sustainable fisheries) still rose from five in 1992 to twenty-four in 2005. By 2021, a study found that 38 per cent of the nation's fish stocks were overfished. And that's with 60 per cent of the nation's catch coming from unassessed stocks. We don't even know what we have, let alone how many to catch.

It's even more precarious in the northern hemisphere, where they're predicting a collapse of most commercial fisheries by 2050. A David Suzuki Foundation report found that Pacific salmon have disappeared from 40 per cent of their range in Canada over the past hundred years, and that there has been extinction of 140 stocks of salmon in one region alone. Canada's Committee on the Status of Endangered Wildlife found that only two out of 29 wild chinook salmon populations aren't at risk of extinction.

A 2008 report by the UN claimed that we could halve the number of boats in the world fishing fleet and still catch the same number of fish. Low numbers of fish are leading to high costs, so if we let numbers rebound, we could catch the same quantity of fish with much less effort. Today, 30 per cent of global fisheries are overfished, a number that has remained unchanged for over three decades. One thing is for sure, wild fish are in demand, and as demand outstrips supply, prices will rise sharply.

In Australia the labelling laws aren't particularly helpful. We don't even know if the tuna in a tin is local, or what species of tuna it is, let alone if it's from a sustainable fishery. I'm no fan of overwrought labelling laws (how many people do you know who actually read the ingredient list and nutrition panel and then put the food back on the shelf?), but knowing where your food is coming from, particularly if it's of questionable origins, isn't a big ask.

WHY FRESH ISN'T ALWAYS BETTER THAN FROZEN

You know the finest prawns (shrimp) and scampi in the best restaurants, and their incomparable flavour? Well even if you don't, it's worth noting that one of Australia's best restaurants uses frozen scampi. The reason is the quick processing time after capture. Some produce, particularly crustaceans — prawns, scampi, crabs — degrades quickly and can be better frozen than fresh. Raw prawns that aren't frozen are usually dipped in sodium metabisulphite to stop their heads turning black, which some people say harms the flavour more than freezing. Wild prawns cooked on board the trawler can be better than fresh if frozen within minutes.

Restaurants in Italy and stores in Japan both have rules saying that labelling must tell you if the seafood has been frozen. Labelling in other countries is less useful.

BUYING SEAFOOD

Seafood shouldn't smell fishy. It should smell of the ocean. The flesh of fish should be glistening, rather than soggy or dry. Whole fish should have a nice gleam to the eye, and perhaps some moist slime on the skin — that's how they are when they come from the ocean.

Prawns shouldn't have black heads, and mussels should be as tightly shut as a boxer's fist.

Frozen seafood is best bought still frozen (rather than 'thawed for your convenience'), and then thawed gently in the refrigerator.

HOW DO I STORE SEAFOOD?

The easy answer? Don't store seafood: buy it to eat the same day, as it loses quality very quickly. If you do store it, keep it very cold — colder than refrigerator cold. Put fish in a container where water can drain off (use a cake rack or upturned saucer in the bottom) and sprinkle with crushed ice. Cover with plastic wrap so it doesn't dry out, and store in the bottom of the refrigerator so raw fish juices don't spill onto anything below.

Some live seafood, such as crabs, oysters and mussels, have different needs (for instance, ice Pacific oysters, but don't ice Sydney rock oysters). Ask your fishmonger, but refrigerate if in doubt.

TO LEMON, OR NOT TO LEMON?

Every culture has its techniques to deal with the complex flavours and aromas of seafood. Lemon, particularly, is considered brilliant in most contexts, thanks to the influence of the English and French. The Chinese use ginger, Italians may use bay leaves.

The trick is to match flavours. Southern hemisphere seafood is often very delicately flavoured compared to many cold-water species popular in the northern hemisphere, so even lemon may overwhelm. But a touch of acid, be it lime or lemon or vinegar, does add nuances and negates any slightly odd aromas.

A general rule is, the oilier the fish — so, the more off-white the colour — the more it benefits from the addition of other flavours. Think sardines versus whiting.

FISH

Wild fish, like animals that can graze rather than being fed only one type of food, can be a more interesting thing to eat than their farmed counterparts. There's more complexity in the flavour. They usually have better texture, because they've been able to swim freely, some up streams, or against currents (and, usually, away from predators). By definition they can be more inconsistent than farmed fish, but on average are possibly better.

WILD FISH

This is the seafood most of us think of when we think of fish and shellfish. It's the stuff that we imagine Greek fishing boats are unloading on Santorini, that the men in yellow waterproof caps are bringing back to shore on the coast of the UK, and weathered Australians are catching off the vast coastline. It's the fish we catch when we dangle a line off a jetty or a tinny, fish that breeds and swims in the wild, and is caught on lines or nets, as it has been for centuries.

If things don't change, however, wild fish will be a distant memory for many people, as fisheries reach commercial extinction, prices skyrocket, and pressure is put on the numerous wild fish populations by increasing world population, pollution and the rapid increase in technology available to fishers.

The thing is, wild fish has been taken for granted for too long. It's not been recognised, until some fisheries have collapsed, that wild fish is a finite resource — a remarkable resource that has been undervalued, if not squandered. Sadly, much is used to feed other animals — chickens, pigs and farmed fish — as well as being used in fish-oil tablets.

FARMED FISH

Like it or not, farmed seafood is here to stay. With 76 per cent of the world's fisheries believed to be in crisis, according to the UN, and others under pressure — with the once innumerable cod now barely catchable in some regions, and wild salmon and herring fisheries devastated — the way of the future, for many, is aquaculture: fish farms.

Already, farmed salmon outnumber their wild cousins fifty to one. Already, the endangered southern bluefin tuna is herded into pens and fattened for sushi before it's had time to mate. Already, fish farming contributes the vast majority of prawns (shrimp) that make it to our tables, thanks to the so-called 'trash fish' that are used to make fish meal and prawn feed. It seems as if the way we've been plundering the world's oceans simply isn't sustainable. By some estimates, the number of large fin fish (that is, fish that aren't shellfish) in wild fisheries has dropped by 80 per cent over the last century.

Aquaculture can be separated into three broad groups. There's inland farming, where freshwater (and sometimes brackish water) is used in ponds, dams, lakes or tanks, and the effluent can be monitored. There's sea aquaculture of shellfish — oysters and mussels — which simply feed off the seawater they filter through their bodies. And there's fish farming in the ocean. Of these three methods, the most contentious is the last, because fish farming in the ocean has no containment for escaped fish, for effluent or for excess feed, and it relies on nature to flush the water clean.

Within this category of offshore fish farming, some of the so-called farms don't actually breed new stock at all. Take southern bluefin tuna 'farming', which isn't true farming at all, but rather a fattening of wild fish. This species, once considered to be on the verge of commercial extinction, is gathered as it migrates around Australia's southern coastline. Only 13 per cent of the original biomass of southern bluefin tuna is left. It's classified as 'overfished' by the Australian government, yet it is unknown whether southern bluefin tuna is still subject to overfishing as I write. Spotted by plane, schools of juveniles are herded into nets, which are then dragged closer to shore, where the fish are caged and fattened. Very few escape the nets to continue their migration east, and none of those caught ever breed to replenish their stocks. The fishermen who learnt the trick have taken the same technology to the Adriatic, where giant bluefin stocks are being similarly decimated.

For the most part, oysters, scallops and mussels are farmed in a way that is considered to have less of an impact on the environment and is therefore sustainable.

CRITICISMS OF SEA-CAGE FISH FARMING

Critics of fish farming are concerned about a few things. A major problem is the feed, much of which comes from bycatch from wild fish stocks. While some might find salmon a nicer fish to eat than much of the bycatch, simply ripping a species from the sea could have long-term ecological implications that we don't know about, given that some fish species are specifically targeted to make fish meal for fish farms. Other things in the feed include chicken meal (from bone and meat), feather meal (from, you know, chicken feathers), mammalian blood and bone, soy beans, canola, and astaxanthin, a colouring agent to turn flesh orange. The problem with changing the protein content from wild fish to chicken meal and blood and bone is that these are low in beneficial omega-3 oil, meaning the omega-3 content of farmed salmon is far lower than that of wild-caught fish.

Some people are worried about the desertification of the seabed underneath fish pens. The concentrated excrement from the fish, along with any uneaten feed, falls to the ocean floor and has been shown to kill existing sea life. Very modern fish farms may have underwater cameras to show when feed is falling through the cages, so they don't waste food, or have as much of an impact on the sea floor. Sea cages are also moved from time to time and areas left fallow to prevent desertification, though this depends on the rules in each area, and the operator's desire to move them. Deep-water locations and areas of high water flow are preferred for sea cages.

Another criticism of fish farms is their use of antibiotics. The fish farm I went to (see the Case Study on page 312), and others near where I live, don't tend to use antibiotics after the first few weeks of life, unless there's a disease outbreak. But the reality is that antibiotics have been found in wild fish that live near the sea cages. The amount of antibiotic used in Tasmania increased from 12 kg (26 lb) in 1997 to 8 tonnes in 2007, but dropped below 2 tonnes in 2019, and lower still in other years.

In the northern hemisphere, farmed salmon have been found to have PCBs (polychlorinated biphenyls) and other toxins in their flesh. This may come from the areas they're farmed in, or the fish meal they're fed. This is less of a problem in the southern hemisphere. Northern hemisphere farms also have to worry about the impact on wild salmon (escapees, antibiotic-resistant bacteria, genetically modified fish, perilous numbers of sea lice), whereas there are no true wild salmon that can interbreed with escapees from fish farms in Australia and New Zealand.

SHOULD I BE AFRAID OF HEAVY METALS?

No. Most fish you'll eat are perfectly fine, so long as you limit your intake to two or three times a week (more in the cleaner southern oceans). Some species such as swordfish, shark (often called flake), marlin, tuna and broadbill do contain mercury in an amount that could, in quantity, pose a risk to pregnant women and nursing mothers, and to children under the age of six years. Everybody else is usually fine. If in any doubt, stick to the recommended serving size of 150 g (5½ oz) of these species for pregnant women, and 75 g (2½ oz) for children under six.

WHAT IS 'SASHIMI GRADE'?

This term recognises what the Japanese hold dear. Because they eat fish raw, there's no hiding its faults: better fishing, better handling, better killing of fish means it is stressed less and tastes better. Line-caught (as opposed to 'net caught') fish, which are brain-spiked, bled (if it's tuna, swordfish or another warmer-blooded fish), and then ice-slurried straight away (iki-jime) have superior eating qualities compared to fish treated with less respect. Hence they're more expensive, and can be eaten raw with confidence, while also being suitable to cook. Sadly, the term 'sashimi grade' isn't enforceable by law.

WHAT SAUCE FOR WHAT FISH?

Oily fish often taste better with a bolder sauce. So while whiting is best with a hint of lemon and a winning smile, sardines can be stuffed with herbed breadcrumbs and served with a caper sauce. The whiter, cleaner-flavoured the fish, the lighter the sauce. Heavier-tasting fish, such as mackerel, is more likely to marry well with robust sauces, such as tomato-based ones, curries and the like.

OCEAN TROUT: A CASE STUDY

It's a diamond-hard morning on Macquarie Harbour on the wild west coast of Tasmania, in 2008. The previous week it was hailing, but today the brackish, tea-coloured harbour, which is about seven times as big as Sydney Harbour, is as smooth as fondant. The surface is being sliced by the bow of the charter boat MV *Second Nature* as we steer our way from the harbour town of Strahan to the sea cages off Table Head. I'm heading out to visit one of Macquarie Harbour's famed fish farms, one specialising in ocean trout. Today, the team from Petuna seafoods are pulling 3500 fish out of the harbour, to be sold across the country and the world.

Ocean trout are rainbow trout that have been transferred to saltwater early in their life and grown out to a much bigger size than inland-farmed trout. They are bred specifically to be ocean trout, and many people find them virtually indistinguishable from farmed Atlantic salmon. They have been in Australia since early last century, and they thrive in the wild in Tasmania's icy inland streams, but can't survive very long, for some reason, out of pens in the saltwater.

A 'hen' trout produces about 6500 eggs per season. That's an awful lot of potential offspring, considering they tend to just replace themselves in the wild, and are lucky to do so, with the deteriorating condition of many of the world's rivers. In captivity, however, many of them will one day become full-sized ocean trout.

Every last fish in this sea cage, which is 120 metres (394 feet) in circumference, will meet its maker today. All 45 tonnes of the fish, which weigh about 3–4 kg (7 –8 lb) each, will be lifted by crane onto the killing ship for a very quick dispatch. They drop down a chute, are stunned by a machine that gives a firm blow to the head, and then pass down to the waiting deck hands, who slit them to allow them to bleed. It looks gruesome, but these fish, compared to wild fish, actually die a very quick, relatively painless death.

Two gleaming trout slip overboard as they thrash to get out of the net that lifts them from the cage. It's a short reprieve, as there's a seal waiting nearby for just such a chance. (One salmon farmer I spoke to offered to show me a seal's head in his freezer.) Even if the seal doesn't get them, the fish's days are still numbered. Ocean trout, just like Atlantic salmon and saltwater charr (a close relative of both trout and salmon), don't survive wild in Australian coastal waters. Instead, they are all fed a steady diet of pellets and separated from the seals in sea cages, 70 of which are owned by this company alone.

Petuna have over a million fish in the water at Macquarie Harbour. Today alone they'll use 12 tonnes of fish pellets to feed them.

These ocean trout start life nearly 300 km (186 miles) away in Tasmania's northern Midlands. At the fish farm in Cressy, female rainbow trout are fed testosterone to make them produce sperm with all-female genetics. Instead of sperm with half X and half Y chromosomes, these are all X, guaranteeing all eggs will be XX — that is, female — when fertilised. Only female fish result, as the jutted jaw of the male fish is apparently considered undesirable by consumers. The eggs are then put under about 4082 kg (9000 lb) per square inch of pressure to produce a third female chromosome (what's called a triploid), meaning the females used for meat never sexually mature, instead putting their energy into growing. A lot of antibiotics are, even sometimes to this day, used right from the egg stage until about two years old, when the immature rainbow trout are sent to the ocean.

It's in the naturally tannic waters that flow from the Franklin–Gordon Wild Rivers National Park into Macquarie Harbour that the fish are fattened for the pot. The top two or three metres of the water is less salty and colder than below, a natural feature of the harbour and a blessing to fish farmers. The fish flush their gills as they surface and dive for pellets. In a more saline environment, the fish would have to be pumped into freshwater tanks twice a year.

The fish we see being pulled from the water look immaculate. They gleam in the sun, the scales shimmering like chain mail, with a fine band of red running head to tail. Each fish looks to be in pristine health. They're not fed antibiotics as adult fish, because the company that grows them believes that if you need to feed antibiotics as a matter of course, there's something wrong with your farming techniques.

For a long time, Petuna has tried to get more reliable size and colour. They can control the orange colour by adding more colouring components to the feed. Most commonly used is a carotenoid called astaxanthin, which is found in krill and algae and in wild salmon with a more natural diet. Without it, the farmed fish would be a dull, greyer colour, which wouldn't please the market. Once the ocean trout have been killed, they're immediately ice-slurried. Today Petuna will use 12 tonnes of ice, and it takes just two hours to harvest 3500 trout.

WHAT'S HAPPENED SINCE THEN?

Tasmania's three big fish farm companies — Petuna, Tassal and Huon Aquaculture — have all expanded their salmon and ocean trout numbers in Macquarie Harbour. And a lot of fish have died (1.35 million) thanks to a lack of dissolved oxygen, a direct result of overstocking in a particularly fragile and unique ecosystem. The science seems to be playing catch-up. Before the expansion, we didn't know what was in Macquarie Harbour, and we didn't know how many farmed fish the harbour could hold. We also didn't know what would happen if, and when, we exceeded nature's limits.

Fish farming, globally, is struggling to get social licence because of issues such as this. While antibiotic use has fallen per kilo of fish produced where I live, we now know that about half the salmon we farm are deaf, thanks to accelerated growth rates. There's also evidence of altered ocean conditions around sea pens that nature isn't able to heal. But we also know that what was deemed sustainable and acceptable to regulators a decade ago has been revisited and updated.

Some fish, such as barramundi, need less feed than tuna or salmon, because they're lazy; they can also cope with brackish water. Kingfish also seem to be a potential aquaculture species for parts of Australia's coastline. Many now think that relying on the oceans to cleanse fish farms is generally more viable than using inland ponds (where the farmer is responsible for the waste that comes from their farm, rather than relying on nature to flush it away). In China, fish have been farmed for thousands of years in land-based ponds, but much of that is carp, and many people prefer the flavour of salmon, which is the most popular fish in Australia by a long, long way.

What we can hope, from Canada, to Chile, from Norway and Scotland to Tasmania, is that our reliance on a handful of closely related species doesn't cost the earth.

Fish stock

Perfect for noodle soups, bouillabaisse, seafood-based risottos and more.

2 kg (4 lb 8 oz) white fish bones (avoid salmon or other oily fish)
2 onions, halved
2 carrots
2 celery sticks
2 bay leaves
2 thyme sprigs
1 tablespoon lemon juice

MAKES 3.5 LITRES (122 FL OZ/14 CUPS)

Place everything in a large stockpot with 4 litres (140 fl oz/16 cups) water, making sure the water covers the ingredients. Place over high heat and bring to the boil. Just as it comes to the boil is the best time to skim it, running a ladle around the edges to scoop off any scum. The lemon juice helps to clarify the stock, but skimming is great, too.

Reduce the heat as soon as it boils, and simmer for 20 minutes. Strain and discard all the bones and vegetables.

This stock keeps well for up to 3 days in the refrigerator (reboiling extends its life), or for 3 months in the freezer.

500 ml (17 fl oz/2 cups) full-cream
    (whole) milk
1 bay leaf
a pinch of ground cloves or nutmeg
2 smoked trout fillets, flaked into
    bite-sized pieces
500 g (1 lb 2 oz) pontiac potatoes,
    peeled and diced
500 g (1 lb 2 oz) skinless blue-eye fillets
    or similar firm white fish, cut into
    2 cm (¾ inch) chunks

30 g (1 oz) butter
2 onions, chopped
2–3 tablespoons plain (all-purpose) flour
1 handful chopped parsley
2 cups fresh, hand-torn breadcrumbs
    tossed in 2 tablespoons melted butter

Fish pie with breadcrumb crust

*Pull out the pots and the casserole dish. Turn on the oven. Invite a few
mates around for Sunday lunch, or just try and get the family in one spot
for a change. Then serve them a fantastic smoky fish pie that uses two
types of seafood that aren't tainted with cheese. Then listen to the sighs.*

SERVES 6–8

Preheat the oven to 200°C (400°F/Gas 6).

Put the milk, bay leaf and ground cloves
in a saucepan and bring to a simmer. Add the
smoked trout, bring back to a simmer, then
turn off the heat and allow the flavours to
infuse for 5 minutes.

Put the potato in a saucepan and pour
in just enough water to cover. Add some
salt, bring to the boil, reduce the heat and
simmer until just cooked through. Drain the
potatoes, reserving the cooking water.

Reheat the milk and when it comes to
a simmer, place the blue-eye into the pan,
making sure it is submerged (push the trout
out of the way). Reduce the heat to low (the
liquid should be barely simmering) and poach
the fish for 4 minutes. Scoop all the fish out
with a slotted spoon and set aside. Discard
the bay leaf, reserving the milk.

Heat the butter in a clean saucepan
over medium heat and fry the onion for
10 minutes, or until really soft. Add the flour
and cook over low heat, stirring occasionally
while it cooks.

Pour in half the reserved milk and stir
until it comes to the boil and thickens. Add
the remaining milk and bring back to the
boil, stirring the whole time. If it goes lumpy,
whisk it. Add about 125 ml (4 fl oz/½ cup) of
the potato cooking water to make a thickish,
but not claggy, white sauce. Season with salt
and freshly milled black pepper, to taste.

Add the fish, potato and parsley, stirring
gently to just combine. (It's nice to add a few
peeled and halved hard-boiled eggs at this
stage.) Pour into a casserole dish, top with
the breadcrumbs and bake for 20 minutes,
oruntil the top is gloriously brown and crisp.

Serve with steamed vegetables.

100 g (3½ oz) tamarind pulp, broken up
125 ml (4 fl oz/½ cup) boiling water
6 dried shiitake mushrooms
60 g (2¼ oz) palm sugar (jaggery),
    or to taste
2 x 3 cm (1¼ inch) strips lime peel
1 teaspoon mandarin or lime juice

3 teaspoons fish sauce
100 g (3½ oz) fresh shiitake mushrooms,
    stems removed and thickly sliced
4 x 160 g (5¾ oz) blue-eye fillets or other
    large-flaked, thick, meaty fish

Blue-eye poached in tamarind broth

Blue-eye trevalla is a firm, white-fleshed fish that holds up well to most styles of cooking, including being poached. It's not dissimilar to cod in texture.

SERVES 4

Make a tamarind paste by mixing the tamarind pulp and the boiling water and mushing up well. Set aside for 10 minutes, then push through a sieve and discard the solids. (You can use prepared tamarind water, but it's not as good.)

Quickly rinse the dried mushrooms, then soak in a little hot water for 10 minutes, or until softened. Reserve the stalks and finely slice the caps.

Put the tamarind paste in a measuring jug and add enough water to make 625 ml (21½ fl oz/2½ cups) total volume. Place in a saucepan with the palm sugar, lime peel and dried mushroom stalks and bring to the boil. Reduce the heat and simmer for 2–3 minutes to dissolve the sugar, then remove from the heat and set aside to allow the lime and flavours to infuse for 15 minutes.

Strain the liquid into a clean saucepan, add the dried mushroom caps and simmer for 10 minutes. Add the mandarin juice, fish sauce and fresh shiitake mushrooms and cook for a few minutes until softened — the mixture should be a bit sour and fragrant.

Poach the fish very gently in this tamarind broth by bringing the broth to the boil and submerging the fish in it, turning it down just as it starts to bubble. It will take only about 3–4 minutes, so long as it has changed colour all the way through.

Place the just-cooked fish in a warmed bowl with a good ladleful of mushrooms and broth. Serve with steamed jasmine rice on the side, which is good for dipping into the broth.

8 thin slices prosciutto or jamón
2 x 250 g (9 oz) whole, fresh rainbow
   trout, scaled and gutted
60 g (2¼ oz) butter

2 tablespoons pine nuts
20 sage leaves
2 teaspoons lemon juice,
   strained

Roasted prosciutto-wrapped trout with sage burnt butter & pine nuts

Fresh trout is so cheap, yet so delectable; perhaps it's a tad subtle for our tastes these days. The resolute flavours in this dish, however, go wonderfully with trout, particularly the hard-to-find brook trout. Pretend you went freshwater fishing.

SERVES 2

Preheat the oven to 200°C (400°F/Gas 6).

Lay four slices of prosciutto next to each other on a clean work surface so that the long edges are slightly overlapping. Lay the trout across the prosciutto to cover the length of the fish, except the head and tail, and wrap the prosciutto around to enclose. Repeat with the remaining prosciutto and trout.

Melt 20 g (¾ oz) of the butter and brush onto the trout. Place the trout in a shallow roasting tin and roast in the oven for about 8–10 minutes, or until cooked through. Place on a serving plate.

Heat the remaining butter in a frying pan over a medium–high heat, add the pine nuts and toss to brown slightly. When the butter turns a nut brown colour, add the sage leaves and remove from the heat. Keep tossing and add the lemon juice. It will fizz and froth, so just keep shaking the pan to stop it burning.

Pour this butter mixture over the trout and devour immediately. I'd probably drink a semillon with it. As the wine flows, you can tell everyone about the D'Meure chardonnay — the one you've heard others on the river talk about, but have never actually seen.

120 g (4¼ oz) butter
1 small cauliflower, cut into small florets
1 onion, sliced
½ teaspoon ground coriander
½ teaspoon ground cumin
¼ teaspoon ground fennel seed

4 x 150g (5½ oz) skinless trevally fillets
(or try dory fillets with the skin on)
½ lemon, for squeezing

Spiced trevally with buttered cauliflower

I like to dream of the ocean, even when the closest I can get is a fishing show on television, or a plate of something fishy. You could serve the cauliflower with Cajun-style blackened fish, but this fennel-seed spice mix is more subtle and goes wonderfully well, too.

SERVES 4

Heat 100 g (3½ oz) of the butter in a saucepan over medium heat and fry the cauliflower for 3–4 minutes, or until it starts to colour. Add the onion and continue to fry, stirring regularly. Season with salt and freshly milled black pepper and cook for as long as you like. I like it when it's starting to break up and the onion and edges are brown.

When nearly ready, mix the spices together in a bowl and sprinkle a little of the spice mixture evenly over each side of the fish fillets.

Heat the remaining butter in a frying pan over medium heat and fry the fish, turning once only, until just cooked through.

Serve the fish with the cauliflower and just a squeeze of lemon juice over each fillet. Baked potatoes make a nice accompaniment.

4 large or 8 small whiting fillets
plain (all-purpose) flour, for dusting
1 egg
1 tablespoon full-cream (whole) milk
100 g (3½ oz/1¼ cups) fresh
    breadcrumbs
40 g (1½ oz) butter or olive oil

Parsley sauce
500 ml (17 fl oz/2 cups) full-cream
    (whole) milk
2 cloves
½ onion
2 bay leaves
20 g (¾ oz) butter
1 tablespoon plain (all-purpose) flour
1 handful flat-leaf (Italian) parsley
    leaves, chopped

Crumbed whiting with parsley sauce

Use a food processor to whiz up fresh bread to make breadcrumbs. They won't be as fine as the dried sort, but have their own distinct character. Having spent the best part of a decade avoiding white sauce, I've finally decided it has its place; with parsley added to the sauce and served with fish or corned beef is one such place.

SERVES 4

Season the fish well with salt and freshly milled black pepper and dust each side with flour. I like to do this in a plastic bag for cleanliness and efficiency.

Lightly beat together the egg and milk in a bowl. Dip each fillet into the egg mixture and then coat each one in the breadcrumbs. Repeat until all the fillets are coated.

To make the parsley sauce, put the milk in a saucepan over medium heat, add the cloves, onion and bay leaves and bring to a bare simmer. Remove from the heat and steep for 15 minutes. Reheat and strain before using, discarding the solids.

Heat the butter in a small saucepan over medium heat until melted, then toss in the flour, stirring well to make a smooth paste. Cook for about 1 minute, then whisk in the hot strained milk. Whisk continuously as the mixture comes to the boil and thickens.

If you can't whisk out the lumps, strain through a fine sieve. Season with salt and freshly milled black pepper, to taste, and stir in the parsley. If the sauce is too thick, add a little more milk to thin it — it should be a good coating consistency but not gluggy.

Heat the butter in a large frying pan over a medium heat (I like to use a mixture of butter and oil). Lay the whiting fillets in the pan and cook for about 2 minutes on each side, or until the breadcrumbs start to brown, then turn and cook the other side, adding more butter or oil if the pan gets too dry.

Lay the fish on plates and spoon the parsley sauce over one end of the fish. Serve with steamed mixed vegetables.

2 eggs
30 g (1 oz) wild rice
2 whole cardamom pods
1 whole clove
2 fresh curry leaves
120 g (4¼ oz) basmati rice
30 g (1 oz) butter

1 tablespoon snipped chives
120 g (4¼ oz) hot-smoked trout fillet,
    broken into large bite-sized pieces

Kedgeree

According to one old recipe book, the classic version of this English dish included smoked haddock served with boiled eggs, rice and, wait for it, curry béchamel. Yes, well. Here it gets a lift with hot-smoked trout, wild rice and soft eggs. I'm afraid I ditched the béchamel, curried or not.

SERVES 2-4

Boil the eggs for six minutes, drain, cool in cold water, then peel and break up roughly with a fork. Set to one side.

Rinse and drain the wild rice. Place the rice in a small saucepan with the spices, curry leaves, a pinch of salt and 125 ml (4 fl oz/½ cup) water. Bring to the boil, then reduce the heat to low. Cover and cook for 30 minutes, taking care not to boil it dry. If it does get too dry, add another 60 ml (2 fl oz/ ¼ cup) water.

Meanwhile, rinse the basmati rice in several changes of cold water and drain well.

When the wild rice is ready, add the basmati rice, stir and add enough cold water to sit nearly 1 cm (½ inch) above the rice. When it returns to the boil, reduce the heat and simmer, covered, for 12 minutes. Turn off the heat. After about 5–10 minutes, open the lid and use a fork to gently fluff the rice.

Add the butter, eggs and chives to the rice and mix with a fork.

Fold in the trout and serve warm or at room temperature, seasoned with freshly milled black pepper, to taste.

CRUSTACEANS & MOLLUSCS

Crustaceans are generally shellfish that can move, meaning things such as crabs and lobsters. They vary from place to place, from warm to cold waters, and everybody has their own idea of what makes a good one. In my view, it's the qualities of being local and very fresh that usually matter more than anything else.

Molluscs, those wonderful shellfish that lounge around on the ocean floor, or in the intertidal zone, have been farmed for years. The native oyster industry along coastal New South Wales, where I grew up, was actually created not for the oyster meat itself, but for the lime that you can harness from burning the shells. Invaluable in building, the result for modern-day eaters is the commercial availability of a wild oyster known as the Sydney rock, or simply rock oyster (to avoid invoking the name of the nation's long-time biggest and most polluted city).

Mostly grown out in clean estuaries, always well away from the city, oysters, mussels and scallops are all filter feeders. They just sit around and suck nutrients from the water (though scallops can actually swim, by snapping closed their shell very fast). For this reason, they're considered environmentally sustainable.

OYSTERS

With oysters, there's not much to their bodies. Some say they're just a gonad with gills, able to filter 50 litres (11 gallons) of seawater a day. That's each little oyster. Because of this, they're an expression of their particular patch of ocean. Brackish waters produce brackish oysters, though usually with some influence from the river mouths in which they sit. Every country, well most, will have its own oysters, differing in shape, size, texture and taste.

On Bruny Island, towards the south of Tasmania, you can find wild native angassi oysters, along with that prolific import, the Pacific. A Japanese oyster, the Pacific grows really fast and big, dominating and often replacing local species. The Pacific now makes up the largest commercially grown oyster fishery in the world, with 80 per cent of the production estimated to be based in China.

The Pacific differs from the native rock oyster in many ways. One is that it doesn't travel well. Sure, it's bigger, more silvery coloured and better-looking than native rock oysters, and it's much cheaper to produce because it grows twice as big in half the time, but three days after it's harvested, the true magic has gone. Even unopened, it converts much of its glycogen to lactic acid in the first day out of the water, which isn't a good thing.

A rock oyster, however, can live for up to three weeks out of the water. They get better, in my view, left for a couple of weeks to plump up in their shell (stored in wet socks, not in the fridge or on ice, as that kills them).

Oysters can be farmed in a way that helps them to gain flavour. Some of the Bruny Island oysters are kept in the cold waters of the D'Entrecasteaux Channel, deeper than you'd find wild oysters. On the south coast of NSW there's a farmer who uses tides, currents and various heights in the water to create different flavours. At their best, oysters have the nuances of a fine wine. At their worst they're smothered in bacon and cheap worcestershire and grilled.

THE DOWNSIDE OF OYSTER FARMING

There is a downside to oyster farming, however. Oysters spawn, producing about 30–40 million eggs at a time. Many of them spawn the first time as a male, the second time as a female, and this massive egg number means that some species out-compete native oysters. This is particularly the case on the NSW coast, where Pacific oysters are considered a noxious pest by native rock oyster farmers, and on the west coast of the US, where Pacific oysters out-compete the native mussel.

Modern farming practices can use a sterile oyster, a so-called triploid (like the salmon with three X chromosomes; see page 312), so spawn from these oysters doesn't contribute to the decline of native species.

WHICH OYSTERS ARE BEST AND FOR WHAT

A good oyster is an expression of the sea or estuary from which it comes, and should be sold unopened. The French consider selling an opened oyster akin to selling opened Champagne; the magic is lost in minutes. Oysters are often slow growing and should smell like a rock pool. They shouldn't be creamy from spawning. Oysters can be seasonal, with certain oysters spawning in warmer weather (such as Pacifics), while others spawn for other reasons, such as after rain (like Australian rock oysters). Oysters are best farmed; only take wild oysters if you really know what you're doing, because you can easily get sick by taking the wrong ones from the wrong place at the wrong time. Remember, they're filtering water as they feed, cleaning it as they go.

Having said that, choosing the best oysters will depend on where you live, as every area often has its own native oysters. Small, well-flavoured oysters are for eating fresh. The native NSW rock oysters, for example, are some of the finest oysters in the world, and are best eaten natural — just-opened and with hardly any flavourings. They can shrivel in seconds when cooked.

The bigger, fleshier, faster-growing and milder-tasting Pacific oyster is better for cooking — especially steamed with a little ginger and soy. Those massive oysters you see in Chinese restaurants are probably wild Pacific oysters — some can be 30 cm (12 inches) long and a decade old.

The native angassi is a flat oyster, not dissimilar to the powerfully flavoured and famed French Breton oyster, and grows in cold southern Australian waters. They're the oyster lover's oysters, but rarely consumed in their own land.

OPENING AN OYSTER

If you can't use a knife to open an oyster (and really, you need to be shown rather than just reading about it), then just lay unopened oysters on a barbecue hotplate or hot pan until they pop open. Then all you need to do is prise the shell open, tip your head back, use your finger to prise the oyster into your mouth and eat it immediately.

HOW TO CHOOSE AND CLEAN MUSSELS

Mussels these days are almost invariably farmed, often on ropes in bays and estuaries. Like oysters, their flavour varies with the variety, where they sit in the intertidal zone and the nutrients that are carried in the water they filter.

Mussels should be tightly shut when you get them. Discard any that are already open and that don't shut when you tap them. Scrub the mussels lightly to remove any grit on the outside, then de-beard them. The beard is the straggly bit that comes from the more rounded side of the shell. Grip it firmly with one hand (a fine cloth helps to grip it) and use the other hand to hold the mussel shell. Wiggle the beard up and down the line where the mussel shell opens until it gives way, which should be as you tug it towards the pointy end.

When you steam the mussels, if they're fresh when you bought them, even the ones that don't open properly can usually be used. Just prise them open, give them a sniff, and if they're good, toss them back into the pot.

WHY NEW ZEALAND MUSSELS ARE ALWAYS DEAD (AND DEAD BORING)

AQIS, Australia's quarantine service, doesn't allow live mussels (and plenty of other seafood) into Australia. So green-lipped mussels from New Zealand arrive already dead. They've already lost that marvellous fresh taste. They're either frozen or cooked, or both, and in the process all that incredible juice they give up when they cook is lost, and with it the ethereal flavour of fresh mussels.

SCALLOPS

There are two types of scallops sold: sea scallops, and bay or estuary scallops. Bay scallops tend to grow closer to shore in colder waters, while sea scallops come from further out and can grow closer to the Equator. Generally, the red roe (sometimes called coral) is removed from sea scallops, but left on bay scallops. A bright red roe means it's a female, a paler roe means it's a male; both are good to eat. This roe has a vaguely bitter character, and is a good foil for the richness of scallops, though some people do prefer to remove it.

Scallops are filter feeders, but unlike mussels and oysters, they can use their shell to move around. To do this, they use their bigger adductor muscle, and it's this white, round muscle, the one that holds the two halves of the shell together, that is known as scallop meat. It's all you get when you buy scallops without the roe.

Typically, scallops are dredged from the ocean floor, and often soaked in a water and phosphate solution, which helps them avoid moisture loss and can lead to water retention. The US forbids the use of too much phosphate because it increases the weight of scallops (which means you're buying water when you buy a scallop). If a lot of water drops from the scallops when cooking, you've bought dud scallops.

It's best to drain scallops on paper towel before cooking, so they're not too wet. And take care when cooking, as it's very easy to overcook them.

Top-shelf scallops are hand-dived, meaning a diver has gathered them from the ocean floor. It's highly unlikely you'll ever get them unshucked, as the shells open soon after harvest, and they tend to dry out unless fully prised open and covered with ice or a damp cloth.

FARMED PRAWNS (SHRIMP)

Prawn farming has been blamed for the destruction of much of the world's mangrove forests, and has met mixed success in helping poor fishing communities find other sources of income in the developing world. Many articles have been written on the problems associated with intensive prawn farming, including the use and residues of cancer-causing chloramphenicol and nitrofuran antibiotics. Farmed prawns are usually soaked in brine post-harvest to add weight.

There are many reputable prawn farms in more developed countries, but for the strictest ethical eaters, it's probably best to avoid farmed prawns altogether, unless you're certain of their origins.

Wild prawns, in many parts of the world, fare little better. The bycatch is between five and ten times as much as the catch itself — in other words, when 1 kg (2 lb 4 oz) of prawns are caught, 5–10 kg (11–22 lb) of other seafood will die. This has a big environmental cost. In Australia, changed fisheries management now means much — if not most — of the wild harvest is classified as sustainable. Fresh raw (uncooked) prawns are usually dipped in sodium metabisulphite to prevent the heads turning dark (which will usually occur within hours of being caught). Some say this chemical has a strong odour you can smell on the cooked shellfish. For this reason it's usually better to buy raw prawns that have been frozen on the boat. The problem is, most retailers thaw them prior to sale, rather than selling them frozen.

WHAT'S THE DIFFERENCE BETWEEN RED AND GREEN PRAWNS?

Red prawns (shrimp) and other shellfish have been cooked. Green ones haven't, simple as that. In this context, 'green' is just a cook's/chef's/marketing term, which can be confusing if your uncooked prawns, crabs or lobsters are a shade of red (though they will go even redder when cooked). For many purposes, raw shellfish adds its own character. If the recipe calls for raw shellfish, don't buy red if you can find a good raw version. But a good cooked product is always better than a dodgy raw product, no matter what the purpose. Just adjust the recipe to suit.

PREPARING LIVE LOBSTERS AND CRABS

The best crabs and lobsters are usually sold live, particularly mud crabs, which can harbour bacteria on the shell. Buying live shellfish is the ultimate test of freshness, and the flavour is incomparable. If not live, it's best to buy cooked or frozen unless you know exactly when they were caught.

To humanely kill a live crustacean, you first have to chill it. Put it in the refrigerator or freezer so it goes gently off to sleep, then kill it when it's stopped moving, with a knife through the brain.

Putting a live lobster or crab into a pot of boiling water is dumb and dangerous, not to mention inhumane.

OCTOPUS, SQUID AND CUTTLEFISH

Octopus and its relatives, squid and cuttlefish, are a completely different kind of seafood, called cephalopods. They can do with very little cooking, or a lot of cooking — seconds versus nearly an hour. Often the tentacles are as good as the head, and tiny octopus may be gutted, leaving the head and legs attached. Pretty much all the outside of octopus, squid and cuttlefish is edible, with the mucky, soggy inside bits being removed, and the hard cuttle or cartilaginous spike removed from squid and cuttlefish.

Fresh cephalopods are amazing to eat, but most are sold frozen, which isn't nearly as nice. Some, such as octopus, can benefit from some beating or tumbling — and most octopus that is sold at the famed Sydney Fish Market is run through dedicated concrete mixers that help to tenderise the flesh. I tend to find long, slow cooking of baby octopus, for about 40 minutes, is enough to tenderise the toughest sort you buy.

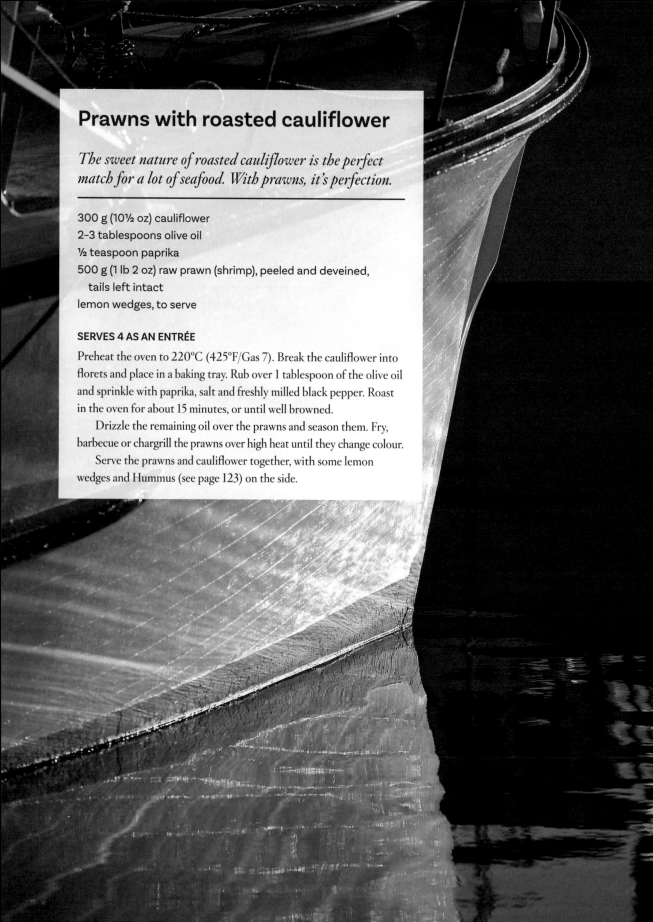

Prawns with roasted cauliflower

*The sweet nature of roasted cauliflower is the perfect
match for a lot of seafood. With prawns, it's perfection.*

300 g (10½ oz) cauliflower
2–3 tablespoons olive oil
½ teaspoon paprika
500 g (1 lb 2 oz) raw prawn (shrimp), peeled and deveined,
 tails left intact
lemon wedges, to serve

SERVES 4 AS AN ENTRÉE

Preheat the oven to 220°C (425°F/Gas 7). Break the cauliflower into
florets and place in a baking tray. Rub over 1 tablespoon of the olive oil
and sprinkle with paprika, salt and freshly milled black pepper. Roast
in the oven for about 15 minutes, or until well browned.

Drizzle the remaining oil over the prawns and season them. Fry,
barbecue or chargrill the prawns over high heat until they change colour.

Serve the prawns and cauliflower together, with some lemon
wedges and Hummus (see page 123) on the side.

Curry paste

3 cm (1¼ inch) piece ginger, grated

3–4 small red chillies, seeded and
    finely chopped

2 teaspoons shrimp paste

1 large lemongrass stem, white part only,
    very finely chopped

1 garlic clove, crushed

½ teaspoon ground turmeric

½ teaspoon salt

40 g (1½ oz) tamarind pulp, broken up

55 ml (1¾ fl oz) boiling water

250 ml (9 fl oz/1 cup) homemade chicken
    stock (see page 163) or water

1½ teaspoons sugar

300 g (10½ oz) snake (yard-long) beans,
    cut into 2 cm (¾ inch) lengths

400 g (14 oz) raw king prawns (shrimp),
    peeled, tails removed and deveined

fish sauce, to taste

juice of ½ lime

Sour yellow curry of prawn

*Homemade curries using homemade pastes are so much better then
pre-packaged ones. Cut or grate everything as finely as you can,
especially the lemongrass — chop it very finely so it's almost minced.
Once the curry paste is made, the curry is quick and easy to cook.*

SERVES 4

Make the curry paste using a mortar
and pestle or small food processor. Blend
together the ginger, chilli, shrimp paste,
lemongrass, garlic, turmeric and salt to make
as close to a paste as possible. Add a little
water if needed.

Make a tamarind paste by mixing the
tamarind pulp and boiling water and mushing
up well. Set aside for 10 minutes, then push
through a sieve and discard the solids. (You
can use prepared tamarind water, but it's
often not as good.)

Place the tamarind paste, stock, curry
paste and sugar in a saucepan over high heat,
bring to the boil, then reduce the heat and
simmer gently for 5 minutes.

Add the snake beans, simmer for a
further 5 minutes, then add the prawns
and fish sauce, to taste. Continue cooking
for about 1 minute, or until the prawns are
barely cooked through.

Add the lime juice, to taste; it should
taste slightly sour, with a small love bite of
chilli. Serve with steamed rice.

1 tablespoon olive oil

1 small onion, grated

1 garlic clove, crushed

500 g (1 lb 2 oz) baby octopus,
    cleaned

250 ml (9 fl oz/1 cup) light red wine,
    or a mix of red and white wine

200 g (7 oz) tinned chopped tomatoes,
    puréed roughly

Baby octopus braised in red wine

Baby octopus are very reasonably priced, and a good fishmonger will clean them for you. If you want to clean them yourself, simply slit between the head and legs and pull out anything that looks unappetising. I reckon there are only two cooking times for octopus — 40 seconds or 40 minutes. And while I love chargrilled octopus, this slow-cooked version is a dream.

SERVES 4 AS AN ENTRÉE

Heat the oil in a small saucepan over medium heat and fry the onion and garlic for about 5–10 minutes, or until they start to colour.

Add the octopus to the pan and continue frying for about 3 minutes, taking care not to darken the onion too much. Stir in the wine and boil rapidly for 2 minutes.

Add the tomato and lots of freshly milled black pepper, reduce the heat and simmer, stirring occasionally, for 40–45 minutes or until the octopus is tender.

Reduce the sauce if necessary (it will be faster in a shallow frying pan if it fits) over a high heat to a thickish consistency. Serve the octopus with chargrilled bread and olive oil.

60 g (2¼ oz) butter
2 x 1 kg (4 lb 8 oz) live or raw lobsters
20-30 kaffir lime leaves
3 cm (1¼ inch) piece ginger, sliced into
    6 rounds

5 coriander (cilantro) roots, washed
150 ml (5 fl oz) unwooded white wine,
    such as riesling

Pot-roasted lobster with kaffir lime leaves

I set out to copy a dish from one-time Sydney restaurant, Pier, and came up with this delicious (but rather different) celebratory meal. Tasmanian southern rock lobsters are the best flavoured, but any fresh lobster is divine.

SERVES 4

If the lobsters are alive, place them in the freezer for about 1 hour, to kill them humanely (see page 333).

Preheat the oven to 230°C (450°F/ Gas 8). Remove all the upper shelves so a big pan can fit in.

Heat the butter in a large ovenproof saucepan (with a lid) over high heat and sear the lobsters well. Don't allow the butter to burn. Add the lime leaves, ginger and coriander roots, cover, and place in the oven for about 7 minutes.

Remove the pan from the oven and allow to stand for 10 minutes. Remove the lobsters from the pan, remove their heads and cut each tail into about 5–6 slices, leaving the shell on if you have a sharp knife, otherwise, you can remove the shell.

Add the wine to the juices in the pan and cook over high heat until reduced by half, adding any juices from the heads and tails. Season with salt and freshly milled black pepper, to taste.

Just before you want to serve the lobster, return the meat to the pan to heat through (and perhaps finish cooking).

Serve warm with the pan juices, the legs and feelers. Some buttered new potatoes would be nice, too.

3 tablespoons extra virgin olive oil
2 red onions, finely diced
3–4 garlic cloves, crushed
125 ml (4 fl oz/½ cup) dry white wine
1 kg (2 lb 4 oz) ripe tomatoes, chopped
    (use tinned out of season)
10 anchovy fillets, chopped
800 g (1 lb 12 oz) spaghetti

1 kg (2 lb 4 oz) mixed seafood (about
    350 g (12 oz) diced boneless fish
    chunks, a few cleaned squid pieces,
    200 g (7 oz) peeled prawns (shrimp),
    300 g (10 1/2 oz) mussels in shell and
    8 fresh oysters)
3–4 tablespoons chopped mint leaves
2 tablespoons chopped parsley

Spaghetti marinara

You can make a good marinara without anchovies, but they do add a savoury 'umami' hit, and it'll be a lesser marinara without them.

SERVES 8

Heat 2 tablespoons of the oil in a large frying pan over low–medium heat and fry the onions for 10 minutes, or until soft — they should gently bubble not sizzle. Add the garlic and cook for 1 minute, then pour in the wine. Bring to the boil and add two-thirds of the tomato and seven of the anchovies and cook over a low heat for 20 minutes.

Bring 8 litres (280 fl oz) of heavily salted water to a rapid boil and add the spaghetti, stirring well as you add it and as it comes back to the boil. Cook until *al dente*.

As you start cooking the pasta, add the remaining tomato and anchovies to the sauce and bring to a simmer. Season with salt and freshly milled black pepper, to taste.

When the pasta is 3–4 minutes away from cooked, add the mussels to the sauce, cover and cook for 1 minute, then add the remaining seafood and herbs. Cover, and cook for 2–3 minutes, or until the seafood has changed colour. Discard any mussels that haven't opened.

When the spaghetti is ready, drain and keep some of the cooking water just in case the pasta sauce is too dry. Toss the seafood sauce through the just-drained pasta with the remaining olive oil. Serve immediately (not with cheese, as it shouldn't need it).

60 g (2¼ oz) butter
½ red onion, finely chopped
200 g (7 oz/1⅓ cups) fresh peas

1 tablespoon of olive oil
24 large fresh scallops, cleaned of grit

Seared scallops with pea paste

*Take two simple flavours and let them do great things together.
You could serve this with crisped pancetta, with a tiny bit of fresh
homemade pasta, or as a snack on bread with drinks. It's not as good
with frozen peas.*

SERVES 4 AS AN ENTRÉE

Heat 40 g (1½ oz) of the butter in a frying pan over medium heat and fry the onion for about 5 minutes, or until translucent.

Add the peas, a pinch of salt and 60 ml (2 fl oz/¼ cup) water. Cover the pan and steam for 5 minutes, or until the peas are just soft. Mash the peas with a potato masher or the back of a fork to resemble a coarse paste, then remove from the heat and keep warm.

Heat the oil and remaining butter in a frying pan over high heat and sear the scallops quickly on both sides, leaving the centres a little opaque.

Divide the pea paste between four plates and arrange the scallops on top to serve.

400 g (14 oz) scallops, cleaned of grit

2 large garlic cloves, crushed

16 snake (yard-long) beans, cut into
2 cm (¾ inch) lengths

1 green mango, peeled

2 tablespoons lime juice

20–30 g (¾–1 oz) palm sugar (jaggery),
grated

1 tablespoon fish sauce

2–3 small red chillies, seeded and
finely chopped

20 small basil leaves (preferably
Thai basil), torn in half

1 teaspoon grated fresh ginger

2 tablespoons chopped coriander
(cilantro) leaves, plus extra to garnish

3 French shallots, finely sliced

1–2 tablespoons peanut oil

2 tablespoons deep-fried shallots
(see note)

Thai-style scallop & green mango salad

You can swap the mango in this recipe for an equivalent amount of green papaya, for a different but interesting result.

SERVES 4 AS AN ENTRÉE

Rub the scallops with half the garlic and allow to marinate for a few hours in the refrigerator if time allows.

Blanch the snake beans briefly in a saucepan of boiling water, then plunge into a bowl of iced water to refresh. Drain and set aside.

Cut the mango into fine slices parallel to the stone, then cut these slices into very fine strips.

Mix the lime juice, palm sugar and fish sauce with the remaining garlic, and stir to dissolve the sugar.

In a large bowl, toss the snake beans, mango, chilli, basil, ginger, coriander and French shallots to combine.

Heat the oil in a frying pan over high heat and sear the scallops quickly on both sides, leaving the centres a little opaque. Add to the mango mixture, pour over the lime dressing, toss and serve garnished with the deep-fried shallots and sprigs of coriander.

Note: Deep-fried shallots are available from most large supermarkets and Asian food stores.

Crab & chilli omelette

Rich egg, sweet crab and the spice of chilli combine to make this one hell of an omelette.

100 g (3½ oz) cooked crabmeat (from about 1 decent
   blue swimmer crab or equivalent)
2 small red chillies, seeded and finely sliced
3 tablespoons chopped coriander (cilantro) leaves
1 teaspoon fish sauce
4 eggs, lightly beaten
1 tablespoon peanut oil
1 large garlic clove, crushed

SERVES 1–2

Mix the crabmeat in a bowl with the chilli, coriander, and fish sauce, then add the remaining sauce to the eggs.

Heat the peanut oil in a large non-stick frying pan over high heat and quickly fry the garlic until starting to colour. Add the egg and stir until it is half cooked. Scatter the crab mixture over the top and press gently into the egg. When the egg is nearly cooked, fold the omelette over, and tip onto a plate.

Halve the omelette and serve with steamed rice.

1 dried shiitake mushroom

80 g (2¾ oz) raw bug or prawn
  (shrimp) meat, finely chopped

40 g (1½ oz) water chestnuts,
  finely chopped

40 g (1½ oz) bamboo shoots,
  finely shredded

2 spring onions (scallions), finely sliced

2 cm (¾ inch) piece young ginger,
  finely shredded

1 tablespoon oyster sauce

16 square spring-roll wrappers,
  trimmed to 12.5 cm (5 inch) squares

1 tablespoon cornflour (cornstarch)

peanut oil, for deep-frying

good-quality chilli sauce, to serve

Bug & bamboo spring rolls

These bug and bamboo spring rolls are gorgeous and taste nothing like the impostors in most Chinese restaurants. There's no need to peel the ginger if it is young and sweet and has a pale coating; otherwise, peel as needed.

SERVES 4

Quickly rinse the mushroom, then soak in a little hot water for 10 minutes, or until softened. Discard the stalk and finely slice the cap.

In a large bowl, mix the mushroom with the bug meat, water chestnuts, bamboo shoots, onion, ginger and oyster sauce.

Lay the spring roll wrappers on a clean work surface and place about 2 teaspoons of the filling mixture in each one.

Mix together the cornflour and about 2 teaspoons water in a small bowl. Fold in the ends to enclose the filling then roll up each to form a roll and seal with the cornflour paste.

The best way to deep-fry is in a wok. Heat enough oil to submerge the spring rolls in a wok over high heat until it sizzles as soon as you sprinkle in a couple of breadcrumbs. Deep-fry the spring rolls, in batches, for about 2 minutes each, or until golden and crisp and the insides are cooked.

Drain on paper towel and serve with the chilli sauce on the side.

1 kg (2 lb 4 oz) mud crab or similar crab
500 ml (17 fl oz/2 cups) peanut oil
2 small red chillies, very finely sliced
2 tablespoons brandy or cognac
1 tablespoon oyster sauce

1 teaspoon sea salt flakes
1 teaspoon coarsely crushed
　black pepper

Salt & pepper mud crab

This is a real finger-licker, which has heat from both chilli and black pepper. It's best if you can coarsely crush the pepper in a mortar, but roughly milled black pepper is the next best thing.

SERVES 2

Take the top shell off the crab and discard. Remove the gills, wash out the guts and cut the body into four even sections. Smack the claws and legs with the back of a knife to crack (this makes it easier to remove the flesh later).

Heat the peanut oil in a wok over high heat until it sizzles immediately when a couple of breadcrumbs are dropped in. Deep-fry the crab for about 5 minutes, or until just cooked through. You may need to do it in batches.

Remove the crab from the wok and set aside. Drain all but 1 tablespoon of the oil from the wok and fry the chilli for a second or two, then return the crab to the wok.

Add the brandy to the wok and cook for 1 minute, then add the oyster sauce and toss to coat the crab. Sprinkle with the salt and pepper, toss and serve.

Chapter 6

VEGETABLES

VEGETABLES

Steve Solomon picks his greens, then delivers them to the restaurant door. Same day. From his plot of about 500 square metres (600 square yards) on the fringes of Launceston in Tasmania's north, he makes enough money to cover all his needs. Solomon is a gardening author, one-time seed salesman, and green thumb philosopher. And what he produces is incredible to behold. For the home cook, what counts with most vegetables is not only how they're grown (from the varieties to the pesticides used), but how recently they were picked. And while Solomon's couldn't be fresher, most so-called fresh produce in the shops has sadly not been picked as recently as you'd think.

Lack of freshness is the great killer of vegetable quality. I've been around the vast wholesale fruit and vegetable markets in Sydney and heard how precise and high paying the supermarkets can be. How hard it is for smaller greengrocers to get quality when the two major supermarket chains that dominate the country are on the spot and on the money. But what happens after the fruit and vegetables leave the market is where some of the difference lies. The local greengrocer takes their produce and puts it on the shelf the same day. The supermarket sends it to a warehouse, from where it will, at some point, be shipped to the stores. A day, two days, a week, can be a long time in terms of quality when it comes to vegetables.

What Solomon and others like him produce bears little resemblance to the stuff available even at the wholesale market. His are small-time vegetables that are grown for a particular demand. There are no strange chemical inputs, no pesticide or herbicide residue to worry about, and seed selection is all about eating quality, not how something will fare when sitting in a refrigerator for a week or three, or trucked across the country. This is real food, and it proves, very simply, just how far removed we are from the origins of what we put in our mouths.

ROOT VEGETABLES

Ian Grubb used to dig all his potatoes by hand. The last time he pushed in the fork to turn the ground over, he uncovered 50 tonnes of potatoes. It was important that the potatoes weren't dug up by tractor like most are, because on Ian's potatoes the skin hasn't set. It's so fine that you can rub the almost translucent skin off with a vague pass of your thumb. Grubb wanted the best eating potato, but hand-forking potatoes isn't that much fun, so Grubb invented a machine that would do the equivalent of hand lifting for him.

Ian Grubb grows arguably the most famous potato in Tasmania, Australia's most famous potato-producing state: the pink eye, a brilliant waxy potato with little rougey highlights ,marketed sometimes as southern gold. Not just any pink eye, however. Ian digs South Arm pink eyes, which are the pink eyes of pink eyes that take their name from the peninsula on which they're grown. So sweet you can eat them with nothing more than a pinch of salt and a glass of water. So yellow they're almost buttery. So freshly dug that a mere rinse under the tap rids them of any of the famed sandy loam that they've grown in, ready for the oven or the pot. It's the potato that is celebrated each spring (yes, potatoes are seasonal, too), not the grower. Yet part of the potato's quality is directly related to Grubb's attitude and respect for the end product.

Like all good food production, Grubb's approach is no accident. He uses chook poo as fertiliser (meaning the ground is full of stinging nettles, which his helpers loathe) and fine cotton gloves to sort potatoes. Most farmers leave the spuds underground for a while as the tops die down so the skin will set (that is, become firmer and less likely to rub off). It's better that way —better for storing, and better for transporting. But Grubb's potatoes are sold as soon as he can dig them, and eaten often the same day, because his pink eyes are grown and harvested with eating as the priority. Not storage. Not transport. It's how good they are in the gob that counts. And these potatoes, just let me assure you, are bloody good eating.

Root vegetables, because they do store well, can be mistreated. And there is an off-season for them, so not everybody can dig and sell potatoes that don't keep. In fact, part of the attraction of many root vegetables is that they do last a while; they're pantry staples. But as with just about anything, freshness counts. Be it beetroot (beets), Jerusalem artichokes, carrots, onions or garlic, there's an optimum time to enjoy them.

Keep an eye out for baby beetroot, which is much sweeter than its grown-up sister. Any type of new potatoes are good, but best are waxy varieties, such as Dutch cream, nicola, pink fir apples and pink eyes. Be sure to use them quickly and store them in the refrigerator. Also, it may be worth searching for wind-free Jerusalem artichokes. I don't suffer too much from the, ahem, after effects of artichokes, but many do. Some varieties are better than others for preventing a following wind.

SOME POTATO VARIETIES AND THEIR USES

Potatoes can be divided roughly into two categories, waxy and starchy. A general rule is that a yellower-fleshed potato is more likely to be waxy, therefore sweeter and less starchy, and more suited to salads or boiling.

Waxy potatoes are generally better for cooking if a recipe calls for potatoes that stay whole, whereas starchy are fine if they are meant to break up. Think of the puffy lightness in a just-baked potato, or the smooth texture of mash. Because there is a higher sugar to starch ratio in a waxy potato, they colour much quicker at high heat (such as frying and roasting) and can over-caramelise and become bitter and unsightly. For this reason starchy potatoes are often preferred for frying and roasting. That said, many potatoes can be substituted with no ill effects, but the right potato for the job can make the meal.

Sweet potatoes aren't actually potatoes, though they are really quite versatile. I find the flavour extraordinarily sweet in some dishes, so I generally use them sparingly, or sour them with vinegar, lemon juice or pomegranate molasses.

MASHING Try desiree, sebago, pontiac or even nicola.

BOILING/SALAD Try pink eyes, bintje, desiree, pontiac, nicola, kipfler (fingerling), pink fir apple, spunta or Dutch cream.

FRYING Try kennebec, russet burbank, spunta, bintje or sebago.

ROASTING Try desiree, pontiac, king edward, sebago or russet burbank.

BAKING Most potatoes are good for baking, but particularly the sebago and king edward; it's the only real good use for coliban (the most common washed variety in shops).

DID YOU KNOW?

While some vegetables, corn and peas in particular, convert sugar to starch the moment they're picked, potatoes do the opposite. Potatoes can convert some starch to sugar after they're picked, meaning that storing some varieties of older potatoes — those that have sat in the ground for longer, as opposed to 'new' potatoes — for a short period can make them taste sweeter.

GENERAL RULES FOR ROOT VEGETABLES

Root vegetables keep really well stored in a cool, dark place that isn't overly humid or dry (ventilated, but not breezy), though beetroot and new potatoes do love being in a paper bag in the crisper drawer of the refrigerator.

Despite keeping well, they're still best eaten within a week of buying.

As root vegetables are generally starchy, they cook better submerged in water or roasted, as opposed to steamed, though that's up to you. They can require peeling, though this is more important with older vegetables, or those that have been stored for any length of time.

DID YOU KNOW?

Carrots will suck moisture out through their leaves after harvest, sending the carrot limp and reducing its crisp, sweet nature. So those expensive baby carrots with the tops left on that you see in the supermarket? A really big waste of money. The tops may look pert, but that could be because they've sucked the life from the carrots. If you do buy (or dig) really fresh carrots with the tops on, cut them off straight away and store the carrots in plastic in the crisper section of the refrigerator.

1 kg (2 lb 4 oz) starchy potatoes
3-4 tablespoons extra virgin olive oil
8-9 garlic cloves, unpeeled

Crashed potatoes

These crashed potatoes could be called smashed, or crushed, but they're kind of between the two. I adore using my knife to squeeze out the soft, roasted garlic from the skins to add warmth to every second mouthful.

SERVES 6

Preheat the oven to 220°C (425°F/Gas 7).

Steam or boil the potatoes until soft; you can peel them if you like. Drain the potatoes, put in a roasting tin and use the back of a spoon to press down and crush them into the tin — they should look like they've crashed, this helps them cook up nicely.

Drizzle well with the olive oil, top with the whole garlic cloves, season with salt and freshly milled black pepper. You could add a rosemary sprig, too, for a more flavoured spud dish.

Bake for 20–30 minutes, or until starting to get crisp edges. Serve hot.

1 kg (2 lb 4 oz) pink eye, kipfler (fingerling) or other waxy potatoes
150 g (5½ oz) cultured butter, softened
2 tablespoons dijon mustard
2 teaspoons lemon juice
2-3 tablespoons chopped dill

Warm potatoes with dill mustard butter

You could use the flavoured butter with fish, but I like the excellent way it moistens potatoes.

SERVES 6

Cut the potatoes if large (I like to leave them whole if they're small enough). Place in a large saucepan with cold, salted water, cover and bring to the boil. Reduce the heat and simmer for about 10 minutes, or until tender.

Meanwhile, mash the butter with the mustard and lemon juice until combined. Mash in the dill.

Toss the potatoes with the butter and add salt and freshly milled black pepper, to taste. Serve with a nice piece of grilled fish, some roasted pork or even a little veal.

500 g (1 lb 2 oz) dutch cream, kipfler
(fingerling) or other small potatoes
1–2 tablespoons olive oil (or duck fat
or lard)

10 garlic cloves, unpeeled
2 rosemary sprigs

Garlic-roasted Dutch cream potatoes

Any small potatoes can be roasted in this way. It's also possible to cook them in a camp oven.

SERVES 6

Preheat the oven to 230°C (450°F/Gas 8).
Put the potatoes in a baking tray and toss them with the oil and garlic to coat well. Add the rosemary, some coarse salt and freshly milled black pepper.

Roast in the oven for about 30 minutes, or until the potatoes are tender, tossing occasionally. The garlic skins may darken, but inside should be fine. Serve with roast lamb or La Gasconnade (see page 246).

1 kg (2 lb 4 oz) jerusalem artichokes
1–2 tablespoons olive oil

Roasted Jerusalem artichokes

The knobbly, only-a-mother-could-love look of Jerusalem artichokes puts some people off. But fresh and sweet from the ground, and roasted to nutty tenderness, they're as good as any roasted vegetable can be. And that's very, very good.

SERVES 6

Preheat the oven to 220°C (425°F/Gas 7).
Scrub the artichokes well and pat dry with paper towel. Place them in a roasting tin and drizzle over the oil; season with salt and freshly milled black pepper, rubbing the oil all over the artichokes.

Roast the artichokes for 30–40 minutes, turning a couple of times, until brown all over. Serve hot.

Chunky roasted carrot paste

Sometimes a simple vegetable takes on a new life when treated differently. A carrot tastes different grated, in sticks, eaten from the ground, simply roasted — and here, crushed a little after roasting.

1 kg (2 lb 4 oz) carrots, peeled
1–2 tablespoons olive oil
40 g (1½ oz) butter or 2 tablespoons extra virgin olive oil

SERVES 6

Preheat the oven to 220°C (425°F/Gas 7).

Chop the carrots if really large and place in a roasting tin. Drizzle with the olive oil and sprinkle with salt and freshly milled black pepper.

Roast the carrots for about 45 minutes, or until starting to brown on the outside and soft inside. Use a potato masher to mash the carrots to make a coarse paste — chunkier is better.

Season again, to taste, and stir through the butter or a good extra virgin olive oil. Serve with roasted or grilled meats.

FLOWERS & LEAVES

Jules Ellis reckons she has the best-fed chooks in Tasmania. She grows some of the finest greens imaginable, mostly for herself and her mum to eat. Apparently, however, 'there's a heck of an excess'.

To be fair, Jules does sell to a local restaurant, as do Clare and Bruce Jackson from Yorktown Organics, a short drive up a nearby valley. The difference is mainly in the size of their operations. Jules is a backyard (or rather, front yard) grower, while Yorktown sells 8 tonnes of baby carrots a year. Like many certified organic growers, the Jacksons are passionate about the organic philosophy. 'Why would you put poison on your food?' Bruce asks about pesticide and herbicide use. A question that doesn't really have a good answer. 'Call me stupid,' he says, 'but most people wouldn't dream of doing it.'

Both Jules and the Jacksons have the same philosophy when it comes to greens: as little chemical input as possible, use them fresh, and get them onto tables while they're at their best.

The great thing about leafy greens for us as consumers is that they give you just about all the indications of freshness. Are the leaves bright coloured and pert? Are they as crisp as they should be? Does the cut stem or base look freshly snipped, or is it dry, brown and cracked? If you've ever seen the glossy, gorgeous leaves for sale in a farmers' market and compared them to supermarket greens, despite all the latter's tricks to get them to gleam in the light, then you'll know what I mean.

Leafy greens often come from a common ancestor. Cabbage, broccoli, cauliflower and brussels sprouts all come from a kale-like ancestor. Silverbeet (Swiss chard) and other chards come from the beetroot (beet) family, which is more closely related to spinach. So what makes one cabbage different from another — better for one use than another? What makes broccoli taste better in one region? Partly it's variety. Partly it's soil. Partly the way they're grown and harvested, how they're stored, transported and how freshly they're sold.

In countries where they've done the groundwork, like Italy, they know that the broccoli of Calabria is better than the broccoli of Friuli. Historical evidence and a passion for flavour help. But even there the noble varieties are being lost to commercial reality. Hence the rise of the Slow Food Movement, which originated in Italy.

It would be much easier for a flavour chaser like me to eat more vegetables if there were more variety among each vegetable. Thankfully we can now add Asian greens to our list of vegetables — particularly Chinese broccoli (gai larn), Chinese cabbage (wong bok) and bok choy (pak choy), a leafy plant eaten in its entirety and often sold young.

HEALTHY SOIL, SUPERIOR FLAVOUR

As I touched on in the early pages of this book, recent research has shown that more biologically active soil (the type you typically find growing organic, small-scale vegetables) produces more compounds in the food you eat — essentially making it more nutrient-dense. The good news is that a lot of those micronutrients provided by healthy soil can be tasted in food, even in the most delicate place of all, in the leaves. What that means is that better soil grows more delicious lettuce, cauliflower, broccoli and everything else that comes from the ground — and that delicious produce is also better for you.

COOKING CABBAGE AND BRUSSELS SPROUTS

I like my cabbage, and my brussels sprouts, cooked in one of two ways. Either cooked for ages so they break down (and usually with a piece of bacon or some duck fat and garlic), or flash-fried (with some bacon or duck fat and garlic ... or okay, with olive oil). The first way is more sulphurous, the second avoids most of that cabbagey smell that many people find reminds them of nursing homes or school dinners.

BROCCOLI

When I was a chef, the only part of broccoli that was served as a vegetable was the tiny end florets, with the stalk going into the ubiquitous 'cream of ...' soup. Later I found that not only does the stalk have more flavour and a more mouth-pleasing texture, but it's also better at holding heat. Broccoli's cousins, gai larn (Chinese broccoli) and broccolini (a broccoli and Chinese kale cross) are more stemmy, and the stem needs less cooking than conventional broccoli. Broccolini is a trademarked vegetable, so I tend to avoid it because it is a hybrid with the rights owned by a single company. Broccoli plants put out shoots after the big head is cut off, and these are better-tasting than broccolini. Market gardeners often sell these shoots, so keep an eye out for them.

LETTUCE

Lettuce and other lettuce-like leaves, such as baby spinach and cress, don't grow as well under the harsh Australian sun as they do in the shade. That's why some versions you buy can be quite harsh on the palate. The best lettuces and mixes, particularly in high summer, are grown under shade cloths, or further from the Equator where the sun is lower in the sky. If you do buy firm-textured leaves, it's best to use a little more acid when dressing them, as this helps to soften and break them down. Dress them with vinegar or lemon juice before adding the oil for best effect.

PREPARING LEAVES

Conventionally grown, unwashed lettuce is one of the most common sources of pesticide residue because of its surface area. Pre-washed lettuce, which may contain slightly less residue, is dipped in a chlorine solution to kill any greeblies that may be crawling on it. While it may look clean, I'd recommend another wash and dry before use.

½ tablespoon olive oil

300 g (10½ oz) broccoli, head cut into
florets

3 garlic cloves, sliced

5 anchovy fillets, chopped

½ tablespoon extra virgin olive oil

30 g (1 oz/about ⅓ cup) shaved Italian
parmesan cheese (Parmigiano
Reggiano or Grana Padano)

Wok-tossed broccoli with anchovies & parmesan

This dish is a delicious way to use beautiful fresh broccoli. It relies on the integrity of the olive oil and the parmesan cheese, so buy the best of both that you can afford.

SERVES 4

Heat the olive oil in a wok over very high heat and stir-fry the broccoli and garlic for a couple of minutes, taking care not to darken the garlic too much. Add the anchovies and 125 ml (4 fl oz/½ cup) water and toss to combine. When the broccoli is cooked the way you like it, add the extra virgin olive oil and remove from the heat.

Serve the broccoli as a light entrée with the cheese on top and some freshly milled black pepper.

20 g (¾ oz) butter
3 thin slices prosciutto, cut into strips
2 large waxy potatoes, peeled and diced
400 g (14 oz/1 large head) broccoli, cut
   into florets, stems sliced
lemon wedges, for squeezing
extra virgin olive oil, for drizzling

Overcooked broccoli with potato & prosciutto

This recipe is a simply delicious use of broccoli that goes beyond the usual crunchy vegetable that we normally see, to become a muddle of gorgeous, friendly flavours.

SERVES 4

Heat the butter in a saucepan over medium heat and fry the prosciutto for 1 minute — there's no need to brown it. Add the potato and just enough water to steam it, about 80 ml (2 ½ fl oz/ ⅓ cup) should do to start. Bring to the boil, cover with a tight-fitting lid and cook for 5 minutes.

Add the broccoli to the pan, check the water level (adding a tablespoon or two if necessary) and keep cooking with the lid on, until the potatoes are cooked through. Remove the lid and continue cooking until the liquid has evaporated and the vegetables are moist but not soggy.

Season with salt and freshly milled black pepper and serve, perhaps with a touch of freshly squeezed lemon juice and some olive oil drizzled over.

500 g (1 lb 2 oz) brussels sprouts
50 g (1¾ oz) duck fat, lard or butter
3–4 garlic cloves, crushed

Duck fat brussels sprouts

I used to call this recipe 'edible brussels sprouts', because the ones I grew up eating weren't. These are slow-cooked with duck fat and garlic, which makes most things taste better. Some people don't like slow-cooked sprouts, so I also do them other ways. Finely slice them and cook as you would the Braised Red Cabbage on page 374, or rub whole sprouts with duck fat, season well and roast them in a hot oven, shaking the pan occasionally until they're quite dark — almost black — on the outside. You can also simply halve them and pan-fry them, cut side down, until soft; a lid helps steam them through while the base browns.

SERVES 6

Cut the bottom from each sprout and remove the dark outer leaves. Cut a little cross into the base of each (some say this allows them to cook evenly, but I know it's so the duck fat can get in).

Put the brussels sprouts and duck fat in wide-based frying pan over medium heat and fry for 5 minutes with the garlic.

Add 250 ml (9 fl oz/1 cup) water, bring to the boil, then reduce the heat and simmer, covered, for 1 hour, shaking the pan occasionally and checking that the sprouts don't dry out.

Remove the lid from the pan and continue cooking to reduce the liquid if too wet. Season with salt and freshly milled black pepper and serve with any meat dish, particularly beef or pork.

12 artichoke hearts (see page 398)
or good-quality artichoke hearts
marinated in oil, cut into halves
1–2 tablespoons extra virgin olive oil
2–3 teaspoons lemon juice

50 g (1¾ oz) shaved Italian parmesan
(Parmigiano Reggiano or Grana
Padano)

Grilled artichokes with shaved parmesan

*Simple, bright-flavoured and desirable; the ingredients do all the work.
To prepare your own artichokes, follow the method in Fava e Carciofi
(see page 398). This dish tastes fabulous, but will taste even better if you
poach a duck egg to go with it. Serve with woodfired ciabatta.*

SERVES 4 AS A STARTER

Brush the artichokes with the oil and cook under a very hot grill (broiler) until just taking on some colour.

Put a few hearts on each plate, drizzle with the lemon juice, top with shaved parmesan and freshly milled black pepper.

400 g (14 oz/about 1 bunch) kale
3 tablespoons olive oil or butter
3 garlic cloves, sliced

Wilted kale with garlic

*Kale is a curly, wonderfully flavoursome green that's a precursor to
cabbage. Think of coarse silverbeet (Swiss chard), which makes an okay
substitute at times. I like to cook kale very simply, just like this.*

SERVES 4

Take each leaf of kale and remove the large rib down the middle — this is quite tough and not good to eat. Wash the leaves well and roughly chop.

Heat the oil in a large saucepan over medium–high heat and fry the garlic just until starting to colour, but only just. Add the kale and stir well. If your pan isn't large enough you may need to wilt some leaves

down before adding more. The water from washing the leaves should be enough, but just make sure the kale doesn't dry out, adding a tiny bit of water at a time if need be.

Cook with the lid on for about 15 minutes. Season well with salt and freshly milled black pepper and serve with just about any meal.

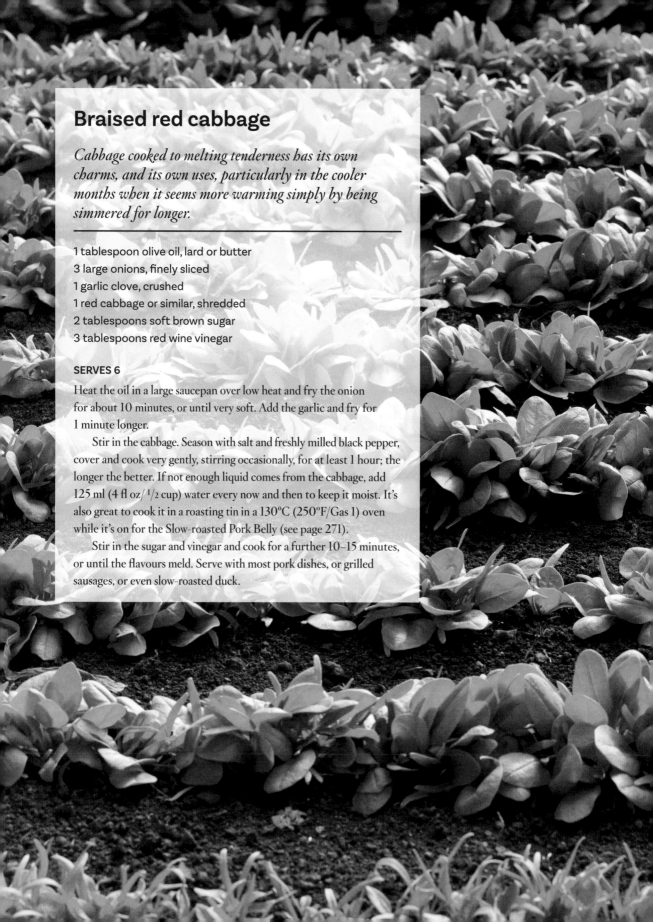

Braised red cabbage

Cabbage cooked to melting tenderness has its own charms, and its own uses, particularly in the cooler months when it seems more warming simply by being simmered for longer.

1 tablespoon olive oil, lard or butter
3 large onions, finely sliced
1 garlic clove, crushed
1 red cabbage or similar, shredded
2 tablespoons soft brown sugar
3 tablespoons red wine vinegar

SERVES 6

Heat the oil in a large saucepan over low heat and fry the onion for about 10 minutes, or until very soft. Add the garlic and fry for 1 minute longer.

Stir in the cabbage. Season with salt and freshly milled black pepper, cover and cook very gently, stirring occasionally, for at least 1 hour; the longer the better. If not enough liquid comes from the cabbage, add 125 ml (4 fl oz/ $1/2$ cup) water every now and then to keep it moist. It's also great to cook it in a roasting tin in a 130°C (250°F/Gas 1) oven while it's on for the Slow-roasted Pork Belly (see page 271).

Stir in the sugar and vinegar and cook for a further 10–15 minutes, or until the flavours meld. Serve with most pork dishes, or grilled sausages, or even slow-roasted duck.

FRUIT VEGETABLES

Some vegetables — many, in fact — are fruits. These include capsicums (peppers), squashes such as zucchini (courgettes), along with pumpkin (winter squash) and that seemingly ubiquitous vegetable, the tomato.

It's difficult to give hard and fast rules for buying fruit vegetables in one fell swoop because of their variety. Tomatoes should be soft but not squishy, and ripe, and never, ever, refrigerated. Pumpkins should be cured for a couple of weeks. Capsicum should be fresh, fresh, fresh and stored in the refrigerator, while zucchini flowers are as delicate as the most perfect rose (and much better to eat), and should be scoffed as soon as practicable after picking.

PUMPKINS

Despite being colonised by Britain — a place where pumpkin (winter squash) was considered pig food — each state in Australia has a favoured pumpkin, the most notable being the Queensland blue. A bold-flavoured, hard, delicious pumpkin, it has fallen out of favour because it's hard to peel, not least because it also has a ribbed skin.

Many now prefer the milder-flavoured but easy to peel butternut pumpkin. What it gives in ease it takes away in taste, being sweeter, but about half as intense in actual pumpkin flavour (as opposed to sweetness) as the Queensland blue.

Jap pumpkin, or kabocha as it's known in Japan, is a 'wet' pumpkin — and is actually a squash, not a pumpkin — so it can be hard to caramelise in the oven. I think it's best in soup.

There are pumpkins that are perfect for northern Italy's pumpkin and mustard fruit tortellini, for carving for North American Halloween, for serving individual soups in, for roasting and for pumpkin pie. There are countless varieties; it all depends on what you can get, what you want it for, and where you live.

TOMATOES

The great example of what has happened to our vegetables can be found in the tomato. Considered poisonous when first imported into Europe from the Americas, it found fame and fortune in the 1700s — and who can imagine Italian food without it? But sadly for the tomato, what is being sold, at least around much of the world today, isn't a patch on what we could be eating. The reality is that the breeding of tomatoes peaked by about the 1950s, and since then, all we've really been doing is trying to make something that will ripen consistently, look good on the shelf and travel thousands of kilometres in a truck.

As anybody who has grown tomatoes knows, the stuff you can buy in a shop is a poor imitator of the real thing. Sold hard, out of season, they offer little of that mouthfilling, satisfying tomato flavour. Hydroponic tomatoes have increased massively in sales in recent years, though there's a lot of talk about their lack of complexity and flavour.

Even if you can buy good tomatoes, it's worth knowing how some of the styles can differ in what they offer. Egg-shaped tomatoes have less moisture and more flesh, which makes them ideal for cooking. Cherry tomatoes are usually the highest in sugar, meaning they can make a very sweet pasta sauce, though I think they are better in salads than cooked, despite their high skin-to-flesh ratio. Low-acid varieties, such as the ox-heart tomato, may never go fire-truck red, but are more of a flesh-coloured deep pink. Round tomatoes vary, too, because they can be different varieties, but generally suit salads more than sauces; most round tomatoes, however, are mass-produced and have no great attributes other than they show up on shelves with monotonous regularity.

GASSING OF TOMATOES

The vast majority of tomatoes for sale in supermarkets are gassed. Growers pick green tomatoes and gas them with ethylene, the odourless, tasteless natural gas that helps to ripen them (and to ripen bananas), and which makes them blush. In goes a green tomato, which has a pale core and a crunchy texture, and out comes a pink tomato — which also has a pale core and a crunchy texture. And not much flavour.

There's nothing wrong with the gas; it's the same gas given off by ripe tomatoes and other fruit, such as apples. (Ethylene is actually a plant hormone, which is also used pre-harvest to thin fruit such as apples and cherries, to get rid of the green tinge on citrus skins, and to loosen nuts on the tree.)

If you want tomatoes 12 months of the year and bananas thousands of kilometres from where they're grown, then it's probably very necessary to use the gas in the way modern food technology does. Imagine having to wait a month or more for your avocado to soften. But, in truth, gassing tomatoes, like gassing bananas, helps the grower, the wholesaler and the supermarket more than the eater. We know slow-ripened fruit, and fruit that is picked as close to ripe as possible, when it's likely to need more care in transport, has far more inherent flavour. The only reason gassing is carried out has nothing to do with the consumer, and everything to do with making money from a product that the farmer and retailer know isn't as good as it could be.

STORING TOMATOES

Tomatoes, contrary to popular opinion, don't necessarily ripen best on the vine. In fact, according to many gardeners, they're best ripened at room temperature, below 25°C (77°F), off the vine. The thing is, however, that they must be picked well after they've turned from green to red, when the skin has turned a shade of pink (if it's a red variety), when there's plenty of gel around the seeds and sugar in the fruit.

The fruit you buy in a supermarket has most likely been picked at the 'mature green' stage, when it's still very much green. It's then kept for six weeks in a predominantly nitrogen-based atmosphere, then gassed with ethylene. Remember the taste of home grown? It is possible to have flavoursome tomatoes in shops, but only if we insist on it.

If you store tomatoes at home, they will lose flavour — *actively* lose flavour — at temperatures below 12°C (54°F), so don't put them in the refrigerator. They also lose about half of their predominant flavour within about 20 minutes of being cut (unless you add salt or other things such as oil). Best to leave them on the kitchen bench, somewhere out of the sun, and only cut them when you're ready to eat.

PEELING TOMATOES

For some recipes, peeled tomatoes are better because the skin can make the dish odd-looking or odd to eat — especially modern varieties that are bred to have a thick skin (so they can be transported and stored). Most of the time, I couldn't be bothered to peel tomatoes if I'm cooking the sauce for any length of time; you just end up with little rolled-up bits of skin in it (and sometimes between your teeth, oh well). Tinned tomatoes, mostly a better option than hard supermarket tomatoes, are usually sold peeled.

To peel a tomato, you need to shock the skin with heat. You can put it close to an open flame, say a gas burner, although most people like to score the skin with a cross at the non-stem end and remove the core, then put it into rapidly boiling water for 10 seconds. Carefully take the tomato from the boiling water and place a bowl of iced water to arrest any cooking that may be going on, try to peel off the skin, and repeat if necessary. A ripe tomato peels really easily; an unripe one can be a bit of a nightmare.

HOW TO ROAST AND PEEL CAPSICUMS

Most capsicums (peppers) in Australia are very watery and don't leave a lot of flesh when roasted and peeled. This has a lot to do with variety rather than the growing of the fruit, though hydroponic fruit is exceptionally wet and unsuitable for these purposes. You can hardly buy any capsicum by variety here, though you can get green, red, yellow and deep purple (almost black) ones, all variations on the same species. While green capsicums will turn red and sweeter, they are usually slightly different breeds of plant than the ones actually sold red. The virtually black ones look just like green capsicums when peeled. In other parts of the world, the array of different capsicums can be dazzling. Recent additions to many greengrocer shelves are yellow (and sometimes red) capsicums shaped like bull's horns. These are usually best eaten fresh, as they don't peel particularly well, and cook down to virtually nothing. In some places, bull's horn peppers (as they're often known) are stuffed and roasted or grilled.

There are two really good methods for roasting and peeling capsicums. The first is to rub the skin of a whole capsicum with a little olive oil. Place in a 230°C (450°F/Gas 8) oven, or roast whole over a flame, until the skin is dark and blistered. Transfer to a plastic bag, tie the bag tightly to seal, then allow to steam for 10 minutes. Remove when cool, discard the seeds and peel off the skin, which should pull back easily. Whatever you do, don't wash the skin off, because just about all the good, smoky, gorgeous flavour will disappear down the sink, too. Cut the flesh into useable-sized pieces and use straight away, or store in olive oil for up to 1 week.

Alternatively, you can cut a capsicum into four quarters and remove the membrane and seeds. Place the pieces, skin side up, on a lined baking tray and brush the skin with a little olive oil. Place under a very hot grill (broiler) until the skin darkens and blisters. Place in a plastic bag and steam, then peel, prepare and store as per the method above.

HOW TO COOK EGGPLANT

In the old days, many people would salt, then deep-fry, eggplant (aubergine). It's still a great way to cook it, though quite messy and expensive, in terms of the oil used.

Despite the fact that most eggplants we can buy are free of bitterness these days, I still like to salt them before cooking. This draws out moisture, so the eggplant softens and cooks more quickly, and I find you can use less oil. First, cut the eggplant into 1.5 cm (5/8 inch) slices, in whichever direction you like. Salt them with fine salt — just a mist, as though you are sugaring the top of shortcake. Do both sides (salting the tray underneath is the easiest way) and leave for 30–60 minutes. Dab them dry with paper towel and leave to drain on paper towel — the more you dry them, the easier they are to cook, because you've already removed water that will need to be evaporated during cooking.

When you're ready to cook, preheat the oven to 220°C (425°F/Gas 7). Brush the eggplant with enough oil so each side glistens (the oil will soak in straight away, so cook the eggplant as soon as it is brushed). Place in one layer in a greased or baking paper-lined roasting tin. Roast until brown, perhaps turning depending on your oven.

Roast eggplant can then be used for antipasto, in a lasagne, or in other dishes such as eggplant parmigiana. The salting and oiling method is also good before using on the barbecue or chargrill, or in a frying pan.

AVOCADOS

To choose an avocado, press it very gently at the stem (pointy) end to see if it gives slightly. Because they ripen from the base up, if the stem end is just ripe, the other end should all be beautifully soft, nutty and ready to gorge on.

To help an avocado ripen, pop it into a paper bag with a banana skin or apple core, and leave on the bench for a couple of days; a room temperature of 20°C (68°F) is best. (You can also use a half-eaten avocado to help ripen a banana.)

Roasted Queensland blue pumpkin with blue cheese

Two ingredients that just taste incredible together are pumpkin (winter squash) and blue cheese. Don't use jap pumpkin, as it is more like a squash — full of water and likely to fall apart before it roasts to golden brown.

---

500 g (1 lb 2 oz) Queensland blue pumpkin (winter squash), skin on and cut into wedges
olive oil, for rubbing
150 g (5½ oz) soft, creamy-style blue cheese (or mix blue cheese with homemade mascarpone, see page 62)

SERVES 4 AS A SIDE DISH

Preheat the oven to 200°C (400°F/Gas 6).

Rub the pumpkin with a little oil, sprinkle with salt and freshly milled black pepper, then place on a baking tray and roast for about 30 minutes, or until brown and cooked through.

Cut a little blue cheese on each piece and return to the oven to melt, then eat lavishly and long.

1 kg (2 lb 4 oz) roma (plum) tomatoes, cored
1–2 tablespoons olive oil
1 onion, diced
¼ teaspoon turmeric

¼ teaspoon ground coriander
½ teaspoon ground cumin
1 tablespoon red or white wine vinegar
1 tablespoon soft brown sugar

Roasted tomato sauce

Use any small breakfast sausages as an excuse to eat this sauce, made with late-season, ripe tomatoes. If your tomatoes are very sweet, as low-acid beefsteak varieties tend to be, you can omit the sugar.

MAKES 400 G (14 OZ)

Preheat the oven to 170°C (325°F/Gas 3).

Place the tomatoes on a small baking tray with at least 2 cm (³/₄ inch) sides and rub all over with just enough olive oil to coat well. Cook for about 90 minutes, or until quite dark.

Allow to cool slightly, transfer to a food processor or use a stick blender to purée the tomatoes, being careful not to make it too smooth and still leave some character.

Heat 1 tablespoon of oil in a saucepan over medium heat and fry the onion for 10 minutes, or until golden. Add the spices and stir to cook for about 1 minute before adding the tomatoes. Use 125 ml (4 fl oz/ ¹/₂ cup) water to wash any remnants from the tomato tray and scrape to remove any stuck-on bits and add to the sauce.

Bring to the boil, then reduce the heat and simmer gently for about 45 minutes, stirring regularly (it will splatter a little as it thickens). Add the vinegar and sugar, and season with salt and freshly milled black pepper, to taste. Simmer for a further 3 minutes to dissolve the sugar and dissipate some of the raw vinegar acid.

Remove from the heat, then pour the hot sauce into sterilised airtight jars. Once cool, store in the refrigerator and use within 2–3 weeks. Serve the sauce warm for late breakfasts, early lunches or dinners.

1 large eggplant (aubergine)

2 tablespoons extra virgin olive oil

1 tablespoon pomegranate molasses (optional)

1 tablespoon balsamic vinegar

2 teaspoons lemon juice

6 mint leaves, finely sliced

150 g (5½ oz) haloumi cheese, cut into four slices

1 pomegranate, seeds removed and skin discarded

Roasted eggplant with haloumi & pomegranate

Thick, sour/sweet pomegranate molasses (available from Middle Eastern food stores and some supermarkets) adds a beautiful complexity to this dish, although you can also make it without.

SERVES 4 AS AN ENTRÉE

Preheat the oven to 180°C (350°F/Gas 4).

Prick the eggplant all over with a fork and bake for about 40 minutes, or until tender. Allow to cool, then peel. Slice the flesh into four portions and arrange on a baking tray lined with baking paper. Place in the oven for 10 minutes to reheat.

Whisk the oil, molasses (if using), vinegar, lemon juice, mint, and salt and freshly milled black pepper in a bowl.

Fry the cheese in a non-stick frying pan over medium–high heat (with a touch of olive oil if necessary), until light brown, turning to colour both sides.

To serve, place the warm eggplant on serving plates, top with a slice of cheese, spoon over the dressing and garnish with the jewel-like pomegranate seeds.

1 tablespoon white wine vinegar

1 teaspoon caster (superfine) sugar

1 teaspoon salt

1 large lebanese (short) cucumber

Quick pickled cucumbers

MAKES 60 G (2¼ OZ/¼ CUP)

Mix together the vinegar, sugar and salt in a bowl to combine well.

Cut the cucumber into quarters lengthways, then slice into 2 mm (1/16 inch) pieces. Place in a bowl and pour the dressing over the top. Set aside to marinate for at least 1 hour before serving.

The pickled cucumbers will keep well, covered in the refrigerator, for up to 2 weeks.

2 tablespoons olive oil
3 large onions, chopped
3–4 garlic cloves, crushed

6 x 400 g (14 oz) tins crushed tomatoes
20 basil leaves

Simple tomato ragu

I've spent some time bagging local tinned tomatoes because they lack the flavour of Italian brands — much to my sadness, because it'd be good to support a local industry. Australian brands are better than they were, but still lack intensity of flavour and that ripe-tomato character. No wonder so many tomato sauce recipes use tomato paste as well.

This recipe makes about 2 litres (70 fl oz/8 cups) of basic yummy tomato sauce, which is so much better than those sold on supermarket shelves. This is more than you will need to make a pasta for dinner (see note), but it can be frozen and is also suitable for braises, with grilled or roasted meats — pretty much everything.

MAKES 2 LITRES (70 FL OZ/8 CUPS)

Heat the oil in a large saucepan or stockpot over low–medium heat and fry the onions for 10 minutes, or until soft and translucent. Add the garlic and cook for 1 minute.

Add the tomatoes to the pan, bring to the boil, then reduce the heat and gently simmer for about 2 hours, or until the oil comes to the top and the flavour becomes rich, unctuous and well rounded. Stir in the basil leaves and cook for a further 10 minutes.

If you are not using the sauce straight away, allow to cool and then freeze in smallish containers for up to 3 months.

Note: To serve with pasta, use about 100 g (3 1/2 oz) dry pasta per person (short, fat varieties are good for this sauce). Cook the pasta in a saucepan of boiling salted water for about 6 minutes. Meanwhile, heat about 100 ml (3 1/2 fl oz) of sauce per person, adding olives, other herbs, chopped pancetta, or nothing if you like. Season the sauce well. Drain the pasta before it's cooked, reserving some of the cooking water. Finish cooking the pasta in the sauce, stirring the whole time and adding a little more reserved cooking water if necessary. The sauce should stick to the pasta by the time the pasta is cooked. Drizzle a little more extra virgin olive oil over the pasta and serve with Parmigiano Reggiano cheese and more pepper on top.

1 kg (2 lb 4 oz) eggplants (aubergines)
3–4 garlic cloves, crushed
2 tablespoons tahini (see note)
1 tablespoon Greek-style yoghurt
1–2 tablespoons lemon juice, to taste

1–2 tablespoons extra virgin olive oil
1 teaspoon salt
¼ teaspoon freshly milled black pepper

Baba ghanoush

The heady smokiness and rounded, in-your-face flavour of this smoked eggplant dip are very seductive. It's best for everyone if you cook the eggplants on a barbecue, if you can, rather than directly on the stove, because it will generate a lot of smoke (see below). The garlic means you need to plan exactly what sort of liaison you are hoping to have, as it cannot be omitted. Baba ghanoush goes brilliantly with most lamb dishes, or chicken cooked on a chargrill.

MAKES 600 G (1 LB 5 OZ)

Grill the eggplants over hot coals, a hotplate or gas flame until the skin has blackened and the inside is very soft. (You can control the smokiness by darkening the eggplant only slightly and finishing off roasting it in the oven.) It sounds scary, but you can also do this straight on an electric stovetop. It will smoke the house out if you don't have a decent extractor fan, but a true baba ghanoush has to be smoky.

Allow to cool, then peel off and discard the skin; rubbing the skin with paper towel and then scraping with a knife is the best way. Chop the flesh.

Put the eggplant in a food processor with all of the remaining ingredients and blend to combine; taste for salt and lemon juice.

Note: Tahini is a sesame seed paste that is available from health food shops and most large supermarkets.

SHOOTS, BULBS, PODS & SEEDS

Peas, they reckon, can turn half their sugars to starch in the first ten hours after picking. So you're unlikely to get a really sweet, fresh pea unless you pick it yourself. That's why frozen peas, often processed within hours of picking, are often sweeter, softer and milder-flavoured than the sort you get at the greengrocer. To a cook they can almost be treated like different vegetables.

Most legumes follow the same rules: fresher is sweeter — and so is younger, with broad (fava) beans being the best example of how youth differs from age. You can eat the entire pod when they're very young, the beans inside are good when they're wearing a tight outer layer that is still Kermit-green, and later they're best either cooked for hours, or double-peeled (see Peeling Broad Beans, opposite).

Corn is the same. A friend who grew up in the cornfields in the southern US was told that if he dropped one cob on his race back from the field to the simmering pot, he should drop the lot and go and pick some more. Freshness, the urgency of picking to pot, was that important.

Not all vegetables are like that. Artichokes can handle some time off the stem. But asparagus is sweet, nutty and incomparable when snapped from the ground and eaten in the field.

HOW TO CHOOSE SHOOTS, BULBS, PODS AND SEEDS

Ask the seller when the vegetables were picked and where they have come from. Then ask if you can try a pod or pea; if not, get their number so you can call them after your guests have gone and berate them if the vegetables were tired-tasting at the dinner table.

Look for vegetables that gleam. Bright colours in things like peas or sugar snap peas, a glossy look on fennel, celery that doesn't appear woody or tired or limp. Even onions should gleam, and brown, white and red onions should be firm when pressed.

Similarly, look for full pods, but not too full. Broad beans and peas can be better if the pod isn't rammed full of overstarchy seeds. Remember, the seller gets paid by weight, not by how good they'll taste.

PEELING BROAD (FAVA) BEANS

To single-peel beans, just attack the pod from the seams, flicking out the beans and discarding the pod. Single-peeled beans can be cooked as is, but some find the casing bitter, and it is much tougher and starchier than the bright green inner, so they need more cooking, particularly if the peeled beans look a bit khaki on the outside, rather than bright green.

To double-peel beans, blanch single-peeled beans in boiling water for 2–3 minutes. Refresh in ice-cold water, then slip off the softened pale khaki shell, using your fingernail to do it (kind of like the way your sister would use her fingernail to pinch you when you were growing up — or was that just me?). The beans are now blanched and shouldn't taste starchy, though they do often benefit from another couple of minutes in a pan.

Generally, 1 kg (2 lb 4 oz) whole bean pods will yield about 330 g (11 3/4 oz) single-peeled beans and roughly 200 g (7 oz) double-peeled ones.

ONIONS: A GUIDE

Onion names change depending on which part of the world, and which part of the country, you live in. Some are interchangeable. Here's a rundown on the most common ones.

BROWN ONIONS A very common, large (often apple-sized) onion with a papery brown skin. Great when cooked, pretty awful (hot, pungent) when raw.

WHITE ONIONS Similar in size and flavour to brown onions. To me there's so little difference between white and brown that they can be used interchangeably. Very occasionally you'll find sweet white salad onions, but this is the exception, not the rule.

RED ONIONS Sometimes called Spanish onions, these onions have a red papery skin and pink-tinged white flesh. Much sweeter and less pungent than white or brown onions, they make more elegant-tasting sauces and can be used raw in salads and the like.

GREEN ONIONS (SCALLIONS) The definition for green onions is confusing. These are also called spring onions, scallions and shallots in various places. These are the onions that have a long, straight stem, with a pale base. Used extensively in Asian cuisine, they're best raw or just barely cooked, though they can be used in place of French shallots (eschalots) for some uses where a mild onion is needed, being better than brown or white onions and just as commonly available. You use the whole of a green onion, apart from the very tips if they're droopy, or any dry outside leaves.

FRENCH SHALLOTS (ESCHALOTS) Also called shallots (getting confused? I am). Small, usually oval, red or golden onions the size of your thumb or smaller. They're sweet and tender, great raw, used extensively to flavour sauces in top-end French cuisine, and in South-East Asia — though there they're often deep-fried.

CHIVES You won't get these confused. Long, very thin, entirely green. Best used raw and snipped with scissors, unless you have a very sharp knife and the skills to use it.

LEEKS Long straight onions, fatter than green onions. Leeks can be as fat as a man's thumb, or as fat as a duck egg. They're best before they get too big, and many people prefer the pale end. While they're relatively sweet, elegant and mild-tasting, they're still favoured in cooking rather than eaten raw. If you ever buy them with a hard centre, that means they've run to seed and should never have been sold.

Leeks are often full of dirt that gets trapped in between the layers of flesh. To get rid of this you need to wash them really well. I like to split the leek down the middle, leaving it intact at the root, pull apart each layer, and wash the dirt out by rubbing each layer with my fingers. A full sink or running water works best. Don't be stingy on the cleaning, or your dish could end up gritty.

GARLIC

It seems odd to give garlic such prominence here. But garlic (part of the onion, or allium, family) has changed, and not for the better. What was once as crisp as an apple, as taut as a ballet dancer's thigh and pungent enough to keep vampires at bay is now just a vague shadow of what it was. The reason, it seems, is cheap imports. Garlic, that marvellous, warming, gently omnipresent fresh herb, has started to taste stale, acrid and dull. About 90 per cent of garlic sold in Australia is imported, mostly from China. It's dipped in a solution to stop it sprouting (and some suggest it's bleached to keep it pure white), as well as sprayed with a pesticide, methyl bromide. And it is the biggest anticlimax come dinner time.

I noticed it when I moved to the countryside and found every second person growing their own. When I helped a neighbour get a trapped donkey out of her fence, she came by with a thank you note (from 'Arthur') and a bag of her own bulbs. Purple, striped, sweet-flavoured garlic is a part of the landscape here. Among the foodies I knew in Australia's largest city, however, it hardly rated a mention, probably because we'd been disappointed by garlic too often. It's so good where I live now that I eat about ten times as much as I did, and it's certainly not cheap (though I do, at the time of writing, have a couple of rows in the vegie patch myself).

It's been reported that the number of commercial growers in Australia has dropped from 1600 to about a hundred, and what we've lost in terms of varieties can never be replaced. That said, there are about 400 commercially recognised varieties in the world, suited to various climates and growing conditions, and most of them taste just great.

Keep an eye out for green garlic. That's right, the spring garlic where it looks like a leek, before the bulb differentiates — it's mild, sweet and delicious.

Purple garlic is also good, and is immediately identifiable as local (not imported) garlic. Russian or elephant garlic has huge, mild cloves that are best roasted, but not good fried. In fact, it isn't true garlic, and doesn't really rock my boat.

200 g (7 oz/1 bunch) asparagus
2 flat mushrooms
200 g (7 oz) snow peas (mangetout)

1–2 tablespoons vegetable oil or olive oil
1 small red onion, sliced
¼–½ teaspoon sesame oil

A spring stir-fry of snow peas, asparagus & mushrooms

I could eat a huge bowl of this with just some rice, or a thin Asian-style omelette and a bit of chilli sauce, but you may want to stir-fry some squid or scallops before you cook the rest, and return them to the pan at the end.

SERVES 2

Snap the woody ends off the asparagus, discard the firm end and cut the tip end into bite-sized pieces, on an angle. Cut the mushrooms into bite-sized fat slices or chunks. Pull the stalk from each snow pea (and try to remove the tough bit up the side as you do it). Cut the snow peas in half on an angle.

Heat the vegetable oil in a very hot wok over high heat and stir-fry the onion until it starts to soften. Add the asparagus and mushrooms and cook for 2 minutes longer, tossing the whole time to keep the vegetables moving. Throw in the snow peas and cook for another minute, or until they start to colour and are hot.

Sprinkle in a generous pinch of salt and some freshly milled black pepper and drizzle in a touch more vegetable oil if the wok is looking dry. When the vegies are done to your liking (I like them browned in spots, but still crisp), remove the wok from the heat, drip in some sesame oil and toss. Taste for salt. If you like it strongly sesame flavoured, add more sesame oil.

Place into a serving dish, and serve with steamed rice and chilli sauce, or with a steamed soy fish or other fish dishes.

80 ml (2½ fl oz/⅓ cup) extra virgin
  olive oil
1 large onion, diced
3 garlic cloves
500 g (1 lb 2 oz) green beans, trimmed

2 large tomatoes, diced, or 400 g (14 oz/
  1⅔ cups) tinned chopped tomatoes
1 bunch fresh dill, roughly chopped
white pepper, to taste

One-hour beans with tomato & dill

The Greeks and Turks and others along the Mediterranean often cook their green beans until they're soft. This is one of my favourite ways of eating them.

SERVES 4

Heat the olive oil in a large saucepan over low heat and gently fry the onion and garlic until soft.

Add the green beans, tomato and half of the dill. Cover and cook for about 50–60 minutes, adding 125 ml (4 fl oz/ ½ cup) water if necessary so it doesn't dry out. Stir the mixture occasionally as it cooks.

Season well with salt and white pepper and finish with the remaining dill. Serve warm or at room temperature.

Buttered peas with speck & lettuce

The lettuce lightens the dish, while the peas add sweetness and the speck depth. In the absence of speck, you can use pancetta or bacon.

40 g (1½ oz) butter
1 small red onion, finely chopped
50 g (1¾ oz) speck or thick-cut bacon, cut into matchsticks
500 g (1 lb 2 oz) frozen peas
200 g (7 oz) iceberg or cos lettuce, fresh outer leaves are good, cut into strips
1 tablespoon chopped mint

SERVES 6 AS A SIDE DISH

Heat the butter in a large frying pan over a low-medium heat and fry the onion until soft. Add the speck and cook for about 3–4 minutes, or until the fat has released from the meat.

Add the peas and lettuce, cover, and stir occasionally as the peas thaw. Once thawed, cook another 3 minutes, or until the peas are hot and soft and the lettuce well wilted. Add the mint and season to taste with salt and freshly milled black pepper. Serve hot.

2 tablespoons extra virgin olive oil,
　　plus extra for drizzling
1 small onion, finely diced
½ lemon
6 globe artichokes (choose firm-
　　headed ones)

1 kg (2 lb 4 oz) broad (fava) beans,
　　single-peeled (see page 391)
2 thyme sprigs
1 tablespoon salt

Fave e carciofi
(broad beans stewed with artichokes)

This is a classic, very rustic Italian dish for those who love the true flavour of the vegetables. This dish is best served as an entrée with some of the juices for dipping good crusty bread into, and perhaps some more olive oil and lemon to dress them up. To cook artichokes for other uses, you can omit the oil, onion and broad (fava) beans and use the same method.

SERVES 6 AS AN ENTRÉE

Heat the oil in a saucepan (choose one that fits all the artichokes snugly when peeled) over medium heat and fry the onion for 10 minutes, or until soft. Remove from heat.

Add 1 litre (35 fl oz/4 cups) water to the pan and squeeze the lemon into the water, adding the lemon half.

Peel the artichokes by cutting off the top third of the leaves and trimming until only the tender, pale innards are left. It's best to remove the furry 'choke' that lies just above the heart — use a teaspoon to do this — then cut the artichokes in half. Place into the lemony water once prepared. When all are done, add the broad (fava) beans, thyme and salt.

Cover and simmer for about 25 minutes, or until the artichokes are very soft. Set aside to stand for at least 30 minutes to let the flavours meld (or even for 4–5 days in the refrigerator if you are getting it ready ahead).

Warm the dish again by heating in a saucepan and serve the warm beans and artichoke (one per person) with a dribble of the cooking water, some more extra virgin olive oil drizzled over the top and freshly milled black pepper.

Serve as part of a lunch with cheeses, meats and bread for lapping up the juices.

2 large fennel bulbs, cleaned and cut
   into eighths through the core
1 large onion, finely sliced
2 thyme sprigs
1 bay leaf

250 ml (9 fl oz/1 cup) white wine, or
   water and some white wine vinegar
olive oil, for drizzling

Fennel braised in white wine & thyme

The way to prepare or clean a fennel bulb is to trim the root and leafy tops off, then peel any slightly coarse outer leaves using a potato peeler; really dodgy ones can come off completely, but you'll lose a lot of the bulb that way. You could brown the cut fennel in a pan or on a chargrill or barbecue prior to cooking, to add another layer of flavour.

SERVES 4

Preheat the oven to 180°C (350°F/Gas 4).

Lay the fennel pieces in an even layer in a deep-sided roasting tin. Scatter the onion and thyme over the top and add the bay leaf. Season with salt and freshly milled black pepper. Pour in the white wine and drizzle with a little oil. Cover with foil and bake for 30 minutes, or until tender.

Remove the foil and bake (maybe increase the oven temperature a notch) until the fennel starts to brown and the juices start to evaporate — a little juice is good, but not a lot. Serve with lamb, or other roast meats, or as part of an antipasti platter, or with fish. Or even at a barbecue.

12 small (4 large) leeks, white part only,
    rinsed and cut into 3–4 cm
    (1¼–1½ inch) lengths
500 g (1 lb 2 oz) baby carrots, peeled
1 large waxy potato, peeled and diced
3–4 tablespoons extra virgin olive oil

a pinch of sugar
white pepper, to taste
1 handful (about ⅓ cup) chopped dill
1 tablespoon lemon juice

Turkish-style braised leeks

This dish is a celebration of good olive oil as well as leeks. I first had it at the house of a Turkish chef, Serif Kaya, where his wife Gulbahar had cooked the most amazing spread of dishes. They very kindly shared the secret of one.

SERVES 4–6

Place the leek in a saucepan with the carrots, potato, half of the oil and 125 ml (4 fl oz/ ½ cup) water. Season with the sugar, some salt and plenty of white pepper.

Cover the pan with a lid and cook gently for about 20 minutes, or until the vegetables are soft. Stir through the dill, then add the lemon juice and remaining olive oil to taste.

Serve the braised leeks at room temperature with roasted lamb or kebabs of some kind.

1 small lemon, scrubbed

2 teaspoons salt

1 bay leaf

400 g (14 oz/2 bunches) asparagus

80 g (2¾ oz) butter

Asparagus with boiled lemon butter

I've found that the most re-gifted item in the food world is the preserved lemon. You buy a jar, use one wedge, then keep it in the fridge for four years. If anybody gives you another one (and for some reason, they do), you just give it to someone else, who gives it to someone else. The thing is, you don't need to waste fridge space on the jar if you don't use them often, because just about any time you need preserved lemon, this boiled salted lemon is just as good.

SERVES 4

Halve the lemon, juice it and keep the juice for another day. Place the lemon in a small saucepan with the salt and bay leaf, then pour in just enough water to cover. Bring to the boil, then reduce the heat and simmer for about 30 minutes, or until tender. Allow to cool, discard the liquid and bay leaf, and cut the lemon into quarters. Discard the pulp and finely dice or purée the skin.

Snap the woody ends off the asparagus and discard.

Heat the butter in a large frying pan over medium heat and gently cook the asparagus, seasoning to taste with salt and freshly milled black pepper, and turning occasionally. When it's nearly done (I like mine with some bite left) add the lemon and heat through to ensure the flavours meld.

Serve the asparagus on a platter with the butter tipped all over for mopping up with bread.

Chapter 7

FRUIT

FRUIT

If there's one area where we've been let down in the quality stakes, it's undoubtedly fruit. Why? Because as consumers, we want every fruit available to us all year round. No longer is there a celebration of the strawberry season at the beginning of summer. No longer are cherries so eagerly anticipated that in the month they're available your hands turn a faith-healer colour of stained red from pitting and gorging on the beauties. Apples are no longer the domain of autumn. It's part of the 'I want it, and I want it now' mentality. What that means, however, is that just about all the fruit you buy, just about all the time, is inferior compared to what farmers could and would grow, if only we let them. This requires a change in consciousness and attitude, which isn't going to happen anytime soon.

So let's do the next best thing. What I hope is that over the next few pages you'll find some tips and tricks for working out how to buy the best produce, and why some of what you may buy will never be as good as it should be unless you grow it yourself.

The good news is that with the rise and rise of farmers' markets, good-quality fruit is starting to become more readily available. Close contact with the grower means that we can tell them exactly what we liked last time, and they can tell us just what the season and growing conditions dictate.

WHY WON'T SOME FRUIT RIPEN ONCE PICKED?
The ripening of fruit is determined by a few things. The cell walls of the fruit break down, making the fruit softer. The starches are converted to sugars, the acid levels drop, and the flavour compounds (mostly aromatic esters) increase. It's how fruit does this that counts. So a watermelon won't ripen once picked, but a rockmelon might.

Fruit can be divided into two general categories — climacteric and non-climacteric — according to whether they will ripen or not once picked. Climacteric fruit continue to ripen after picking (respiring substantially and releasing ethylene), whereas non-climacteric fruit don't. This ripening is supposed to increase the fruit's sugar content (though I have my doubts when it comes to peaches). Non-climacteric fruit may soften off the tree, but that doesn't mean it will develop more flavour, or increase its sugar content. Acidity may drop, however, making it taste sweeter.

But — and in this book there always seems to be a *but* — climacteric fruit can be further classified into those with starch reserves and those without. Which explains my distrust of peaches and nectarines. They don't have substantial starch reserves that can be turned into sugar, and therefore can't produce more sugar from starch once they are picked. They can, however, 'ripen' by softening and dropping in acid levels. What they definitely *don't* do is gain any more aromatic compounds, those marvellous things that make a peach smell like summer. Plums and mangoes tend to fall into this category too.

Climacteric fruits produce ethylene (see Gassing of Tomatoes, page 377), whereas non-climacteric fruits don't — so, in theory, putting climacteric fruit in contact with other riper climacteric fruit will help them ripen (or over-ripen if you're not careful).

SOME CLIMACTERIC FRUIT These fruits will ripen more, in theory, once picked, so long as they have been picked late enough. Just because they can ripen off the tree, however, doesn't mean they are as good as if ripened on the tree (though some, such as pears, are actually better picked unripe). Peaches, for instance, only gain about one-fifth of the flavour components when picked and ripened off the tree compared to being picked fully ripe from the tree, so you're only getting 20 per cent of the flavour.

Apples	Feijoas	Mangosteens	Plums
Apricots	Figs	Nectarines	Quinces
Avocados	Guavas	Papayas	Rockmelons
Bananas	Jackfruit	Peaches	Tomatoes
Blueberries	Kiwi fruit	Pears	
Durians	Mangoes	Persimmons	

SOME NON-CLIMACTERIC FRUIT There can be some softening and change in colour with these fruit after picking, but there is no real change in aromatics, flavour or sugar content.

Blackberries	Honeydew melons	Raspberries
Cherries	Longans	Strawberries
Citrus	Lychees	Watermelons
Eggplants	Olives	
Grapes	Pineapples	

POME FRUIT: APPLES AIN'T APPLES

Bob Magnus has 220 varieties of apples. Sounds like a lot if, like me, you grew up with just two types: red and green. Even today, the availability of apples to most people is limited to between four and ten varieties. But the former apple research station at Grove in Tasmania, only a three-quarter hour drive from Bob's orchard, has 500 varieties (cultivars), which in the season are on show at the local apple museum. This, however, is just the tip of the apple iceberg; Brogdale farm in the UK has the British national collection, numbering 2200 apple varieties (plus 500 varieties of pears, 350 of plums and 320 of cherries). Sounds amazing, but that's just 2200 out of an estimated 7500 varieties. Meanwhile, the US grows a reputed 2500 varieties (thank you, Johnny Appleseed). What most of us think of as apples barely touches on the varieties that we could have, if there was commercial demand.

Apples are so readily eaten in so many cultures, and yet they seem to be so poorly understood. Despite the fact that I live on an island enticingly called the Apple Isle (because in the 1960s it exported an awful lot of apples to the world), even here we have relatively little culture of apple varieties, little appreciation or knowledge that there are apples for cooking (that cook hard or soft), apples for eating today, apples for cider, apples that are mealy, or fragrant like fennel, with bouncy acidity that can suck your undies up your bum, or crisp like the frost that blankets the naked orchards come winter. Apple varieties can do all that, and much, much more.

Apples are the best known of the so-called pome fruit. It's a complex definition, but pome fruits all have seeds held in with a coarse membrane surrounded by flesh. So we're talking apples, pears, quinces and nashis as the main commercial crops. The trees are deciduous and need quite a bit of cold weather to set fruit properly. When they pollinate, they cross-pollinate, so the seeds of an apple won't give birth to the exact same kind of apple tree. This cross-pollination, however, leads to the plethora of varieties that exist today. (If you plant the seed of an apple and it grows into a tree, probability says you've got a one in 100,000 chance of a decent apple that has qualities as good as, or better than, those of the parent tree the apple you first ate came from.) That's why apple trees are grafted.

Commercial apples are grown for their looks (russet or patches of coarse, cinnamon-coloured skin, are selected against, as are fine lines), their keeping qualities, their size and colour. It's also imperative that the apple isn't easily bruised, so it can travel a long,

long way. Most modern apple growers aim at producing a crisp, sweet, good-storing and good-transporting apple because that's what the market favours.

These aren't sound criteria. The so-called 'red delicious' apple variety invariably isn't delicious, and in fact the floury texture it develops in storage put me off eating apples for a decade until I realised its season was only for about two weeks each autumn. When we bought our 70 acre (28 hectare) farm, we inherited 50 red delicious trees, and I discovered the apples are usually rubbish from day one.

A FEW APPLES AND THEIR USES

Apple varieties are often named rather poetically. Rather than offering an exhaustive guide, given there are thousands of varieties, this is just a taste of what you may be able to buy if you live near an apple-growing region.

BRAMLEY Britain's favourite cooking apple cooks down to very soft. It's not very nice to eat fresh, however, as the texture is rough and the flavour sour.

CATSHEAD Sour, sour, sour. Gorgeous green skin and blistering acidity, best cooked. When large, the shape resembles a cat's head. Dates from the 1600s.

COX'S ORANGE PIPPIN Rated as one of the world's top eating apples, this fruit is complex (some suggest melon and 'Florida orange juice'), fragrant, and good-looking to boot.

FUJI Sweet and crisp, Japan's favourite apple has great keeping qualities.

GEEVESTON FANNY Just love the name. A very local apple for me, found in southern Tasmania and named after the town of Geeveston, where it was first discovered, and the wife of the grower who popularised it, Fanny Evans. Small and blushed, the flesh is tender, white and very aromatic.

GOLDEN DELICIOUS When left to turn truly golden and eaten off the tree this apple is nothing like the green stuff you buy in shops. Crisp, sweet yet acid, it's a brilliant cooking apple when you need it to hold its shape (see Tarte Tatin, page 426).

GRANNY SMITH A green-skinned Australian variety that keeps really well, named after Maria Ann Smith, who propagated it from seed in the late 1800s. A decent eater and cooker, it isn't the best at either, but it does grow in warmer climes than most — and, importantly for a commercial crop, it stores really well, so is available all year.

PINK LADY Developed in 1973 in Western Australia by crossing a golden delicious with a lady williams. A crowd-pleaser that has done very well in recent years, thanks to its crisp texture, high sweetness and refreshing acidity.

STURMER This apple ripens late, and ripens fully off the tree, making a good cider apple. With a thick skin (that gets a 'greasy' feel) these fruit are best stored for a month before eating. Great flavour, though the texture can get slightly rubbery.

YARLINGTON MILL Punchy acidity, great sugar, lively flavour, named after the water mill where a pip took root in the stonework, in Somerset, England. A bittersweet apple that's perfect for cider.

WAXED APPLES

Some apples, even in today's enlightened times, are waxed, with a small drop of food-grade wax used per fruit. This is done mostly for aesthetic reasons (they look like an apple you've just picked and rubbed on your shirt), and because waxing does help preserve the fruit. Apples have a much finer, natural waxy coating, but it's very difficult to remove added wax without scrubbing, detergent and heat, all of which I wouldn't recommend on apples. It's better to buy unwaxed apples, in season.

PEAR VARIETIES

Pears, sometimes seen as the apple's poor cousin, come in many varieties, some, if not most, used in cooking and processing. A ripe pear, however, has a shorter shelf life than a ripe apple, a delicate melting flesh and a wonderful aroma. To me, it's one of the finest fruits to put with chocolate (see Pear and Chocolate Tart, page 555).

ANJOU America's favourite pear, available both red and green. A good eater, and not bad for cooking if used before fully ripe (as with many pears).

BEURRÉ BOSC A terrific russet pear with a luscious elongated shape, named because it's buttery, and after Monsieur Bosc, who headed Paris's botanical gardens and propagated the pear in the early 1800s. When ripe, it's the perfect pear for cooking, as it gets sweeter earlier in the ripening process (before it's fully soft), and holds its shape better, rather than cooking to mush.

COMICE A sometimes large, fat-necked, very juicy green pear that can come with a sexy blush. It breaks down quite quickly and should only be eaten fresh.

CONFERENCE A decent green, elongated pear with white flesh.

CORELLA A blushing, low-chill pear that comes late in the season and has a firm texture.

JOSEPHINE A green pear with a hint of russet, this is a great Belgian eating pear.

PACKHAM'S TRIUMPH Known colloquially as just packham, this is the bulbous greeny yellow pear with white flesh that is common in Australian markets. A great, simple eating pear.

SENSATION A great name for a modest, tender pear that comes in green or red varieties.

WILLIAM'S BON CHRÉTIEN Also called a william or bartlett, this is another extremely common green pear that ripens to yellow, with buttery-coloured flesh and a musky flavour.

WHY PEARS ARE SOLD UNRIPE

Pears, unlike most apples, like to ripen off the tree. Left on, they turn mealy, or rubbery. That's why when you buy a pear, it is usually firm, when you may want it soft. This is a great thing for us, the consumers, because it means we're able to buy pears at the perfect point to get ultimate ripeness. The downside is that it does mean you usually need to shop a few days ahead.

Pears ripen best at room temperature (below 25°C/77°F), not in the refrigerator. You can put them in a paper bag, perhaps with a banana skin, to speed up the ripening if need be.

To check a pear is ripe, press gently at the stem end: if it gives, it's ripe.

NASHI

A relatively new fruit to the commercial scene in Australia is the nashi. There are currently about 25 types of nashi grown in the country, and a lot more in Japan, where they're loved for their crisp texture. The nashi is sometimes known as a crisp version of the pear, with a fairly watery flavour by comparison. They're mostly about texture, but if you can get fruit straight from the tree, some have seductive, fleeting aromas that make them an autumn joy.

QUINCES

Quinces are the pome fruit that you only eat cooked. Raw, the flesh is astringent, tough, and decidedly unappetising. Cooked — especially if slow-cooked — they turn a gorgeous pink to rouge colour, their fragrance lifts to become intoxicating, and their lack of sweetness means they work well in both sweet and savoury dishes.

The two main varieties of quince are the smyrna and the pineapple quince. Smyrna are smoother, less fragrant, and hold together far better when cooked in liquid. Pineapple quinces are often large, more knobbly, and smell like pineapple (or at least pineapple essence). Both are green to gold in colour and keep well in cold storage for a month or two. Both are best picked slightly green if you want to make pastes (that way they'll contain more pectin, a natural fruit thickener), and both will fill the kitchen with their heady aroma if left whole in a bowl.

Like other pome fruit, quinces will go brown once cut. Rubbing the cut surfaces with an acid such as lemon juice can help prevent this.

HOW TO CHOOSE POME FRUIT

Only buy pome fruit in autumn — or perhaps some apple varieties in late summer and early winter.

Buy apples to eat straight away, pears to eat in a few days, and quinces that could sit on the bench for a week perfuming the kitchen before cooking.

Ask for a taste. A good apple should have great eating qualities, all of which are lost with long storage. A good merchant will know their qualities and be able to explain them.

Apples should be crisp, pears may have started to yield a little, and quinces should be as hard as a chef's heart.

1 kg (2 lb 4 oz) cooking apples, peeled, cored and cut into 1.5 cm (⅝ inch) dice
200 g (7 oz) raw (demerara) sugar
2 eggs, lightly beaten
a few drops natural vanilla extract
125 ml (4 fl oz/½ cup) extra virgin olive oil
200 g (7 oz/2 cups) walnuts, roughly chopped
250 g (9 oz/1⅔ cups) self-raising flour
1½ teaspoons ground cinnamon

Ye oldey appley cakey

Okay, so it's not that old, but this recipe does apparently come from a school recipe book from Western Australia, although I don't have the original. Even though I've adapted it, the basis is still an old-fashioned, delicious cake, which is mostly apple coated in a cake batter.

SERVES 12

Preheat the oven to 180°C (350°F/Gas 4). Grease a round 28 cm (11¼ inch) cake tin and line the base and sides with baking paper.

Mix the apples in a bowl with the sugar, egg, vanilla, oil and walnuts. Sift in the flour, cinnamon and a pinch of salt and stir to coat the apples in the batter.

Smooth the mixture into the prepared tin and bake for about 45 minutes. Allow to cool in the tin for 5 minutes, before turning out onto a wire rack to cool completely.

This is a very moist cake that is delicious at room temperature and gets better on the second day after it's made. Store in an airtight container and eat within 3 days.

Brandy cream

6 cloves

200 g (7 oz) sour cream

2 egg yolks

30 g (1 oz) sugar

1 tablespoon brandy

Apple pudding

1.5 kg (3 lb 5 oz) cooking apples, peeled, cored and cut into eight wedges

1 tablespoon finely diced candied lemon peel (see page 468)

100 g (3½ oz/1¼ cups) fresh breadcrumbs

150 g (5½ oz) caster (superfine) sugar

75 g (2¾ oz) butter, chilled and cubed

½ teaspoon freshly grated nutmeg

Apple pudding with brandy cream

This pudding recipe is adapted from Dorothy Hartley's apple charlotte in her seminal book, Food in England.

SERVES 8

To make the brandy cream, put the cloves and half of the sour cream in a very small saucepan over low–medium heat and heat carefully, stirring as the cream softens, until it starts to bubble around the edges. Remove from the heat and allow to steep for 15 minutes, or until cool.

Whisk the egg yolks, sugar and brandy in a bowl until pale. Stir in all the sour cream (including the clove cream) until combined. Refrigerate for 1 hour before serving.

To make the pudding, place the apples in a large mixing bowl with the candied lemon peel, two-thirds of the breadcrumbs, 100 g (3½ oz) of the sugar and 50 g (1¾ oz) of the butter and toss to combine.

Preheat the oven to 180°C (350°F/ Gas 4). Grease a deep 28 cm (11¼ inch) casserole dish and sprinkle with 1 tablespoon of breadcrumbs and half the nutmeg and toss them around to line the dish. Tip the apple mixture into the dish and press down well. Cover with foil or a lid and bake for 1 hour, or until the apple is soft. Flatten the top with a spoon.

Put the remaining breadcrumbs, sugar, butter and nutmeg in a food processor and pulse to make a crumble-type mix (or you could do it by hand). Sprinkle over the top of the apple mixture and bake for a further 20 minutes, or until the crumbs are golden.

Allow to cool slightly and serve with the brandy cream.

750 g (1 lb 10 oz) cooking apples, peeled, cored and thinly sliced
750 g (1 lb 10 oz) sweet shortcrust pastry (see page 150 — you will need to make 1½ times this recipe and then weigh it)
100 g (3½ oz) caster (superfine) sugar, plus extra for sprinkling
1 teaspoon finely grated lemon zest
150 g (5½ oz) blackberries (frozen ones are fine)

Lady grey custard
600 ml (21 fl oz) pouring (whipping) cream (35% fat)
1 vanilla bean, split lengthways
125 ml (4 fl oz/½ cup) boiling water
1½ teaspoons lady grey tea leaves
4 egg yolks
150 g (5½ oz) caster (superfine) sugar
100 g (3½ oz) homemade mascarpone (see page 62)

Apple & blackberry pie with lady grey custard

SERVES 10

Preheat the oven to 200°C (400°F/Gas 6). Put the apples in a large saucepan over low heat, cover, and cook, stirring occasionally, for 5 minutes, or until soft but not pasty. Cool completely, discarding any excess liquid.

Roll out two-thirds of the pastry into a circle with a 30 cm (12 inch) diameter and use it to line the base and side of a deep 25 cm (10 inch) round pie dish. Sprinkle 2 teaspoons of the sugar over the pastry base.

Toss the apple with the remaining sugar and lemon zest and place in the pastry case. Top with the blackberries.

Roll out the remaining pastry to create a circle with a 25 cm (10 inch) diameter for the pie lid. Lay over the pie and press the edges to seal. Cut a slit in the top of the pie lid to allow steam to escape. Sprinkle the top with some extra sugar. Bake for 35–45 minutes, or until the pastry is golden and cooked.

Meanwhile, make the custard. Put the cream and vanilla bean in a saucepan over high heat and bring almost to the boil. Remove from the heat, whisk and set aside for 20 minutes. Pour the boiling water over the tea leaves in a cup or bowl and let stand for 10 minutes, then strain the tea into the cream. Beat the egg yolks with the sugar. Reheat the cream over medium–high heat and whisk into the egg mixture. Return to medium heat in a clean saucepan and stir until the custard thickens slightly. Don't let it boil, or it will curdle.

Strain the custard and whisk in the mascarpone. Serve warm with the pie.

Alternative: To make a petal custard, omit the tea and substitute 125 ml (4 fl oz/¹/2 cup) Homemade Rosewater (see page 504) or 1 teaspoon bought rosewater, and stir it through after the custard is removed from the heat.

2 kg (4 lb 8 oz) quinces, peeled, quartered
    and cored
3 cm (1¼ inch) strip lemon peel, white
    pith removed

1 vanilla bean, split lengthways
1 tablespoon sugar, plus extra,
    to taste

Baked quince

*Quinces are not the easiest fruit to peel, and can be tricky to core — you
can do both once the quinces are cooked if you like (see note), but I prefer
to do it at the start. You can also cook them for less time, and they'll be
good, but the longer you let them cook, the more intense the flavours
become — four hours is better than two. The smyrna variety will hold
together better, but you can also roast pineapple quince this way.*

SERVES 6-8

Preheat the oven to 200°C (400°F/Gas 6).

Place the quinces around the bottom of
a wide based, baking dish (preferably with a
lid). Add the lemon peel, vanilla bean and
750 ml (26 fl oz/3 cups) water. Cover, reduce
the oven temperature to 160°C (315°F/
Gas 2–3), and cook for 1 hour.

Add the sugar to the dish and cook for
another 2 hours, or until tender and fragrant
— check it doesn't dry out and add some
more water if necessary. Remove the lid, baste
with the cooking liquid and cook for another
10–15 minutes, or until the liquid has reduced
to a thick, heavenly flavoured syrup.

Serve very simply, perhaps warm with
the cooking syrup and a dollop of natural
yoghurt or ice cream. Baked quinces also
make an amazing accompaniment to brie-
style cheese.

Note: For those of you who don't want to
peel and core the quinces when they are raw,
there is another way to cook them so they
come out purple and soft. Take the whole
fruit, making sure the skin is clean, and
immerse in sugar syrup (made up of equal
parts sugar and water) in a deep baking tray.
Add the lemon peel and vanilla if you wish.
Cover with baking paper and a lid or foil,
and place in a preheated 120°C (235°F/
Gas ½) oven. Cook for 4 hours, or until soft
and purple; the quinces barely simmer. Allow
to cool in the syrup. The skin will slide off
easily and the core can now be removed,
although the friend who taught me this
method then shoves the whole fruit into
custard and onto a tarte tatin.

40 g (1½ oz) butter
1.2 kg (2 lb 10 oz/about 8) golden
   delicious apples, peeled, halved
   and cored

100 g (3½ oz) sugar
3 tablespoons water
400 g (14 oz) pâte brisée (see page 148)

Tarte tatin

This incredible dish, made famous by the Tatin sisters from Lamotte Beauvron in France, is the essence of technique: you simply caramelise the apples, cover with pastry, bake, then invert and serve upside down — and the more you do it, the better you get at it. I use windfalls when I make this, as it's a good way to use up recently bruised fruit. The ingredient amounts above will vary depending on the size of the apples and the pan you use. Turn the oven on when the apples are nearly cooked.

SERVES 6

Heat the butter in a very wide heavy-based ovenproof frying pan, about 30 cm (12 inch) wide, over low heat. I have a dedicated cast-iron tatin pan that I carted around France in a mad moment. But in the town where the sisters made the cake famous, they use any old frying pan, then put the caramelised apples in a spring-form cake tin. If you are going for the tin option, grease a 30 cm (12 inch) spring-form cake tin to transfer the apple into before topping with pastry.

Add the apples to the pan, cut side down, and cook really slowly until they have caramelised. You may not fit them all in the pan at the start, but you can take a couple out once they soften and squeeze more in, then return them all to the pan. Sprinkle the sugar over the apples, then turn them over and cook the other side, splashing in some water if needed to make the caramel.

This whole process may take about 1 hour, though probably slightly less. Cook until the sugar starts to caramelise and the apple is cooked through — the water will slow the sugar caramelising. I like to add a bit of water just at the end to soften the caramel, too.

When the apples are nearly cooked, preheat the oven to 200°C (400°F/Gas 6). Roll the pastry into a circle with a 30 cm (12 inch) diameter to fit the pan, about 5 mm (¼ inch) thick all over.

Remove the pan from the heat. Cover the apple with the rolled-out pastry so it covers the apples completely and tuck in the edges. Bake in the oven for about 20–30 minutes, or until the pastry is well browned.

As soon as you remove the pan from the oven, gently invert the tart over a plate or platter (the caramel will be hot, so be careful). Serve warm with vanilla ice cream.

125 g (4½ oz) butter, softened
150 g (5½ oz) caster (superfine) sugar
3 eggs
100 g (3½ oz) sour cream
100 g (3½ oz/⅔ cup) self-raising
   flour, sifted
150 g (5½ oz/1½ cups) ground almonds
2 pears, cored and perhaps peeled,
   cut into 1 cm (½ inch) dice

Walnut crumble
150 g (5½ oz) butter, chilled and cubed
135 g (4¾ oz) plain (all-purpose) flour
80 g (2¾ oz/⅓ cup) soft brown sugar
75 g (2½ oz/¾ cup) walnuts, crushed

Pear & sour cream cake with walnut crumble

The sour cream adds a smooth richness, the pears add moisture, and the crumble is thick and crunchy with walnuts. The perfect cake, really.

SERVES 10

Preheat the oven to 170°C (325°F/Gas 3). Grease a 23 cm (9 inch) round spring-form cake tin and line the base and side with baking paper.

To make the pear and sour cream cake, cream the butter and sugar until pale and light. Beat in the eggs, one at a time, then beat in the sour cream. Fold in the flour and the ground almonds, just until it's an even consistency. Fold through the pears and spoon the mixture evenly into the base of the cake tin.

To make the walnut crumble, use your fingertips to rub the butter into the flour and sugar (or pulse in a food processor), until the mixture is crumbly. Stir in the walnuts.

Sprinkle the walnut crumble over the top of the cake and bake in the centre of the oven for about 60–70 minutes; test with a skewer. The cooking time can vary depending on the type and ripeness of the pears and your oven. It should be moist in the centre, but not doughy. Rub your fingers up the skewer to make sure — if you have any wet mixture on your fingers, give it another 5 minutes.

Remove from the oven and allow to cool in the tin for at least 10 minutes before removing to a wire rack to cool completely (don't invert the cake). Serve on its own, or perhaps with some Clotted Cream (see page 61).

2 kg (4 lb 8 oz) pink lady apples,
    peeled, cored and thinly sliced
finely grated zest of 1 lemon
juice of 1 lemon
4–5 tablespoons honey
8 eggs
375 g (13 oz) block puff pastry

Egg wash
1 egg
2 tablespoons milk

Apple amber

Apple amber is an old recipe idea where you make an apple paste, thicken it with eggs and sweeten it with honey. I've turned it into a pot pie as some did in times gone by, but I don't like to call it a pie because it doesn't have pastry on the bottom.

SERVES 6

Put the apples with a tiny bit of water — about 2 tablespoons — in a saucepan over very low heat. Cover and cook for about 15 minutes, stirring regularly, or until very, very soft. Allow to cool.

Preheat the oven to 200°C (400°F/ Gas 6). Beat the lemon zest, lemon juice, honey and eggs into the cooked apple using a wooden spoon, and taste for sweetness, adding more honey or some sugar to taste.

Spread the apple in the base of a 2 litre (70 fl oz/8 cup) capacity square casserole dish, about 20 x 20 cm (8 x 8 inch). Roll out the pastry on a lightly floured surface to 3 mm (1/8 inch) thick. Cover the dish with the pastry, cutting it to shape. To make the egg wash, combine the egg and milk and brush over the top of the pastry

Bake in the oven for about 30 minutes, or until the pastry is crisp and brown, and serve with Clotted Cream (see page 61).

Spiced pears

500 g (1 lb 2 oz) sugar

1 teaspoon green cardamom pods

4 star anise

½ teaspoon coriander seeds

10 black peppercorns

8 pears, ripe but not too soft, peeled, quartered and cored

unsalted pistachios or roasted almonds, crushed, to garnish

Rosewater chocolate sauce

300 ml (10½ fl oz) pouring (whipping) cream (35% fat)

200 g (7 oz/1⅓ cups) finely chopped dark chocolate

1 teaspoon rosewater or orange blossom water (see page 504)

caster (superfine) sugar (optional)

Lightly spiced pears with rosewater chocolate sauce

Remember when you were a kid and you'd steal ripe pears from the neighbour's orchard to eat on the long walk home from school? Remember his gruff voice when he'd yell out menacingly (yet, you knew it was half-heartedly), to send you on your way? Remember the flavour of fruit fresh from the tree, before mass transport and cold storage destroyed our palates? Well, neither do I. But I do remember growing up on tinned pears, and these are nothing like that. The spice, particularly the star anise, makes a wonderful play on the pears before leaping into a matrimonial state with the chocolate.

SERVES 8

To make the spiced pears, put the sugar and spices in a saucepan over high heat with 1 litre (35 fl oz/4 cups) water. Stir until the sugar dissolves. Add the pears to the simmering liquid and bring to the boil. Turn off the heat and allow the pears to steep in the poaching liquid for about 5 minutes, checking to make sure they don't overcook. They will keep cooking for a while once removed from the liquid, too, so don't wait until they are mushy. Place the cooled pears and the poaching liquid in an airtight container. They will last for up to 1 week in the refrigerator.

To make the rosewater chocolate sauce, heat the cream in a small saucepan over high heat until nearly boiling. Add the chocolate and stir until all the chocolate has dissolved, using only enough heat to help the chocolate melt. Cool slightly, then add rosewater, to taste. You may also need to add some sugar if your chocolate is quite dark and/or bitter.

Drain the pear halves, warm them just gently (in a microwave would be good) and serve with a good spoonful of lightly warmed chocolate sauce on top. Garnish with the crushed nuts. The syrup makes a lovely cordial; you can also use it on ice cream.

Apple butter

This apple butter makes a great accompaniment to pancakes (try blueberry), as a spread for toasted fruit bread (see Bara Brith, page 482), or melting over hot banana fritters.

1 large apple, peeled and cored
1 tablespoon caster (superfine) sugar
100 g (3½ oz) butter, softened
ground nutmeg or cinnamon, to taste (optional)

MAKES 200 G (7 OZ)

Cut the apple into bite-sized pieces. Place in a saucepan over very low heat with ½–1 teaspoon water and cook, covered, for 10–15 minutes, or until soft. Stir regularly so the apple doesn't stick. Add the sugar and mash to a pulp. Allow to cool.

Beat the apple in a bowl with the softened butter. Flavour with a little more sugar if necessary, and possibly a little nutmeg or cinnamon. Use while at room temperature, or refrigerate if not using straight away.

STONE FRUIT

The Japanese buyers will stay close to Tim Reid's farm in southern Tasmania's Derwent Valley for several days. So will the scouts from the supermarket giants; both sets of buyers nibbling on cherries every few hours or so. When this fruit is ready, it's ready, no waiting, and a matter of hours can make the difference between good fruit to transport and sell, and fruit that is too soft to sell. Particularly if the cherries make the journey from southern Australia all the way to Japan.

Tim Reid specialises in the firm, crisp, pale pink cherries favoured by the Japanese. Knowing the Japanese eye for consistency of fruit size, shape and colour, matched to their intolerance for certain sprays, these cherries are grown in a relatively clean way. They're also grown with no local market in mind, the fruit sprayed with calcium to toughen the skin, which helps in transporting and prevents them splitting.

HIGH-CHILL VERSUS LOW-CHILL FRUIT

Cherries, like most stone fruit, are still highly seasonal despite what we've managed to do with so many other fruit and vegetables. That's partly because they don't store for long, but also because they like a certain number of cold nights each year, and are susceptible to late frosts that can wipe out a crop if it happens after bud burst, the moment when the young tree's buds open, ready to sprout forth to revel in spring.

Reid's cherries are high-chill fruit, but there's been a big move to low-chill varieties, particularly of peaches and nectarines. Crops traditionally grown in cold climates are progressively being grown in warmer (low-chill) climates, stretching the season for peaches in Australia, at least, from November to April. The problem with low-chill varieties is that, quite frankly, they don't taste as good. They taste lower in acid (the modern trend is to favour high-sugar, low-acid varieties), and the aroma and the flavour seem less exciting.

There's a massive breeding program going on worldwide to create better low-chill varieties, which should result in improvements in flavour. In the meantime, many of the breeding programs are aimed at getting low-chill, non-melting flesh peaches, the sort favoured by canneries because their flesh doesn't break down easily when cooked. ('Non-melting' is industry doublespeak for what are sometimes known as 'rubber' fleshed peaches, or firm fleshed, both of which aren't particularly appetising terms.) These peaches don't get that melt-in-the-mouth juiciness you want of the best peach, but rather stay firm. This allows them to be ripened on the tree more easily, which is perfect if they are going to be handled or transported very much. Again, and I know this is getting repetitive, it's farming for the benefit of farmers and wholesalers, not for us, the consumers. It doesn't address what we want, which is the best-quality fruit in terms of flavour and texture.

CHERRIES

As is the case with peaches, cherry growers favour different fruit for various reasons, many to do with ripening time. The variety of cherry you're eating one day may be different from the variety you'll eat a week or two later (with names such as ron, van, bing and stella). The good news is that despite breeding programs aimed at lengthening the cherry season, it's still a fleeting crop that is at its peak in summer, and usually only for about a month or two each year.

One type of cherry that has fallen out of favour where I live is the sour cherry, most notably the Kentish and morello, from a slightly different species of plant than sweet cherries. Sweetness has taken over, and the use of sour cherries for savoury dishes has virtually disappeared from our culinary culture. Most savoury dishes now use the inappropriate sweet cherry.

WHAT TO LOOK FOR IN PEACHES, NECTARINES AND APRICOTS

Good peaches, nectarines and apricots are only available during summer. The fruit should be properly tree-ripened; aroma is a great guide, and so is texture, so ask your retailer to give you a slice to taste before you buy. If they don't let you, give the fruit a gentle squeeze at the stem end, and it should yield under modest pressure. The fruit — and the whole shop or stall — should smell strongly aromatic in the case of peaches and nectarines.

I once asked a peach orchardist how I could tell when a peach was at its peak for eating. He looked at me like I was a crazy person. 'When it falls from the tree,' he said. That's when the sugars, aromas and flavours are at their peak. Sadly, that means the best fruit is for the grower, rather than consumers.

Look for high-chill varieties. Basically, the colder the winter climate they grow in, the better they'll taste (so long as summer is hot enough). Locally grown and tree-ripened is more important than high-chill, however.

If you see fruit at a farmers' market, ask the grower if they're 'melting flesh' varieties, as this will ensure better fruit — the kind you need to eat over a bath, shirt off.

Choose a variety of varieties. Each breed of fruit is good for about a week or two at the most, so many growers have several varieties that they use to span the season.

Nectarines, by the way, are just peaches without the fuzz.

PEELING PEACHES OR NECTARINES To peel peaches or nectarines and give them some colour, put them into a saucepan of rapidly boiling water for 10 seconds to blanch them, then refresh in cold water. Leave for 5 minutes and the colour from the skin will seep into the flesh. Peel. If they don't peel easily, repeat the blanching — it's a sign they weren't ripe enough when picked.

POACHING PEACHES OR NECTARINES Poached peaches and nectarines are simply stunning. Poaching preserves fruit that is ready to eat, which can then be used in a variety of desserts — though they're wonderful just as they are, perhaps with some very good Homemade Yoghurt (see page 44).

To poach peaches or nectarines, mix twice the quantity of water to sugar (for example, 2 cups water to 1 cup sugar) and heat until simmering in the smallest saucepan that will fit the fruit in one layer — being sure to have enough liquid to completely submerge the fruit. You can flavour this syrup with a bay leaf, perhaps, or cinnamon, a vanilla bean, star anise or nutmeg, though it's best to let any spices steep in the hot liquid for 15 minutes before adding the fruit.

When ready to poach, make sure the liquid is simmering, then add the whole peaches or nectarines. Turn off the heat and allow the fruit to 'cook' in the cooling liquid, weighed down gently with an upturned saucer or plate. Firmer fruit may need to be simmered for a couple of minutes before you switch off the heat.

Store the fruit in the poaching liquid (which you can re-use) in the refrigerator. Serve with cream or mascarpone, or yoghurt and some fresh berries.

If you poach peaches or nectarines with the skin on, then peel later, the blush of the skin transfers to the fruit. It will, however, wash out again if the fruit is left in the syrup.

4 x 3–4 cm (1¼–1½ inch) bread slices,
 cut from a dense, unsliced white loaf
2 poached peaches or nectarines, pitted
 and sliced (see page 438)
5 eggs, lightly beaten with a pinch of salt
80 ml (2½ fl oz/⅓ cup) full-cream (whole)
 milk

1 teaspoon natural vanilla extract
2 tablespoons maple syrup, plus extra
 for drizzling
20 g (¾ oz) butter
150 g (5½ oz) raspberries, dusted well
 with icing (confectioners') sugar
lightly whipped cream, to serve (optional)

French toast stuffed with peaches

*To stuff French toast, you make a pocket in the bread to fill with fruit.
It's easier to handle than making a sandwich. If you don't have time to
poach the fruit (you can also use in-season pears), soften the peaches in
a little butter in the frying pan before cooking the toast.*

SERVES 4

Cut a slit into the side of the slabs of bread, through the crust, to make a large flat pocket through the middle. Slip a quarter of the sliced peaches into each piece of bread.

In a bowl, mix together the egg, milk, vanilla extract and maple syrup until combined. Transfer to a large, shallow bowl.

To cook the toast, heat a large frying pan over medium heat and add the butter. Working with one piece of bread at a time, dip each slice into the egg mixture until well sodden, then transfer straight to the frying pan where the butter should have just started to sizzle. Cook until brown on one side, then turn over and cook the other side. You may

want to use a lid to warm it right through — you'll probably need to cook the toast in two batches.

Serve the toast with a drizzle of maple syrup, some scattered raspberries, and some cream on the side if you like. Make sure there's plenty of maple syrup on the table for those greedy enough to want more. If you prefer, you can use the peach poaching liquid in its place.

1 litre (35 fl oz/4 cups) full-cream (whole) milk

1 vanilla bean, split lengthways (or use 2 teaspoons natural vanilla extract)

3 x 3 cm (1¼ inch) strips lemon peel taken with a potato peeler, white pith removed

100 g (3½ oz) caster (superfine) sugar

160 g (5¾ oz) arborio rice (or other risotto rice)

200 g (7 oz) halved, pitted cherries

a pinch of ground nutmeg or mace

Cherry breakfast risotto

Fans of porridge or rice pudding will adore this sweet breakfast dish. If you want to round out the flavours a little, try replacing some or all of the sugar with raw (demerara) sugar, or maybe even a hint of honey. I like to add a little extra milk and let it sit for an hour before eating.

SERVES 4–6

Put the milk, vanilla bean, lemon peel and sugar in a large saucepan over high heat. Add the rice and reduce the heat when it starts to simmer. Cook for about 20 minutes, stirring every few minutes. Stir in the cherries and the nutmeg. Keep simmering, stirring occasionally, until the rice is very soft — about another 10 minutes.

The risotto will thicken up a lot more as it cools. Remove the vanilla bean and lemon peel. Serve warm or at room temperature with some more fruit — Baked Rhubarb with Brown Sugar and Elderflower (see page 453) is nice.

100 g (3½ oz) raspberries (frozen are fine)

100 g (3½ oz) sugar

300 ml (10½ fl oz) sauternes-style dessert wine, plus 2 tablespoons extra

1 vanilla bean, split lengthways

4 ripe nectarines, peeled (see page 437)

Sauternes cream

150 ml (5 fl oz) pouring (whipping) cream (35% fat)

2 egg yolks

2 teaspoons icing (confectioners') sugar, sifted

Raspberry-poached nectarines with sauternes cream

The classic peach Melba uses vanilla ice cream, raspberry sauce and peaches. It's a stunning marriage of flavours. Here, I've used the same flavours (with nectarines for a change, though you could use peaches), and put them all in the one pot. I reckon a bit of scalded cream would go amazingly well, but good-quality ice cream would also be lovely.

SERVES 4

Put the raspberries, sugar, dessert wine and vanilla bean in a small saucepan over high heat until just simmering, stirring to dissolve the sugar. Add the nectarines and poach in this liquid for about 5 minutes, or until they are soft but not soggy — it will depend a lot on the fruit. Sometimes, if really ripe, you can just bring them to the boil and turn off the heat immediately.

Leave to steep in this liquid overnight, covered in plastic wrap in the refrigerator.

To make the sauternes cream, whisk the cream with the yolks, extra dessert wine and sugar in a bowl until thickened slightly.

Serve the nectarines at room temperature in a little pond of poaching liquid, with a drool of sauternes cream over the top.

BERRIES & SOFT FRUIT

Richard Clark has been selling raspberries since he first set up a roadside stall at the age of fourteen. When I first met him, despite working for the Reserve Bank in Sydney, he would return once a year to the family farm near Plenty, just north-west of Hobart, to harvest and market raspberries as fine as just about any on the market.

The first sign that these are ripe raspberries, harvested ready to eat, is that the pickers take the fruit straight from the raspberry canes and put them directly into punnets. An absence of double-handling limits any damage to the berries. Up to 5 tonnes of fruit is picked like this every day during the season, then delivered to Hobart within about 24 hours, and sold at the best foodstores and markets as fresh fruit. This is an old American variety, the willamette, which has fallen out of favour because, despite tasting heavenly — despite being brightly coloured, juicy, full of sugar and acid, and being soft and succulent to eat — it doesn't keep very well. About 90 per cent of the williamettes grown by Richard's family's farm can't be picked and sold fresh within the narrow ripening window, so were sold for crushing into juice.

Over at Carl Sykes' berry patch, about an hour south of Richard's, pickers are busy at the tail end of the season. Carl's blueberries are little bliss bombs of flavour. He puts it down to the grass — the fact he doesn't spray underneath his blueberry bushes, but rather likes the grass to thrive, to trap carbon that will break down as the grass mulches into the soil. Blueberries have a firmer skin than raspberries, so their shelf life is much longer, but still they have to be picked ripe if they're going to have any flavour worth raving about.

The clue to what's wrong with modern, commercially available soft fruit is in the name. Soft fruit should be picked, and eaten, soft. But that doesn't work if you're picking one day, sending them to a wholesaler the next, who sells them to a supermarket where a half-trained casual staff member will put them on the shelf in a week's time. It just doesn't work, and every time you've bought a punnet of strawberries you've probably been wondering just what happened to the flavour.

Well, the flavour was never there in the first place. Berries have been bastardised. We've been led to believe that strawberries should have a white heart and be able to sit in the refrigerator for a week. That raspberries will hold their shape after picking, that blueberries have a six-month season and that blackberries can be sold in a punnet rather than eaten with sticky fingers from a dangerously spiky bush.

The season for most soft fruit is summer. That's it. That's the time when there's heat in the day, and the berries, which all originated in cold-climate countries, become laden with fruit, and you get the mix of bracing acidity and succulent sweetness that marks properly ripened fruit. It's supposed to be a celebration of a remarkable, fleeting season, of berries that make your hair stand on end and your tongue hang out and your knees tremble.

Instead, shop-bought berries, just about all the time, are a shadow of the way the fruit could, and should taste. The thing to remember about berries and soft fruit, just like stone fruit, is that they can't be improved, only maintained after picking.

FIGS

There are thousands of cultivars of fig, some grown just for pollination, and there is at least one grower in Australia who has about fifty varieties in the ground.

A fig is actually a bunch of flowers, with thousands of the flowers internalised within each fruit. When you eat a fig, you consume a very fertile seedbed (and other, more protein-based bits, see below) and a lot of sweet, gorgeous nectar.

Figs, like other soft fruit, need to be picked ripe, and eaten within a day or two. At their best, the skin is fragile, the base heavy with sweet nectar, the fragrance pronounced and the giggles from grown men a little embarrassing. At their worst they're a bit dry, hardly sweet, light in the hand and grainy in the mouth.

VEGANS, VEGETARIANS AND FIGS

Figs are fertilised by a wasp that has to enter the fruit through the small hole at the end. As she enters, the female wasp loses her wings, and, after laying her eggs, she dies inside the fig. When her eggs hatch, the males will mate with the females, then dig a hole for the females to escape through, before they, too, die inside. The females fly off to fertilise another fig.

To eat a fig, therefore, is to eat the dead body of the mother wasp, and consume eggs or perhaps the bodies of other wasps, a fact some vegans and vegetarians may want to consider.

WHAT TO LOOK FOR IN BERRIES

Soft fruit should be ready to eat — and needs to be eaten — virtually as soon as it's picked. Berries are cold-climate fruits, and those that are grown in colder areas have a more intense, sharper, more aromatic flavour, and usually more racy acidity. The best berries I've eaten came from above the Arctic Circle in a Finnish summer.

It's usually better to eat locally grown fruit than anything that has been transported, because transported fruit is usually picked while still under-ripe.

Look for fruit with a bright or deep colour, as colour is a sign of flavour. When choosing berries, however, be aware that they will soften and change colour after picking, without gaining any more flavour or sugar. Raspberries are the classic example, getting darker but not sweeter once picked.

Strawberries, whose Latin genus name is *Fragaria*, should be fragrant. If you can't smell them before you see them, they aren't good strawberries.

WHY IS MY JAM SO RUNNY?

If you're making jam, it's always good to use some unripe fruit in the pot. Great, perfectly ripe, soft, squidgy berries will make a great sauce, but not a firmly set jam. The reason? Pectin, the same thing that makes fruit firm, and which breaks down as the fruit ripens, is the ingredient that makes jam set. So, despite its joyous colour and flavour, perfectly ripe fruit is unlikely to set. You can add pectin, use the seeds from citrus fruit in the jam (wrapped in muslin/cheesecloth for easy extraction) and add some lemon juice, the acid of which helps the pectin that's in the fruit to set. Fruit set is a complex interplay of pectin, acid, sugar and the fruit's consistency. I cover this in depth in my book, *Not Just Jam*.

I like to eat the ripest fruit, and use some that are under-ripe in the jam. I'm happy with runny jam that tastes of summer in a jar rather than the commercial, dull-coloured, very thick jam that they sell in supermarkets.

RHUBARB

While not a soft fruit, or a fruit at all by definition, rhubarb is a remarkably sour, wonderfully fragrant stem that cooks to succulent softness. Rhubarb can be bright red, have patches of green, or even be fully green. I've found the green variety has more fragrance and higher acidity, but different cultivars have different properties.

To choose rhubarb, pick bright, pert stems with glossy leaves. Discard the leaves (they're poisonous) before cooking.

200 g (7 oz/1⅓ cups) plain (all-purpose) flour
120 g (4¼ oz) caster (superfine) sugar
120 g (4¼ oz) butter, chilled and cubed
3 rose geranium leaves, washed
500 g (1 lb 2 oz) rhubarb, washed and chopped

500 g (1 lb 2 oz/3⅓ cups) strawberries, hulled and halved if large
3–4 tablespoons honey
1 teaspoon natural vanilla extract

Strawberry, rhubarb & rose geranium crumble

Strawberry and rhubarb seem to complement each other in ways words can't describe. Made into crumble, they release their flavour even more. If you don't have rose geranium, you should. And if you really, really don't have it and can't get it from someone's garden, you can try a few drops of Homemade Rosewater (see page 504) in the fruit, which will create a similar effect.

SERVES 6

To make the crumble, mix together the flour, sugar and a pinch of salt. Rub in the butter with your fingertips until it looks crumbly. You could pulse this mix very gently in a food processor but it won't be as good. Refrigerate for 30 minutes.

Put the rose geranium leaves and 125 ml (4 fl oz/½ cup) water in a saucepan over high heat. Simmer for a few minutes until quite fragrant. Preheat the oven to 200°C (400°F/Gas 6).

Toss the rhubarb and strawberries with the honey and vanilla (heat the honey if it is too thick to work with). Press the rhubarb and strawberry mixture into the bottom of a 25 cm (10 inch) square baking dish or similar and splash with a little strained rose geranium water to flavour but not drown.

Just before baking, sprinkle the crumble evenly over the fruit. Bake for about 30–40 minutes, towards the top of the oven, until the crumble has browned. Serve warm with vanilla ice cream or bay leaf custard (see variation to Good Old-fashioned Cornflour Custard, page 48).

1 kg (2 lb 4 oz) gooseberries or other
    berries
110 g (3¾ oz/½ cup) sugar
500 ml (17 fl oz/2 cups) good old-
    fashioned cornflour custard
    (see page 48)

500 ml (17 fl oz/2 cups) pouring
    (whipping) cream (35% fat), whipped
    until thick

Gooseberry fool

*A fool is something stirred through custard or cream. Here I've used
both custard and cream. You can use the same philosophy to make other
summer fools, such as raspberry or strawberry. Gooseberries are super
sour, but aromatic and joyous when cooked with plenty of sugar. Look for
them at the start of summer.*

SERVES 4–6

Remove any stems from the gooseberries
and wash well. Drain and place them in a
saucepan over medium heat with the sugar,
and stew for 10 minutes, or until really soft.
Push vigorously through a sieve, reserving
the pulp and juice and discarding the skins.
Allow to cool.

Push the custard through the same sieve
as you did the berries. Fold the gooseberries
very gently through the custard and whipped
cream, adding more sugar to taste, if needed.

Serve in small bowls or glasses. You can
serve it immediately, but it gets better if left
to stand for 3–4 hours, if you have the time.

Baked rhubarb with brown sugar & elderflower

The bracing acidity of rhubarb is usually best married with sugar, and brown sugar has more complexity than white. The elderflower adds a new layer of fragrance. In its absence, you could add a teaspoon or two of full-flavoured honey.

---

500 g (1 lb 2 oz) rhubarb, trimmed and chopped into
   3 cm (1¼ inch) lengths
2–3 tablespoons dark brown sugar
2 tablespoons elderflower cordial
100 ml (3½ fl oz) pouring (whipping) cream (35% fat)
1 teaspoon caster (superfine) sugar
a few drops natural vanilla extract (optional)

SERVES 4

Preheat the oven to 220°C (425°F/Gas 7). Lay the rhubarb on a baking tray, sprinkle with the brown sugar and elderflower cordial and bake for about 10–15 minutes, or until soft.

While the rhubarb cooks, whip the cream with the sugar and vanilla until soft and moussey.

Serve the rhubarb in bowls with a dollop of cream on top.

600 ml (21 fl oz) moscato wine

3 teaspoons powdered gelatine

120 g (4¼ oz/about 8) savoiardi
(lady finger) biscuits

300 g (10½ oz) raspberries

4 eggs, separated

50 g (1¾ oz) caster (superfine) sugar

130 g (4¾ oz) icing (confectioners')
sugar, sifted

500 g (1 lb 2 oz) homemade mascarpone
(see page 62)

80 ml (2½ fl oz/⅓ cup) elderflower
cordial

Raspberry & elderflower trifle with moscato jelly

Raspberries are a celebration of summer. Soft, bright in colour and acidity, sweet and packed full of flavour, they're brilliant in desserts. I like to use them with elderflowers, which also have a tremendous summery perfume, and are now sold as a cordial in many supermarkets. Failing that, just use freshly squeezed orange juice. If you can't get moscato, dilute a dessert wine with half its volume in water. It's best to make the trifle a day before you plan on eating it to let it set. A little weeping in the bottom of the bowl is just fine.

SERVES 4–6

Put the moscato in a saucepan over high heat and bring to almost boiling. Whisk in the gelatine until it dissolves, then remove from the heat.

Arrange the savoiardi biscuits in the base of a 25 cm (10 inch) square casserole dish, about 2.5 litre (87 fl oz/10 cup) capacity, and pour over the moscato to coat. Allow to cool, then refrigerate overnight so it sets.

The next day, tip half the raspberries over the top. Whisk the egg whites with the caster sugar until stiff peaks form.

In a separate bowl, whisk the yolks with the icing sugar until pale and light, then beat in the mascarpone, being careful not to overmix or it will split. Stir in the cordial, whisk again, and then gently fold in the egg whites.

Smear this thickly over the biscuit mix and raspberries, top with more raspberries, cover, and refrigerate for 1–2 hours before serving with a glass of moscato.

500 g (1 lb 2 oz) greek-style yoghurt
1 teaspoon natural vanilla extract
2 tablespoons honey
1 tablespoon finely grated lemon zest
500 g (1 lb 2 oz/3⅓ cups) strawberries
3 peaches or nectarines, stones
    removed, cut into chunks

2 bananas, peeled and cut into
    bite-sized chunks
1 tablespoon lemon juice
5 basil leaves, finely sliced

Warm strawberry salad with vanilla drained yoghurt

I love strawberries as much as I love Hobart on a sunny Sunday afternoon. And that's a lot. Unlike Hobart, however, I only love fresh strawberries in summer.

SERVES 4

Place the yoghurt in a strainer lined with muslin (cheesecloth) or strong, clean, absorbent paper. Cover the yoghurt, place a bowl underneath the strainer, and place the whole lot into the refrigerator to let the whey drain out overnight. The next day, put the thickish yoghurt into a bowl and stir in the vanilla extract.

In a large frying pan, heat the honey and zest over medium heat. Add the strawberries, peaches and bananas and toss to warm through. Add the lemon juice and basil and serve warm with the yoghurt.

2 rose geranium leaves, or 30 rose petals,
    washed
60 g (2¼ oz) sugar
1 teaspoon powdered gelatine

500 g (1 lb 2 oz/3⅓ cups) strawberries,
    stem removed, halved or quartered
    if large

Strawberry & rose geranium jelly

Strawberries that bruise when you pick them, that lovingly give up their juices at the touch of a knife, are what good food is all about. And that means you should only buy them in summer. Choose really ripe, deeply coloured berries, and avoid very large ones as they tend to be all show. This soft jelly works well with mango, too, and it's worth begging, borrowing or stealing the rose geranium leaves. Just so long as it's not from my house. You will need to make this one day in advance to allow the jelly to set.

SERVES 4

Put 400 ml (14 fl oz) water in a saucepan over high heat and bring to the boil. Add the rose geranium leaves, remove from the heat, and allow to infuse for 15 minutes.

Discard the leaves, bring the water back to the boil, add the sugar and sprinkle in the gelatine, stirring to dissolve. Remove from the heat and allow to cool until nearly set.

Pour half the jelly into the base of four parfait glasses (you knew you'd be able to use them one day!) and add the strawberries. Refrigerate for 5–6 hours, or until set.

Pour over the remaining jelly and refrigerate overnight. Serve as a dessert (or a honeymoon breakfast), with a late-harvest sauvignon blanc.

Figs with jamón & gorgonzola

This recipe uses gorgonzola dolce latte, a softer, sweeter version of this wondrous blue cheese. There's the playfulness of the soft, nectar-laden figs with the salty jamón and sour cheese.

6 fresh figs
60 g (2¼ oz) gorgonzola dolce latte
6 thin slices jamon or prosciutto

SERVES 2

Cut the figs in half if large. Press a small nugget of gorgonzola into the middle of each fig and drape the jamón over the top. Cook under a hot preheated griller (broiler) or bake in a 200°C (400°F/Gas 6) oven until they're warm throughout (the cheese will melt) and serve warm.

CITRUS FRUIT

Just about all citrus is the result of crossing just a few citrus fruits — the pomelo, the citron and the mandarin. From these we get multiple crosses that have produced the astounding range of beautifully acidic fruit we know today, from lemons to tangelos, from oranges to grapefruit.

Citrus fruit comes in relatively few varieties compared to pome fruit. It also comes from hotter climates, where summers are fierce or subtropical, and winters not too scathing — think Israel, south-west and south-east US (Florida and California), Spain, southern Italy and the hot, inland Riverina region of Australia. With the exception of the lemon, which can cope with fierce winters, most citrus is at home in the subtropics.

What makes citrus fruit good is the variety, the weather and the way it's stored. Luckily for us, citrus keeps very well, barely changing in character (except, perhaps, for a drastic loss of its all-important vitamin C) for weeks and sometimes months.

ORANGES

The truth is, the best-tasting orange isn't actually completely orange. Not to me, anyway. The best commercial variety, one of two that dominate the local market, is the valencia.

The best-looking orange is the Brazilian-originated navel orange, bred to be highly orange in colour. Its popularity comes from this, the fact that it is a hybrid and doesn't produce seeds, and that it comes at the far end of the season from valencia oranges.

Good citrus, particularly oranges, need a cranking-hot summer. A dry summer helps too. They don't grow at all well where I live, but out on the irrigated, baking hot plains of north-western Victoria and the Riverina in NSW, where the winters are cool enough but not too icy, and there's little humidity compared to the tropics, oranges thrive. The good news for eaters is that oranges keep fairly well, and travel exceptionally well, so they can be picked fully ripe and make it to shops and markets a long way from the source.

SEVILLE This is a bitter, sour orange best suited to savoury sauces (duck a l'orange, or the peel in Beef Shin Daube, see page 227) or marmalade.

NAVEL Sometimes called washington navels (despite originating in Brazil), these oranges grow during summer and are usually ripe in autumn. Along with other related navels — all of which take their name after the orange's flower end, which produces a second, mini orange that looks like a belly button — these are usually bright orange and harvested before winter frosts. They're a seedless hybrid and good for eating and juicing fresh (see page 465).

VALENCIA Also known as murcia, these oranges, despite what the name implies, probably didn't come from Spain, but are named after the famed town in Spain where majestic orange trees line the streets and riverbank. Never fully orange, even when ripe, they do have seeds and are usually ready at the start of summer. Like navel oranges, they are good for eating and juicing, and also make fantastic sweets.

BLOOD ORANGES This fruit has a deep red colour through the flesh and produces a juice that resembles ox-blood. They are highly aromatic and complex, and favoured by many for their juice. The main Italian variety is moro, which is sharp and sweet, and deep red. Another variety, maltese, is only flecked with red and doesn't have as much acid.

CUMQUATS

A tiny citrus that is usually too sour to be eaten fresh, cumquats are prized in cookery and in marmalade; wherever both the flesh and pulp can be used. The nagami cumquat is an oval-shaped Japanese variety that can be eaten fresh and whole because the flesh isn't anywhere near as sour, or the skin as bitter, as everyday cumquats.

MANDARINS

This is the collective name for a group of citrus where the skin is easier to peel and the fruit smaller than that of oranges. They're orange in colour. Tangerines are a subgroup of mandarins that are a darker orange than other mandarins. They're the same when it comes to cooking. Always choose heavy fruit, because the heavier they are, the more likely they are to be full of juice. The honey murcott variety is firmer-fleshed and skinned, which makes it better for cooking than the early-season, more common imperial mandarin.

LEMONS

Lemons have a curious habit of ripening off the tree. Well, not exactly ripening, but of converting pith to a juicier centre over a period of two weeks. That said, eureka and lisbon lemons will always have a much thicker skin than cool-climate meyer lemons. As meyer lemons have a more delicate aroma, and less acidity, many consider them a superior cooking lemon. Because of their thinner skin, they don't store or transport as well, making them an item of rare and unusual value. It's been suggested that they're a cross between a mandarin and a lemon.

LIMES

Originating in the eastern Mediterranean, limes tend to be sourer than lemons, and more aromatic in a perfumed kind of way. The juice oxidises very quickly and is best squeezed immediately prior to use. The most popular types are the key lime, which takes its name from being popularised in Florida in the US, and the Tahitian lime, named for the island in the Pacific. Australia has some native limes, the most commercial being the highly prized finger lime, which comes in a rainbow of colours from pink to yellow to green, with fantastic coarse-grained flesh that forms caviar-like, highly acidic pearls that add sparkle to dishes.

KAFFIR LIMES (MAKRUT)

Knobbly limes native to South-East Asia, kaffir limes are highly aromatic and not as sour as normal limes. They usually don't give up much juice, and with such a convoluted skin the zest is hard to grate. For this reason their characteristic double leaf is used more often than the fruit itself, usually to flavour curries, soups and sauces, though you can try it in custard, too.

CLEMENTINES

A cross between an orange and a mandarin, clementines are more savoury than mandarins, as well as being quite aromatic and easy to peel.

GRAPEFRUITS

A cross between the pomelo and the sweet orange, one common cross produces a delightfully bitter grapefruit. Modern grapefruit are bred to be less bitter, particularly the pink and red varieties perfected by the Americans.

POMELOS

A large, pithy, wonderful citrus found in the US and Mexico, across southern China and into other parts of Asia. The pomelo is the precursor of the modern grapefruit. The fruit, which can easily be the size of an orangutan's head, has very large segments of relatively dry, sweet and not-too-bitter fruit (especially compared to its progeny, the grapefruit, which has some role as a substitute in recipes). Pomelo can be used in salads, as it is through Asia and the Americas, but is terrific eaten as a fresh fruit. The pink pomelo is the best flavoured.

TANGELOS

A cross between a mandarin and a grapefruit (or pomelo), which gives it sugar, acidity and an abundance of juice, and also makes it easy to peel. Tangelos have a little nipple on the top and are a hybrid, so have few seeds.

STORING CITRUS

When you get them home, it is best to refrigerate citrus fruits or eat them quite soon. Don't store them with ethylene-producing fruit, such as pomes, bananas or avocados, because this will cause them to go off sooner.

According to a Department of Agriculture website, grapefruit and lemons are best stored at 12°C (54°F), navel and valencia oranges at 7–10°C (45–50°F), and mandarins at 5°C (41°F). At these temperatures grapefruit, valencia and navel oranges and lemons can be expected to keep for 3 months, and mandarins for 1–2 months, depending on variety, maturity and storage conditions.

FRESHLY SQUEEZED IS BEST

Most of the so-called orange juice you buy in shops is made from concentrate. That's why it doesn't taste like the juice you get if you squeeze your own oranges. Frozen and shipped around the world, most orange juice comes from countries far from ours, with growing practices that can be questionable, or at least can't be questioned from such a distance. If it says made from local and imported ingredients, the local ingredient could be the water that is used to reconstitute it. The best orange juice you can get is the stuff you squeeze yourself.

The juice from navel oranges will go bitter about 30 minutes after you squeeze them.

4 egg yolks
125 ml (4 fl oz/½ cup) full-cream
    (whole) milk
200 g (7 oz) sugar
1 vanilla bean, split lengthways
4 tablespoons Grand Marnier or
    Cointreau (or other distinct liqueur)

2 teaspoons finely grated orange zest
300 g (10½ oz) thick (double/heavy)
    cream (over 45% fat)
300 ml (10½ fl oz) pouring (whipping)
    cream (35% fat)

Orange semifreddo

This is quite an adult dessert — although you can omit the grog for the children's sake and substitute a little orange juice instead, which can make it icier.

SERVES 8

Beat the egg yolks in a bowl until very pale and thick.

Put the milk in a saucepan over high heat and add the sugar and vanilla bean. Stir to dissolve the sugar, bring to the boil, then reduce the heat and simmer for 3 minutes. Remove from the heat, whisking well, and discard the vanilla bean.

Pour the milk in a thin stream onto the egg yolks, whisking the yolk mixture as you do so. Continue whisking until cool (use a cold-water bath under the bowl if doing this by hand). Beat in the Grand Marnier and orange zest.

Mix the creams and lightly whip until soft peaks form. Fold gently into the egg mixture until just combined.

Spoon into a 1.5 litre (52 fl oz/6 cup) mould or eight 200 ml (7 fl oz) individual dariole moulds or ramekins and freeze until set, about 4–6 hours.

Note: If the semifreddo is ever a shade too firm, place it in the refrigerator for 30 minutes before serving.

1 teaspoon finely grated tangelo zest
1 portion crepe batter (see page 199)

Tangelo and cumquat sauce
120 g (4¼ oz) cumquats
½ cinnamon stick
1 green cardamom pod
50 g (1¾ oz) sugar, plus 1 tablespoon
    extra

250 ml (9 fl oz/1 cup) tangelo juice,
    strained
1 tablespoon brandy, Grand Marnier
    or Cointreau
1 egg white
100 g (3½ oz) homemade mascarpone
    (see page 62)

Tangelo & cumquat crêpes suzette

I like to fill crepes with a lightened mascarpone mix (you could use sweetened ricotta), and flavour them with this intense, citrussy sauce.

SERVES 4

Mix the tangelo zest into the crepe batter and cook the crepes as you would normally. Keep warm stacked on a plate, covered, in a low oven while you make the sauce.

Wash the cumquats and cut them into quarters lengthways, discarding the seeds. Place in a saucepan over high heat with the cinnamon stick, cardamom and 60 ml (2 fl oz/¼ cup) water. Bring to the boil, then turn off the heat and allow to sit for 10 minutes. Strain and reserve the cooking water and fruit separately.

Sprinkle the sugar over the base of a frying pan over high heat, shaking the pan occasionally, until the sugar melts and starts to caramelise. Add the cooking water from the cumquats and simmer until nearly caramelising again.

Add 185 ml (6 fl oz/¾ cup) of the tangelo juice to the pan and continue to reduce the syrup by half. Add the remaining juice, brandy and cumquats. Flambé if you must, and cook for 3–5 minutes until the cumquats are tender.

Whisk the egg white with the extra sugar until soft peaks form. Fold into the mascarpone.

When the sauce is ready, spread the mascarpone mixture thinly over the crepes, fold into quarters, place on plates and spoon the sauce over the top, to serve.

1 grapefruit
1 teaspoon dark brown sugar

Grilled grapefruit with brown sugar

You're hardly likely to make the kids want grapefruit if you don't add sugar. The sharply acidic nature of some grapefruit alters with the warmth of a grill and the light caramelisation of brown sugar. If you want to turn it into a bit of a party breakfast dish, add a splash of rum.

SERVES 2

Cut the grapefruit into even halves and sprinkle half of the sugar over each side. Place under a hot grill (broiler) on high and cook until they start to caramelise. Did someone say something about a splash of rum?

4 oranges or 6 lemons
500 ml (17 fl oz/2 cups) boiling water,
    plus extra for blanching
440 g (15½ oz/2 cups) sugar

Candied citrus peel

You can use this recipe to make lemon or orange candied citrus peel, both of which can be used in fruit cakes (see Janette's Mother's Christmas Cake, page 485) or Hot Cross Buns (see page 137).

MAKES 155 G (5¾ OZ) CANDIED ORANGE PEEL, OR 100 G (3½ OZ) CANDIED LEMON PEEL

Remove the peel from the fruit using a sharp knife — cutting to ensure you are removing the skin and pith and leaving behind the fruit

Place the citrus peel in a bowl and pour over enough boiling water to cover. Blanch for 1 minute. Rinse the peel and blanch again for 1 minute in fresh boiling water.

Place the peel in a small saucepan with the boiling water and add the sugar. Bring to the boil, then reduce the heat and simmer for 30 minutes, or until glacé (meaning it should look translucent). Drain well. Citrus peel stores well in an airtight container in a cool pantry for weeks if not months.

3 tablespoons self-raising flour, sifted

345 g (12 oz/1½ cups) caster (superfine) sugar

200 g (7 oz/2 cups) ground almonds

4 tablespoons finely grated mandarin, tangelo, lemon or lime zest (I prefer 3 tablespoons mandarin to 1 of lime)

3–4 teaspoons green cardamom seeds, ground

8 egg whites

150 g (5½ oz) butter, melted and cooled slightly

Fragrant citrus & cardamom cake

The biggest danger with this cake is undercooking it. To check, press the top firmly, pierce with a skewer or allow extra time if uncertain. The cake is very moist, so you can get away with overdoing it a little, just so long as the underside doesn't become too dark. After all, there's nothing as unappealing as a burnt bottom.

SERVES 10

Preheat the oven to 160°C (315°F/Gas 2–3). Grease an 18 cm (7 inch) round spring-form cake tin and line the base and side with baking paper.

Sift the flour into a bowl with the sugar and ground almonds and add the zest and cardamom. Stir in the egg whites, then the reasonably cool melted butter, and mix well.

Pour the mixture into the prepared tin and cook for about 90 minutes (fan-forced ovens will tend to brown the outside more quickly) or until completely cooked.

Allow to cool for 10 minutes in the tin, then remove and place on a wire rack to cool completely.

Serve at room temperature. This cake is a little like a curry, the leftovers taste even better a couple of days later, if you can leave any. It will store in an airtight container for up to 5 days.

250 g (9 oz) sugar

80 ml (2½ fl oz/⅓ cup) lemon juice, strained

1½ tablespoons elderflower cordial

400 ml (14 fl oz) full-cream (whole) milk

Lemon & elderflower sherbet

A sherbet, in the old-fashioned sense, is an iced dessert that uses milk (unlike a sorbet), but doesn't use eggs (unlike an ice cream). This works well even if you don't have an ice-cream machine or anything too fancy.

MAKES 1 LITRE (35 FL OZ/4 CUPS)

Put the sugar and 250 ml (9 fl oz/1 cup) water in a saucepan over high heat, stirring until the sugar is dissolved. Allow to cool (you can speed this process up by placing the base of the pan in cold water). Add the lemon juice and stir well. Then, stir in the elderflower cordial and milk. It could well look curdled, but don't worry about that.

Place in a large plastic tray in the freezer (big enough to whisk it up in later) and freeze for 1 hour. Pull from the freezer and whisk (use a hand beater) to break up all the ice crystals and redistribute them. Do this every 30 minutes or 1 hour for the next 2–3 hours while the mixture freezes. If you forget it,

or your freezer is super efficient and the ice becomes too firm, use a food processor to turn it back into slush.

When the mixture is light and airy, smooth over the top and freeze for 1 hour more so it's more like a sorbet than a slushie.

2 limes
2 tablespoons sugar
1 kaffir lime leaf (optional)
300 g (10½ oz/2 cups) ripe blueberries
1 large mango

500 g (1 lb 2 oz/3⅓ cups) ripe
    strawberries, hulled, and halved if large
150 g (5½ oz/1¼ cups) ripe raspberries

Summer fruit salad with lime syrup

This recipe makes a luscious summery fruit salad where you plump up the flavours using heat, lime and sugar. The lime and kaffir lime leaf are what take it from the realms of ordinary fruit salad to another level altogether, though you can substitute lemon or cumquat leaves for the kaffir lime leaves if you have them. Add chunks of peach or nectarine if you want, too, and serve at any time from breakfast to after dinner.

SERVES 4

Grate the zest from the limes and juice them. Put the sugar in a saucepan over medium heat and add 80 ml (2½ fl oz/⅓ cup) water; warm gently. Add the lime zest and kaffir lime leaf and simmer for 2 minutes. If any of the fruit seems a bit lacklustre, in particular the blueberries — which often taste of little until warmed — add to the hot syrup. Allow this syrup to cool a bit, but not completely.

Meanwhile, cut the cheeks from the mango and peel and dice the flesh. I use a big kitchen spoon to remove the flesh from the peel, sliding the spoon around just under the skin. Mix all the fruit in a big bowl, splash in the lime juice and toss it all together with the now cooler lime syrup.

Serve with natural yoghurt, or even better, buffalo milk yoghurt.

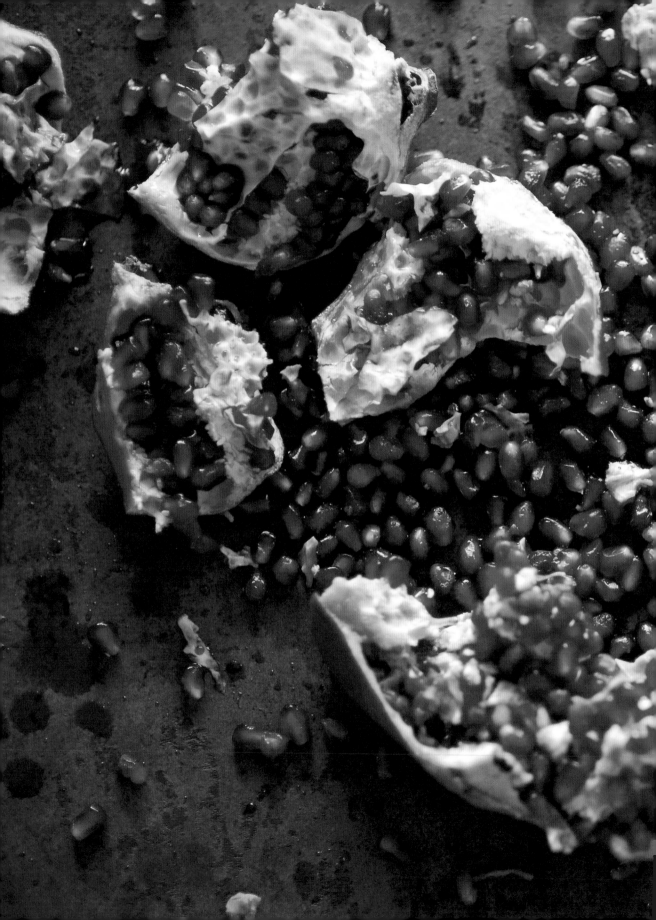

TROPICAL & VINE FRUIT

There aren't many recipes for tropical fruit in this book. Partly because I live a long way from the tropics, but mostly because a perfectly fragrant mango, a rouge-red papaya, a jaw-drenching rambutan, a slice of golden-coloured pineapple, even a slow-ripened banana can be a thing of beauty and needs nothing more than to be eaten. Slowly, appreciatively and lustily. Good tropical fruit needn't be, and probably shouldn't be, messed with.

The thing about tropical fruit is that there are endless varieties. One farm alone has more than 500 at last count, according to Tropical Fruit World, which claims to have the largest collection on the globe. There are sapote, sapodillas and breadnuts among the more familiar mangoes, pineapples and papaya. It's what we do, or don't do, with these varieties that matters. We have fifteen types of banana in Australia, but only two appear to be available commercially. There's little difference between one farm's bananas and another's, most coming from genetically identical stock — bananas grow from a pseudostem that shoots out of a dividable corm, and most are the seedless variety, cavendish.

SO, YOU DON'T LIVE IN THE TROPICS?

Too bad. You'll never be able to truly appreciate the way tropical fruit should taste unless you visit. Good tropical fruit, virtually without exception, ripens to sticky, gooey, soggy softness. It just doesn't transport well, let alone keep for any length of time. The further you live from the tropics, the worse the produce will be.

You may be able to buy some half-decent lychees, which have a naturally resilient casing. Papaya can ripen a little off the tree, though it's still going to be picked quite hard and green. Mangoes, well, you'll get something hard and good to make a Thai green mango and chilli salad with. Bananas? Well, they can be good, but never truly great.

So what to do if you're looking to buy decent tropical fruit? Buy ungassed bananas (see A Few Words on Bananas, opposite, and Gassing of Tomatoes, page 377), buy mangoes only in summer, and use a little sugar and lime juice to bring out the flavours hiding in well-travelled fruit. But don't expect any tropical fruit to taste as good as it would at the source.

A FEW WORDS ON BANANAS

Bananas should be ripened slowly (gassing with the naturally occurring gas ethylene is a fast-ripening process done in huge chambers at the fruit markets). Ungassed bananas can be eaten when the skin has quite a lot of brown spots, because the fruit inside takes longer to soften, but gets more flavour. Refrigerated bananas will get a dark bloom over the skin, and once refrigerated it's very hard to get them to ripen properly. The ideal storage temperature is 18–22°C (64–72°F), which usually means in air-conditioned rooms in the tropics, or at comfortable room temperature elsewhere.

To speed up the ripening of bananas at home, keep them in a paper bag to trap their natural ethylene, and pop in an apple or its core if you have one. This process is usually slower than commercial gassing, but may be necessary in some cool-climate areas where the bananas just aren't ripening.

Sugar bananas should be almost black when eaten. Yellow, they're still starchy. But if they ripen slowly, the inside goes almost like caramel, and the aroma increases.

Plantains are very similar to bananas, though they are usually larger and starchy. By rough definition plantains are for savoury cooking, where bananas are for eating fresh or for using in sweet dishes, though this definition is not exclusive.

HOW TO TELL A RIPE PINEAPPLE?

Forget pulling a leaf from the top. It means nothing. The best way to tell a ripe pineapple is to pick it up, check the colour, the feel and the smell. Pineapples ripen from the base up, and don't ripen any more once picked, so the fruit should be a sunset-gold colour most of the way up. All over is better. Press it, and it should give gently all over, though more towards the base. And then smell the prickly fruit at the base, because it should smell ripe and make your mouth water. If it smells sour or fermented, it's gone bad. I actually prefer to buy fruit that has a soft spot and cut that out, rather than buy green, hard, boring pineapples.

HOW TO CHOOSE TROPICAL AND SUBTROPICAL FRUIT

As mentioned above, all tropical fruit varieties should be soft. The quality will be better the closer you are to where the fruit is grown.

Tropical fruit often has bold colours and distinct aromas, giving you a head start on how to choose it. It should be fresh. Even coconuts can go rancid inside.

A rockmelon will have a heavenly scent when ripe, especially at the non-stem end. Watermelons will be heavy, and make a good loud thunk when flicked. Most of the time you'll be buying them cut, so look for one with bold colouring and a thinner rind.

Mangosteens, arguably the most delectable fruit in the world, are very hard to select because they're shrouded in a leathery casing and have no aroma, and there are few clues about ripeness. Best to buy twice as many as you need and check the quality when you open them up; with any luck, you'll have to eat twice as many. Often tropical fruit is very sweet, so it tastes better with a squeeze of lime juice.

VINE FRUIT

While the most common use of vine fruit (okay, let's call them grapes) is in wine, plenty of them end up dried. Until recently, Afghanistan provided most of the sultanas (golden raisins) for the world. There's also a massive business in sun-drying fruit in Australia's Riverina, while the US makes good use of the long, hot, dry Californian summers to produce dried fruit.

For a long time the dried fruits of the vine — currants, raisins, sultanas, along with dates — were so prized, they were symbols of celebration. Think Christmas and wedding cakes made with a dense fruit loaf. Before mass transport and the use of controlled atmosphere and cold storage, dried fruit was virtually the only way to feast on the glut out of season. All throughout Europe there are Easter breads with currants, pastries dotted with raisins, and sweets laced with dried fruit of the vine.

Vine fruit can, of course, be eaten fresh. Some cultures make use of sour, unripe grapes (see Chipolatas with Sour Green Grapes, page 285), or the juice of unripe grapes, which is known as verjuice or verjus. With its lightly acidic, flavoursome nature, verjuice makes a nice change from lemon juice or vinegar, especially boiled into sauces and the like, though its cost in Australia is often prohibitive for common use.

Grapes for wine are virtually always different from those used on the table. They are often more sour, have thicker, unappetising skins, and plenty of seeds, whereas table grapes are usually hybrids, so there are no seeds, they favour sweetness over all other characteristics (including flavour), and they have thinner skins. Because this makes them easier to eat, table grapes are more likely to be used dried than those used to make wine. One exception is the seeded, but exceptional, muscatel.

DID YOU KNOW?

478

Currants, the dried fruit you put into your Eccles cakes and Christmas pudding, aren't really currants at all. Instead of being dried black or red or white currants (sold fresh in mid summer), they're actually dried, seedless zante (black corinth) grapes, which originated in Greece.

What are known as sultanas where I live are called golden raisins in the US. In fact, raisins could imply any dried grapes in the US. In most Commonwealth nations, a sultana is the dried, golden-coloured fruit from a thompson seedless grape, while a raisin is a fleshier product always from a larger, darker grape.

300 ml (10½ fl oz) unwooded sauvignon blanc

60 g (2¼ oz) sugar

2 teaspoons powdered gelatine

2 large mangoes

200 g (7 oz) natural yoghurt

pulp of 1–2 passionfruit, strained

grated lime zest, to serve

Fresh mango with sauvignon blanc jelly & passionfruit yoghurt

This dish is a great brekky option, although when in season mangoes are good for serving any time of day. The exact quantity of sugar you'll need in this recipe will depend on how much residual sugar there is in the wine and the acidity of your sauvignon blanc. I prefer an aromatic wine, like most from the Adelaide Hills, or even a New Zealand drop. Don't spend too much on the wine, just as much as you feel you can afford, as sugar covers a heap of faults. You will need to prepare the jelly a day in advance and let it set overnight.

SERVES 4

Heat the wine, sugar and 200 ml (7 fl oz) water in a saucepan over medium heat and stir until the sugar is dissolved. Bring almost to the boil (simmer if you want to dissipate the alcohol) and sprinkle in the gelatine, stirring rapidly to dissolve.

Remove from the heat and allow to cool to room temperature.

Cut the mango cheeks from the stone, then peel off the skin and cut the flesh into 5 mm (¼ inch) cubes. Place the mango in the bottom of four serving bowls and pour over the jelly. Allow to set overnight in the refrigerator.

Combine the yoghurt and passionfruit pulp and serve on the table with the lime zest for guests to help themselves.

500 g (1 lb 2 oz) mixed dried fruit, such
  as sultanas (golden raisins), raisins
  and currants
100 g (3½ oz) sugar
300 ml (10½ fl oz) hot black tea,
  strained

500 g (1 lb 2 oz/3⅓ cups) self-raising
  flour, sifted
2 tablespoons marmalade
2 teaspoons mixed (pumpkin pie) spice
1 egg, beaten
1-2 tablespoons honey, warmed, to glaze

Bara brith

*This is a very simple Welsh fruit bread that has just a touch of spice and
a nice hint from the tea. Older versions of the recipe use yeast instead of
self-raising flour, and a bit of lard to make it taste even better. Depending
on your fruit, it may need a touch more liquid when you go to mix it.
You'll need to soak the fruit the day before you wish to make this.*

MAKES 1 LOAF

Mix the dried fruit and sugar together
in a bowl and pour the still hot tea over
the fruit. Stand until the fruit is swollen.
Leave overnight if you can, or warm it in
a saucepan to help speed up the process.
There should still be some liquid when you
go to make the bread.

Preheat the oven to 170°C (325°F/
Gas 3). Grease a 20 x 12 x 11 cm (8 x 4½ x
4¼ inch) loaf (bar) tin and line the base and
sides with baking paper.

Put the tea-soaked fruit in a big bowl,
stir in the flour, marmalade and mixed spice
and then the egg until well combined. Spoon
the mixture into the prepared tin, pressing

to avoid air bubbles and to even out the top.
Bake for about 1 hour 15 minutes, or until
a skewer comes out clean. Brush the top
with the warmed honey just as it comes
from the oven.

Allow the loaf to cool in the tin for a
few minutes, then turn out onto a wire rack
to cool completely. Cut into slices and serve
with a good spread of soft butter.

Bara brith keeps well stored in an airtight
container for up to 1 week.

100 g (3½ oz) sugar
350 ml (12 fl oz) pouring (whipping)
    cream (35% fat)
1 vanilla bean, split lengthways or
    1 teaspoon natural vanilla extract
2 eggs
5 egg yolks

120 g (4¼ oz) caster (superfine) sugar
140 ml (4¾ fl oz) sauvignon blanc
100 g (3½ oz) dried muscatels, seeds
    removed if you like
100 ml (3½ fl oz) muscat wine or brandy

Boozy crème caramel with drunken muscatels

This wine-scented crème caramel is a recipe best attempted by experienced cooks. The reason is that caramel can be tricky, and you want the custard to set gently, and the line between cooked and overcooked is relatively fine. It's worth the challenge, though, because the result is heavenly.

SERVES 6

Preheat the oven to 150°C (300°F/Gas 2).

Place the sugar and 125 ml (4 fl oz/ ½ cup) water in a stainless steel saucepan; aluminium will cause the sugar to crystallise, rather than cook and caramelise smoothly. Bring to a rapid boil until the sugar is a deep caramel colour. I like to get it to a point where there's just a spot of dark brown appearing somewhere on the base of the pan, to get a slightly bitter caramel. Working quickly, put the base of the pan in a basin of cold water to arrest the cooking, then tip the molten sugar into the base of six 125 ml (4 fl oz/½ cup) dariole moulds or ramekins. Set aside.

Heat the cream and vanilla bean in a clean saucepan over high heat until it starts to foam, but don't boil. Remove from the heat, whisk, and allow to infuse for 15 minutes. Discard the vanilla bean.

Beat the eggs and yolks in a bowl with the caster sugar. Reheat the cream and whisk into the egg mixture. Heat the wine without boiling and whisk it into the egg mixture. Strain into the moulds over the now-set caramel.

Place the moulds in a deep baking tray and pour in enough hot water to come one-third of the way up the moulds. Bake for 35–45 minutes, or until set. After 25 minutes, check every 5 minutes so as not to overcook. Allow to cool, then refrigerate, preferably for 1–2 days.

The night before you plan on serving, soak the muscatels overnight in the muscat.

To serve, run a knife around the inside edge of each mould and invert the crème caramel onto the plate. You may need to jiggle it to break the vacuum underneath. The caramel should flow out and around. Garnish the caramels with the drunken muscatels. They can be stored for up to 1 week in the refrigerator.

484

500 g (1 lb 2 oz) butter

500 g (1 lb 2 oz) soft brown sugar

9 eggs

1 tablespoon sweet sherry

500 g (1 lb 2 oz/3⅓ cups) plain
(all-purpose) flour, sifted

1 teaspoon baking powder

½ teaspoon salt

500 g (1 lb 2 oz/4 cups) raisins

500 g (1 lb 2 oz/4 cups) sultanas
(golden raisins)

500 g (1 lb 2 oz/2¾ cups) pitted dried
dates, chopped if large

250 g (9 oz) mixed peel (mixed candied
citrus peel); see page 468

250 g (9 oz) quality glacé fruit, chopped

125 g (4½ oz) maraschino cherries

125 g (4½ oz) almonds

125 g (4½ oz/1¼ cups) walnuts, chopped

3–4 tablespoons brandy, for brushing

Janette's mother's Christmas cake

*This cake recipe is better than the one that was passed down in my family,
and comes from a family friend, whose cooking was always superb. It
takes an awfully long time in the oven, so don't start cooking it unless you
can be there (and conscious) to take it out 5 hours later.*

MAKES 1 CAKE

Preheat the oven to 200°C (400°F/Gas 6).
Grease a deep 30 cm (12 inch) square
cake tin and line the base and sides with
baking paper.

Beat the butter, sugar, eggs and sherry
until pale. Fold in the flour, baking powder
and salt and stir to combine. Add the fruit
and nuts to the batter and stir to mix well.
Spoon into the prepared tin.

Line the bottom and outsides of the tin
with newspaper (about 8 sheets) and tie with
kitchen string to hold in place. The paper
can catch fire in some gas or fan-forced
ovens, so try not to leave a lot of loose edges
for that to happen or use another insulator,
such as cloth.

Bake for 20 minutes, then reduce the
oven temperature to 175°C (330°F/Gas 3)
for 20 minutes, then reduce the temperature
again to 125°C (240°F/Gas ½) for 4 hours
and 20 minutes. The cake will be burnished
brown on top, it won't have risen much and
the fruit on top shouldn't be burnt.

Brush the hot cake with the brandy,
then allow to cool in the tin. Store the cake
wrapped in foil in the refrigerator — it
should last for months if well stored.

400 g (14 oz) sweet shortcrust pastry
   (see page 150)
500 g (1 lb 2 oz) bananas
3 egg yolks
70 g (2½ oz) soft brown sugar

1 teaspoon natural vanilla extract
300 g (10½ oz) sour cream
50 g (1¾ oz/⅓ cup) unsalted macadamia
   nuts, chopped

Banana & macadamia sour cream pie

I do reckon that the flavour of bananas is the perfect match for brown sugar. Throw in some sour cream and some wonderful native Australian macadamia nuts, and you've got a rich, decadent way to spoil yourself.

SERVES 8

Preheat the oven to 180°C (350°F/Gas 4). Grease a shallow 22 cm (8½ inch) round pie dish.

Roll out the pastry to about 5 mm (¼ inch) thick and use it to line the base and sides of the dish. Line the pastry with baking paper and fill it with baking beads or rice. Blind bake the pastry for about 10–15 minutes, or until the edges are cooked. Remove the weights and paper and cook for a further 5 minutes, or until the base is just cooked. Allow to cool.

Increase the oven temperature to 200°C (400°F/Gas 6). Peel the bananas and cut into thick slices on a sharp angle.

Beat the egg yolks with the brown sugar and vanilla, then whisk in the sour cream. (Place the egg whites in the refrigerator, telling yourself you'll make a meringue some time. Two weeks later, find them in the refrigerator and throw them out.)

Scatter the banana over the base of the pastry, pour over the sour cream mixture and bake for about 10 minutes. Top with the macadamias and continue baking for about 20 minutes more, or until browned and set.

Remove from the oven and allow to cool. Slice and serve at room temperature.

488

Chapter 8

WILD FOOD, NUTS, OLIVES & OILS

WILD FOOD, NUTS, OLIVES & OILS

I'm a great fan of the forage. Of looking for food that grows wild. When I lived in Sydney I used to balance on a chair on a busy street corner, stealing olives so I could brine them myself. On my little plot of land there are five types of mushrooms, along with watercress, blackberries and nuts. There are many foods that can be foraged from the sides of roads, from forests, from the shoreline of pristine beaches — although it's best to get a local expert to show you as some are poisonous.

While not usually wild these days, nuts and olives are also often found in public places. They're some of the original peasant foods that are now appreciated for how good they are, rather than just how common they are. In Hobart, locals can be found gathering walnuts from beneath the trees in the streets come autumn. Olives grow feral around the Adelaide Hills, around Orange in central west NSW, and in other places where southern Europeans planted them or let them seed. Those who know what they're doing can get food (and oil, if olives are abundant) to help see them through the year.

WILD FOOD

Keep an eye out for samphire and pigface by the shoreline, purslane where it's damp, and watercress in clear running streams. There's wild fennel, the leaves of which are brilliant in sauces. Dandelions can be blanched and used in cooking; the bitter young leaves are often favoured by some cultures in salads. Stinging nettles make great sauces and are wonderful used to flavour risotto, with the cooking process rendering the stinging chemical inert. Buck's horn plantain pops up all over. Blackberries are forgiven their 'weed' status each summer. Rose petals, while not wild in most places, make terrific found food, simply tossed into sugar syrup (just make sure they're super fragrant and not sprayed). And many parts of the world boast nuts that can be foraged on the byways. If you live in a country where truffles grow wild, then you are particularly lucky — but of all the wild food scenes, by far the biggest is centred on mushrooms.

TRUFFLES

Jack leaps towards me, dragging Sue behind. They look like they've been having the best fun, foraging for truffles, that incredible black subterranean fungus. They've been looking, with great success it seems by their grins, in a 25-year-old, three-hectare truffiere (truffle farm) in the north of Tasmania. Jack is pulling at his lead and isn't the only one with mud on his face. Sue, his handler, has a dirty nose and hands and knees, and wellies that are lacquered in muck. I've arrived just as they are leaving and hope to finish the job, foraging along the last few rows of hazelnut trees, evergreen and English oaks, whose roots may carry the magnificent tuber melanosporum, the prized black winter truffle.

Harvesting truffles in Australia is a very scientific venture compared to in the wild, which is possible in certain parts of Europe, from France and Spain to Italy and even further east. In Australia truffles are farmed, so the soil is constantly monitored, and the size, quality and position of every truffle recorded. However, even on this truffiere, where the trees are planted specifically in a way to try to ensure success, the mystery remains. Why do some sites, some trees, produce prolifically, and others not at all? Which tree will come up with the finest-smelling truffle today, and which one next week? But best of all is that in these more modern times they're managed forests, so — unlike the wild version, where the first finder always keeps — these truffles can be left in the ground as long as they need to fully ripen. For the aroma to become sweet and pungent. For that strange mix of earth, death and sex to become apparent to the dogs' handlers, who are the most critical link in getting the finest black truffles to the table.

492

In the countries where they originated, such as Italy and France, black truffles are supposed to be hard to find. But when you show up to a proven site, in a forest that has been planted specifically to produce truffles — the roots of the trees inoculated with the spores of the subterranean fungus — it seems, on the surface, remarkably easy.

First a specially trained dog leads the way. It scratches the dirt, ideally just once, on the patch where it can smell a truffle. With a nose that is at least one thousand times more powerful than a human's, it can smell a truffle a long way away. About 94 metres (308 feet) into a breeze, according to Duncan Garvey, part owner of Perigord Truffles in northern Tasmania.

On this brisk winter's day I'm with Garvey's business partner, Peter Cooper, whose dog Ocki was salvaged from the pound. A black 'bitsa', the gorgeous mongrel has found hundreds if not thousands of truffles. A few metres after entering the trees, with his nose to the ground, Ocki pauses above a spot in the earth and scratches gently with one paw. He's rewarded with a treat and Peter bends to the earth. Using a well-honed, soft but tactile truffle-digging tool — his finger — he scrapes the earth away from the fungus, revealing what could easily be a muddy stone. Before prising it from the earth, he clasps a handful of the dirt between weathered hands and gestures for me to smell it. All I can think of is mud. Then the smell. That smell. The sweet, penetrating, high-nostril notes of truffle come through at the end. A primordial smell. One that has me salivating and my spine arching and my toes tingling.

A good truffle smells amazingly good. But it's a very personal thing. A good truffle doesn't smell like truffle oil. It smells much deeper, much older, much more complex. It's like a slow-ripened banana compared to banana flavouring. Or a fine old burgundy compared to cheap cordial. And each truffle has its own aroma, some more earthy, some more lifted, some almost touching on the forbidden. It's the smell of life at its most pleasant.

And so within seconds we have found our first truffle. I say we, but I'm really nothing more than just an overjoyed spectator. And while it looks easy, this is the satisfying end point of an amazing operation that started with an overheard conversation in a café in a nearby town, where the then fresh-faced agronomist Garvey learnt of these magical black truffles that were worth an absolute fortune. He thought it would be great to have something so pricey growing in his native state, so he set out to find out more about them. When Duncan suggested they grow truffles Peter said, 'Well, if you can grow chocolates, you're a better farmer than me.' Like most Australians the chocolate truffle, named after the subterranean one, was all he knew.

Back in the truffiere, the dog is pulling at the leash. Ocki is eager to find more, and soon he does; the next isn't ripe, and I'm given a lesson on what to smell for, and just when to harvest. 'A harvester needs to love the cold,' says Garvey. 'They need to love to walk, they need to love dogs. And they really need to love red wine.' And by that he doesn't mean it helps for the harvester to have a hangover, but rather to have a nose that can tell differences in aroma to a vast degree. It's not the dog, rather the dog's handler, who decides just when a truffle is ripe and ready to harvest, and when to leave it for another week.

The bagged truffles are weighed back at the truck. About 12 per cent of the weight we record will be washed off. That's mud, and with truffles costing thousands of dollars a kilogram, it will be scrubbed off before they're sold. We choose a truffle from the selection; my favourite has an aroma bordering on the feral, as well as a slug hole — 'It's the best one,' says Peter, 'the slugs know which ones are really ripe' — and a curious ring around it that doesn't show up until I brush it clean with a toothbrush. It's okay to soak the truffle and wash it well, unlike mushrooms. In fact, it'd be hard to remove the grit any other way.

Back at the house, I scrub the knobbly 50 g (1¾ oz) tuber clean. The truffle is then trapped inside an airtight container with eggs fresh from the chook house, and some tissue to stop the truffle sweating when left overnight. The next day it has ripened the eggs, exuding just a fraction of its intense perfume, which the eggs have soaked up through their porous shells. I whisk three of them with a fork and toss the mix in a pan with a bit of butter and make a thin, still slightly moist-topped frittata (see page 501). The truffle is shaved over the top, I smell a scent of the forbidden, and the rest is too personal to relate.

BLACK TRUFFLES

The best truffles don't come as an oil, as a paste or in a tin. Real truffles are an acquired taste; the more you smell and taste them, the better they taste and smell. First timers, having heard the hype, are often underwhelmed. The best guide to buying good black truffles is your nose. Truffles should smell heavenly, be very, very fresh (they are only available in winter) and have a firm texture.

WHITE TRUFFLES

While the black truffle has been famed in France and parts of Italy for years, the Italian white truffle is even rarer. It has an incredibly intense aroma and a mouthfilling, satisfying taste, which leads some to claim it is the closest thing we have to the perfect flavour. There has been little success in trying to farm the white truffle, however, so it remains an indulgence for those who visit parts of Europe where they find them in the wild.

White truffles are also only available in winter, and cost about three times as much as black truffles. They should never be cooked, rather just warmed to about 70°C (158°F), by being shaved onto warm food before eating. There is a far lesser variety of white truffle that is now cultivated, which is insipid by comparison with the real thing.

COOKING WITH TRUFFLES

Don't get fancy. Truffles are small and taste best when warmed. They are at their most obvious when used with a carbohydrate, such as pasta, risotto, potatoes or bread. Use a few slivers in potatoes baked with cream, or shave truffles over a pasta dish (ideally, make the pasta with truffled eggs). Truffles also go really well with fat and salt; try a buttered truffled toasted sandwich. They are also fantastic shaved over a meat dish, such as steak, roast duck or venison, or put a few slivers under the skin of a chicken with a knob of butter prior to roasting.

Avoid using them with onions, which seem to take away the nuance of truffles, yet add little in return.

WHAT'S THE DEAL WITH TRUFFLE OIL?

Truffle oil, virtually without exception, is a result of food technology, not nature. It's grown in a factory, not a forest. It may have truffle in it, or other mushroom flavours, but the elusive truffle also has an elusive flavour that resists most attempts to put it in a jar or tin, or other products, for any length of time.

WILD MUSHROOMS

Be afraid. Very afraid. If you don't know what you're doing when gathering mushrooms, you're in trouble. There are mushrooms that will make you mildly sick. There are some that will make you sick the third time you eat them. There are some that half the population can eat with impunity, while the other half get stomach troubles. Some are okay cooked, but not raw, that are fine if you don't drink alcohol, or eat them after they're blanched. And some will just plain kill you or leave you on dialysis for the rest of your life.

If you know what you're doing, however, foraging for wild mushrooms is one of the great joys of food gathering. You can find some incredible-tasting mushrooms in different types of forest, some to dry for later use, some to cook up with garlic and parsley the minute you get home. In Europe the local chemist or greengrocer often knows which species are edible. In the absence of expert advice, however, do what the mycologist (mushroom scientist) who showed me what to eat says her professional brethren do. Look, admire, take a photo of all those amazing wild mushrooms, and eat the cultivated ones you buy in a shop.

CULTIVATED MUSHROOMS

There's nothing wrong with cultivated mushrooms — although some find the fact they often use poo from factory chicken farms a bit hard to deal with ethically. To be honest, I adore them. The small button mushroom is mild and delicate and terrific raw or lightly cooked. Bigger, when they're called (wrongly) field mushrooms, they're full-flavoured and great for long cooking. And there are the magnificent shiitake, enoki, shimeji and other wood mushrooms, such as oysters. For your money, Swiss browns are usually good value, considering their elegant flavour — though if you can find lilac wood blewits, buy them. Cultivated mushrooms have no season.

3 truffled eggs (see note)
1 tablespoon extra virgin olive oil
30 g (1 oz) truffle

Truffled egg frittata

Truffles go brilliantly with the simplest of dishes — over pasta with butter and cheese, in with potatoes and olive oil, in a very straight white wine risotto, in a sandwich with lots of butter. They like starch, fat and salt, so don't skimp on the oil or butter, and they don't love onions, but do love garlic. This frittata is the classic thin Italian version.

SERVES 1

Preheat a grill (broiler) to high.

Whisk the eggs with a fork, adding a little water and plenty of salt and freshly milled black pepper. Heat the oil in an omelette pan or similar non-stick frying pan until hot, then quickly tip in the eggs, stirring fast to move the cooked egg from the base of the pan and allow all the egg to set. When it's nearly set, flash the top under the grill to firm it up (I like it if it has a still moussey texture inside).

Quickly shave over the truffle, using a mandolin or a potato peeler if, for some reason, you don't have a dedicated truffle slicer, and serve hot with chargrilled bread drizzled with more oil.

Note: To truffle an egg, you allow the egg to absorb the intoxicating aroma of truffle through its porous shell. Simply put the truffle in an airtight jar with the 3 eggs and keep for at least 1 day in the refrigerator. You can easily do a dozen eggs this way.

40–60 g (1½–2¼ oz) butter
1 large red onion, finely chopped
1 teaspoon salt
3 tablespoons chopped flat-leaf
    (Italian) parsley
1.5–2 litres (52–70 fl oz/6–8 cups)
    homemade chicken stock
    (see page 163) or water
400 g (14 oz) risotto rice (arborio,
    vialone nano or carnaroli)

1 large handful nettles (or use cavolo
    nero), washed and chopped
150 ml (5 fl oz) dry, unwooded white wine
80 g (2¾ oz) Italian parmesan cheese
    (Parmigiano Reggiano or Grana
    Padano)

Nettle risotto

Once, when writing a book on the food of Italy, I found myself on a mountainside in Val D'Aosta, staying at a goat dairy where the cheesemaker cooked incredible food. One of the best things she did was turn the otherwise quite scary stinging nettle into a great-tasting risotto. I'm a fan of the relatively expensive vialone nano rice, as you can be less careful about the cooking and it still, miraculously, retains its texture. Australian arborio rice, sadly, tends to break while cooking, and the result is a bit more porridge-like.

SERVES 6 AS AN ENTRÉE

Heat the butter in a large, heavy-based saucepan over a medium heat. Add the onion and salt and cook for 2–3 minutes, then add the parsley and continue cooking until soft.

Bring the stock to the boil in a separate saucepan; keep simmering until needed.

Add the rice to the pan and stir to combine. Fry gently until the grains are all warm inside (you can tell this by picking up one grain and squeezing between thumb and finger and feeling the heat). Increase the heat, toss in the nettles, slosh in the wine, and stir constantly until it has been incorporated. Reduce the heat again.

When all the wine has been absorbed add the stock, one ladleful at a time. Stir fairly constantly as you wait until each spoonful is absorbed. I find good stirring for the first 5 minutes is more important than stirring the whole time. After 15 minutes, start to test the rice occasionally to ensure it doesn't overcook.

The rice is cooked when it has a creamy consistency, being firm inside, but not nutty. When it reaches this stage (you may have a little stock left over, but if you run out, use water), add two-thirds of the parmesan and season with salt and freshly milled black pepper, to taste. Stir to dissolve.

Remove from the heat and allow to rest for about 3–4 minutes to settle the texture. Serve the risotto sprinkled with the remaining cheese.

Homemade rosewater

You can make quite an intense, distilled rosewater by using a bowl as a lid on a wide pot, and a smaller bowl in the middle of the petals in the pot to collect any drips of condensation. Steam rises off the simmering petals and condenses on the base of the top bowl, which forms drips that you collect in the smaller bowl. However, I like to make my rosewater with just a simple sugar syrup, stuffing in as many rose petals as I can. The result is much more delicate than commercial rosewater. You can make a more intense syrup, although less of it, by repeatedly adding petals. Try rose geranium leaves for a different character.

---

400 g (14 oz) sugar
petals from about 40 unsprayed roses, rinsed well

MAKES 1 LITRE (35 FL OZ/4 CUPS)

Put the sugar and 1 litre (35 fl oz/4 cups) water in a large saucepan over high heat and stir until the sugar dissolves. Bring to a simmer and push in as many petals as the water will hold. Bring back to a simmer, then turn off the heat and allow to steep until cool. Drain and discard the petals. You can intensify this syrup by repeatedly adding petals and steeping, though you do lose some liquid each time. Store in an airtight container in the refrigerator for up to 2 weeks.

Variation: To make orange blossom water, follow the method for rosewater above, but substitute two handfuls of orange blossoms for the rose petals. You can also use lemon, cumquat or lime blossoms.

NUTS

For such a simple ingredient, nuts have been needlessly debased. You'll find you've been missing the taste of a walnut when you finally crack your own and taste its truly fresh flavour as you eat the nubbins of nut from the shell. You'll see that ground almond, known as almond meal, is a bland impostor, a shadow of what it could taste like, if you grind your own nuts.

The trick is to get nuts fresh. Shell your own nuts if you can spare the time (I know, I know, it's a tedious job, but it's worth it). Buy just enough to eat in a short time, and try to find a supplier who prides themselves not on price, but on the flavour of the nuts that they sell.

HOW TO ROAST NUTS

The best way to roast nuts is to cook them on a baking tray in a 180°C (350°F/Gas 4) oven. Spread the nuts in one even layer and check them regularly, shaking the tray regularly so they cook more evenly. The trick is not forgetting them, because their high oil content means they go from seemingly raw to burnt and acrid in minutes, after sitting in the oven for what seems like ages doing nothing.

The nuts are ready when they have started to change colour inside. Check by cutting one open on a chopping board, but don't bite into it, unless you have a heatproof mouth. Don't let them get to the colour you want (a lovely golden colour is often the aim); rather, remove them from the oven earlier because they will keep cooking for a minute or two even after they're removed. If you are rubbing off any skins, do it while the nuts are still warm.

Roasted nuts have a much shorter shelf-life than raw nuts, so only roast what you need.

HOW TO CHOOSE NUTS

The best nuts are sold in the shell. Otherwise, choose your nuts based on the turnover of the shop. Fresh is best because once shelled, they will oxidise far more quickly, losing flavour and aroma, and eventually they'll go rancid. A good shop will get them from somewhere that shells constantly throughout the year. For most nuts, the season is autumn, though some, like walnuts, benefit from some time (weeks not months) in the shell before eating.

Some people are worried that nuts may contain extra pesticide residue because of their high oil content. It's true that many are sprayed quite heavily, but the residue isn't necessarily any greater than the amount you'll find on a conventionally grown lettuce leaf. If you're worried, buy unshelled nuts (because the shelled ones are usually fumigated), and buy organic nuts where possible.

400 g (14 oz) sweet shortcrust pastry
(see page 150)
8 fresh figs, halved

Frangipane
100 g (3½ oz/⅔ cup) blanched almonds
100 g (3½ oz/¾ cup) pistachio kernels
100 g (3½ oz) caster (superfine) sugar
120 g (4¼ oz) butter, softened
2 eggs

Fig & pistachio frangipane tart

*Figs and pistachios were made to go together. Here you blend almonds
and pistachios for a fragrant frangipane mixture (a traditional almond
paste used in tarts), then press fresh figs into the mix. In the absence of
fresh figs, use soaked dried ones, or poached pears, or nothing.*

SERVES 10

Preheat the oven to 180°C (350°F/Gas 4).
Grease a 26–28 cm (10 ½–11 ¼ inch) round
loose-based flan (tart) tin.

Roll out the pastry on a well-floured
work surface or between sheets of baking
paper to make a circle with a 30 cm (12 inch)
diameter. If you have the time, put the pastry
on a tray and refrigerate for 30 minutes. Use
the pastry to line the base and side of the tin.

Line the pastry with baking paper and fill
it with baking beads or rice. Blind bake the
pastry for 15 minutes, or until the edges are
cooked. Remove the weights and paper and
cook for a further 5 minutes, or until the base
is just cooked. Let it cool while you make
the frangipane.

To make the frangipane, put the almonds,
pistachios and sugar in a food processor and
process until fine. Add the butter and eggs,
blending well to combine.

Spread the frangipane evenly over
the cooked pastry base. Press the figs into
the frangipane, carefully but firmly, cut side
up, in a ring about 1 cm (½ inch) in from
the edge. Fill the middle with any remaining
fig halves, making a nice uniform pattern
if possible.

Sit the tin on a baking tray (in case it
leaks) and bake for about 30–40 minutes,
or until the top is coloured lightly and the
middle has set. Allow to cool completely
before removing from the tin.

Serve at room temperature.

300 g (10½ oz/1 recipe) very short sweet
    shortcrust pastry (see page 150)
500 g (1 lb 2 oz) sugar
1 cinnamon stick
½ whole nutmeg, cracked
8 very small pears, ripe but still firm
125 g (4½ oz) butter, softened
2 eggs

45 g (1¾ oz) caster (superfine) sugar,
    plus 1 tablespoon extra
185 g (6½ oz/1⅓ cups) hazelnuts, roasted
    (see page 506) and crushed
60 g (2¼ oz) ground almonds

Pear, hazelnut & burnt butter tart

*I've used small whole pears in this tart, arranged standing up, but you can
use bigger pears cut into quarters and laid on their side.*

SERVES 8

Preheat the oven to 180°C (350°F/Gas 4).
Grease a 23 cm (9 inch) round loose-based
flan (tart) tin.

Roll out the pastry between two sheets
of baking paper to make a circle with a
26 cm (10 ½ inch) diameter. Use the pastry
to line the base and side of the tin and trim
any rough edges. Refrigerate for 1 hour
before using.

To prepare the pears, put the sugar in
a large saucepan over high heat with 1 litre
(35 fl oz/4 cups) water and stir to dissolve
the sugar, then add the spices. Peel the pears
and core from the bottom, leaving the stalks
intact. Place the whole pears in the syrup
and poach for 5 minutes, or until tender.
Drain well and allow to cool. The syrup
can be stored in the refrigerator and re-used
for more poaching, or used on pancakes or
ice cream.

Melt the butter in a frying pan over
medium–high heat, shaking constantly until
it turns a nut brown colour. Remove from
the heat, pour into a heatproof bowl and
allow to cool. Beat the eggs with the caster
sugar to dissolve the sugar, then fold in the
hazelnuts and ground almonds. Add the
butter and stir to combine.

Sprinkle the extra caster sugar over the
pastry, and pour in the hazelnut mixture.
Push the base of each pear into the mixture,
spacing evenly around the tart, and wrap the
stalks in a little foil to prevent them burning.
Bake in the oven for 40–45 minutes, or until
the filling is brown and set. Allow to cool
before removing from the tin, then remove
the foil from the pear stems.

Serve at room temperature, with cream
if desired.

6-8 sheets of confectioners' rice paper
    (optional) (see note)
250 g (9 oz) caster (superfine) sugar
2 teaspoons golden syrup or light treacle
    (optional)
300 g (10½ oz) honey
750 g (1 lb 10 oz) roasted unsalted
    mixed nuts (brazil nuts, almonds,
    macadamias and hazelnuts)
750 g (1 lb 10 oz) mixed dried fruit
    (such as dates, figs, raisins, citrus peel)

75 g (2½ oz) dark chocolate, grated
1 tablespoon ground cinnamon
1 teaspoon ground cloves
1 teaspoon ground nutmeg
1 teaspoon ground mace
1 teaspoon allspice
240 g (8¾ oz) plain (all-purpose) flour,
    sifted

Panforte

Panforte is Italian for 'strong bread'. In Siena, where it originates and still reaches its zenith, you can buy it dark, light, with pepper or without. You can also eat it all year, but it has all those Christmassy fruit and nuts we enjoy, so it's particularly appropriate in the festive season. This panforte isn't like the ones from Siena, especially with its golden syrup and Brazil nuts, but I really like its character.

SERVES 40

Preheat the oven to 180°C (350°F/Gas 4). Grease two 21 cm (8¼ inch) round sponge tins and line the base and sides with baking paper. Line it again with 3–4 rice paper sheets, overlapping if necessary. (I actually cook it without the rice paper often when I can't find the right stuff in the shops.)

Heat the sugar, golden syrup and honey in a large saucepan over medium–high heat. Whisk until dissolved, then simmer for a further 3 minutes.

In a separate bowl, mix together the nuts, fruit, chocolate, spices and flour and fold into the sugar mixture while still warm, using your hands when the mixture has cooled enough.

Divide the mixture into two and press firmly onto the rice paper in each tin, trying to make it as even as possible. The mixture can stick to your fingers, so take care not to lift it off the paper. Cover the top of

each round with the remaining rice paper to make an even layer and press down well. You can tear off the overlapping paper once the panforte has been cooked. Even if not using paper, be sure to press the mixture well into the tin to avoid air pockets.

Bake in the oven for 20 minutes; it just needs to heat through but not darken noticeably. Allow to cool and set slightly before trying to remove the panforte from the tin. To serve, cut into very thin slices (about two bites worth each).

Note: Confectioners' rice paper is traditionally used in Italian and other European sweet cookery. It is available from Italian delicatessens and specialty food stores.

300 g (10½ oz) raw almonds
2 tablespoons soy sauce

1 tablespoon olive oil

Soy smoke-roasted almonds

The trick with these lip-smacking snacks is to get the soy sauce cooked into the almonds until it starts to smoke. You can toss a generous pinch of smoked paprika through the nuts as they come from the oven, too, for a smokier end result.

SERVES 4

Preheat the oven to 200°C (400°F/Gas 6).

Toss the almonds with the soy in a large bowl, then toss with the oil. Pour the nuts onto a lined baking tray, using a spatula to scrape all the oil and soy from the bowl over the nuts.

Roast the nuts, tossing regularly to coat them in the soy and oil mixture, for about 12–15 minutes, or until the marinade is all gone and the almonds are smoking as the soy scorches on the tray.

Remove from the oven, allow to cool really well, then store in an airtight container. They should keep about 2 weeks.

200 g (7 oz) fresh chestnuts
100 ml (3½ fl oz) unwooded white wine
60 g (2¼ oz) sugar

3 cm (1¼ inch) strip lemon peel
80 g (¾ oz) homemade mascarpone
 (see page 62)

Sweet chestnuts with mascarpone

Once a peasant food, the humble chestnut is often now only seen in posh restaurants, because it's a bit of work to cook. Here's a simple way to match its sweet mealiness with the light acidity of mascarpone for richness.

SERVES 2

Preheat the oven to 180°C (350°F/Gas 4). Use a sharp knife to cut a cross in the domed top of each nut. Roast for about 20 minutes, then peel while hot (wear rubber gloves). If the inner brown husk hasn't come off, blanch in boiling water for 3–4 minutes, drain and rub or scrape to remove.

Heat the peeled chestnuts in a small saucepan over high heat with the wine, 100 ml (3½ fl oz) water, sugar and lemon peel. Simmer until they become tender; about 5–10 minutes is usual. Remove the chestnuts with a slotted spoon, discarding the lemon peel, and keep cooking the liquid until reduced to a thickish syrup.

To serve, reheat the chestnuts in the syrup, place in bowls, melt the mascarpone into the remaining syrup and pour over the top.

12 sheets filo pastry

80 g (2¾ oz) butter, melted, plus 150 g
   (5½ oz) butter, extra

40 g (1½ oz) sugar

2 tablespoons honey

60 ml (2 fl oz/¼ cup) pouring (whipping)
   cream (35% fat)

3 tablespoons finely grated mandarin
   or orange zest

250 g (9 oz) unsalted macadamia nuts

200 g (7 oz) slivered almonds

Macadamia & honey tart

*This rich tart can be made with a Sweet Shortcrust Pastry base (see
page 150), which is first blind baked, but filo pastry adds a different
dimension altogether. Cut it thinly to serve, unadorned.*

SERVES 12

Preheat the oven to 180°C (350°F/Gas 4).
Grease a 27 cm (10¾ inch) round loose-
based flan (tart) tin. Line the base and side
of the tin with layers of filo pastry, brush
each layer with a little of the melted butter
before adding the next. Trim the edges.

Put the extra butter, sugar, honey and
cream in a large saucepan over high heat then
reduce the heat and simmer for 3 minutes.

Add the mandarin zest and simmer for
1 minute more. Fold through the macadamia
nuts and almonds and spread evenly over the
prepared pastry case.

Bake in the oven for 25–35 minutes, or
until the top is a nice caramel colour. Cool
for 30 minutes in the tin before removing.

Store the tart in an airtight container in
the refrigerator for a couple of days at most,
but serve at room temperature.

OLIVES & OILS

The olive, that ancient, almost mystical fruit that is inedible until cured, underpins so much of the great food of the Mediterranean. When they're good, they're so good. Oven-warmed black olives, tossed with garlic, rosemary and olive oil, can make a memorable start to a meal. A smear of green olive tapenade on the skin of a just-roasted chicken can heighten the senses. Flecks of olive through bread dough can scent the whole loaf.

Good olives are never marinated when sold. This is reserved for the dodgy ones. Good olives are usually lightly, but not overtly, bitter. They're not too salty, just enough to wake you up, not slap you over the head. And good olives are never the cheapest on the shelf.

There's been a rise in locally produced olives, which means they haven't travelled around the globe before arriving at the local store. This, from the quality of some I've tried, is a very, very good thing.

Always rinse olives before using. The brine on many commercial olives is best not eaten, and if they're overly salty, soak them in cold water for a few hours or a day to draw out some of the brine.

CURING YOUR OWN OLIVES

I like to cure olives each autumn or winter, playing around with various methods. My favourite is to use fresh water to start a gentle fermentation inside the olive, then brine them for three months before using. It pays to start with very good, unbruised olives; if in doubt, good greengrocers can sell you some.

For black ones, simply immerse the washed olives in fresh water in a plastic container, keeping them under the water using an upturned plate or similar if they float. Taste one on day one, so you can see how vile raw, uncured olives are. Keep them somewhere safe, out of the refrigerator. Change the water every day, and taste them after 10 days. They won't taste like cured olives, but should have lost some of that metallic, super-bitter flavour.

It's just the same method for green olives, though if they're hard they'll need cracking first. Simply hit each one gently with a hammer to split the flesh. This allows the water to infiltrate and draw out some of the harsher flavours. Firm green olives can take up to twice as long as soft black olives in the first water-bath stage. Again, taste after 10 days to see how they are. They'll probably take at least two weeks to become ripe for the brine.

BRINING OLIVES

Once the olives have come from their water bath, they need brining. The easiest way to make the brine is to take water and stir in enough salt so a fresh egg rises to the surface. This is about five tablespoons of salt for each 1 litre (35 fl oz/4 cups) water. Steep the olives in this, again weighing them down with a plate or saucer (they'll float a lot more in brine) and cover with a lid. Put them somewhere cool and out of the way for three months, checking from time to time that they're not getting mould on top. This mould isn't terrible, but it's not great either. Scoop it off and sprinkle the top with more salt to prevent it happening again. After 3 months brining, they'll be ready to eat. I like to drain and rinse mine, and keep them in oil in the refrigerator, but this does make them messy to eat. You can make a fresh brine solution (use about half the salt) — or put them in vinegar, which is my least favourite method of finishing them.

OILS

Good table olives are different from those that make oils. And good oils are usually, but not always, a bit pricey. The best news is that a great oil, fat with flavour and dripping with antioxidants, is only used in small quantities. The better flavoured the oil, the less you can eat of it.

It's important that your oils be fresh. As fresh as practicable. Buy only what you'll use in a month, unless you can store them properly. Good storage is cold, dark and dry. Whether it's a nut oil, an olive oil, or a seed oil, they can all go rancid, and oxygen, light and heat are the enemies of freshness. Buying bulk oil in a tin is sensible, in glass it's not.

A lot of people buy vegetable oils, such as canola (rape) and sunflower. These are relatively flavourless oils, sometimes made using quite harsh chemical processes. Being light in flavour means you're more likely to eat more of these oils. I rarely use them; if I do it's for oiling my chopping board, and to make my mayonnaise more lightly flavoured. Avoid palm oil, which has a bad environmental reputation, usually destroying the habitat of orangutans and other tropical animals. Palm oil is often simply labelled 'vegetable oil', so if it comes from Indonesia, Malaysia or Thailand, don't buy it.

WHAT IS EXTRA VIRGIN?

There's a complex definition, and a simple one. The most pure, most flavoursome, best olive oil, one that is extracted mechanically, is called extra virgin. The worst sort of olive oil is called pomace oil, and is chemically extracted. I only buy extra virgin (of varying prices) and use it for most things. There's a testing and tasting process that helps ensure extra virgin olive oil adheres to good principles and standards. As consumers, that's all we need to know, really.

Artichoke & green olive paste

Spread this paste sparingly on chargrilled bread, served with fish, veal or lamb. I used roasted artichoke hearts when I came up with this recipe because that's what I had in the fridge. You can use normal preserved ones, but if buying them, choose those preserved in oil.

60 g (2¼ oz) preserved artichoke hearts (see page 398)
100 g (3½ oz) pitted green olives, rinsed
2–3 anchovy fillets
1½ tablespoons extra virgin olive oil
½ teaspoon lemon juice

MAKES 200 G (7 OZ)

Put the artichokes, olives and anchovies in a food processor and process until fine. Add the oil and blend until smooth. Season with salt and freshly milled black pepper, to taste. Add the lemon juice, and blend to combine. Store in a sterilised airtight jar in the refrigerator for up to 2 weeks.

200 g (7 oz) pitted green olives, rinsed
2–3 anchovy fillets
1 small red chilli, seeded and chopped
1 tablespoon salted capers, rinsed

1 tablespoon basil leaves
2–4 tablespoons extra virgin olive oil

Green olive tapenade

Green olives are firmer and more bitter than their black cousins, giving a very different flavoured tapenade.

MAKES 250 G (9 OZ)

Put the olives, anchovies, chilli and capers in a food processor and process until fine. Add the basil and pulse to combine, then drizzle in enough olive oil to make a paste.

Store the tapenade in an airtight container in the refrigerator for 1 week.

Note: You can use this tapenade to create a wonderful olive-scented chicken. Roast a chicken until cooked through but still moist. Smother the flesh with 2–3 tablespoons of the tapenade, cover with foil and allow to rest for a few minutes before serving.

1–2 garlic cloves
200 g (7 oz) pitted black olives, rinsed
2–3 anchovies
1 tablespoon salted capers, rinsed

2 tablespoons coriander (cilantro) leaves
1 small tomato, chopped
2–3 tablespoons extra virgin olive oil

Black olive tapenade

This is not a traditional tapenade, which in theory should have more capers. The addition of tomato helps cut the richness and add another layer of flavour, but it does mean the tapenade won't keep quite as long.

MAKES 250 G (9 OZ)

Put the garlic, olives, anchovies and capers in a food processor and process until smooth. Add the coriander leaves and pulse, then blend in the tomato. With the motor running, drizzle in the olive oil until you have

a loose paste. Season with lots of freshly milled black pepper (it shouldn't need salt), to taste.

Keeps well stored in an airtight container in the refrigerator for 1 week.

1 tablespoon raisins

2 large red capsicums (peppers), roasted and peeled (see page 378)

30 g (1 oz) blanched almonds, lightly roasted (see page 506)

4 anchovy fillets

3 teaspoons anchovy oil (from bottle of anchovies)

1 garlic clove

8 drops orange blossom water (see page 504)

3–4 tablespoons walnut oil or other nut oil

¼ teaspoon fennel seeds, crushed

Anjou funny stuff

In the words of Edina from the once popular TV show Absolutely Fabulous, *'I don't want to sound selfish, but ... me, me, me, me.' This is my recipe, with advice, of course, from chef George Biron who ran Victoria's stunning regional restaurant Sunnybrae, who took the idea from British food writer Elizabeth David, who borrowed the idea from a French chef, who apparently found it in the Loire region — where everybody probably makes it all the time. Hmmm ... It may not be original or even authentic, but it's sensational with seafood.*

MAKES 400 G (14 OZ)

Soak the raisins in hot water for 15 minutes, then squeeze out the excess moisture.

Place all of the ingredients, except for the walnut oil and fennel seeds, in a food processor and purée to a pulp. With the motor running, add enough oil in a thin stream to form a nice, slightly runny, paste consistency.

Season to taste with salt and freshly milled black pepper. Add the fennel seeds and stir through. Transfer the paste to a sterilised airtight jar and store in the refrigerator for up to 2 weeks.

2 large unpeeled garlic cloves
50 g (1¾ oz/⅓ cup) blanched almonds
1–2 anchovy fillets
1 large red capsicum (pepper), roasted
and peeled (see page 378)
1 small red chilli, seeded and finely
chopped

80 ml (2½ fl oz/⅓ cup) extra virgin
olive oil
lemon wedge, for squeezing (optional)

Romesco

This is a Spanish sauce, traditionally made with pounded almonds and romesco peppers. We don't get romesco peppers where I live, so I've stolen the idea and used roasted capsicum (pepper) to achieve a similar effect.

I first ate this sauce just north of Barcelona with calçots (like thin leeks or green/spring onions), which had been roasted over grapevine coals). We pulled the black outer skin from the calçot, dipped it in the sauce, tipped our heads back and giggled like schoolgirls at the incredible flavours. Unfortunately, you also can't get calçots in Australia, so use the paste with bread, meatballs, fish — or anything, really.

MAKES 200 ML (7 FL OZ)

Preheat the oven to 220°C (425°F/Gas 7).

Wrap the garlic in foil and roast in the oven for 15 minutes. Alternatively, put the garlic in a dry frying pan over medium heat and toss fairly constantly until the garlic is soft within (the skin may brown a little and that's just fine).

Squeeze out the soft garlic, discarding the skin, put in a food processor with the almonds and process until fine. Add the

anchovies, capsicum and chilli and blend well. With the motor still running, pour in the oil in a thin stream until it forms a thickish but smooth paste.

Season to taste with salt and freshly milled black pepper and perhaps a squeeze of lemon juice.

2 tablespoons salted capers, rinsed
  and finely chopped
2 small garlic cloves, crushed
2 tablespoons finely chopped basil
2 tablespoons chopped rocket (arugula),
  oregano or coriander (cilantro) leaves

4 tablespoons finely chopped parsley
3–4 teaspoons lemon juice
4–6 tablespoons extra virgin olive oil

Salsa verde

Salsa verde literally means 'green sauce', so there are as many salsas verdes as there are cooks. I've made the same number of versions as times I've made it — depending on what's in the herb garden and fridge. This one is terrific on steak, and is best hand-cut. The idea with the herbs is to use 8 tablespoons in total, and you can vary it as you see fit. Rosemary and thyme are very strong, as is sage, so use sparingly. Use good-quality olive oil for best results. This recipe makes enough to flavour the meat for at least six people.

MAKES 125 G (4½ OZ/½ CUP)

Put all of the ingredients in a bowl and mix together well. Season with salt and freshly milled black pepper. It is preferable to let the sauce stand for 30 minutes before using.

Note: If you are using the salsa verde to accompany steak, let the meat rest, slice and push the slices back together. Then rub the salsa across the top so the flavour permeates.

1 tablespoon balsamic or wine vinegar
2 tablespoons extra virgin olive oil or
  nut oil

A nice short salad dressing

This is a simple salad dressing, perfect for leaves, and good on tomato and goat's cheese.

MAKES 60 ML (2 FL OZ/¼ CUP)

Whisk together the vinegar and oil and season with a generous amount of salt and freshly milled black pepper.

Toss the dressing through washed and dried lettuce leaves with just enough dressing to coat.

Vinaigrette dressing

This is a great dressing to use on warm potato salad, salade nicoise, over beans, sliced tomatoes, or just on lettuce leaves.

2 teaspoons dijon mustard
2 tablespoons extra virgin olive oil
juice from ½ lemon
2 teaspoons chopped oregano or basil leaves
1 teaspoon chopped parsley leaves (optional)
1–2 garlic cloves, crushed
a pinch of sugar

MAKES 80 ML (2½ FL OZ / ⅓ CUP)

Whisk the mustard in a bowl with the oil, lemon juice, oregano, parsley (if using), garlic and sugar. Taste for lemon juice, and season with salt and freshly milled black pepper.

528

80 g (2¾ oz/½ cup) pine nuts
2–3 garlic cloves
70 g (2½ oz/about 2 cups gently pressed)
  basil leaves
250 ml (9 fl oz/1 cup) extra virgin olive oil

40 g (1½ oz) italian parmesan cheese
  (Parmigiano Reggiano or grana
  padano), finely grated
40 g (1½ oz/⅓ cup) finely grated
  pecorino, mature but not astringent

The papa's pesto

*The real thing is beautiful to behold. Classically served over a firm,
medium-length pasta with beans and potatoes, pesto can also be used
to flavour fish, as a dabbing sauce served on the table with chargrilled
eggplant (aubergine) and other antipasti, or added to tomato sauce
as it comes from the stove.*

MAKES 430 G (15¼ OZ/1¾ CUPS)

Put the pine nuts and garlic in a food
processor and process to form a paste.

Add the basil leaves, then pulse, scraping
down the sides regularly. Add half of the oil,
continue processing, then add the cheeses
and the remaining oil and pulse to just
combine. The pesto will remain bright green
in colour unless you over-process it. Season
with salt and freshly milled black pepper,
to taste.

Store the pesto in a sterilised airtight
jar in the refrigerator for 1 week, although
it is best consumed within a few days
of making.

Chapter 9

SWEET FOODS

SWEET FOODS

Sugar. It taps into some part of the brain that brings extraordinary pleasure. We seek it out. But sugar, as we know it now, hasn't been readily available in many cultures for all that long. Up until about 300 years ago, in Anglo-Saxon cooking, sugar was rare, and totally sweet dishes and desserts, relatively unusual. Sugar was used in savoury food, as it still is today, in Thai food and some North African dishes, although in earlier days most commonly in the form of honey, or fruit.

Sugars, including honey, keep well. In fact they preserve other things, such as jams or bacon. They also help transform the bitter cocoa bean that was once used to make a savoury drink with chilli, into that incredible modern experience, chocolate.

We probably use too much sugar these days. Those who study our preferences know that putting sugar in snack food, even savoury snack food, is a quick way to seduce the palate. But used wisely, used where it should be, sugar and honey are remarkable things. If you must put it in savoury food, always try to use a flavoursome variety, be it a good palm sugar (jaggery) or molasses, and marry the sweetness with an acid of some kind (vinegar, lemon juice, lime juice all help) — and don't be afraid to use chilli as a counterpoint. The Thais have a marvellous way to showcase the versatility of sugar, where they sprinkle it on a noodle dish with roasted ground red hot chilli, and then splash on lime juice and fish sauce. A lot goes on in the mouth at one time, like the most amazing fireworks on the tongue — and far from the sugary sweetness so many Western cooks now emphasise. If tomatoes need sugar to make them shine, they aren't good tomatoes.

HONEY

Yves Ginat's honey room smells of blossom. There are bees, of course, buzzing around the flyscreens, eager to consume the nectar. Some have become studded into slicks of the ambrosial sticky syrup; they are the few that have arrived inside by accident when the hives were stripped of their honeycomb. There's the smell of warm wax, too, but the overriding aroma is one of good, floral leatherwood honey, as it smells when harvested from the hives.

This honey room is different to some. All honey is removed from the wax comb — stolen, as some vegans would say, from bees that have spirited it away for winter from the blossoms they visit. But the difference is the way the honey is extracted. There's no extra heat involved in Yves' method of extraction. Honey, like oil, runs more freely when hot, but just like oil, honey retains far more of its volatile aromatic compounds (that is, flavour and fragrance) the less it is heated.

It's okay to heat the honey to about 27°C (81°F) because this is the constant temperature inside most beehives — it's a bit like being in the tropics all year round. In winter the bees use the honey as an energy source, beating their wings vigorously to create warmth as they turn the honey to physical energy. In summer the bees bring in water and fan the air, creating their own evaporative cooler. So honey is used to being heated to 27°C (81°F), the temperature where it softens and runs freely from the hive. Hotter extraction takes far less time, however, so most beekeepers favour it.

Honey is a miracle of location. It tastes of the geography, of the plants where the nectar is gathered. And it helps to know a little about how the honey is won to get a sense of its value. It's one of the first truly sweet additives that humans would've been able to harvest readily. Honey can replace sugar in so many uses, but is, essentially, an expression of the land from where it comes, and the hand that helps harness it.

Yves fashions his hives from timber during the winter months and captures a swarm from another hive to put in them. These timber hives are left in pockets of native bush adjacent to World Heritage areas in Tasmania's south. The best honey, many would say, comes from the famed native leatherwood, which produces about 70 per cent of the island state's honey each year.

Leatherwood honey comes from one of only two native species of *Eucryphia*, to be precise — in Yves' case, *Eucryphia lucida*. It's usually a secondary canopy (that is, the trees form tufts of leaves under the top canopy provided by taller trees). The trees grow in areas of high rainfall, and flower only in the warmer months. A good stand of leatherwood will produce an enormous number of blossoms for about six weeks a year, but many of the remaining stands are too high in altitude for bees. Bees don't really like the climate above 600 metres (1968 feet) in altitude, they don't like it cold, and they don't like rain. They don't like wind, either, and yet cold, windy, rainy country is now virtually the only habitat of any great stands of leatherwood.

Against all odds the bees do manage to brave the air on sunny, still, warm days, and the leatherwood is a prolific producer of pollen and the all-important nectar within its flowers. Yves has selected the European honey bee for its efficiency, as a healthy hive can produce up to 150 kg (331 lb) of honey in a short season, compared to the Australian native bee, which only produces about 500 g (1 lb 2 oz) in the same time.

The commercial European honey bee is a remarkable worker. The queen is prolific, laying up to 2000 eggs a day, while the worker bees, sterile females, gather honey, tend the young and the queen, as well as feed and tend the more sedentary males (drones).

Male bees really don't do much, just lounge about on the couch (or bee equivalent) getting fed and watered and treated like royalty. I guess they do service the queen, but it does seem a stretch to call them all kings.

When a virgin queen is born, she flies upwards from the hive and a whole mob of male drones, ready to mate and swarm, spring into action, the first to nail her thinking he's onto a winner. But she hangs on to his member (which has developed in place of a sting) and he dies shortly after. She may mate with several drones this way. The disconsolate other males return to their original hives and live off the fat of the hive until autumn when (in cold climates) the worker bees decide not to waste honey needed for winter on lazy males, and kick them out and to their deaths.

From this simple interaction, we get honey. The bees fly from flower to flower and collect nectar that is then dehydrated by enzymes in their stomach. They then transfer it into the cells of the hive where it thickens even more into the honey we know and love.

The leatherwood that Yves' bees have collected is run through a centrifuge, then stored in large vats, and dribbles from the tap easily when poured. It will form super-fine crystals over the coming weeks, a result of not being heated. These crystals are spreadable and melt on the tongue like butter, releasing the aroma that was so expertly harnessed in a forest miles away.

As I mentioned, honey, by its nature, is an expression of place. In Italy, there are famed chestnut, wild strawberry or bitter corbezzolo honeys. In France they also love chestnut honey, along with lavender, buckwheat or fir varieties. The honey section in a French foodstore can be impossibly big, with the French choosing each honey by its predominant blossom. In the UK keep an eye out for honey made from the nectar of heather, in the US pumpkin blossom honey is a distinctly flavoursome syrup, and Spain does an amazing orange blossom version. New Zealand is best known for its manuka honey, which also appears, though in less quantity, in parts of Australia.

WHAT IS GOOD HONEY?

Good honey is usually from a single source, so the predominant flavour is of one type of blossom (though some good honeys can be a blend of flowers).

It's unheated and unfiltered, so offers the full expression of the flower that bore it and the place it originated. Good honey may be finely crystallised; this is not a negative, however, and over time some crystallisation can be expected of unheated honey.

6 mandarins

4 green cardamom pods (or use other whole spices, such as cloves or a cinnamon stick)

115 g (4 oz/⅓ cup) honey

100 g (3½ oz) sugar

200 g (7 oz) homemade mascarpone (see page 62)

2 tablespoons icing (confectioners') sugar, sifted

2 teaspoons orange blossom water (see page 504)

Honey-poached mandarins with orange blossom mascarpone

Try to get firmish mandarins for this recipe, such as clementine or honey murcott. If any of the mandarins are dry, sadly you can't cook with them, just like you can't eat them fresh: next time you're at the shop, give the owners a jolly along, because it's just lazy buying on their part.

SERVES 6

Scrub the mandarin skins, then peel off the skin and retain each mandarin in one piece, reserving the peel.

Place 500 ml (17 fl oz/2 cups) water in a saucepan and add the cardamom, honey, sugar and mandarin peel. Bring to the boil, then reduce the heat and simmer for about 5 minutes. Remove from the heat and allow to steep for 10–15 minutes. Remove the peel (you don't have to get it all).

Bring the syrup back to the boil and add the mandarins. Reduce the heat and simmer for 5 minutes, then turn off the heat and allow the fruit to cool in the pan.

Mix together the mascarpone, icing sugar and orange blossom water (or you can use some of the poaching syrup). Serve the mandarins whole, perhaps slightly warm but room temperature is good, with a blob of mascarpone and some of the cooking syrup drizzled around.

Alternative: For a much quicker dessert idea you can cut fresh mandarins in half, sprinkle a little brown sugar on top and grill (broil) them until the sugar caramelises. Serve the mandarins with some mascarpone, or a cream whipped with a pinch of ground cardamom and icing (confectioners') sugar.

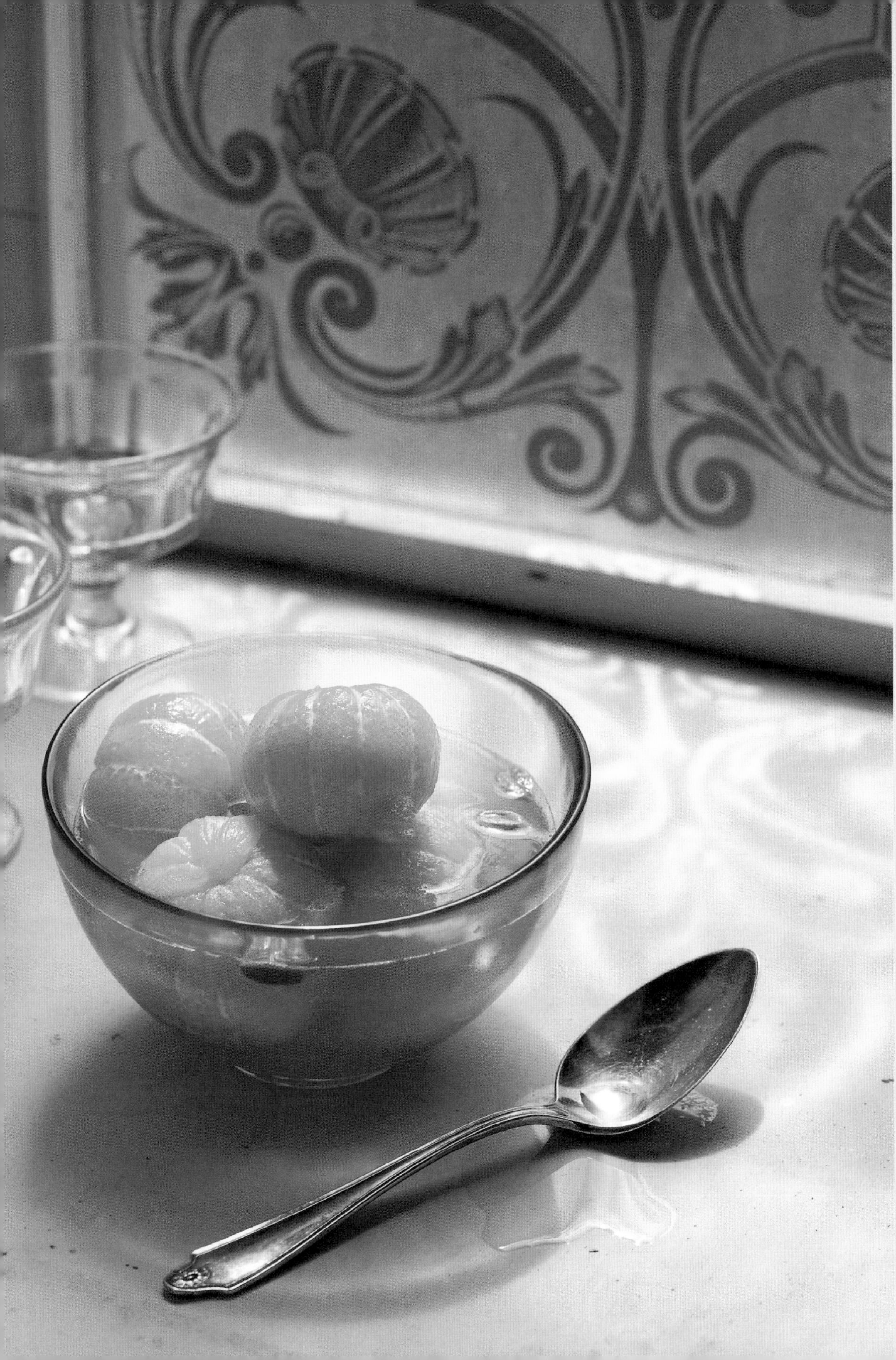

100 g (3½ oz/1 cup) rolled (porridge) oats

135 g (4¾ oz) plain (all-purpose) flour, sifted

200 g (7 oz) caster (superfine) sugar

70 g (2½ oz) shredded coconut

125 g (4½ oz) butter, cubed

2 tablespoons honey

1½ teaspoons bicarbonate of soda (baking soda), sifted

Honeyed Anzac biscuits

I like my Anzac biscuits (cookies) chewy, and it may take a couple of attempts to get them just right. Honey makes a nice change from the golden syrup that is used in most traditional recipes.

MAKES 25

Preheat the oven to 180°C (350°F/Gas 4). Line two baking trays with baking paper.

Mix the oats, flour, sugar and coconut together in a large bowl. Make a well in the centre.

Heat the butter and honey in a saucepan over medium heat and stir until melted and combined. Stir in the bicarbonate of soda to combine (it will foam up, this is normal).

Pour the honey mixture into the dry ingredients and mix to combine. If it seems too stiff, add 1–2 teaspoons water. Place dessertspoon-sized blobs about 5 cm (2 inches) apart on the prepared trays, allowing room for them to spread.

Bake for about 15–20 minutes, or until the biscuits are golden. They will keep in an airtight container for up to 1 week.

Leatherwood honey & vanilla milkshake

I like this milkshake without ice cream, but for a sweeter, richer, thicker version you can add a large scoop of vanilla ice cream.

---

500 ml (17 fl oz/2 cups) full-cream (whole) milk
2 tablespoons unheated leatherwood honey
90 g (3¼ oz/⅓ cup) natural yoghurt
1–2 teaspoons natural vanilla extract
¼ teaspoon freshly grated nutmeg

SERVES 2

Put all the ingredients into a blender and blend well until smooth and light. Taste for honey, adding more if desired, or some sugar to taste.

Serve the milkshake in tall glasses with a big wide straw for making slurping noises.

SUGAR

Sugar is sugar is sugar. It tastes, primarily, sweet. Unless, of course, you can get your hands on fine, naturally processed sugars. Then you will discover that the impurities that are removed to make pure white crystals of normal sugar are part of the attraction of the flavour.

Sugar can come from any plant that has a high sugar content. In colder climates it's made from sugar beets, but global transport and the discovery of the super high-yielding sugar cane has meant that the all-important source is now the tropical sugar cane. Today, 70 per cent of sugar comes from cane, the vast majority usually refined to white sugar.

SUGAR (REFINED WHITE SUGAR) Ordinary white sugar is virtually pure sucrose in relatively largish crystals. This is the white, everyday sugar you most likely have in your tea or coffee.

CASTER (SUPERFINE) SUGAR A more finely sieved or ground version of ordinary white sugar. The only difference is the crystal size, which makes it easier to dissolve in cakes and biscuits, so it is favoured in some cooking. A slightly higher cost makes it an inefficient sugar to use in syrups and the like.

RAW SUGAR Large, gently brown crystals of sugar that come from boiling down the syrup extracted from sugar cane or beets, with minimal chemical intervention. The large crystals make them ideal for when you want some crunch, such as a crumble cake or similar, though most raw sugar is used in coffee.

DEMERARA SUGAR Similar to raw sugar in texture — in fact, it's arguably a sub-species of raw sugar, but with a stronger taste of molasses.

SOFT BROWN SUGAR In most instances brown sugar is just a fine caster sugar, with some of the treacle and molasses that is removed in processing added back to it. Muscovado sugar, most famously promoted by Billington's, a company in the UK, is a brown sugar that is unrefined, and its flavour is far more interesting and complex, though it does cost a lot more, too.

Brown sugar has a high moisture content, and when it dries out it can harden. To help prevent this, store it in an airtight container. If it does dry out, a soaked piece of porous porcelain, or a wedge of apple, lodged in the sugar for a few hours can help bring it back. Or you can just dissolve it on your porridge like I do.

DARK BROWN SUGAR Soft brown sugar with more molasses added back to it.

ICING (CONFECTIONERS') SUGAR A very, very fine version of ordinary white sugar that dissolves almost immediately. Again it can be sieved or ground from refined white sugar.

ICING MIXTURE The same as icing sugar, but with cornflour (cornstarch) added. It helps to keep some water icings (frostings) thick, but its real advantage is that it doesn't dissolve on top of cakes or pastries it is dusted over a few hours ahead of serving.

JAM SUGAR A coarse white sugar that contains some added pectin. The coarse grains dissolve more slowly, which helps the jam set without problems of crystallisation.

PALM SUGAR (JAGGERY) The dried syrup of one of several palms from South-East Asia. The flavour is quite attractive in a gentle, caramelly kind of way, similar to raw sugar or a very light brown sugar.

TREACLE The syrup that forms as a byproduct of making refined white sugar. The palest form is called golden syrup, the darkest is molasses, and the intermediate forms are sold simply as treacle.

MOLASSES The syrup produced by a later process in the refinement of white sugar, molasses is more bitter than treacle or golden syrup.

GOLDEN SYRUP A magical syrup that is the result of harnessing a pale syrup from an early stage in sugar processing. It is sweeter than sugar (higher in fructose than sugar), so you use less to get a similarly sweet result. Golden syrup has more nutrients than plain white sugar and is less likely to crystallise.

GLUCOSE SYRUP (CORN SYRUP) A perfectly clear honey-like syrup used in some cooking. It's mostly glucose rather than sucrose, and is an invert sugar, meaning it has different properties, including the ability to freeze without forming crystals, so it's good for use in ice cream to prevent that crunchy, icy texture.

MAPLE SYRUP The pure sap from maple trees in North America is reduced to between one and four per cent of its original volume to make the syrup (the amount depends on the weather and the season). In its unadulterated form, it's a thing of joy. Fake flavoured syrups (such as maple 'flavoured' syrup, which contains a factory-made chemical substitute for maple) are a very poor substitute, and while some pancake syrups may be a mix of real syrup and glucose syrup, you're paying for a watered-down flavour.

Maple syrup can be further reduced to make maple cream (a lightly crystallised structure) or maple sugar, which is in a hard block form.

200 g (7 oz) butter, softened

150 g (5½ oz) caster (superfine) sugar

2 tablespoons golden syrup or
  light treacle

3 eggs

1 tablespoon finely grated mandarin
  or orange zest

150 g (5½ oz/1 cup) self-raising flour,
  sifted

50 g (1¾ oz/½ cup) ground almonds,
  sifted

125 ml (4 fl oz/½ cup) maple syrup

Sticky mandarin pudding with maple syrup

Toast and marmalade. Pork and fennel. Chicken and mayonnaise. Some things are just sublime together. Mandarin and maple syrup do it for me every time. If you have loose-skinned mandarins, lightly freeze the fruit for 30 minutes or so to firm it up enough to grate or zest. Late-season honey murcott mandarins (or similar) are the perfect variety because of their firm skin.

SERVES 6

Preheat the oven to 200°C (400°F/Gas 6). Grease a 2 litre (70 fl oz/8 cup) casserole dish.

Beat the butter, sugar and golden syrup in a bowl until light and well combined. Beat in the eggs, one at a time. Fold in the mandarin zest, flour and ground almonds, then spread evenly over the base of the casserole dish. Tip the maple syrup over as evenly as possible and cover with foil.

Place the dish in a shallow roasting tin and pour enough hot water into the tin to come 2 cm (³/4 inch) up the sides of the dish. Bake in the oven for 1 hour. Remove the foil, lower the oven temperature to 180°C (350°F/Gas 4) and continue baking for about 20–30 minutes, or until a skewer comes out clean when inserted into the centre of the pudding and the top springs back when pressed. It should be golden on top.

Serve warm, with a rich cream such as Scalded Cream (see page 59).

150 g (5½ oz) caster (superfine) sugar,
plus extra for sprinkling

300 g (10½ oz) butter (preferably French
and cultured), softened

300 g (10½ oz/ 2 cups) plain (all-purpose)
flour, sifted

150 g (5½ oz) cornflour (cornstarch),
sifted

My mum's shortbread

*Mix this really gently, and don't let it brown. Then you'll have the
world's best shortbread. Just like Mum's.*

MAKES 24 PIECES

Lightly beat the sugar and butter in a bowl until combined. Fold in the flours and stir together using a spoon until it gets too stiff to handle, then use your hands to form into a ball.

Preheat the oven to 150°C (300°F/ Gas 2). Line two 25 cm (10 inch) wide baking trays with baking paper. Divide the mixture into two even-sized portions, place on the trays, and press into two circles with a 20 cm (8 inch) diameter, about 1 cm (½ inch) thick all over.

Crimp the edges of each circle between two fingers and thumb to create a scalloped effect, prick all over with a fork and bake in the centre of the oven for about 1 hour, swapping shelves and turning the trays around after 30 minutes. Be very careful not to allow the shortbread to brown on top.

When it comes out of the oven and is still hot, cut each round into twelve slices as you would a cake. Sprinkle a little extra caster sugar evenly over each round and allow to cool. Store in an airtight container, not in the refrigerator, and eat them within 1 week.

200 g (7 oz) sweet shortcrust pastry
  (see page 150)
200 g (7 oz/2 cups) walnuts (about
  500 g/1 lb 2 oz nuts in shell)
2 slices white bread
80 ml (2½ fl oz/⅓ cup) full-cream
  (whole) milk
100 g (3½ oz) treacle

1 teaspoon finely grated mandarin zest
  (freeze the fruit for a little while to get
  the skin to firm up if need be)
2 egg yolks
scalded cream (see page 59), to serve

Walnut & treacle tart

One of the things my mother used to do on an annual basis was bring me a big bag of gorgeous Victorian walnuts in their shells, and I created this tart to use up the surplus. It's a variation on the French classic tarte aux noix, with the addition of a little old-fashioned treacle. Mandarin zest helps to lift the flavours, but you can use orange zest if you prefer. And yes, it is a bit of mucking around shelling your own walnuts, but this tart tastes twice as good if you can be bothered to put in the effort.

SERVES 6–8

Preheat the oven to 180°C (350°F/Gas 4). Grease an 18 cm (7 inch) round loose-based flan (tart) tin.

Roll out the pastry on a well-floured board or between two sheets of baking paper to make a circle with a 22 cm (8½ inch) diameter. If you've got the time, cover the pastry and refrigerate for 30 minutes. Use the pastry to line the base and side of the tin and trim to fit.

Line the pastry with baking paper and fill it with baking beads or rice. Blind bake the pastry for 15 minutes, or until the edges are cooked. Remove the weights and paper and cook for a further 5 minutes, or until the base is just cooked.

Roughly chop and scatter 50 g (1¾ oz/ ½ cup) of the walnuts evenly into the pastry base.

Put the bread in a bowl and pour over the milk to completely soften the bread. Squeeze the bread to remove the excess milk and mush up the bread.

In a food processor, grind the remaining nuts until fine, pulse in the bread and place in a bowl. Add the treacle, mandarin zest and egg yolks and mix well. Pour this mixture into the pastry case, smooth the top, and bake for about 20–25 minutes, or until set. Allow to cool before removing from the tin.

Serve at room temperature, in slices, with a dollop of scalded cream.

60 g (2¼ oz) butter, chopped
135 g (4¾ oz) self-raising flour, sifted
1 egg, lightly beaten
½–1 tablespoon full-cream (whole) milk
160 g (5¾ oz) sugar

1½ tablespoons golden syrup or light
  treacle
lemon wedge, for squeezing (optional)

Golden puff dumplings

Many thanks to at least four generations of O'Donnell women, who all cooked with this recipe. My version originates in hand-written form from west of Melbourne. If you can't get golden syrup, a light treacle is the best substitute.

SERVES 4

Cut 25 g (1 oz) of the butter through the flour and a pinch of salt (you can rub it in a bit using your fingers if you like). Add the egg and enough milk to make a dough. Roll the dough out and divide into 10–12 portions, rolling each into a small ball.

To make the sauce, heat 375 ml (13 fl oz/ 1½ cups) water in a saucepan over high heat with the sugar, golden syrup and remaining butter. Bring to the boil, stirring to combine.

Add the dumplings to the pan, reduce the heat to low–medium, cover, and simmer for 15 minutes, adding a little squeeze of lemon juice to make it a little more adult if you like.

Serve hot with bay leaf custard (see variation to Good Old-fashioned Cornflower Custard, page 48) or vanilla ice cream.

CHOCOLATE

Chocolate. Just say the word, close your eyes and you can feel the best chocolate in your mouth. Good chocolate, the result of mixing fermented cocoa beans, a hint of sugar and not much else, is about as fine a food as you can get. We know that cocoa imitates the release of hormones in the body, the same ones that you get when you fall in love.

At its most pure, chocolate is made from cocoa liquor (the dry part of the ground cocoa bean, which looks a little like clumps of dirt and tastes a lot like bitter mud), cocoa butter (the miraculous fat that has been extracted from the cocoa bean), and sugar. The fat melts at body temperature into a product that has a very slinky, sexy mouthfeel. The sugar balances the bitterness of the cocoa liquor.

But what happens with most chocolate is that the manufacturers want it to travel, so cocoa butter is replaced with other fats that melt at higher temperatures. (It's also expensive to buy cocoa butter, and much cheaper to buy vegetable oil.) The more sugar you add to chocolate, the more faults in the cocoa liquor you can hide. And the more you water down the flavour, the more the chocolate might need boosting with added aromas and flavours.

Cocoa liquor is a coarse, grainy substance. To get it into chocolate it is conched (run between metal rollers to make it smoother). This is an expensive and time-consuming exercise, so cheap chocolate is barely conched (a few hours, perhaps), while excellent chocolate, such as Valrhona, Zokoko or Kennedy and Wilson, is conched for up to three days.

Good chocolate — which, by definition, has a high cocoa content (hence less sugar or other additives) — is also a bit bitter, and can be an acquired taste. It does, however, contain less fat and less sugar, and has a greater effect on those who find chocolate a substitute (or reinforcement) for their love life. One small square is more satisfying, if you savour it, than a block of everyday milk chocolate.

White chocolate isn't chocolate. It contains no cocoa liquor, but is rather made with condensed milk or cream. Good versions, however, may be made with cocoa butter, and so have a super-refined mouthfeel.

Poached pears
600 g (1 lb 5 oz) sugar
1 cinnamon stick
4 beurre bosc pears, peeled

Ganache
125 ml (4 fl oz/½ cup) pouring (whipping)
  cream (35% fat)
250 g (9 oz) milk chocolate, chopped
1½ tablespoons Kahlua
1 kg (2 lb 4 oz) shortcake pastry
  (see page 149)

Pear & chocolate tart

Pear goes better with chocolate than many other fruits do, and in this tart, they're both amazing. This tart will need to be made the day before you wish to serve it.

SERVES 8–10

Preheat the oven to 190°C (375°F/Gas 5). Grease a 24 cm (9½ inch) round pie dish, about 4 cm (1½ inch) deep.

To poach the pears, put the sugar in a saucepan over high heat and add the cinnamon stick and 600 ml (21 fl oz) water. When simmering, add the pears (the liquid should cover them, although you may need to weigh them down with a saucer so they don't float) and poach at just below a simmer for about 5 minutes, or until tender. Allow to cool (store them in the liquid if not using at once).

To make the ganache, put the cream in a saucepan over high heat and add the chocolate, whisking until smooth. Remove from the heat and add the Kahlua. Allow to cool.

Roll out two-thirds of the pastry between sheets of baking paper, as it is quite sticky, to create a circle with a 28 cm (11¼ inch) diameter.

Line the base and side of the dish. Place in the freezer for 10 minutes — this will help avoid shrinkage. Line the pastry with baking paper and fill it with baking beads or rice. Blind bake the pastry for about 15 minutes, or until the edges are cooked. Remove the weights and paper and cook for 5 minutes, or until just cooked. Allow to cool.

Meanwhile, roll out the remaining pastry between sheets of baking paper, to create a circle with a 25 cm (10 inch) diameter for the lid. Refrigerate until ready to use.

Spread the ganache over the baked pastry case. Cut the drained pears into quarters, removing the cores and stems. Arrange the pears over the ganache. Sit the pastry lid over the top and press the edges to seal. Cut a small hole in the top to release air.

Place the pie dish on an oven tray and bake for 20–25 minutes, or until the pastry is cooked. Allow to cool, then refrigerate overnight to set. Serve at room temperature.

150 ml (5 fl oz) full-cream (whole) milk

100 ml (3½ fl oz) pouring (whipping) cream (35% fat)

100 g (3½ oz) good-quality dark chocolate (60–70% cocoa), chopped

1 tablespoon unsweetened cocoa powder

1–2 tablespoons brandy, cognac, kirsch or whisky

sugar, to taste (optional)

The world's best hot chocolate

This hot chocolate is best enjoyed in front of a fire, on a sheepskin rug, in your ugg boots and after you've popped the hot water bottle in the bed. You could put less cream, less chocolate or less alcohol in this recipe, but you could also put your tongue on an ice cube to see if it sticks. I don't recommend you do any of that. This is the ultimate adult hot chocolate that you may not even want to sweeten — or share, for that matter, though it is very rich.

SERVES 2

Put the milk and cream in a small saucepan over high heat. Cook until it's warm, then whisk in the chocolate and cocoa until the chocolate has melted. Bring to nearly boiling point, then remove from the heat and whisk in the alcohol.

The chocolate will add a little sweetness, but you can add more sugar to taste if you like. Pour evenly into two mugs and serve hot.

400 g (14 oz) dark chocolate (60-70% cocoa), chopped

400 g (14 oz) butter, just melted but not hot

250 g (9 oz) caster (superfine) sugar

8 eggs, separated

250 g (9 oz/2½ cups) ground almonds

unsweetened cocoa powder, sifted (optional)

clotted cream (see page 61), to serve

Flourless chocolate cake

With its almost fudgy middle and a good hit of chocolate, this cake keeps well. But I can tell you now it won't last. If you can't find high-cocoa chocolate, use some cocoa powder in the mix as well, to add flavour.

SERVES 10-12

Preheat the oven to 180°C (350°F/Gas 4). Grease a 26 cm (10½ inch) round spring-form cake tin and line the base and side with baking paper.

To melt the chocolate you can either do it in the microwave on a very low setting, or in a heatproof bowl over a saucepan of hot but not boiling water. Stir it often to distribute the heat — too hot and it will go hard. Water spilt into the chocolate will also cause it to stiffen and become as unmanageable as a three-year-old.

Beat the butter and sugar until it is creamy looking. It could still be runny and split when you stop beating. This is fine. Beat in the egg yolks and whip well. Beat in the melted chocolate, then fold in the ground almonds until combined.

Beat the egg whites in a separate bowl until firm (but not stiff) peaks form. A good indicator is that the whites won't slide easily from the bowl when it's tilted. Gently fold the egg whites into the chocolate mix, using a quarter of the whites at first to lighten the batter, then fold in the remainder only until just combined.

Scrape the mixture into the cake tin and bake in the middle of the oven for about 40–50 minutes, testing with a skewer to see if it's cooked. The skewer won't come out clean, but less messy. It's a fudgy cake, and undercooking isn't the worst thing that can happen. Allow to cool in the tin before turning out.

Serve dusted with cocoa powder and clotted cream.

135 g (4¾ oz) self-raising flour

3 tablespoons unsweetened cocoa
powder (sifted if it's lumpy), plus
3 tablespoons extra

100 g (3½ oz) caster (superfine) sugar

125 ml (4 fl oz/½ cup) full-cream
(whole) milk

1 egg, lightly beaten

60 g (2¼ oz) butter, melted

120 g (4¼ oz) dark brown sugar

500 ml (17 fl oz/2 cups) boiling water

Chocolate self-saucing pudding

I have tested various quantities of this recipe several times to come up with one I really liked. It's bigger on cocoa than most, and might frighten the children. It has been suggested that 1 teaspoon instant coffee in the sauce mixture makes it even better.

SERVES 6

Preheat the oven to 180°C (350°F/Gas 4). Lightly grease a 1.5 litre (52 fl oz/6 cup) capacity casserole dish.

Mix the flour, cocoa and sugar in a bowl, then pour in the milk and egg and stir until it turns into a nicely even, wickedly dark batter. Fold in the butter and pour into the base of the dish. Sprinkle the brown sugar over the top, dust with the extra cocoa, then tip the boiling water over the top.

Bake in the centre of the oven for about 35 minutes (the sides should be bubbling). Cool just a little, before serving with cream or ice cream.

ACKNOWLEDGMENTS

It's been nearly two decades since I started work on *Real Food*. In that time I've been lucky enough to visit so many people, so many farms, sharing countless meals, all helping to build up a body of knowledge that is recorded within these pages. From the initial commission by publisher Jane Lawson at Murdoch Books, to the early editors, Jacqueline Blanchard and Sonia Greig, along with brilliant design work from Reuben Crossman, all overseen by Kay Scarlett, that first edition was a work that spanned decades and genres, droughts and floods and pandemics. I'm forever grateful to Sue Hines for putting her trust in me from up high as director at Murdoch Books.

For this edition, it's a massive thanks to my publisher Jane Willson for seeing the incredible value in a revised and updated tome. You've breathed new life into the old book (and the old cook!), and taken it in a fantastic new direction, not least with this stunning cover. To Sarah Odgers for finding Yuko Kurihara for the cover and giving the entire 400-plus pages a delightful fresh look, thank you from the bottom of my heart. I never envisaged such a gorgeous layout. I'm very lucky to have had Katri Hilden as editor for my third book in a row, a woman who finds the best in my words, and also finds the mistakes I make and fixes them (though any mistakes that remain in the text are mine alone). The whole team at Murdoch have been so fantastic to work with, including Justin Wolfers who kept the process running like a well (olive) oiled machine at breakneck speed to get it out on time. Thanks also to Sue Bobbermein, a publicist who was already excited about the book a year out from release, while still working on the previous one — I'm so lucky to have you on my side. Massive gratitude as always to Jane Morrow, Publishing Director, for championing so many of my projects over the years. The body of work we have amassed together is astonishing in its scope, depth and clout.

For inspiration in the first place, I'm indebted to cheesemaker Nick Haddow, whose idea of artisan (spelt HARDisan) framed much of my knowledge and journey into growing and producing food in the first place. Along with mates and fellow chefs Ross O'Meara and Alan Benson, he took my understanding of food to new depths, and new heights.

A special thanks to the food producers who took me in and gave me counsel, including Andrew Cameron, Ian Grubb, Morrie Wolf, Steve Solomon, Jules Ellis, Yves Ginat, Fred and Anne Leaman, Joe Bennett, David and Rita Stephens, Joe and Antonia Gretschmann, Gerard Crochon, Carl Sykes, Rob and Richard Clark, Will Brubacher, Tim Reid, the Cowen family, Bob Magnus, Peter Cooper, Duncan Garvey, John, Jill and Will Bignell, Hans Stutz, Esther Haeusermann, Maureen Dowd and Annie Nutter, along with Clare and Bruce Jackson.

Help came from all angles, including Dean Stevenson, Danielle Campbell, Paul Rubie, Jen Owens and Julian Stevenson, as well as stylists Lynsey Fryers and Mary Harris. Gil and June Tutty at Armytage House were the kindest hosts for the original one-week shoot.

A lot has changed in the last dozen or so years. And a lot hasn't. Photographer par excellence Alan Benson has remained a steadfast mate throughout the years, our lives filled with all the pleasures, challenges, grief, births, gluttony and countless photo shoots that only a full life can boast. Thank you, mate, for all you do to make our farm look better than it does, for capturing the seasons, the pleasures, on your camera. And thanks for updating my author photo with a greyer, hopefully wiser, version of me.

After four decades at the stove, and a decade and a half on the land, there are still things to cook, things to grow, amazing producers yet to be met, their stories yet to be told. I hope I get to meet you in the coming years. Meanwhile, the things that matter to me now are not so different from those that mattered when I was still a lad, or fresh into trade school. Good food, good company, a joyful home life.

I have all that, thanks to the grace and magnificence of Sadie Chrestman, who shares a love of soil, shares a community, a home with me in southern Tasmania. We have always been a family, Sadie, Hedley and I, since that first year on Puggle Farm, our original farmhouse near Cygnet. We have laughed, screamed, danced, wept, sang praise and bled on our new piece of land for over a decade, making our own way, as best we can, with what we have and what we bring. Thank you from the bottom of my heart, Sadie, for making me the best I can be.

And this book is a thank you to someone who probably won't understand what he has given me for a few years yet. To Hedley, thanks for the laughs, for the motivation to do better, for the crinkle-cut hot chips cooked in beef fat. From the time you slithered, blinking, into the world, fattening nicely on your mother and leaking like a colander, I feel like I've been given a new best friend who I don't want to share with anyone. As I watch you come into your teens, I see you finding a new place in the world, looking outward from our cocoon, and wanting to explore the globe in all the ways open to a young man. It's a world I hope I have helped to make more joyful, and better, even if only in a small way, and even if it's only better for you. Thank you for the trust you place in me every day. It's my wish that I can live up to even a fraction of that.

BIBLIOGRAPHY

Alm, R & Cox, M, *Myths of Rich and Poor: Why We're Better off Than We Think,* Basic Books, New York, 2000.

Amendola, J & Rees, N, *Understanding Baking: The Art and Science of Baking,* John Wiley and Sons, Milton, 2002.

Angus Society of Australia, *The Impact of Hormonal Growth Promotants on Carcass Composition and Meat Quality,* Armidale, 2007.

Barber, D, *The Third Plate,* Hachette UK, 2014.

Bassi, D & Layne, D, *The Peach: Botany, Production and Uses,* CABI Publishing, Oxfordshire, 2008.

Burg, SP, *Postharvest Physiology and Hypobaric Storage of Fresh Produce,* CABI Publishing, Oxfordshire, 2004.

Clover, C, *The End of the Line: How Overfishing Is Changing the World and What We Eat,* Ebury Press, London, 2005.

Commercial Chicken Meat and Egg Production, ed. Bell, DD, Weaver WD & North MO, Springer, Massachusetts, 2002.

Dalrymple, L & Hilliard, G, *The Ethical Omnivore,* Murdoch Books, Sydney, 2020.

David, E, *English Bread and Yeast Cookery,* Penguin Books, London, 1977.

Evans, M, *On Eating Meat: The Truth About Its Production and the Ethics of Eating It,* Murdoch Books, Sydney, 2019.

Evans, M, *Soil: The Incredible Story of What Keeps the Earth, and Us, Healthy,* Murdoch Books, Sydney, 2021.

Fairlie, S, *Meat: A Benign Extravagance,* Chelsea Green, Vermont, 2010.

Fearnley-Whittingstall, H, *River Cottage Meat Book,* Hodder & Stoughton, London, 2004.

Fox, PF & McSweeney, P, *Dairy Chemistry and Biochemistry,* Springer, Massachusetts, 1998.

Gray, L, *The Ethical Carnivore,* Bloomsbury, London, 2016.

Grescoe, T, *Bottomfeeder: How the Fish on Our Plates Is Killing Our Planet,* Pan Macmillan, London, 2008.

Grigson, J, *Jane Grigson's Vegetable Book,* Penguin Books, New York, 1978.

James, M & P, *The Tivoli Road Baker,* Hardie Grant, Melbourne, 2017.

Marcilla, A, Zarzo, M & Del Rio, M, 'Effect of storage temperature on the flavour of citrus fruit', *Spanish Journal of Agricultural Research*, vol. 4, no. 4, 2006, pp. 336–344.

McGee, H, *On Food and Cooking: The Science and Lore of the Kitchen,* Simon & Schuster, London, 2004.

Owen, S, *The Rice Book: History, Culture, Recipes,* Frances Lincoln, London, 2003.

Pollan, M, *The Omnivore's Dilemma: A Natural History of Four Meals,* Penguin, New York, 2006.

Pollan, M, *In Defense of Food,* Penguin Books, New York, 2009.

Postharvest Technology of Horticultural Crops, ed. Adel A Kader, ANR Publications (UC), California, 2002.

Reineccius, G & Heath, H, *Flavor Chemistry and Technology,* CRC Press, Florida, 2006.

Singer, P & Mason, J, *The Ethics of What We Eat,* Text Publishing, Melbourne, 2006.

Stuart, A, *Low Tox Life Food,* Murdoch Books, Sydney 2021.

Sudheer, KP & Indira, V, *Post Harvest Technology of Horticultural Crops,* New India Publishing, New Delhi, 2007.

UK Health and Safety Executive, 'Pesticides Residues Monitoring: Report of the Pesticide Residues Committee', UK Government; see www.prc-uk.org

WEBSITES

allaboutapples.com
amcs.org.au
dairyaustralia.com.au
fishnames.com.au
gffoodservice.com.au
msc.org
sydneyfishmarket.com.au
chicken.org.au
goodfishbadfish.com.au

INDEXES

strangozzi 286
strawberries 446, 450
streaky bacon 267
sucker lambs 243
sugar bananas 477
sugars 533, 544–5
sumac 143
sunflower oil 517
Sunnybrae 522
sushi rice 101
sustainable agriculture 23
    regenerative agriculture 210
sweet potatoes 355
sweetcorn 97
    see also corn
Swiss brown mushrooms 497
Swiss chard 364
Sydney Fish Market 333
Sykes, Carl 446

T

table grapes 478
tahini 387
Tahitian limes 462
tangelos 463
tangerines 461
Tasmania 220, 244, 311, 312,
    412, 414, 534
Tatin sisters 426
Texas longhorns 219
Thailand 533
thick cream 55
Third World 26
Thorpe Farm 96
tipo 00 flour 127, 132
tofu 114
tomato sauce 378, 383, 386
tomatoes 376–7
    egg-shaped 377
    gassing 377, 378
    hydroponic 377
    peeling 378
    storing 377–8
    and sugar 533
    tinned 378
Tongola dairy 72
treacle 545
triticale 99
tropical fruit 476–8
Tropical Fruit World 476
truffles 492–7, 501
tub-set yoghurt 37
tuna 303, 308, 309
turkeys 174, 175
two-tooth sheep 243
typicity 73

U

UHT milk 34
ultrafiltration 35, 39
ultra-pasteurised milk 34
umami 75
unbleached flour 127

V

Valencia oranges 460, 461, 463
Valrhona chocolate 552
veal 35, 205–9, 213–15
veal crates 214
vegetables 353
    fruit vegetables 376–9
vegetarian cheese 78–9
vegetarianism, and milk 35
venison 286, 289
verjuice 478
vine fruit 478

W

wagyu beef 215, 218, 219
wagyu–angus cross beef 212, 219
wagyu–friesian cross beef 35
wallaby 286
walnuts 506, 550
    wild 491
washed rind cheese 78
watercress 492
watermelon 409, 477
Wessex saddleback pigs 206, 258, 260
West Country Farmhouse Cheddar 75
wet-aged meat 221
wet-cured ham 265–6
wheat 95, 96–7
wheat flour 96–7, 126
whey 56, 72
white chocolate 552
white mould cheese 77–8
white truffles 496
wholemeal flour 129
wild fennel 492
wild fish 308, 309
wild foods 492–7
wild game 286, 290–1
    buying 291
wild mushrooms 492, 497
wild prawns 332
wild rice 101
willamette raspberries 446
Wiltshire horn sheep 242
wine grapes 478
winter squash (*see* pumpkins)
Wolf, Morrie 301
world hunger 26

Y

Yarlington Mill apples 413
yearling beef 215
yeast 130
yoghurt 31, 32, 36–7
York ham 265
Yorkshire curd cheesecake 88
Yorktown Organics 364

Z

zucchini flowers 376

First published in 2010 by Murdoch Books Pty Limited
This edition published in 2022 by Murdoch Books,
an imprint of Allen & Unwin

Murdoch Books Australia
83 Alexander Street
Crows Nest NSW 2065
Phone: +61 (0)2 8425 0100
murdochbooks.com.au
info@murdochbooks.com.au

Publisher: Jane Lawson
Photographer: Alan Benson
Concept and Design: Reuben Crossman
Project Manager and Editor: Jacqueline Blanchard
Food Editor: Sonia Greig
Stylists: Lynsey Fryers and Mary Harris
Production: Alexandra Gonzalez

2022 EDITION
Publisher: Jane Willson
Editorial Manager: Justin Wolfers
Editor: Katri Hilden
Design Manager and Designer: Sarah Odgers
Additional Photography: Alan Benson
Cover Design: Andy Warren
Cover Illustration: Yuko Kurihara
Production Director: Lou Playfair

Murdoch Books UK
Ormond House
26–27 Boswell Street
London WC1N 3JZ
Phone: +44 (0) 20 8785 5995
murdochbooks.co.uk
info@murdochbooks.co.uk

We acknowledge that we meet and work on the traditional lands of the Cammeraygal people of the Eora Nation and pay our respects to their elders past, present and future.

OVEN GUIDE: You may find cooking times vary depending on the oven you are using. For fan-forced ovens, as a general rule, set the oven temperature to 20°C (35°F) lower than indicated in the recipe.

We have used 20 ml (4 teaspoon) tablespoon measures. If you are using a 15 ml (3 teaspoon) tablespoon add an extra teaspoon of the ingredient for each tablespoon specified.

10 9 8 7 6 5 4 3 2 1

ISBN 9 781 92261 636 4 Australia
ISBN 9 781 91166 859 6 UK

A catalogue record for this book is available from the National Library of Australia

NATIONAL LIBRARY OF AUSTRALIA

Colour reproduction by Splitting Image Colour Studio Pty Ltd, Clayton, Victoria
Printed by C&C Offset Printing Co. Ltd., China

'What's old is new again! Knowing where your food comes from is more important now than ever, for the health of our planet and ourselves. Mathew and his book are an inspiring source of information on how to get started or keep going in the right direction.'
GUY JEFFREYS, MILLBROOK WINERY, CHEF

'Matthew Evans is the real deal. He talks the talk, walks the walk, and cooks the kind of food we could all use more of in our lives.'
ALICE ZASLAVSKY, AUTHOR AND BROADCASTER

'In a world where so many people are completely disconnected from where their food comes from, this book offers a bridge of connection. It's exactly what the world needs, more now than ever.'
EMMA GALLOWAY, MY DARLING LEMON THYME FOUNDER AND AUTHOR

'Matthew Evans makes the kitchen a site of quiet protest and a space where we can all form new habits to create the future of food. It's the kitchen companion I've been seeking, and I know it will become a stained, dog-eared and much-loved book before I hand it down to my child. It is a joyful and urgent book.'
NICOLA HARVEY, FARMER, PODCASTER AND AUTHOR

'A truly inspiring book to make you want to consider how you source your food, and cook beautifully achievable recipes with the seasons. Soil-to-stomach eating was the past but it is imperative that it be the future too. Food grown the right way to benefit the soil and your health.'
MICHAEL JAMES, BAKER AND AUTHOR

'Matthew Evans writes with the passion of a man possessed. Possessed by all the good things. A care for hospitality, a call for generosity and a plea to embrace the environmental and regenerative farming practices that can make a huge difference to our future.'
ANNIE SMITHERS, DU FERMIER, CHEF AND AUTHOR

'I had the good fortune of having access to nothing but this book while camping in Gippsland, Victoria's beef country. Reading it in the wilderness made me think about my surroundings, of produce quality and of simple, yet well prepared, food. So much so that I ended up feeding the insatiable urge to cook a piece of locally sourced steak over my camp fire once I was able to put the book down.'
THI LE, ANCHOVY, CHEF

'Matthew Evans is a big-hearted farmer, considered conservationist, witty philosopher and modern crusader. At best, *The Real Food Companion* will make you think about all that is important in our world and at worst, you will be extremely well fed.'
NICK HADDOW, BRUNY ISLAND CHEESE COMPANY FOUNDER AND AUTHOR

'Matthew's real food philosophy is not aspirational, it is imperative in this age of climate action. To know Matthew and read his thoughtful approach is to be inspired. I challenge everyone to embrace 'soil to stomach' wholly, and just try – go ahead, try – to read this compendium of food wisdom and not want to join us in this food movement.'
PALISA ANDERSON, FOUNDER BOON LUCK FARM ORGANICS